Poetry and the Global Climate Crisis

This book demonstrates how humans can become sensitized to, and intervene in, environmental degradation by writing, reading, analyzing, and teaching poetry. It offers both theoretical and practice-based essays, providing a diversity of approaches and voices that will be useful in the classroom and beyond.

The chapters in this edited collection explore how poetry can make readers climate-ready and climate-responsive through creativity, empathy, and empowerment. The book encompasses work from or about Oceania, Africa, Europe, North America, Asia, and Antarctica, integrating poetry into discussions of specific local and global issues, including the value of Indigenous responses to climate change; the dynamics of climate migration; the shifting boundaries between the human and more-than-human world; the ecopoetics of the prison-industrial complex; and the ongoing environmental effects of colonialism, racism, and sexism. With numerous examples of how poetry reading, teaching, and learning can enhance or modify mindsets, the book focuses on offering creative, practical approaches and tools that educators can implement into their teaching and equipping them with the theoretical knowledge to support these.

This volume will appeal to educational professionals engaged in teaching environmental, sustainability, and development topics, particularly from a humanities-led perspective.

Amatoritsero Ede is an international award-winning poet who was born in Nigeria, and he is a literary scholar and Assistant Professor of English at Mount Allison University, New Brunswick, Canada.

Sandra Lee Kleppe is a Professor of English-Language Literature at Inland Norway University of Applied Sciences.

Angela Sorby is an award-winning poet and a Full Professor of English at Marquette University in Milwaukee, Wisconsin.

Research and Teaching in Environmental Studies

This series brings together international educators and researchers working from a variety of perspectives to explore and present best practice for research and teaching in environmental studies.

Given the urgency of environmental problems, our approach to the research and teaching of environmental studies is crucial. Reflecting on examples of success and failure within the field, this collection showcases authors from a diverse range of environmental disciplines including climate change, environmental communication and sustainable development. Lessons learned from interdisciplinary and transdisciplinary research are presented, as well as teaching and classroom methodology for specific countries and disciplines.

Environmental Consciousness, Nature and the Philosophy of Education
Ecologizing Education
Michael Bonnett

Theatre Pedagogy in the Era of Climate Crisis
Edited by Conrad Alexandrowicz and David Fancy

Institutionalizing Interdisciplinarity and Transdisciplinarity
Collaboration across Cultures and Communities
Edited by Bianca Vienni Baptista and Julie Thompson Klein

Interdisciplinary Research on Climate and Energy Decision Making
30 Years of Research on Global Change
Edited by M. Granger Morgan

Transformative Sustainability Education
Reimagining Our Future
Elizabeth A. Lange

Poetry and the Global Climate Crisis
Creative Educational Approaches to Complex Challenges
Edited by Amatoritsero Ede, Sandra Lee Kleppe, and Angela Sorby

For more information about this series, please visit: www.routledge.com/Research-and-Teaching-in-Environmental-Studies/book-series/RTES

Poetry and the Global Climate Crisis

Creative Educational Approaches to
Complex Challenges

**Edited by Amatoritsero Ede, Sandra Lee Kleppe,
and Angela Sorby**

LONDON AND NEW YORK

from Routledge

Designed cover image: © Turgut Birgin / iStock

First published 2024
by Routledge
4 Park Square, Milton Park, Abingdon, Oxon OX14 4RN

and by Routledge
605 Third Avenue, New York, NY 10158

Routledge is an imprint of the Taylor & Francis Group, an informa business

British Library Cataloguing-in-Publication Data
A catalogue record for this book is available from the British Library

Library of Congress Cataloging-in-Publication Data
Names: Ede, Amatoritsero, editor. | Kleppe, Sandra Lee, editor. | Sorby, Angela, editor.
Title: Poetry and the global climate crisis : creative educational approaches to complex challenges / edited by Amatoritsero Ede, Sandra Lee Kleppe, and Angela Sorby.
Description: Abingdon, Oxon ; New York, NY : Routledge, 2023. |
Series: Research and teaching in environmental studies | Includes bibliographical references and index.
Identifiers: LCCN 2023026283 (print) | LCCN 2023026284 (ebook) |
ISBN 9781032508566 (hardback) | ISBN 9781032508542 (paperback) |
ISBN 9781003399988 (ebook)
Subjects: LCSH: Poetry—History and criticism. | Climatic changes in literature. | Global environmental change in literature. | Ecology in literature. | Poetry—Study and teaching. | LCGFT: Literary criticism. | Essays.
Classification: LCC PN1065 .P64 2023 (print) | LCC PN1065 (ebook) |
DDC 808.1/071—dc23/eng/20230830
LC record available at https://lccn.loc.gov/2023026283
LC ebook record available at https://lccn.loc.gov/2023026284

ISBN: 978-1-032-50856-6 (hbk)
ISBN: 978-1-032-50854-2 (pbk)
ISBN: 978-1-003-39998-8 (ebk)

DOI: 10.4324/9781003399988

Typeset in Times New Roman
by codeMantra

Contents

Contributors

Niyi Akingbe is a Professor of Comparative Literature and Poetics. He is at present a Distinguished Research Fellow in the Department of English Studies, University of South Africa, Pretoria. He received a PhD from the University of Lagos, Akoka, Nigeria, where he studied Protest Literature. He was born in Nigeria but now lives in South Africa. He has taught in different Nigerian and South African universities in the past 20 years. His scholarly interests include Comparative, Postcolonial, Commonwealth, Protest and African literatures, Cultural studies, Music in literature, and the intersection of literature and Film studies. His work has been published internationally, in reputable accredited journals in Africa, Asia, Australia, Europe, and the United States. He is co-editor of *English Academy Review*.

Christian Jil Benitez is a poet, scholar, translator, and educator from the Philippines. He earned his AB and MA in Literature from the Department of Filipino at the Ateneo de Manila University, where he teaches literature and rhetoric. He is currently pursuing his PhD in Comparative Literature at Chulalongkorn University, Thailand. Hailed as the Poet of the Year 2018 by the Commission on the Filipino Language, his critical and creative works in both English and Filipino have been published in various anthologies and journals, including *The Routledge Handbook of Ecofeminism and Literature (2022)* and the special issue of *eTropic* on tropical materialisms. His first book, *Isang Dalumat ng Panahon (2022)*, which intuits the Philippine notion of time through the rubrics of the tropical, the poetic, and the (neo)material, was published by the Ateneo de Manila University Press.

Dean Anthony Brink, originally from the Puget Sound, now with dual citizenship in Taiwan, teaches literature and thought at National Yang Ming Chiao Tung University, Hsinchu, Taiwan. He is the author of *Philosophy of Science and The Kyoto School* (Bloomsbury 2021) and *Poetics and Justice in America, Japan, and Taiwan* (Lexington 2021). His creative work has appeared in *New Writing, Nimrod, Helios Quarterly, Cordite Poetry Review*, and *Technoculture*.

Aidan Coleman is a Senior Lecturer in English Education and Creative Writing at Southern Cross University. As well as numerous scholarly articles and book chapters, he is the co-author of a series of Shakespeare textbooks and three collections of poetry. *Thin Ice: A Life of John Forbes* (Melbourne UP) is forthcoming in 2024.

Melanie Duckworth is an Associate Professor of English Literature at Østfold University College, Norway. She has a BA from the University of Adelaide, an MA from the University of York, and a PhD from the University of Leeds. She has published on contemporary poetry, Australian literature, and children's literature in journals including *Environmental Humanities, Australian Literary Studies*, and *Bookbird*, and in several edited collections. She is co-editor of *Plants in Children's and Young Adult Literature* (Routledge 2022) and *Storying Plants in Australian Children's and Young Adult Literature: Roots and Winged Seeds* (Palgrave 2023).

Amatoritsero Ede is an international award-winning poet born in Nigeria. He has published three highly acclaimed poetry collections, *A Writer's Pains & Caribbean Blues* (1998), *Globetrotter & Hitler's Children* (2009), and *Teardrops on the Weser* (2021). The first collection won the 1998 All Africa Okigbo Prize for Literature and the second was nominated for the Nigerian Literature Prize in 2013. A widely anthologized poet, Ede also won second prize in the First May Ayim Award: International Black German Prize in 2004. He is a literary scholar and an Assistant Professor of English at Mount Allison University, New Brunswick as well as the Publisher and Managing Editor of the *Maple Tree Literary Supplement*.

Rasaq Malik Gbolahan is currently a PhD student in the Department of English at the University of Nebraska, Lincoln. His research interests include African Literature, Digital Humanities, Oral Poetry, Ecocriticism, and Indigenous studies.

Knut Øystein Høvik is an Associate Professor of English Literature, Culture, and Didactics at Inland Norway University of Applied Sciences. He has published on the history of English teaching in Norway and on Indigenous voices. His latest contribution discusses the Australian rock band Midnight Oil's environmentally themed lyrics in the context of the climate crisis.

Katharina Maria Kalinowski is originally from Northern Germany, studied in England, and completed a joint PhD "Dr Europaeus" in English and Poetry at the Universities of Cologne, Kent, and Dublin. Her creative-critical research explores ecopoetics and (eco)translation and can be found in *Ecozon@*, *Magma*, and the *Irish Poetry Reading Archive*. She currently teaches Creative Writing at Düsseldorf University.

Sandra Lee Kleppe is a Professor of English-Language Literature at Inland Norway University of Applied Sciences. She is currently heading a project with the working title, "Literature, Teacher Education and the Climate Crisis" that aims to prepare pupils, students, and teachers for the climate-ready classroom using tools from literature/literary studies. Some of her publications include *Poetry and Sustainability in Education,* edited with Angela Sorby (Palgrave Macmillan 2022); *Poetry and Pedagogy across the Lifespan: Disciplines, Classrooms, and Contexts,* edited with Angela Sorby (Palgrave Macmillan 2018); and *Raymond Carver's Poetry: Against the Current* (Ashgate, 2013).

Heidi Silje Moen is an Associate Professor of English-Language Literature at Inland Norway University of Applied Sciences. She has published on Ezra Pound and animal poems in an educational context. Her latest contribution argues that tree poems read through the lenses of biospheric egalitarianism could aid in the preservation of biodiversity.

Hanna Musiol hails from Poland. She holds a PhD from Northeastern University (US), and is a Professor of Literature at NTNU in Norway. Her interests include American literary studies, transmedia storytelling, and critical theory, with emphasis on migration, political ecology, and human rights. Musiol regularly organizes city-scale curatorial and public humanities initiatives, and she collaborates actively with grassroots storytelling ensembles such as *Literature for Inclusion* and Poetry without Borders in Trondheim, Norway.

Janet Newman lives in New Zealand. Her essays, poems, and reviews have been published in New Zealand and Australia. She has a PhD from Massey University for her thesis *Imagining Ecologies: Traditions of Ecopoetry in Aotearoa New Zealand* (2019). Her first poetry collection is *Unseasoned Campaigner* (Otago University Press, 2021).

Mariam Salaudeen is currently a PhD student in the Department of English and Literary Studies, Osun State University, Nigeria. Her research interest covers African Literature and Environmentalism as well as cultural and film studies.

Caitlin Scarano is a writer based in Bellingham, Washington. She holds a PhD from the University of Wisconsin-Milwaukee and an MFA from the University of Alaska Fairbanks. Her second full-length collection of poems, *The Necessity of Wildfire*, was selected by Ada Limón as the winner of the Wren Poetry Prize and won a 2023 Pacific Northwest Book Award. Caitlin is a member of the Washington Wolf Advisory Group. She was selected as a participant in the NSF's Antarctic Artists & Writers Program and spent November 2018 in McMurdo Station in Antarctica.

Angela Sorby is a Full Professor of English at Marquette University in Milwaukee, Wisconsin. She received her PhD from the University of Chicago and has published a critical monograph (*Schoolroom Poets*), three award-winning poetry collections (*Distance Learning, Bird Skin Coat,* and *The Sleeve Waves*), two co-edited collections with Sandra Kleppe (*Poetry and Pedagogy Across the Lifespan* and *Poetry and Sustainability*), a co-curated historical anthology with Karen Kilcup (*Over the River and Through the Wood*), and many academic articles. Her past and current research projects involve interdisciplinary cultural studies, focused on sustainability, mass incarceration, and creative pedagogy. She is involved in sustainable curriculum development at Marquette and in the wider Milwaukee community, including high school, college-age, and incarcerated/re-entry student populations.

Anne Buchanan Stuart grew up in Australia and lives near Byron Bay. She has a doctorate in Philosophy and Poetry and is an Adjunct Research Fellow at the Griffith Centre for Social and Cultural Research at Griffith University on the Gold Coast. Anne teaches Literature in the School of Humanities.

Ronnie K. Stephens is a Full-Time Assistant Professor at Tarrant County College and a graduate student in the University of Texas at Arlington PhD program. His research centers on poetry and pedagogy in the 21st-century classroom, with a particular interest in poetry as an act of resistance.

Christina Thatcher is an American poet and scholar now working as a Lecturer in Creative Writing at Cardiff University in Wales, UK. She has published two poetry collections with Parthian Books: *More Than You Were* (2017) and *How to Carry Fire* (2020). Her third collection-in-progress, *Breaking a Mare*, won a Literature Wales Writer's Bursary in 2018. Follow her @writetoempower.

Marzia Varutti, born in Italy, was a Post-Doctoral Fellow in the School of Museum Studies, University of Leicester, and subsequently Associate Professor in Museology and Cultural History at the University of Oslo, Norway. She is currently M. S. Curie Research Fellow at the Center for Affective Sciences, University of Geneva, Switzerland.

Rosanne van der Voet is a Lecturer in environmental humanities and urban studies at Leiden University in the Netherlands. She recently completed her PhD on storytelling and the environmental crisis of the oceans at the University of Sheffield, where she developed "medusa poetics" as a literary structuring device inspired by the life cycle of jellyfish. Her research spans across various interdisciplinary strands of the blue humanities, with particular focus on nonhuman experience of environmental issues, creative-critical, approaches and applied ecocritical analysis of new nature-based water management projects in urban and industrial environments in the Netherlands. Her work can be found in journals such as *ISLE, Ecozon@, Journal of Posthumanism, Book 2.0,* and *The York Journal*.

Introduction

The term "ecocriticism" was first used by William Reichert in a 1978 essay that calls poems "renewable source[s] of energy, coming as they do from those ever-generating twin matrices, language and imagination" (108). Almost a half-century later, the internet allows students, teachers, and scholars to access a complex global ecosystem of poetry, moving beyond the Eurocentric Romantic canon that underpins Reichert's essay. From indigenous New Zealand to a Wisconsin prison and online *scifaiku* (science fiction haiku) communities, poetry continues to generate energy, as the essays in this volume show. That said, the metaphor has its limits: poems won't replace the oil extraction industry or reverse bee colony collapse. Can poetry still be relevant as the global climate crisis accelerates? Many of us who teach have heard this question – *why bother with poetry?* – in our classrooms, often most urgently posed by students in STEM fields. It is a question that this volume of essays aims to take seriously.

Poetry and the Global Climate Crisis began, not with a fixed thesis, but with an open-ended call for papers that would bring scholar-teachers from around the world into conversation with one another. As with all productive conversations, common threads quickly emerged, and we editors used three central issues to select and organize the material. All of the essays in this volume address, in some way, (1) the possibility of forging authentic connections across individuals, human societies, and more-than-human lifeworlds; (2) the perils of "making connections" that fail to acknowledge power asymmetries; and (3) the practical ways that poems can help readers navigate our shared (but not equally shared) global biosphere. Poetry challenges readers – perhaps especially students, who might be reluctant readers – to consider the diverse ways that language and imagination can pose familiar problems, such as water contamination, in new ways.

In this book, we focus on poetry, but the need for more global conversations is not limited to any one area of the sciences or humanities. Indeed, reading these essays has reminded us that for most of human history (in Indigenous North American oral traditions for instance or even in early European Romantic science writing), nature has not been understood through atomized "fields" but rather via hybrid sources that integrate multiple material, cultural, and affective perspectives. To be poetic is not to be anti-scientific; it is, rather, to integrate old, new, and emergent knowledge(s), honouring complementary ways of seeing that can help us dream *and* engineer a habitable future.

Many of the essays in this book are from emerging scholars, and all of them focus on specific poets and poems located in particular global communities. Rather than attempting sweeping theories, individual chapters provide materials that are immediately usable in educational settings: Nigerian environmental poetry, Philippine ecopoetic riddles, three poems about Australian trees, and so on. This is a deliberate editorial choice, meant to encourage comparative reading, teaching, and learning. Of course, this runs the risk of facile or oversimplified equivalencies. So, for scholars, such readings must be the first step in an ever-widening and deepening

DOI: 10.4324/9781003399988-1

project. Nevertheless, we hope that juxtapositions will generate surprising insights as students, teachers, and readers mix and match the poems found in these eclectic ecocritical experiments. For instance, how might a Midnight Oil song relate to G'ebinyo Ogbowei's *Marsh Boy*? Rather than answering such questions, we simply make them possible to ask.

The first section of the book, "Perspectives on Indigenous Poetries," contains three chapters that all approach teaching poetry at the crossroads of native and settler cultures. Chapter 1, "Embodiment and Solace: The Entanglement of Culture with Nature in Contemporary Aotearoa New Zealand Ecopoetry" by Janet Newman, proposes that ecopoetry can contribute to a bicultural education that is specific to Aotearoa New Zealand. The chapter triangulates between the New Zealand biome, Māori (native) worldviews, and Pākehā (settler) experiences through the reading of three ecopoets. These are Brian Turner, Robert Sullivan, and Airini Beautrais. Turner's work, which stems from the literary nationalist tradition, appears to be Wordsworthian in its use of nature as a tool for constructing and healing the individual self. Sullivan, whose literary heritage includes traditional Māori poetry, extends and transforms more individualistic settler ecologies by fusing humans, culture, and nature. Beautrais takes a postcolonial ecocritical approach by recognising the colonial constructedness of ecologies in a settler country and the detrimental effects of such constructions on the indigenous ecological and cultural landscapes.

Chapter 2, "From Burning Beds to Rising Seas: Environmental Issues in the Song Lyrics of Midnight Oil," by Knut Øystein Høvik, examines ecological issues in nearby Australia as they have developed over the long career of the rock band, Midnight Oil. The chapter illustrates how close readings of poetic song lyrics can have significant educational potential. In a classroom setting, the lyrics can be used to promote awareness of global challenges amongst learners since the story of Midnight Oil, in many ways, teaches about that of the Australian environmental movement as it gradually grew from a settler-focused protest movement in the 1970s. That movement eventually merged with issues of Aboriginal rights from the 1980s onwards, culminating in The Makarrata Project, a mini album inspired by the Uluru Statement from the Heart by the First Nations National Constitutional Convention (2017). Prior to this album, the band's music has been mostly *about* First Australians, but now it is *with* them. This means that the fact that such collaborations can carry colonial baggage does not render them impossible.

The final chapter in this section, "From Standing Rock to Flint, Michigan: How Indigenous Poets Contextualise the Fight for Clean Water" by Ronnie K. Stephens, moves to North America, where water rights have been the topic of much public attention in recent years, both concerning Flint, Michigan, and the Dakota Access Pipeline near Standing Rock Sioux land. Stephens argues that Indigenous poets like Natalie Diaz and Layli Long Soldier invert white colonial understandings of water. He notes that their poems can act as an effective entry point for student-led discussions about climate change and its impact on freshwater sources. The chapter also discusses the inherent danger of imagining water solely through a utilitarian lens. Framing the conversation for students in terms of both New Materialist and Indigenous ideologies, Stephens, not unlike Newman, demonstrates how both settler and native approaches can contribute to bicultural learning.

Section II, "Perspectives on the More-than-Human," engages life forms including the avian (Chapter 4), arboreal (Chapter 6), aquatic (Chapter 7), and mammalian (Chapter 8). The section opens with Chapter 4, "Last Migrations: The Poetry of Migratory Birds" by Melanie Duckworth and Aidan Coleman. It brings together migratory bird poetry from two hemispheres in the works of Scotland-based poets, Kathleen Jamie, Don Paterson, and Jen Hadfield in conversation with Australian poets, Judith Wright, Les Murray, and Jill Jones. Birds, as the authors point out, do not recognize national borders. It is then apposite that while some of these poets may share nationalities they inhabit and write from different bioregions. With reference to the literal birds the poems address – and drawing on zoopoetics, extinction studies, and ecocriticism – the chapter nudges teachers and students to consider the complex lives of migratory birds. This, in turn, presents unique opportunities to engage affectively – to *care about* – questions of extinction, climate change and global belonging. Humans and birds share a precarious dependency on the vagaries of climate. Chapter 5, "Animal Politics and Ecological Haiku" by Dean Anthony Brink situates short poetic forms as a global phenomenon. It argues that the traditional Japanese conventions of indirection can lead to subtle, non-didactic eco-poems. Strategies for writing short-form poetry in general can be taught by example, showing how, in English, very short verse forms can be deepened by intertextual connections from within and beyond Asia. In educational contexts, one under-explored variant of interest to ecological poetry is the *scifaiku*, a new subgenre of haiku that draws on the surging popularity of science fiction. Cultural energies from Japan can be transformed and re-circulated, even by poets (including student-poets) who do not speak Japanese, resulting in vibrant trans-Pacific creative communities.

Chapters 6–8 depart from academic conventions (outdated, we would argue) by discussing ecopoems about animals, written by the scholar/poets themselves. These essays thus model increasingly popular pedagogical strategies that ask students to produce hybrid creative/critical writing. In Chapter 6, "Greeting a Ginkgo: How Anthropomorphism in Poetry Can Inspire Eco-Empathy," Christina Thatcher provides close readings of two poems from her collection, *Breaking a Mare*. She highlights how empathizing with a ginkgo or a river can elicit in readers the desire to act in ways that protect and respect the non-human. This self-reflexive chapter defends the much-maligned genre of "anthropomorphism." It shows how writing poetry that puts a human face on trees and waterways might help readers to feel the consequences of climate change and encourage a more hopeful attitude. To this end, Thatcher highlights the debates surrounding anthropomorphism and empathy using, among other methods, Poetry Inquiry (PI) to discuss how localized data is linked to climate change. This is a strategy that can be employed both in and outside the classroom to connect readers to concrete climate issues.

Chapter 7 demonstrates an even more experimental attempt at creative hybridization. In "Of Jellyfish, Lichen, and Other More-Than-Human Matter: Ecopoethical Writing Research as Transformative Politics," Katharina Maria Kalinowski and Rosanne van der Voet model how to stimulate behavioural change in readers and learners by writing and re-presenting their own ecopoems, in this case about organisms that grow symbiotically in saltwater and in forests. The chapter showcases how innovative writing-as-research can swerve away from anthropocentric worldviews and make environmental concerns material on the page, demonstrating the educational potential of linguistic turns to force unpredictable insights. When Kalinowski and Van der Voet note that "we arguably need not only scientific knowledge but also imaginative interventions and emotional connection to the earth," they are stressing an issue that is central not only to this section, but to the book as a whole.

Section II closes with Chapter 8, "Using Poetry to Learn from the Animals We Brought to Antarctica," in which Caitlin Scarano explores the fate of sled dogs used during human expeditions. As with the two previous chapters, Scarano presents readings of her own poems, written during her extraordinary residency in Antarctica. Scarano merges historical and archival approaches with affective expression to expose the impact of colonialism and exploration on non-human beings, in particular dogs. Drawing on the theories of human-animal studies (HAS) and posthumanism, this chapter demonstrates how poetry can complicate the relationships between humans and animals. It also explores the complex networks of relationships between technology, capitalism, science, and the Antarctic landscape. The poems generate empathy for the dogs in question and can teach us how to question human exceptionalism and human-centrism embedded in acts and narratives of exploration, specifically in the Antarctic context.

Section III is titled "Critical and Theoretical Perspectives," but Chapters 9, 10, and 13 extend certain themes from the previous section, since they also concern poetry about plants and animals, while using more conventionally scholarly lenses. Chapter 9, "Imaging the Real in Times of Crisis: Empowerment and Ecosophy in Shaun Tan's Tales from The Inner City" by Heidi Silje Moen, explores a picture book by Australian-born artist Shaun Tan, showing how the visual-verbal poetry and the visual artwork in the collection as a whole can create in learners epistemic self-doubt. Tan's collection nudges young readers to unlearn their reflexive (as in habitual, unthinking) anthropocentrism and to embrace an ecosophical worldview more beneficial to all life. Moen's readings of animal poems and illustrations portray powerful and poignant relationships among creatures: an orca and its baby, for instance, or a human and a dog. Moen concludes that

> through imaging and imagining our essential dependence on and interconnectedness with the non-human as intrinsic to the self and, by simultaneously enabling learners to read critically and empathetically, poetry can empower learners to take responsible action on behalf of the living earth.

This conclusion echoes other chapters in the volume, while adding a unique focus on picture books and illustration.

Chapter 10, "Vegetal Relationality: Three Australian [Eco]poets" by Anne Buchanan Stuart, seeks to re-imagine human ecological relations by way of poetic encounters with the vegetal world. Her theoretical approach outlines four types of ecosocial literary texts, ecophobic, ecophatic, ecoliterate, and ecophilic, showing how the latter two apply to three Australian poets, Oodgeroo Noonuccal, Martin Harrison, and Judith Wright. Her readings demonstrate how poetry can help readers, teachers, and students think in new ways about climate change through an engagement with the vegetal, illustrating that plants can have agency and that poetry can provide cross-ontological alliances with the nonhuman. Moreover, her theoretical framework, applied here to specific poets, has wide application to "vegetal" poems from many literary traditions.

Chapter 11, "Carceral Climates: Poetry, Ecology, and the U.S. Prison System" by Angela Sorby, moves the conversation into the prison-industrial complex. Sorby offers ecological readings of five poems, all of which appeared in a special issue of Poetry magazine on writers affected by the American prison system. From her own teaching experiences, Sorby explores how prisoners can and do use poetry to locate themselves in ecosystems that are larger, more diverse, and more generative than any prison space. At the same time, the essay addresses the ways that ecosystemic imagery invites non-incarcerated readers to understand how prison poetry engages with what ecocritic, Donna Haraway, calls "intentional kin making" across significant ecosocial barriers. Importantly, this chapter also teaches that "ecological" poetry is not limited to poems about nature, by showing how the relationship between works generated from within the prison-industrial complex can resist toxic confinement, creating kinship communities with human and more-than-human worlds beyond prison.

Moving from carceral to black ecologies, and from industrial to weather climates, Chapter 12, "Black Ecologies, the 'Weather,' and 'Renegade' Poetic Sensorium" (Sharpe 104) by Hanna Musiol proposes that weather systems, and the climate itself, can be inherently antiblack. Drawing on Christina Sharpe's understanding of "antiblackness" as a "total climate," Musiol examines the poetry of two African American poets, Afaa Michael Weaver and Evie Shockley. Emphasizing that Black poetic ecologies need to be read more carefully and taught more often, the chapter concludes with a reflection on how Black ecopoetics may also activate the sustaining potential of poetry to act on the readers' breathing bodies, sensing, and imagining other weathers, other climates.

Embodiment is also central to Chapter 13, "'Everything Depends on Us:' The Ecofeminist Vision in Naomi Shihab Nye's Honeybee" by Sandra Lee Kleppe. The focus of this chapter is an examination of bees and other animals in the poetry of Palestinian-American Nye from a perspective that echoes the concerns of ecofeminists, Maria Mies and Vandana Shiva. Mies and Shiva's long-term environmental activism insists that workers, especially women and people of colour, have been disproportionately affected by industrialized agriculture and its harmful pesticides. It is precisely such chemicals alongside industrial beekeeping, as Nye points out in her poems, that have led to both bee colony disorder and the large-scale poisoning of our natural environment. Kleppe's chapter concludes that there is much to be learned from teaching *Honeybee*. These poems can sensitize learners not only to the plight of bees, but to the living conditions of a host of other species and how these interact with – and are interdependent on – humans of different genders and many cultural backgrounds.

Our final section, "Global Juxtapositions," offers readings of poets from such diverse countries as South Africa (Chapter 14), Nigeria (Chapter 15), the Philippines (Chapter 16), and Italy (Chapter 17). The opening Chapter 14, "Mitigating Ecological Threats: Amplifying Environmental Activism in Gabeba Baderoon's Poetry" by Niyi Akingbe, makes a point that is pertinent not only to this section but to the volume as a whole:

> While the trajectory of ecocriticism is indebted to the exceptional intersection of literature and the environment as aptly illustrated in the American and English literary traditions, a broader approach would seek to probe the essence of ecology within the larger context of phases of world literary history.

Akingbe illustrates this idea using the works of Gabeba Baderoon, an important political voice in post-Apartheid South African poetry whose work is just beginning to be understood as ecopoetic. We can learn through Baderoon's strategies – informed by the struggle against apartheid – that moderation in language is often more effective in climate discourse than unbridled anger.

African poetry is also the focus of Chapter 15, "Capitalism and Environmental Activism in Selected Nigerian Poetry" by Mariam Salaudeen and Rasaq Malik Gbolahan. Salaudeen and Gbolahan investigate two poetry collections, G'ebinyo Ogbowei's *Marsh Boy and Other Poems* (2013) and Magnus Abraham-Dukuma's *Dreams from the Creeks* (2015), in light of the devastation of the Niger-Delta by crude oil capitalism. This chapter shows how Nigerian poets play critical roles in shifting our gaze to the losses occasioned by ecological destruction in a place like Nigeria's coastal Niger-Delta region. This example also challenges readers to rethink the politics of land ownership and capitalism in other contexts. Teaching this topic, as the authors note,

> can also reflect how poetic intervention can be studied for the purpose of creating important conversations around the need to protect the land and animals, and also offering a space to think about how we can collectively work against ecological hazards.

The final two chapters continue to fuse the local and the global, taking us to bioregions not examined elsewhere in this volume: the Philippines and Italy. Chapter 16, "Bugtong, or the Philippine Riddle as an Ecopoem," by Christian Jil Benitez, introduces the folk *bugtong* – a genre not likely familiar to most English speakers – and argues that the *bugtong* takes a hyper-local, vernacular approach to ecological literacy. The chapter outlines the predominant definition of ecopoetry in the current Philippine literary landscape – a definition that ignores the *bugtong*. However, figuring out the riddles of the *bugtong* can teach students how to work with the material ecology of local objects. In this sense, this genre emerges as a Philippine ecopoem that powerfully activates in humans an ecological literacy that is also a certain love for matter, allowing students and readers to realize our most intimate entanglements with the material world writ large.

The closing chapter of the book, Marzia Varutti's "Poetry and Ecological Awareness: Inspiration from Pierluigi Cappello's Poetry," encapsulates the themes of interrelatedness and entanglements that connect many of the essays. "If ecology is essentially about inter-relatedness, about relationships between organisms and their environments," Varutti notes, "then poetry is ecology as it is intrinsically about relationships – with ourselves, fellow human beings, the planet; indeed poetry can be seen as the art and craft of putting those relationships into words." Though Varutti applies this statement to lucid readings of poems by Pierluigi Cappello, her emphasis on relationships can serve as an appropriate reflection for the theme of this book as a whole. As Varutti and the other authors in this book suggest, poetry remains a renewable form of energy. Of course, poetry alone can't save the planet – but neither can discursive or political or even technical innovation alone. As students, teachers, readers, and scholars, we must integrate our multiple cultural knowledge(s) and power sources. Poetry matters, and it is especially important in school settings if we hope to prepare students for the collective global action that climate change requires. All forms of education are also forms of relational entanglement, and all are, in turn, affected by the ecosystems that contain and connect us.

Part I

Perspectives on Indigenous Poetries

1 Embodiment and Solace

The Entanglement of Culture with Nature in Contemporary Aotearoa New Zealand Ecopoetry

Janet Newman

Introduction

This chapter teaches about the triangular affiliation between nature, Māori[1] and Pākehā that is specific to Aotearoa New Zealand. Although such triangulation between nature, Indigenous and settler culture is not unique, it takes a distinctive form in this country. Much can be learned from exploring these affiliations and the tensions they give rise to as represented in the ecopoetry of three contemporary poets. The methodology of the chapter is a relatively comparative analysis with an earlier Western ecopoetic tradition in the background and makes critical departures from a purely Western ecocritical analytical model.

Ecopoetry is a distinct form of nature poetry that acknowledges and explores the relationships between human culture and nature. It opposes human degradation of the natural world and perceives nature as both essential for human survival and necessary in its own right. It sometimes explores connections between nature and human consciousness which British critic Jonathan Bate describes as "the relationship between external environment and ecology of mind" (252). American critic J. Scott Bryson contends that ecopoetry is "a version of nature poetry generally marked by three primary characteristics" (5). They are "an emphasis on maintaining an ecocentric perspective"—that is, foregrounding the natural rather than the human world—"that recognises the interdependent nature of the world" and "leads to a devotion to specific places and to the land itself, along with those creatures that share it with humankind" (5–6), "an imperative towards humility in relationships with both human and nonhuman nature" and "an intense scepticism concerning hyperrationality … that usually leads to an indictment of an overtechnologized modern world and a warning concerning the very real potential for ecological catastrophe" (6). Bryson asserts that "while adhering to certain conventions of romanticism" ecopoetry "also advances beyond that tradition and takes on distinctly contemporary problems and issues" (5).

The ecopoetry of contemporary Aotearoa New Zealand poets Robert Sullivan, Brian Turner and Airini Beautrais can teach us how notions of ecological loss and senses of belonging are complicated by Indigenous and colonial histories. Robert Sullivan, (b. 1967), (Ngāpuhi and Kāi Tahu iwi) is also an academic and editor whose writing links contemporary social and racial concerns to Māori and Pacific cultural traditions. His ecopoetry extends Western notions of encroachment and ecology by embodying culture in nature. That is, it represents the natural world as comprising human elements. Sullivan writes back to a 'classic' Aotearoa New Zealand poem, "The Magpies," by Denis Glover (b. 1912) who was working within the literary nationalist tradition from which the work of Brian Turner (b. 1944) stems. Turner is the country's most prominent conservationist poet. He is also an essayist and environmental activist. His poetry appears to be Wordsworthian in its use of nature as a tool for constructing and healing the individual self and might thus be described as Romantic ecopoetry. The youngest of the three

DOI: 10.4324/9781003399988-3

poets, Airini Beautrais, (b. 1982), is also a prose writer. Her ecopoetry recognises the colonial constructedness of now familiar ecologies, and the detrimental effects of such construction on indigenous plants, animals and Indigenous people. It thereby takes a postcolonial ecocritical approach to the relationship between culture and nature in a settler country.

Robert Sullivan (b. 1967)—A Moanan Perspective

When Aotearoa New Zealand poet and academic Robert Sullivan (Ngāpuhi and Kāi Tahu iwi) writes, "the spirits soar in the wild wind around us,/wind strong enough to break the wind mills/ littering the field," he writes beyond the eco-friendly sustainability of wind power generation to a sense of windmills as pollution. Spirits of ancestors inhabit the "wild wind" of Sullivan's lyric and the wind farm is figured as a spiritual contamination. In his poem, "South Point, Hawai'i" from *Voice Carried My Family* (2005), the presence of ancestral spirits is portrayed as uplifting despite the wind farm's violation of the site of early Hawaiian settlement:

> How could the ancestors know such desecration
> would arrive in this place? Such sadness.
> And yet their spirits soar here. They fly here.
>
> (15)

The ancestral spirits are depicted as more affecting than the physical remains of the ancient temple and the contemporary information centre, and stronger than the physical presence of the windmills. They provide a "spiritual harbour," a place of shelter in contrast to the windmills which are "littering." Such a sense of spiritual violation, we learn from this poem, lies outside the usual measures of environmental pollution gauged by a Western worldview that acknowledges violation of graveyards yet does not generally ascribe such encroachment to places where no physical remains are present—except, perhaps, war memorials—and certainly not to the elements of nature. Sullivan thus expands Western notions of ecopoetry and ecology by embedding culture in the nonhuman world such that the wind is conceived as part of the human realm.

In "49 (*environment I*)," from *Star Waka* (1999), Sullivan employs the image of a hydroelectric power project to figuratively portray the loss of Māori culture to Western modernity. The poem asks if waka makers, who are representative of Māori culture, will "live in submarines." Submersion of Māori culture by "the mechanical heat/of organised industry" is compared with the literal flooding of the South Island township of Cromwell following the 1993 construction of the Clyde Dam. The floodwater appears to represent colonial capitalism and to imply an ongoing threat to Māori culture, including Māori literature. The poem urges the poet to "write more":

> before he's dammed
> into poems clutching reeds
> waka bobbing above
>
> (53)

Thus, Sullivan confronts the Western worldview in which hydroelectric power generation is generally considered to be beneficial to the environment because it produces sustainable energy. He frames hydroelectric power projects—as he frames wind farms in "South Point, Hawai'i"— as an exemplar of Western industrialisation that stifles Indigenous culture.

Sullivan further depicts the embodiment of Māori culture in ecology through his poetic representation of stars—important navigation aids to Polynesian ocean voyagers not only as astronomical points but also as guiding lights of ancestors. In a joint introduction to *Whetu Moana: Contemporary Polynesian Poems in English* (2003), Sullivan and co-editors Albert Wendt and Reina Whaitiri explain:

> The people of Polynesia carefully and meticulously recorded their whakapapa, or lineage, thus establishing and strengthening their links with the earth, the sky, the gods and each other. Polynesians also believe that when we die we become stars that help to guide the living across that huge body of water Te Moana Nui a Kiwa.
>
> (1)

Sullivan's poetry collection, *Star Waka*, imparts Pacific Islanders' history of ocean navigation and discovery, and reliance on connection between human and nonhuman worlds. He draws these worldviews into the present to reveal tensions with Western comprehensions of nonhuman ecologies as being distinct from the human realm. According to poet and scholar Alice Te Punga Somerville, the numbering of the poems in the collection suggests not only "the precise mathematical foundation of navigation" but also "whakapapa" (51) which involves counting through genealogies. By drawing close connections between Pacific migrations and whakapapa, "Sullivan reflects on Māori as ocean people: voyagers, navigators, travellers, deeply embedded in specific land because of, not despite, previous migrations" (52). Bringing the maintenance of voyaging and navigation into the present, "demonstrat[es] the understanding that ancestors live on through successive generations" (53). Somerville's reading raises the centrality of ancestry to Sullivan's work, including the comprehension that ancestors reside in places and natural elements. Therefore, environmental degradation of these places or elements not only affects physical and emotional connection to them but also erodes their cultural associations.

One poem in *Star Waka* explicitly contrasts Western approaches to astronomy with Māori acknowledgement that stars embody spirits of ancestors. "*Waka 16 Kua wheturangitia koe,*" which takes its title from a traditional Māori proverb, begins:

> Beloved
> sent to Hawaiiki
> to become a star
> (20)

The poem goes on to consider how Māori connection to the nonhuman world via stars is diminished, figuratively and literally, through the loss of the brightness of starlight due to the "machines" of industrial capitalism that:

> lighten blackness
> when many stars
> are lost in the lightning
> (20)

Starlight lost to the artificial nightlights of modernity is only visible "in the papakainga" and "from middle of ocean." These images portray the technologically driven power of modernity outshining the lights of stars—which are comprehended as guiding ancestors—and the natural world generally. The inability to see stars due to light pollution, except from physically and culturally isolated places, figuratively portrays the shrinking of the space for Māori culture in a technological, ecologically damaged Pacific region. Such embodiment of culture in ecology thus expands the definition of ecological encroachment beyond the physical disappearance of plants and animals, and beyond the loss of nature that is familiar or produces solace. Rather, Sullivan portrays a sense of spiritual and communal loss. That is, the ecology here is not just the effects of industrial action on nature and consequently nature on human conditions but also the effect of cultural expression, such that ecology takes on not just physical and emotional connections but cultural ones.

Spirituality informs Sullivan's portrayal of ecological degradation of specific terrestrial places. "*xviii Similitude*," also from *Star Waka*, compares cutting a sewage pipe through Ōtuataua stonefields with "sticking a pipe/through Stonehenge –" (22). Likening the ancient stonefields to the globally recognised Neolithic monument in England compares the importance of the ancient site to Māori with the significance of Stonehenge to European culture. Yet the poem does not focus on air, water and seabed pollution caused by the proximity of a wastewater treatment plant but rather on the "violation of the lifeblood/of its guardians" (22). Like the windmills in "South Point, Hawai'i," the sewage pipe in South Auckland yields a spiritual contamination which, through the embodiment of culture in ecology, expands the idea of encroachment.

Sullivan's poetry explicates what he terms "Moanan" (2015: i) spirituality. 'Moana' means 'body of water,' specifically the Pacific Ocean, and Sullivan's poetry can thus inform us about what distinguishes the worldview of Polynesia, including Māori, from that of European, or Pākehā.

Brian Turner (b. 1944)—A Pākehā Perspective

Aotearoa New Zealand's most prominent conservationist poet, Brian Turner, connects his poetic persona with the landscapes of the remote regions of Central Otago in the South Island where he lives. Turner's Romantic poetic inheritance can be traced to Wordsworth's *The Prelude* (first published in 1850) in which the protagonist experiences nature's influence on consciousness from a rowboat. The protagonist in "Man in a Boat" from Turner's first collection, *Ladders of Rain* (1978), also escapes in a rowboat from modernity to a comforting nature:

> For a time the sounds of Civilization
> came muted across the water
> till eventually they faded away entirely
> (38)

Throughout Turner's work, a sense of solace and well-being derived from the presence of the nonhuman world is an enduring theme.

His poetic persona is portrayed like, a part of, and inhabited by, the rivers, ranges and open grasslands of Central Otago. In "High Noon" from *Bones* (1985), "the water pushes into my mouth, a thickening tongue" (45), suggesting that the river, and by extension nature, speaks through him. "October on the Otamita," from the same collection, renders the water as blood: "Walking upstream it's as if the water's/flowing through me, jigging my heart" (43). In "The River in You" from *Taking Off* (2001), "you sense the pull/that draws you back is the river in you" (51). Metaphors for habitation of the poetic speaker by the land are employed in "Home Ground" from *Taking Off* (2001): "the land takes you in" (67) and "Van Morrison in Central Otago" from *Beyond* (1992):

> It's not picturesque,
> it's essential, almost grand
> and it aches
> (10)

In this poem, the presence of the hills is figuratively linked to physical revival which

> makes it heart-stopping,
> articulate, hurtful
> like resuscitation.
>
>   (10)

In "Hawkdun Summer" from *Elemental* (2012), a sense of selfhood—of "when you're most like you" (198)—arises from proximity to the Hawkdun Range. In these ways, Central Otago's distinct landscapes and dramatic cloud formations are portrayed as comprising a measure of Turner's poetic speaker who requires specificity of place to be complete and whose sense of self is founded, in part, on his presence in the landscape.

Turner's sense of connection to nature, interpreted as a notion of belonging and, indeed, of selfhood, imparts the importance of the presence and preservation of Central Otago's remote landscapes. In his collection of poems and essays, *Into the Wider World: A Back Country Miscellany* (2008), he relates his opposition to the $2 billion Meridian Energy wind farm proposed for the Lammermoor Range. The project was abandoned in 2012 after a court battle with an environmental group, which included Turner who opposed the scheme for its visual impact on the tussock-covered highlands. He writes: "Up there on a fine day is like being surrounded by fields of gold that fortify and fuel the spirit" (353). His love of the uplands for "their aura, their unique character" is "evidence of a deep attachment and connection" and "one feels, at times, a sense of other forces at work there, perhaps a sense of the numinous" (354–355). Turner shares with Sullivan the notion of windmills as pollutants but his view of them as destructive to his sense of belonging to, and "spiritual" (355) connection with, the natural vista differs from Sullivan's conception of them as desecrating sacred ground. Rather, the proposed presence of the windmills is an affront to Turner's sense of solace and well-being derived from his location in a landscape he portrays as otherwise devoid of human impact.

In 13 collections of poetry published over more than 40 years, Turner often relates his sense of connection with nature through accounts of the sport of fly fishing. He chronicles his passion for both angling and the river environs through a poetic speaker whose connections with trout and their Central Otago river habitats are portrayed as communions. Over time, we learn how this relationship with nature changes, suggesting a perceptive arc, somewhat like a narrative arc, with three distinct postures. The first is an exposition of the excitement of the sport of fly fishing with some tension between the catching of trout and an appreciation of them as part of the nonhuman world. The second constitutes an evasion of the act of fly fishing. Although the poems are still centred on this activity, they focus rather on a sense of well-being afforded by the presence of the nonhuman world. The third shift is a move away from the earlier poems' Romantic imagery to practical language and ecopolemic that imparts a sense of the loss of the natural world due to human activities: increased tourism, hydroelectric power schemes which dam and alter the flow of rivers, and intensive dairy farms which draw river water for irrigation.

In these later poems, trout and the poetic angler are rendered as victims of the toxic effects of modernity, as in "Lament for the Taieri River" from *Into the Wider World*:

> The Taieri River stinks from effluent,
> is soured by pesticides and fertilisers.
> The flow is sluggish, low;
>
>   (364)

This poem recalls a past when fish flourished, blaming "progress" and the "Regional Council" (365) for decisions that "turn country I love,/… into country it was never meant to be" (364). "Last Songs," also from *Into the Wider World,* evokes a disquieting sense of irrevocability regarding the polluted state of the river—"all the great songs/are last songs" (318). It suggests a lack of learned insight—"the finest moments/…toss us among the rocks/of our generation's experience"—as the poet grows to understand that "nothing bores deeper than the knowledge/of loss" (318). Trout appear only as "shadowy dreams," a metaphor that also describes those places which once afforded solace from modernity:

> Like spent spinners our dreams at dusk
> fall back to the river
> and drift away.
>
> (319)

Like Sullivan, Turner perceives hydroelectric power schemes as environmentally degrading but not because they portend a cultural loss. Rather, along with other forms of modernity that threaten trout habitats, they signal the loss of those remote places that provided Turner with a sense of solace, belonging and, crucially, selfhood. While Turner's poetry is founded in a particular Aotearoa New Zealand geography, the sentiments about that environment and his connection to it are in sympathy with the traditional Romantic aesthetic of the relationship between nature and human consciousness. His sense of belonging to nature is generic, without a sense of what makes Aotearoa New Zealand 'nature' of particular significance.

Notions of belonging to the land are a specific issue for ecopoetical writing in Aotearoa New Zealand. Literary historian Alex Calder, in *The Settler's Plot: How Stories Take Place in New Zealand* (2011), uses the phrase "belonging through nature" (172) to describe "the affection for place felt by Pakeha" (4), which he says differs as a sense of belonging from the Māori concept of belonging described by the concept of tūrangawaewae. Calder writes:

> We Pakeha are at home here, we identify as New Zealanders, this is our place, we belong –
> and yet, without denying any of those things, there is another degree of belonging that we
> do not have that is available to Maori (or perhaps to the Maori side of you).
>
> (5)

He describes a "syndrome" he calls "Pakeha turangawaewae" as "an oxymoron" because as well as describing a different sense of belonging from that of Māori, it posits belonging by Pākehā who "are not only relative newcomers and strangers but also beneficiaries of the historical marginalisation of Maori" (4). Calder's problematical notion of 'belonging through nature' describes a Pākehā approach to nationhood of which Turner's poetry is an exemplar.

Turner perceives his notion of belonging to be the same as, rather than different from, a sense of belonging conceived by Māori. The title of his poem, "Tangata Whenua" from *All That Blue Can Be* (1989), deliberately appropriates the Māori term 'tangata whenua' to assert a notion of Pākehā Indigeneity. This assertion is in tension with the customary meaning of 'tangata whenua,' which is 'Indigenous people' and references Māori cultural practices and beliefs that locate whānau in traditional lands. Turner's poem employs images of historical and present-day European occupation of Central Otago and the metaphor of habitation of his poetic speaker by nature—"the country/rolls through me" (18)—to assert his alternate sense of Indigeneity. He claims this notion even more assuredly in "Southern Tribesmen" from *Taking Off* (2001), in which a sunset over the Hawkdun Range is the occasion for reflection on Pākehā belonging, writing that "because it's there/and we're here to see/it … that defines the meaning/of indigenous" and "my sense of belonging here/rises defiantly out of the dark" (72). Pākehā belonging is Turner's acknowledged subject but what is unacknowledged is the extent to which this elides other histories and Indigenous perceptions of belonging. Although he may seek to assert a sense of dual Indigeneity—as discussed extensively in books by prominent historian of Turner's own generation, Michael King—the elision of Māori history in his poetry risks a sense of substitution: that of one Indigenous culture for another. Turner's short poem "Toi-Toi and Tussock" from *Footfall* (2005), which is written in memory of King, metaphorically connects the historian with indigenous and exotic species and a sense of nationhood:

> You were toi-toi and tussock,
> trout and hapuku:
> what makes us us.
>
> (30)

But the word 'us,' with its suggestion of nationhood, elides those who may not feel that trout are a part of a notion of belonging. When learning about these cultural differences between Pākehā and Māori, it is important to note that trout are an introduced species which displaced some indigenous fish species which were Indigenous food sources.

Writing Back to Denis Glover (b. 1912) and Literary Nationalism

The Pākehā notion of 'belonging through nature' as portrayed in Turner's poetry and by extension the tradition from which Turner's work stems is problemised not only by Sullivan's evocations of Indigenous conceptions of belonging based on ancestry, cultural representations and oral history but also through the impact of colonialism. To enter this discussion, it is worth a close look at Sullivan's poem "Took: A Preface to 'The Magpies,'" from *Shout Ha! To The Sky* (2010). It is useful because the poem explicitly signals a sense of belonging based on cultural norms prior to European settlement by writing back to a poem by Denis Glover (b. 1912), who was working within the literary nationalist tradition from which Turner's work stems.

The first stanza of Glover's poem "The Magpies" (1964) begins, "When Tom and Elizabeth took the farm" and ends, "And *Quardle oodle ardle wardle doodle*/The magpies said" (32). The poem then recounts a European couple's loss of farmland to a mortgagee sale during the Depression. Sullivan's poem, however, recounts an earlier dispossession: the loss of Māori land through colonial settlement. "Took: A Preface to 'The Magpies'" highlights the cultural gap between settler and Māori notions of occupation and belonging. In it, the farmers are "shooing/us down the dusty trail. Your talk sounds like the magpies—/all quardling oodling ardling wardling and doodling." The poet speaker responds: "Do you mean korero, uri, arero, wairua, ruruhau perhaps sir?" (25). This final line of the poem compares the incomprehensibility to European settlers of the Māori words, "korero, uri, arero, wairua, ruruhau," and by extension Māori culture, with the meaningless "Quardle oodle ardle wardle doodle" of the ambivalent magpies in Glover's poem, suggesting little interest on the part of the European farmers (and by extension, Glover, the Pākehā poet) in comprehending the Māori situation and plight.

Sullivan's poem hinges on the word 'took' in the title, which appears in Glover's first line: "When Tom and Elizabeth took the farm" and which Sullivan reads to mean they appropriated it. In his essay "A Poetics of Culture: Others' and Ours, Separate and Commingled,"

Sullivan says, "the word 'took' in the first line implies that it was taken rather than 'given'" (11). (Glover, himself, seems more likely to have meant bought because 'took' can also mean 'took over' or 'purchased'—but Sullivan seems to suggest that the word's other denotation is nevertheless historically apt, and the very fact that Glover would not have meant to employ the double denotation is more or less Sullivan's point.) In his essay, Sullivan says the phrase "Not understood" in his poem relates to Thomas Bracken's poem "Not Understood" (1879), which laments a loss of Christian values. (Thomas Bracken, 1843–98, is best known for author-ing Aotearoa New Zealand's national anthem "God Defend New Zealand" (1876)). Sullivan appears to use the phrase ironically to suggest that a confiscation of Māori land was counter to Christian values. In "Took: A Preface to 'The Magpies'" Sullivan explicates what he calls "the absence (I am tempted to say 'erasure') of explicit historical and political references in many works of NZ literature" which "are as political and historical, when we notice, as the inclusion of them" (10). His poem provides an alternative, Māori perspective to Glover's poem, which describes the indifference of the exotic magpies to the hardships of farming during the Depres-sion. In contrast, Sullivan's poem describes the loss of Māori culture as well as land and indig-enous birds following European colonisation, revealing a Māori ecological consciousness. By writing back to Glover's "The Magpies"—described by Wellington poet Bill Manhire as "the single New Zealand poem to have achieved a kind of 'classic' status" (11)—Sullivan aims to educate readers about the issue of the erasure of Māori culture through both land confiscation and literature. Such erasure exists then in Aotearoa New Zealand's long tradition of ecopoetry, of which this poem turns out to be a part, because Māori connection to the land is, for Sullivan, a part of the land's ecology.

Sullivan's poem enacts the erasure of language while also speaking the language. That is, it works one way if you don't understand the Māori words (revealing them as indecipherable noise like the chatter of the magpies in Glovers' poem) and another if you do (their meanings—talk, descendants, tongue, spirit and shelter—reveal the affiliation of Māori to the land, to each other and to a willingness for conversation.) These Māori words signify connection to land based on oral and ancestral histories and a sense of home, in contrast with the commercial relationship to the land of Glover's hard-worn settlers. In his poem, Tom and Elizabeth are forced by mort-gagee sale to leave the farm, which is deemed worthless because the bank is unable to sell it. This is in opposition to the Māori valuing of the land—in Sullivan's account—for its ancestral history, a sense of belonging and provision of home.

Such difference between Māori and non-Māori notions of relationship with the land is described by fiction writer and poet Keri Hulme in her essay "Mauri: An Introduction to Bicul-tural Poetry in New Zealand" (1981): "The Maori relationship with the land is intense. Land is not an exploitable resource: it is Papatuanuku, earth mother" (302). Through spotlighting the particular version of Eurocentricity of Glover's celebrated poem—by in turn contrasting the meaning of the Māori words with the meaninglessness Europeans ascribed to them and by high-lighting a denotation of 'took' that remained seemingly invisible to Glover—Sullivan reveals Māori belonging to the land as more complicated than Glover's settler colonial sense of own-ership or indeed Turner's subjective notion of 'belonging through nature.' Sullivan represents land—ecology—not as a resource or as a place of solace but as inherently tied to culture through spirituality, ancestry and rites of occupation.

Airini Beautrais (b. 1982)—A Postcolonial Ecocritical Approach

An alternative Pākehā approach to Turner's representations of nature and the human relationship with it is taken by Whanganui poet, Airini Beautrais, in her collection *Flow: Whanganui River*

Poems (2017). Beautrais is almost 30 years younger than Turner and her poetic heritage stems not from Wordsworthian Romanticism but more readily aligns with the relatively recent field of postcolonial ecocriticism. In *Flow,* the nonhuman world is portrayed not through Turner's Romantic lens but rather from a postcolonial approach that depicts the land in a state of colonially constructed malaise. Beautrais shows connection between people and nature through portrayals of trout and fishing, characterising trout in a polluted river as symbols of reduced human connection with nature akin to Turner's later poetic representations. But she recognises trout as an introduced species that supplanted, and in some cases caused the extinction of, indigenous fish.

Flow's opening poem, "Confluence *Taumarunui, 2013,*" portrays the speaker's brother Joe catching a trout, cooking it over a fire and, together with the speaker, eating it. At the end of this narrative, Joe remarks: "'I think I'll remember these as the good old days,'" (22) implying that trout fishing—an activity many New Zealanders consider a right of citizenship—will soon become a thing of the past. Like Turner's later poems, Beautrais's poem carries lessons about the impending loss of the connection between people and nature that the sport of trout fishing affords. But in contrast with Turner's earlier Romantic depictions of trout inhabiting an unspoilt nature, Beautrais portrays the fish as part of a degraded modernity arisen from the spoliation of ecologies by the settler colonial project.

As its title indicates, "Confluence *Taumarunui, 2013,*" is set at the confluence of two rivers. The Ōngarue River where Joe fishes is "clean-looking" at "this time of year" because "there's no run-off" (21)—a reference to nitrogen leaching from farmland. But the Whangaehu River that joins it is "*never* clean" (21). On the riverbanks are introduced willows, poplars, Japanese walnuts, cherries, corn; and one indigenous tree—but it is not whole: "half a tōtara" (21)—and pollution: "disposable nappies, circles of bourbon bottles" (22). Joe's trout is eaten with "wild greens harvested from New World" (22)—a supermarket chain. He has taken to

braining trout with a rock,
rather than knifing between the eyes, like he taught me.
People will do all kinds of things to come down to earth.

(22)

This violence against the fish in an attempt "to come down to earth" suggests that the degraded nature has had a degrading effect on Joe. At the poem's conclusion, he maintains, for now, his off-the-grid lifestyle, drifting to sleep in his car. But even "the sound of water" is subject to exotic modification: "the poplar leaves slapping" (22). Such representations portray the relationship between people and nature within a settler colonial country as a lack of indigenous nature and the presence of nature that has been constructed by human agency, notions that are absent from Turner's Romantic appreciation of the colonially constructed trout habitats of Central Otago.

Beautrais explicitly tackles the degrading effects of the introduction by European settlers of trout into Aotearoa New Zealand's rivers in the 1860s for the sport of angling. In "Trout/*Oncorhynchus mykiss/Salmo trutta*," she employs rhyme and line-ending verbs—"translucent, light-bending/freckled and blending" (91)—which heighten the colours and liveliness of trout and the excitement of fishing—"pooling/where the wide-spooling/hook shimmers, dangling" (93). While these representations would seem to recall Turner's early angling poems, Beautrais adds a layer to his appreciation of trout and fishing by explicating the dominance of trout over the smaller, indigenous fish, "A weeding/of weakness, of small things" (92), and "That which was here first is caught in the jawing,/the gnawing … then fall to a culling:/newcomers spread and their numbers keep swelling" (93). The poem's penultimate stanza critiques the global culture of fly-fishing:

> The small and the slimy are fit for ignoring
> the roaring
> of rapids calls to the rover.
>
> (93)

It implies that the practice of anglers coming from other countries to experience trout fishing in Aotearoa New Zealand is an act of forgetting those ecologies—"The small and the slimy"—that are now reduced or extinct due to European colonisation.

In the subsequent poem, Beautrais explicitly mourns an indigenous fish species displaced by trout. "Grayling/Upokororo/*Prototroctes oxyrhynchus*" employs unadorned language and brevity to mimic the small, plain fish. It begins:

> Small, insignificant fish.
> Even your name is formless.
>
> (95)

By contrasting with the rich language and long length of "Trout/*Oncorhynchus mykiss/Salmo trutta*," this four-line poem illustrates in form and content the striking differences between trout and grayling, implying the dominance of the exotic over the indigenous.

Through Beautrais' portrayals of trout as connecting people and nature, and as responsible for human-caused ecological loss, we learn about the layered complexity of human entanglement with nature in a settler colonial setting. She draws attention to what American postcolonial ecocritic and academic Elizabeth DeLoughrey calls, "our very assumptions about what is a natural landscape" (2011: 266). Beautrais's poetry recognises that trout habitats—which Turner depicts as places of escape from the human world to a soothing nature—are in fact sites of colonial construction and that 'wildness' is not always what it seems. Trout swimming in Aotearoa New Zealand rivers are in fact products of human intervention, which have displaced 'wild,' or indigenous, nature.

Furthermore, Beautrais recalls the impact of the introduction of such exotic species on the pre-colonial Māori lifestyle. Like "Grayling/Upokororo/*Prototroctes oxyrhynchus*," six other short poems have titles that include the species' Māori names alongside English and Latin names, thereby raising cultural complications regarding the circumstances of their decline. These poems—"Kākahi/*Freshwater mussel/Echyridella spp.*," "Kōura/Freshwater crayfish/*Paranephrops planifrons*," "Lamprey/Piharau/*Geotria australis*," "Spoonbill/Kōtuku ngutupapa/*Platalea regia*," "Tuna/Longfin eel/*Anguilla dieffenbachii*" and "Whio/Blue duck/*Hymenolaimus malacorhynchos*"—suggest that Indigenous cultural associations are as crucial to the ecological and intrinsic significance of these species as are Western notions of their importance.

These titles in turn carry implications in the bodies of the poems. "Kākahi/*Freshwater mussel/Echyridella spp.*" ascribes farming, and by extension Pākehā colonialism—"The water low,/the run-off thick"—as culpable for a lack of mussels for consumption, suggesting the harmful effects of farming on Māori customary fishing rights:

> Twenty-two sites,
> only one fit
> to harvest from.
>
> (85)

In other poems, Beautrais brings home connections between natural losses and cultural ones by suggesting the way that both are preserved more in symbol than reality. "Hīnaki" invokes the pre-colonial Māori lifestyle, dispensing with an English translation of its title which means eel trap. The lines "hung in a glass case over a model weir" and "your cup will never hold an eel again" (108) make explicit the loss of a viable Māori food source, contrasting the elevation of the trap preserved as a cultural relic in a museum with the living Māori culture that has been undermined. Similarly, "Whio/Blue duck/*Hymenolaimus malacorhynchos*" contrasts the image of the blue duck on the New Zealand $10 banknote with the duck in nature, which is as "Hard to come by" (87) as money. This poem even more overtly than "Hīnaki" critiques a tendency to value symbol over substance, representation over thing. Just as the picture of the duck is a representation, money itself is merely a representation of value, suggesting, perhaps, a misplacing of value—the substitution of the valuing of capitalist consumerism, rather than the valuing of nature that sustained pre-colonial Māori culture.

Beautrais is careful to note the difference between her own cultural position and that of Māori. While Turner deliberately confronts Māori as he seeks to assert an equal sense of belonging to the land—and by disregarding cultural difference implicitly produces an attitude of monoculturalism—Beautrais is mindful of such difference, writing in her dedication to *Flow*: "the significance of the relationships between Whanganui iwi and the river cannot be adequately addressed by a Pākehā writer" (13). She describes herself as a sixth-generation descendant of European settlers including a land surveyor from the time of colonial deforestation. The poems in *Flow* trace the Whanganui River catchment's geology, ecologies and histories of human settlement from 1864 until 2014, including the ecological violation of colonialism and changing Pākehā attitudes towards the environment over time.

"Tributaries/*Taumarunui to Piropiro, 2014*," describes the poet and her parents—it uses the 'Beautrais' family name—cleaning family gravestones, an action which connects her family to a history of colonial settlement and environmental degradation. While they do this work, the conversation turns to her father's history of environmental activism. By juxtaposing actions that honour the family's settler past with discussions about environmental protection, Beautrais can educate us about a generational shift in Pākehā attitudes towards nature. And by employing the Māori word whakapapa to describe her family lineage—"This cemetery/is as far back as we know our Beautrais whakapapa" (67)—she suggests her own generation's increasing familiarity with, and adoption of, some Māori words and concepts.

The poem relates conflict between environmental activists and logging companies in the 1970s, suggesting comparatively recent resistance to the felling of indigenous forests. The Pureora Forest that remains due to the 1978 anti-logging protest is portrayed as now shared by people and nature through recreational activities such as the "Timber Trail" cycleway. The poem's concluding lines, "A robin follows us out, hiding in the mānuka,/reappearing, disappearing, returning" (68), invoke the return and resilience of those indigenous birds that were absent from the felled landscape and from the European settler consciousness portrayed elsewhere in *Flow*.

"Treetops/*Pureora, 1978*" projects the ecologically empathetic point of view of an activist lodged in a tree who is portrayed as courageous for undertaking this life-threatening action. Empathy for ecologies that live in the forest alongside the trees and vines underlies this portrayal of the successful protest by the Native Forest Action Council. But this success is somewhat reduced by recognition of the extent of deforestation and the difficulty of protecting indigenous species in the patches of forest that remain:

—the hardest push
was working to restore the bush,
to stitch these fragments up again.

(65)

This poem is a ballad, a form Beautrais uses for many poems that she sets in colonial and more recent times. Speakers present many environmental perspectives, ranging from bushmen who promote commercial logging to the activists who celebrate the forest's preservation. Repetition of the traditional form conjures a sense of continuity and connectivity between the various voices. It draws together Pākehā viewpoints into a shared history of settlement and of place, creating a sense of complicity and mutual responsibility for environmental degradation and rehabilitation.

Alongside changes in Pākehā environmental attitudes, Beautrais portrays a generational shift towards a greater understanding of Māori concepts relating to nature. Poems that include her children—who would seem to represent the future—portray Pākehā and Māori valuing nature in its own right rather than as a resource. Resonance between Māori, Pākehā and nature, as represented by the river and the stars, is evoked in "Puanga." By alternating between the names "Puanga" and "Rigel," the Māori and English terms, respectively, for the brightest star in the constellation of Orion, this poem foregrounds Māori and European mythologies from which the names originate. It also references "Subaru," the Japanese name for Matariki, connecting Whanganui with its sister city Nagaizumi-cho in Japan, another Pacific culture. But it asserts the dominance, locally at least, of the Māori name over the others:

> But in Whanganui,
> Puanga is the star
> we look for in the new year.
> (78)

The "hunter" in the sky is the star cluster Orion, which takes its name in Western culture from the mythical Greek hunter. "In a tank a real eel./The silver of īnanga." (79) Juxtaposing the image of the "hunter" with the "real" eel in the tank and the īnanga—an indigenous fish species—contrasts Western preservation of the hunter only in myth with a pre-colonial Māori lifestyle in which eels and īnanga were hunted for food.

The poem evokes a sense of burgeoning resistance to the present state of ecological degradation through the adoption of bicultural education: "The children are making the river" (77) via a model comprising representations of indigenous birds and plants, and aspects of Māori culture. It incorporates Māori words that have become familiar to non-Māori New Zealanders in the last 15–20 years: piupiu (flax skirts), poi (soft woven balls on strings), harakeke (flax), whare (house), Matariki (Pleiades) (77–78). Protection of the natural environment is evoked through images of belonging and renewal—"A time to prepare new ground. … Where can we plant this tree? (79). Similarly, "Huihui/*Taumarunui 2014*,"—"Huihui: to gather. Like water does" (70)—ascribes the importance of iwi while acknowledging dual cultural pasts and a sense of two cultures coming together through a shared history of place.

In her dedication to *Flow*, Beautrais highlights the 2014 deed of settlement between Whanganui iwi and the New Zealand government which made the Whanganui River the first waterway in the world to be legally recognised as a living entity. Historian and anthropologist Anne Salmond describes the settlement as an example of "a willingness by a non-Māori majority in New Zealand to recognise the value of Māori conceptions" (410). Māori terms in Aotearoa New Zealand's Resource Management Act (1991) and Local Government Act (2002) requiring councils "to take into account the relationship of Māori and their culture and traditions with their ancestral land, water, sites, wāhi tapu (ancestral sites) and other taonga," are altering New Zealand law as the legal process is required to acknowledge "'the persistence and creativity of a distinctly Māori register of value'" (Thinking Through Things 2007, qtd. in Salmond 313).

Beautrais's poems expand on this notion of integration by imparting the proposal that ecological recuperation is occurring beyond legal frameworks, that is, in everyday life.

Conclusion

The ecopoetry of the three contemporary Aotearoa New Zealand poets examined in this chapter can teach us about varying notions of nature and the human relationship with it alongside changing societal attitudes towards ecologies and Indigenous culture over time.

In Turner's work, we learn that ecological loss and preservation manifest in reflections on the spoliation of remote Central Otago landscapes due to the effects of wind farms and hydropower schemes, increased tourism and irrigated agriculture. Turner's project is to preserve the 'nature' that remains. His poetry portrays notions of escape from encroaching modernity by venturing into, and meditating on the psychic benefits of, Central Otago's remote landscapes. Thus, his work aligns with the Romantic tradition and the British/American model of ecopoetry within an Aotearoa New Zealand setting. This approach is complicated by the fact that much of the 'nature' Turner admires was humanly constructed through the colonial project.

Sullivan's lessons about ecological loss and preservation focus on the loss of Māori ancestors embodied in natural elements, the loss of tapu (sacred) natural elements and the loss of kaitiakitanga—the ability to fulfil customary duties of environmental guardianship over particular places. These Indigenous conceptions of ecological loss and encroachment problematise and expand Turner's approach by drawing attention to the imposition of the Anglophile notion of solace in nature onto landscapes apprehended by Māori as inherently tied to the human world.

For Beautrais, recognition of ecological loss centres on indigenous plants and animals and the effects of their losses on the pre-colonial Māori lifestyle. Her collection, *Flow: Whanganui River Poems,* portrays the achievements and failures of colonialism, describing towns and farmland created by settlement as ugly and lacking indigenous species. But it also describes shifts in Pākehā environmental attitudes over time, from a focus on resource-driven degradation to a desire for preservation. Beautrais's approach aligns with the field of postcolonial ecocriticism in which literature plays a part by "conceptualizing both the legacies of rupture and the possibilities of imaginative recuperation and transformation" (DeLoughrey et al. 2015: 5).

A sense of belonging and nationhood is integral to Aotearoa New Zealand ecopoetry in ways that show specific tensions between settler colonial and Indigenous cultures here. For Turner, a sense of belonging derives from appreciation and occupation of colonially constructed environments. His poetry describes belonging through nature centred on figurative emotional and physical attachment to place, arising from birthright, occupation and a lifetime of outdoor recreation in Central Otago. Being a New Zealander is expressed as a combination of exotic and indigenous species. This narrative—founded on what Turner sees as "essential"—is open to interrogation within a postcolonial ecocritical framework in which "scholars have emphasized that empire is constitutive to knowledge of place and its representation" (DeLoughrey 2014: 325). Turner's notion of belonging, which stems from a sense of attachment to a particular Aotearoa New Zealand landscape, follows the country's tradition of literary nationalism—which strove to assert a sense of settler belonging in a new land—and therefore exemplifies a particular Pākehā approach.

Sullivan's poetry implicitly problemises approaches such as Turner's by raising Indigenous conceptions of belonging. These centre on ancestry recorded in oral history within a wider Pacific homeland with its own spiritual epistemology. Sullivan expresses belonging to Aotearoa New Zealand and the Pacific region through the "Moanan" perspective and "culturally inherited ways of being" (2015: ii). His poetry imparts the centrality of genealogy to selfhood, and the importance of ancestry to community both in the past and in the present, tracing communal belonging through lineages dating back to first discovery and original habitation.

Beautrais relates multiple narratives of history to portray culturally different stories and interpretations of belonging to place. Acknowledgement of her own limited comprehension of Māori notions of belonging suggests awareness of cultural difference. By embedding now commonly used Māori words and names into her English verse, Beautrais suggests that her own sense of belonging in Aotearoa New Zealand is attuned to connection with both Pākehā and Māori cultures. This connection is enlarged in poems where acceptance by Pākehā of Māori understandings of nature provides a pathway for environmental recuperation.

Different ways of perceiving ecological loss in Aotearoa New Zealand reveal tension between appreciation of so-called 'natural' environments that have in fact been constructed by colonialism, and Māori and nonhuman ecologies that have, at times inadvertently, been supplanted. The embodiment of ecology in culture—such as in Sullivan's poems that describe spiritual desecration of natural elements—raises tension between so-called environmentally friendly projects, such as wind farms and hydropower schemes, and their potential spoliation of places of cultural significance. Pākehā notions of, often individual, belonging through nature and of nationhood are in tension with a Moanan sense of belonging to the wider Pacific region founded on community, spirituality and ancestry.

These tensions bring into question terms such as 'ecocentric' and 'nonhuman nature' that underlie foundational definitions of ecopoetry. They raise questions such as, which ecologies? Whose nonhuman nature? Rather than interdependence between people and nature, a phrase that currently underlies definitions of ecopoetry yet implies nature on the one hand and culture on the other, contemporary ecopoetry from Aotearoa New Zealand portrays a wider sense of entanglement. It exemplifies what DeLoughrey et al. describe as the ways in which "the history of colonialism necessitates the imbrication of humans in nature" (2015: 1) because "postcolonial environmental representations often engage with the legacies of violent material, environmental, and cultural transformation" (2015: 5). By problemising accepted notions of what constitutes nature, this approach suggests new ways of learning about how Aotearoa New Zealand ecopoetry aligns with and differs from formative definitions of the field of ecopoetry.

Contemporary ecopoetry located within a particular cultural setting expands current understandings of ecopoetry and of ecology in ways that may not occur elsewhere. Aotearoa New Zealand has its own unique flora and fauna, which have been "violently modified" (Steer 85) by comparatively recent European colonial settlement. As Pawson and Brooking note, "relations between people and environments in New Zealand share many of the characteristics of such interactions elsewhere, when migrants arrive in new lands" but "both the context for these interactions and the manner in which they have intersected with this context and each other have produced very particular outcomes" (17–18). The result of these outcomes for Aotearoa New Zealand ecopoetry is a unique local variant. The ecopoems analysed in this essay provide examples of the kinds of narratives about ecology and culture that are "essential for understanding the social, cultural, and political experiences of global ecological change in specific locations and across different time frames" (DeLoughrey et al. 2015: 2). The role of Indigenous culture in this country and its literature makes Aotearoa New Zealand ecopoetry a significant contributor to such global understandings. Reading Aotearoa New Zealand ecopoetry by poets such as Sullivan, Turner, and Beautrais side by side can promote the adoption of bicultural education and nurture a future where the triangular affiliation between nature, Māori and Pākehā that is specific to Aotearoa New Zealand is better understood.

Glossary of te reo Māori Words

Aotearoa   North Island—now used as the Māori name for New Zealand.

arero   tongue.

atua   ancestor with continuing influence, god, demon, supernatural being, deity, ghost, object of superstitious regard, strange being—although often translated as 'god' and now also used for the Christian God, this is a misconception of the real meaning. Many Māori trace their ancestry from *atua* in their *whakapapa* and they are regarded as ancestors with influence over particular domains.

hāpuku   groper, grouper, *Polyprion* oxygeneios—a large heavy-bodied fish with a big head and a wide mouth found in warm seas.

haka   performance of the haka, posture dance—vigorous dances with actions and rhythmically shouted words. A general term for several types of such dances.

harakeke   New Zealand flax, *Phormium tenax*—an important native plant with long, stiff, upright leaves and dull red flowers. Found on lowland swamps throughout Aotearoa/New Zealand.

hīnaki   eel trap, wicker eel basket, wire eel pot.

huihui   to put or add together, come together, meet, gather, assemble, congregate.

īnanga   inanga, whitebait, *Galaxias maculatus*—a small silvery-white native fish with a slender body. Found in streams, rivers, lakes, swamps and pools throughout the coastal regions of Aotearoa/New Zealand up to 215 km inland.

iwi   extended kinship group, tribe, nation, people, nationality and race—often refers to a large group of people descended from a common ancestor and associated with a distinct territory.

kaitiakitanga   guardianship, stewardship, trusteeship, trustee.

kākahi   freshwater mussel, *Hyridella menziesi*—a bivalve mollusc which lives in fine mud or sand in freshwater lakes, ponds, streams and rivers. Has a dark, olive-brown coated shell and the inside is greyish-white.

kapa haka   concert party, *haka* group, Māori cultural group, Māori performing group.

kōrero   speech, narrative, story, news, account, discussion, conversation, discourse, statement, information.

kōtuku ngutupapa   royal spoonbill, *Platalea regia*—a large white bird with a long, black, spoon-shaped bill and black legs which feeds on tidal mudflats by sweeping its bill from side to side.

kōura   salt-water crayfish, the southern rock lobster, red rock lobster, spiny rock lobster, *Jasus edwardsii*—a species of spiny lobster found throughout coastal waters of southern Australia and New Zealand including the Chatham Islands.

mānuka   tea-tree, *Leptospermum scoparium*—a common native shrub bush with aromatic prickly leaves and many small, white, pink or red flowers.

Matariki   Pleiades, Messier 45—an open cluster of many stars in Te Kāhui o Matariki, with at least nine stars visible to the naked eye…. The first appearance before sunrise of Matariki in the north-eastern sky, in the Tangaroa phase of the lunar month, indicates the beginning of the Māori year—about mid-June—and is the cause for celebrations.

moana   sea, ocean, large lake.

Moana-nui-a-Kiwa, Te   Pacific Ocean.

Pākehā   New Zealander of European descent—probably originally applied to English-speaking Europeans living in Aotearoa/New Zealand.

papa kāinga   original home, home base, village, communal Māori land—sometimes written as one word, *papakāinga.*

Papatūānuku   Earth, Earth mother and wife of Rangi-nui—all living things originate from them.

piharau   lamprey, *Geotria australis*—an eel-like fish that has a sucker mouth with horny teeth and a rasping tongue. A highly valued food of Māori. Found around North, South, Stewart and Chatham Islands coasts, penetrating inland to 230 km.

piupiu   waist-to-knees garment made of flax—has a wide waistband and is used in modern times for *kapa haka* performances.

poi   a light ball on a string of varying length which is swung or twirled rhythmically to sung accompaniment.

Puanga   Rigel—the seventh brightest star in the sky and seen above Tautoru (Orion's Belt) in the eastern sky in the early morning. With some *iwi* Puanga heralded the beginning of the Māori year.

ruruhau   shelter, refuge, protector.

tangata whenua   local people, hosts, indigenous people—people born of the whenua, that is, of the placenta and of the land where the people's ancestors have lived and where their placenta are buried.

taonga   treasure, anything prized—applied to anything considered to be of value including socially or culturally valuable objects, resources, phenomenon, ideas and techniques.

toetoe   *Cortaderia* spp.—native plants with long, grassy leaves with a fine edge and saw-like teeth. Flowers are white, feathery, arching plumes. Grow on sand dunes, on rocks and cliff faces, along streams and swamp edges.

tōtara   *Podocarpus totara, Podocarpus cunninghamii*—large forest trees with prickly, olive-green leaves not in two rows. Found throughout Aotearoa/New Zealand.

tuna   eel of various species, including the longfin eel *(Anguilla dieffenbachii)* and shortfin eel *(Anguilla australis).*

tūrangawaewae   domicile, standing, place where one has the right to stand—place where one has rights of residence and belonging through kinship and *whakapapa.*

upokororo   New Zealand grayling, *Prototroctes oxyrhynchus*—a small slender fish, silvery, sometimes with a reddish back. Was caught in large numbers and found only in lowland rivers and streams. They spawned in freshwater streams and developing to maturity in salt-water. Their length was between 20 and 40 cm. Although once common in Aotearoa/New Zealand streams, it is now extinct, possibly because of the introduction of trout.

uri   offspring, descendant, relative, kin, progeny, blood connection, successor.

wāhi tapu   sacred place, sacred site—a place subject to long-term ritual restrictions on access or use, e.g., a burial site, a battle ground or a place where tapu objects were placed.

wairua   spirit, soul.

waka   canoe, vehicle, conveyance, spirit medium, medium (of an *atua*).

whakapapa   genealogy, genealogical table, lineage, descent—reciting *whakapapa* was, and is, an important skill and reflected the importance of genealogies in Māori society in terms of leadership, land and fishing rights, kinship and status. It is central to all Māori institutions.

whānau   extended family, family group, a familiar term of address to a number of people—the primary economic unit of traditional Māori society. In the modern context, the term is sometimes used to include friends who may not have any kinship ties to other members.

whare   house, building, residence, dwelling, shed, hut, habitation.

whetū   star—sometimes also used for other celestial bodies, e.g., comets. Stars were observed carefully as they were important indicators of time and particular stars and star clusters were omens of aspects of life, including crop success.

whetūrangitia   to appear above the horizon (a star or the moon).

whio   blue duck, *Hymenolaimus malacorhynchos*—blue-grey duck with a pale pink bill found along fast-flowing mountain streams and rivers in native forest and tussock grassland. Named after the call of the male bird.

Notes to Glossary

Definitions, some of which have been abbreviated, and current spellings are from Te Aka Māori Dictionary at maoridictionary.co.nz. which is based on the book *Te Aka Māori-English, English-Māori Dictionary and Index* (2011) by John C Moorfield.

toetoe is commonly misspelt as toitoi or toi-toi.

The whakataukī (proverb), "Kua whetūrangitia koe," in this context means, "Return, take your place amongst the stars along with your ancestors that adorn the sky." (https://wheturangitia. services.govt.nz accessed 23 February 2023).

Note

1 With digital access to macrons, their use in Māori words is now commonplace. This chapter cites quotations exactly as they appear and many did not include macrons at the time of publication.

Works Cited

Bate, Jonathan. *The Song of the Earth*. Picador, 2000.

Beautrais, Airini. *Flow: Whanganui River Poems*. Victoria UP, 2017.

Calder, Alex. *The Settler's Plot: How Stories Take Place in New Zealand*. Auckland UP, 2011.

DeLoughrey, Elizabeth M. "Ecocriticism: The Politics of Place." *The Routledge Companion to Anglophone Caribbean Literature*, edited by Michael A. Bucknor and Alison Donnell, Taylor & Francis, 2011, pp. 265–275.

——, et al. "Introduction: A Postcolonial Environmental Humanities." *Global Ecologies and the Environmental Humanities: Postcolonial Approaches,* edited by E. DeLoughrey et al., Routledge, 2015, pp.1–32.

Hulme, Keri A.L. "Mauri: An Introduction to Bicultural Poetry in New Zealand." *Only Connect: Literary Perspectives East and West*, edited by Guy Amirthanayagam and S.C. Harrex, Flinders UP, 1981, pp. 290–310.

Manhire, Bill. *Denis Glover Selected Poems*. Victoria UP, 1995.

Pawson, Eric and Tom Brooking. *Making a New Land: Environmental Histories of New Zealand*. Otago UP, 2013.

Salmond, Anne. *Tears of Rangi: Experiments Across Worlds*. Auckland UP, 2017.

Somerville, Alice Te Punga. *Once Were Pacific: Māori Connections to Oceania*. Minnesota UP, 2012.

Steer, Philip. "Colonial Ecologies: Guthrie-Smith's Tutira and Writing in the Settled Environment." *A History of New Zealand Literature*, edited by Mark Williams, Cambridge UP, 2016, pp. 85–97.

Sullivan, Robert. "Mana Moana: Wayfinding and Five Indigenous Poets: A Thesis Submitted In Fulfilment of the Requirements for the Degree of Doctor of Philosophy in English." *University of Auckland*, 2015, http://hdl.handle.net/2292/25497. Accessed 2 May 2018.

——. "A Poetics of Culture: Others' and Ours, Separate and Commingled." *Landfall*, 1, no. 211, 2006, pp. 9–18.

——. *Shout Ha! to the Sky*. Salt Publishing, 2010.

——. *Star Waka*. Auckland UP, 1999.

——. *Voice Carried My Family*. Auckland UP, 2005.

Turner, Brian. *All That Blue Can Be*. John McIndoe, 1989.

——. *Beyond*. McIndoe Publishers, 1992.

——. *Bones*. John McIndoe, 1985.

——. *Elemental: Central Otago Poems*. Random House, 2014.

——. *Footfall*. Random House, 2005.

——. *Into the Wider World: A Back Country Miscellany*. Random House, 2008.

——. *Ladders of Rain*. John McIndoe, 1978.

——. *Taking Off*. Victoria UP, 2001.

Wendt, Albert et al. *Whetu Moana: Contemporary Polynesian Poems in English*. Auckland UP, 2003.

2 From Burning Beds to Rising Seas

Environmental Issues in the Song Lyrics of Midnight Oil

Knut Øystein Høvik

Introduction

February 2022 saw the release of *Resist*, the final studio album by the Australian rock band Midnight Oil. The closing chapter of a career that started 46 years earlier is a concept album with the climate crisis as its central focus. With *Resist*, the band calls for urgent action, criticizing political apathy and apologizing on behalf of their generation for failing the youth through inaction on climate change. Few musical artists can be said to have done more than the members of Midnight Oil in terms of advocating environmental values and raising awareness of the global climate change. As frontman Peter Garrett (2017) reflects in his memoir: "Midnight Oil's message wasn't in the songs by themselves [...] The message was in joining the music and its lyrics with actions that matched what was being sung" (185).

This essay discusses Midnight Oil's environmentally-themed lyrics in the context of educational perspectives on the climate crisis. A close reading of some of the lyrics from the band's back catalogue, which consists of 144 songs spread out across 13 albums and 2 EPs, forms the basis for the discussion. The educational potential that lies in close reading and repeated listening to song lyrics to get a better understanding of environmental challenges is significant. Although the focus of this essay is on environmental issues, it should be pointed out that the lyrics often discuss intersecting topics. I have structured this argument with reference to four significant thematic categories in the lyrics: (1) the impact of environmental change on natural ecosystems, (2) the impact of environmental change on humans, (3) nuclear fallout and (4) Indigenous collaborations.

In *Ecomusicology*, Pedelty (2012) addresses the question of popular music's engagement with the environmental crisis and looks for reasons "for the relative dearth of songs about environmental matters", asking to what extent environmentally-themed songs "effectively communicate environmental messages to audiences", and what listeners do with these songs (47–48). While song lyrics and poetry are often considered to belong to different areas of culture and cultural production, they are also closely connected. Pattison (2012) simplifies the main difference between the two by suggesting that poetry is made for the eye and lyrics for the ear. Eckstein (2010, 10) argues that while lyrics and poetry share certain similarities, they differ in at least one respect: the voice in poetry is generally perceived as *internalized*, while the voice of lyrics is by definition *external*. For Aadland (2013, 242), song lyrics involve a negotiation between language and voice. And because in music voice adjusts to the formal requirements of patterned sound, Pedelty (2012, 147) draws on Boucher and Frith and argues that "the lyricist faces a range of constraints that the authors of poetry, prose and spoken word do not", such as meter, rhythm and rhyme – although of course poetry in print has a long tradition of dealing with such constraints, from sonnets and rondeaux to villanelles and haikus. The ballad form has often

DOI: 10.4324/9781003399988-4

been adopted for lyric poetry in print. Ong (1982) has examined the relations between orality and writing and demonstrated how modern high-technology culture has led to a "secondary orality" with the introduction of voice technologies and devices like the telephone, television, radio and other electronic devices. In this sense, rock lyrics are best considered in terms of orality, as opposed to literature in print. Printed poems may adopt forms and styles drawn from oral culture but do not engage in oral cultural transmission or practice as such.

At the same time, poetry and song lyrics have a long, shared history. In ancient Greece, a lyric was a song to be accompanied by the lyre, a harp-like instrument (Cuddon 1992, 514). In its current usage, the term 'lyric' is hard to define. It has in some ways become an umbrella term that encompasses most versified literature and thus become a synonym for 'poetry' (Wolf 2005). Deutsch (1974) defines 'lyric' as "[a] poem composed to be sung or appropriate for singing" (81). The clear connections between poetry and song are underscored by Gray's (1992, 268) definition of the term 'song' as "[a] short lyric poem intended to be set to music". This corresponds with Gadamer's (1980) view that

> [o]ral poetry is already always on the way to being text, just as poetry transmitted in rhapsodic elocution is always on the way to being 'literature'. Song, too, which intends to be sung more than once, appears to be already on such a path, indeed on the way to both poetry and music.

(6)

While song lyrics must be considered as a holistic expression where attention is also paid to the music, the distinction between song and printed lyrics is not necessarily that sharp (Diesen 2018). John Stuart Mill (1883) saw lyric poetry as "more eminently and peculiarly poetry than any other" (719). Karlsen (2013, 2) argues that song lyrics are the dominant form of poetry of our time, reaching a much larger audience than the book. The Irish poet Paul Muldoon (1998) similarly sees the song as belonging to the world of poetry, and his own work often draws on popular music, or is composed for musical performance. It can therefore be argued that the shared history and characteristics between poetry and song lyrics at the very least invite an examination of the latter in the context of poetry. A similar view would seem to be held by the Swedish Academy, which awarded the Nobel Prize in Literature for 2016 to Bob Dylan "for having created new poetic expressions within the great American song tradition" (The Nobel Prize 2016). While Midnight Oil may not have attained Dylan's exalted literary status, few could argue against the band's contribution towards creating new poetic expressions in the Australian rock tradition. It is some of these poetic expressions, and their relevance to learning about the global climate crisis, that will be explored in the following discussion.

Background

Midnight Oil is an alternative rock band hailing from Sydney's northern suburbs. Since the formation of the band in 1976, its line-up has consisted of Peter Garrett (vocals), Rob Hirst (drums), Jim Moginie (guitar) and Martin Rotsey (guitar). Past members include bass players Andrew James (1976–80), Peter Gifford (1980–87) and Bones Hillman (1987, until his death in 2020). Firmly established as part of the Australian social and political landscape, the band has for many years been among the most politically active and socially aware acts in the music industry.

The years from 1978 to 1986 were the band's most productive period, during which its members established its political outlook. Emerging from the punk and rock scene in the 1970s, the band toured relentlessly in its early years, gaining a large and dedicated following on the notoriously hard to please pub circuit. As a band inspired by the punk movement, their anti-establishment stance was almost a given. The songs on the band's first three albums, *Midnight Oil* (1978), *Head Injuries* (1979) and *Place without a Postcard* (1981), largely reflect the views of a frustrated younger generation which had grown tired of older men in suits running the country, whether due to the conservatism of Malcolm Fraser's government, the influence of the Murdoch press, or just anger and frustration with profit makers and the political status quo in general.

A watershed came with the career-defining album *Diesel and Dust* (1987), which brought global attention to environmental challenges in general and the plight of Indigenous Australians in particular. Another defining moment came at the closing ceremony of the 2000 Olympics in Sydney when the band performed their signature song "Beds are Burning" (1987). On stage, the band made a political statement by donning black outfits with the word "sorry" on them in response to John Howard's Liberal government's refusal to apologize for historical governmental actions, in which Indigenous children were taken from their families and would become what is now known as the Stolen Generations. During the 1990s, the band's international role diminished somewhat, but they remained active in Australian politics and society. In 2002, the band broke up, leaving Garrett to pursue a high-profile political career, before reuniting again in 2016.

Activists

Peter Garrett has always argued that Midnight Oil was not a political band, but a band that found itself intersecting with politics. In his view, the band's purpose was not to push political views onto their audiences, but it was something that merely happened (Zuel 2002). Breen (2006), however, claims that the band's "almost didactic approach to popular music-making was unashamedly political. 'The Oils' used music as a tool for educating Australians about the issues of the day" (60). Stratton (2006) has observed that

> as Midnight Oil became more and more outspokenly a political band, they did so using a quite different, and more modern, form of political address. That is, rather than narrativizing a story with which the audience could identify [...], Midnight Oil lyrics are more likely to describe situations in a general, abstracted way and affirm what should be done.
> (250)

Yet, despite Garrett's outspokenness on stage and the band's obvious left leanings, concerts never turned into openly political rallies. Instead, the band sought new audiences by constantly evolving musically and reinventing themselves, while remaining committed to their ideals.

Tall, bald, hampered by a limited vocal range and with his manic dance moves, Garrett cut an unlikely figure as a rock star. Yet, his striking and charismatic on-stage appearance proved to be a formidable asset when championing political issues, as he lent his voice to the anti-uranium movement and work done by Greenpeace, while also serving two terms as President of the Australian Conservation Foundation (the country's leading environmental organisation). Having run as a candidate for Senate for the Australian Nuclear Disarmament Party in 1984, he entered into politics full time 20 years later with the Labor Party. Garrett's political career saw him reach some of the highest offices in the country, holding ministerial posts in both Kevin Rudd and Julia Gillard's cabinets.

Over the years, the band has lent support to various causes through protesting and performing at benefit concerts (Garrett 2017; Hirst 2012; Lawrence 2016). The band's most notable environmental "stunt" came in 1989, when – at the height of their popularity – they responded to the natural disaster caused by the spill from the oil tanker *Exxon Valdes* by staging an impromptu lunchtime concert on the back of a truck outside the Exxon Building in New York under the banner "Midnight Oil makes you dance, Exxon makes us sick". A year later, *Blue Sky Mining* became the first music album with covers, sleeves and long boxes manufactured entirely from recycled paper, while in Los Angeles, a huge banner promoting the upcoming concert read "Earth Day is a great idea. What about the other 364 days?" (Goldstein 1990).

For Midnight Oil, activism and song lyrics have always been closely connected, as explicit political commentary by the band members has gone hand in hand with their musical career and performances. Through their own activism the band summoned "their fans to step ahead and become something more than an audience" (Bonastre 2011, 61), often demanding action. An early example of this can be found in "No Reaction" (1979), where the band provocatively challenges the audience to do something. In the recurring questions in the lyrics, the listeners are asked about their aspirations, the direction they will take to get there, what they are willing to do to achieve this and who they will take their inspiration from. The audience is thus put in a position where they have to take a stand on whether they are "doers" or "talkers", "runners" or "walkers", "givers" or "takers", and whether they follow "movers" or "makers". This uncom-promising style was to characterize Midnight Oil's activism throughout the band's career. As the band continued to "inscribe their protest within the discourses of social power", protest became their musical lore, what for them became the "art of the possible" (Steggles 1992, 147–148).

The Impact of Environmental Change on Natural Ecosystems

It was perhaps not so surprising that five liberally-minded, educated, urban baby boomers of the Australian post-war generation should take an interest in the environment, as their forma-tive years coincided with the emergence of the environmental movement. The protests in 1972 against the decision to flood Lake Pedder in Tasmania had seen the birth of modern environ-mentalism. That same year also saw the formation of United Tasmania Group, the world's first political party with an openly green profile (Warde, Robin & Sörlin 2018, 172). Meanwhile, the Australian Conservation Foundation, formed in 1965, united enthusiasts of the left and the right, as well as people from different social backgrounds, in support of the environmental cause (Blainey 2009).

It was Tasmania that provided the setting for Midnight Oil's first environmentally-themed song. "Burnie" (1981) is about industrialization in the port town of the same name on Tasmania's north coast, pleading against allowing industry to define the town's future. This perspective highlights the environment left for coming generations in particular, of the children writing their contract in the sand, whose future seems eternally "grey". The hesitant sense of optimism relies on a sense of attachment to place, and "a hope" that everything will somehow turn out right in the end.

"Burnie" is not the only song that highlights how the urban environment, too, requires atten-tion, and can either foster or become hostile to its inhabitants. In "Who Can Stand in the Way?" (1984), the band criticizes the urban sprawl that Sydney has become, with its heavy traffic and helicopters criss-crossing the sky above shopping malls and apartment blocks. It is a place where big business rules. At the end of the song, listeners are addressed by a directly speaking, rather than singing voice, and the voice uttering the final lines of the lyrics at the end of the song depicts a futuristic scene where Sydney has become a desert where emus graze in the city centre, telling us that lessons must be learnt, and that Mother Nature will one day reclaim what is rightfully hers.

Such resilience on Mother Nature was to be reflected, 13 years later, in "Underwater" (1996), the opening track of the largely ignored album *Breathe*. In the lyrics, the band pays tribute to the natural beauty that can be found beneath the surface of the ocean, in a "realm", which, despite its inaccessibility to humans, has the potential to "make believe". Great mysteries are hidden in the deep, but the untamable power of the ocean can also be witnessed "overland".

The urban and commercial focus of many songs also addressed the idea of "development" both as economic growth based on the unsustainable approach to natural resources in general, and in the specific context of construction. In many of their early songs, Midnight Oil attacked property development and the building boom along Australia's East coast. The band demonstrated a connection between the destruction of habitats and ecosystems, and the demolition of man-made heritage of cultural rather than commercial value. In "Dreamworld" from *Diesel and Dust* (1987), the lyrics lament the disappearance of the giant Norfolk Island pines that once stood along Manly's beachfront on the outskirts of Sydney, and that have since been replanted. The song also references the Cloudland Ballroom, a heritage-listed building in Brisbane, which in 1982 was demolished without prior warning to make way for blocks of flats. The title of the song was inspired by the Dreamworld theme park on the Gold Coast, and which was exactly the kind of commercially driven and tourism-oriented event machine that the band openly deplored.

In the gloomy but beautiful "River Runs Red" (1990), from their next internationally successful album, *Blue Sky Mining*, the band vents their anger at companies who exploit natural resources. In a world where there should be enough for everyone, we are ruled by commercial interests. The speaker addresses previous generations, blaming them for their excesses. The chorus describes a dark, grim, almost apocalyptic scene where the "river runs red" (a metaphor for a bleeding planet), while "black rain falls".

Despite the bleak pictures presented in many of their songs, Midnight Oil are not immune to romanticism and praising the pastoral and the beauty of the Australian countryside. Inspired by Xavier Herbert's historical novel *Capricornia* (1938), the band's album with the same title from 2002 sees their usual criticism of Australian society being sprinkled with nature imagery. In their homage to the land, the band paints a sensory landscape where the sunrise reveals mountains in the distance ("World That I See"), the jacaranda are in bloom ("Golden Age"), the scent of tropical rain giving way to a "heat wave" ("Tone Poem"), while dingoes howl at the moon ("Under the Overpass") under star-filled skies ("Golden Age"). But it is also a land of harshness and remoteness that takes a special kind of breed ("World That I See"). Touching ground, feeling once again Australian soil under their feet and breathing in the "fresh air" ("Been Away Too Long"), hints at the homesickness that members of the band would have felt on tour.

In *Nature's Economy* (1994), Donald Worster writes about how agriculture has led to ecocide on a scale unmatched by factory owners or bomb makers. On the "The Barka-Darling River" (2022) from Midnight Oil's last album, *Resist*, Garrett shares some his frustrations from his years in Parliament, in particular conflicting interests between states and federal government over the Murray-Darling Basin, which accounts for 41 per cent of the nation's gross value of agricultural production and for 70 per cent of all water used for irrigation (Garrett 2017, 155; Gergis 2018). Resenting Canberra's lobbying culture and political backstabbing, Garrett describes it as a derelict house with "a fatal flaw" in the building construction. Hoping to secure a sustainable future for the main artery of inland Australia and its surrounding lands, of which 40 different First Nations and 35 endangered species of animals are dependent, Garrett, as Minister of the Environment, found himself duped by political shenanigans. Instead, the bush landscape "surrenders" to the excavator, leaving only a faint memory of the once free-flowing river.

The traditional (Western) idea of wilderness as nature uncontaminated by civilization has been increasingly challenged in recent theory and scholarship, particularly in the context of ecocriticism or environmental humanities. The romanticized idea of wilderness focused on places where humans are strangers and must approach nature with humility and portrayed wilderness as offering a sense purity and the possibility of spiritual renewal. The planet's ultimate remaining wilderness is a part of the world that Australia lays claim to. In "Antarctica" (1990), the band addresses the importance of good custodianship for the planet's last great wilderness uninhabited by humans. Hoping that Australia can take a leading role in the Antarctic Treaty and leave the continent's fragile ecology to itself, the hauntingly soft song offers hope of a place where water is "real and clean". In presenting the first-person voice of a "settler's son", however, the song also recognizes the destructive impact of previous generations on open and wild landscapes and thus implicitly pleads for a different outcome. The concerns over the use of resources in "Antarctica" were already anticipated in "Arctic World" (1987), another song addressing the fragility of polar landscapes. The song denounces the destructive effects of mining and oil drilling in Greenland and Alaska. Again, its perspective is not unified, and it evokes both a frustration with the exhaustion of resources for profit and the idea of empty polar landscapes as void of life and value, inviting material exploitation.

Having started out with an anti-establishment stance, the band is now itself more or less the Establishment. Still, the band has not mellowed over the years; they appear to remain as angry and impatient as when they started out and are not afraid to vent their anger at politicians, industrialists, property developers and media tycoons who should do more to create a sustainable and green future. As grandparents about to enter retirement, in the confrontational "Rising Seas" (2022) the band issues an apology to their grandchildren and future generations for political and economic inaction when it comes to tackling the climate crisis, addressing carbon pollution and promoting renewable energies. The music video, released just days before the UN Climate Conference in Glasgow in 2021, featured footage courtesy of Greenpeace of the consequences of climate change for humans, such as melting glaciers, polar bears jumping from one sheet of ice to the next, floods in various parts of the world and Sydney Harbour shrouded in bushfire smoke, and water levels around the Opera House rising as a result of torrential rain. Back in the 1980s, at the height of the MTV dominance of the music industry, the band had been reluctant to produce music videos to promote record sales. With the timing of the release of "Rising Seas", however, the band used the medium for a completely different purpose: to effectively teach about the dangers of the climate crisis to a younger audience, the millennial YouTube generation.

The impact of environmental change on natural ecosystems has always been an integral part of Midnight Oil's lyrical content. By addressing these issues in their lyrics, the band has continuously sought to educate their audience about the hazards of climate negligence, trying to get their listeners to reflect on the impact of environmental change on themselves as human beings and what actions they can take in order to make the world a greener, safer and more sustainable place to live.

The Impact of Environmental Change on Humans

Several song lyrics portray the negative impact of environmental change on humans and thus bolster the indirect didactics of the group's climate activism. Such lyrics, when they enter the minds of fans, can in turn impact their attitudes and lead to climate action.

In the song "Blue Sky Mine" (1990), the band remembers the asbestos mine at Wittenoom in Western Australia and one of Australia's saddest industrial and job-related health disasters, where as many as 2000 people may have died from asbestos-related illnesses. The mine had been owned by Australian Blue Asbestos, referred to as the Blue Sky Mining Company in the song lyrics. The narrative of the song is told from the viewpoint of a miner who is torn between his deteriorating health (as a result of working at the mine) and the need to feed his family. Meanwhile, the company directors, whose only concern is to ensure that the balance sheet can break even, lie to the shareholders and hope that no one finds out. For a company seeking to maximize profits, there is nothing more valuable than "a hole in the ground", regardless of the social and environmental costs (Stratton 2004). Garrard (2012, 103–104) has argued that a classic feature in environmental writing is to portray villains as faceless bureaucrats or salesmen, like in this song.

Another song, "Too Much Sunshine" (2002), mocks those who would question the veracity of the concept of global warming. Climate change "scepticism", a mix of valid scientific uncertainty, popular misunderstanding , politically motivated misrepresentation and conspiracy theories, is a major barrier to progress on reducing greenhouse gas emissions in some democratic countries, such as the USA, Canada and Australia where some groups have rejected evidence of climate change (Garrard 2012, 20; Warde, Robin & Sörlin 2018, 163). Addressing the inhabitants of a town called "Pissitaway", where the only thing that changes is the inhabitants' "hue", the band issues a strong statement, criticizing suburban complacency, general ignorance and a lack of imagination when it comes to creating a better, greener, more sustainable future. In the lyrics, the assonance between "sleep" (which the inhabitants are capable of) and "dream" (which the inhabitants are incapable of) highlights how these two activities are closely connected but also stand for oppositional attitudes to one's future: one is passive, and the other a means of imagining an alternative way of living. As Yeats (1914/1994, 148) famously wrote: "In dreams begin responsibility".

The band has always taken a keen interest in what Australia should be, playing its part in shaping the future of their home country and being a significant contributor in redefining Australian nationhood in the modern age. In "One Country" (1990), the band sought to heal a divided nation, telling its listeners that divisions between people are so miniscule that instead they should rally around loftier, worthier and more ambitious causes, such as healing a wounded planet. Rather than simple romanticized unity, however, the lines also reflect a sense of urgency that has less to do with spiritual connection than a need for action in an emergency: without a sense of shared purpose, people remain "defenceless" in the face of an environmental catastrophe threatening the continent and the surrounding ocean. The "landmass" and ocean are "one" in the sense that they are shared by all, but also "one" in the sense that they are irreplaceable, and once lost no second chance will present itself. The interconnectdness between life below water and life on land is reflected in the United Nations' (2023) Sustainable Development Goals 14 and 15.

Nuclear Fallout

In the early 1980s, the fear of nuclear warfare and destruction was becoming increasingly real with the escalating arms race between the Soviet Union and the USA. With "Armistice Day" (1981) and "US Forces" (1982), the band took a clear stand against the Australian-American military alliance and denounced US military intervention in foreign nations' affairs. Both songs seemed to strike a chord with their Australian audience and became their first successful forays into the singles charts. "US Forces" appeared on the band's fourth album, *10, 9, 8, 7, 6, 5, 4, 3, 2, 1*, a title suggesting countdown to imminent destruction of the planetary ecosystem.

Few things rouse apocalyptic thinking more than the unimaginable threat of nuclear weapons (Garrard 2012, 110). By the time the band released the album *Red Sails in the Sunset* in 1984, Garrett made his first venture into politics, with the Nuclear Disarmament Party. The album was recorded and produced in Tokyo, and the Japanese experience – especially visiting Hiroshima – deeply impacted the band. With the album cover by the Japanese artist Tsunehisa Kimura, depicting Sydney Harbour after a hypothetical nuclear strike, and songs like "When the Generals Talk" and "Minutes to Midnight" (a reference to the Doomsday Clock) the band issued a clear warning against military propaganda and the threat of nuclear apocalypse.

The threat of nuclear holocaust is also central to the concept of environmentalism in a wider context. As Worster (1994) writes: "Under the threat of the atomic bomb a new moral consciousness called environmentalism began to take form, whose purpose was to use the insights of ecology to restrain the use of modern science-based power over nature" (343). This, he claims, lead to "a sense of urgency, bordering at times on apocalyptic fear" (353).

In "Harrisburg" (1984), about the Three Mile Island nuclear reactor's meltdown near Harrisburg, Pennsylvania, in 1979, the band prophetically warned about the particular kind of devastation that would follow nuclear disasters. The fallout that we cannot see, nor smell, is "twenty times" worse than anything we can imagine.

In "Hercules" (1985), the band reacted angrily to the sinking of the Greenpeace vessel *Rainbow Warrior* outside Auckland Harbor by French intelligence agents, calling it an unforgettable and unforgivable act. At the time, France was carrying out nuclear testing in the South Pacific, and *Rainbow Warrior* was on its way to protest against the tests. The song's title refers to the military transport airplanes used by both the American and Australian armed forces. New Zealand's antinuclear stance in the face of strong international pressure was something that the band greatly admired (Garrett 2017, 104–105).

"Hercules" contrasts with the sombre, pleading pacifist anthem "Put Down That Weapon" (1987), in which Australia's harbours have become what the great battleships "call home", referring to US naval vessels, including nuclear submarines, anchoring up in Sydney and other Australian ports. Appealing to common sense, the lyrics stress the futility and danger of armed struggle and how perceived strength can be delusional. Moreover, the band uses apocalyptic rhetoric, which seems a necessary component of environmental didactics, as it is capable of galvanizing activists, converting the undecided and ultimately, perhaps, of influencing government and commercial policy (Garrard 2012, 113). The song's lyrics also employ a tension between darkness and light, both as hidden agendas and impact, and as revealing visibility: hiding under water is of little use if the sky above has gone "dark with rain" (possibly radioactive), and secrets are brought to light "with the torchlight on". The phrase "point the finger" as a sign of accusation implies a countermove to pointing a gun, a weapon of war that should now be "put down". The lyrics imply a looming gun fight between two parties, like the two nuclear states of the Cold War, which would destroy both if allowed to escalate. Strength, as the final line suggests, is of little consequence in such a disaster.

Nuclear testing had also been the subject of "Maralinga" (1982). In 1952–57, the British had carried out nuclear tests on the Nullarbor Plain at Maralinga, South Australia. The tests were kept secret, even from Prime Minister Robert Menzies. The result was that the Pitjantjatjara and Yankunytjatjara peoples were forced off their traditional lands for over 30 years (Knightley 2001, 298–300). In the song, the lines are spoken, told from the perspective of an Aboriginal person witnessing the horrors of the testing. Looking back, the displaced speaker remembers home as a warm and peaceful place "of wide open spaces". But this peaceful, idyllic image turns suddenly dark and apocalyptic as "ashes fly" in the air and the ground turns black. Still, despite the obvious dangers and horrors of destruction, the speaker wants to be there, at what is home. Not only that, he has to be there "at the end".

"Maralinga" is not just about loss of land, but also about a way of life. As McCredden (2007) writes: "The dialectic between home and homelessness, voiced in 'Maralinga' has its own trajectory for indigenous Australians, emerging out of a deeply traditional relationship to the land, to ancestors and to dreamings" (224–225). The "Australian geo-human landscape" (Steggles 1992, 148) and its impact on the nation's original inhabitants would eventually become a particular focus for the band, but also an area where the members of the band would have to educate themselves before they could educate their audience.

Indigenous Collaborations

Indigenous issues, such as land rights, cosmology, vulnerability to ecological disruption etc., and how these are tied up with ecology have been a central aspect in Midnight Oil's repertoire since the mid-1980s. The issue of Indigenous land rights in particular was something that caught the attention of the band, and especially Peter Garrett, a qualified lawyer. In 1986, Midnight Oil joined the Aboriginal band The Warumpi Band on a tour of remote places in the Australian outback for what became known as the Blackfella/Whitefella Tour. For the band, this experience was to prove both life-changing and career-changing.

Few could have anticipated the enormous success that the album *Diesel and Dust*, and in particular the hit song "Beds are Burning" would bring to the band. One of the chapters in Garrett's (2017) memoir is titled "The time had come", a reference to one of the lines in "Beds are Burning". For Midnight Oil, it certainly was a case of the timing being right. By the time *Diesel and Dust* was released, the music industry had fallen prey to the commercial interests and demands of MTV. Musical tastes were changing, and following Live Aid in 1985 there was a need and desire for artists who could engage with more "serious" matters in their songs (Breen 2006). Furthermore, 1986 had seen the Chernobyl disaster. At the same time, people were becoming increasingly aware of the greenhouse effect. The year 1986 had also seen the phenomenal international success of *Crocodile Dundee*, a film that made the outside world aware of Australia's Indigenous population, which had been consistently overlooked by successive governments. Into all of this, *Diesel and Dust* and "Beds are Burning" fit perfectly, as the band was "able to transfer their politics and their music onto the global (especially the US) stage" (Breen 2006, 61).

Using cultural and geographic references to situate the song in an Australian context, a place of dry heat, derelict vehicles and almost impenetrable to modernity (McCredden 2007), "Beds are Burning" addresses the injustice suffered by generations of Australian Aboriginal people and the need to repay the debt that the country's white settlers owe them. Through repeated rhetorical questions about dancing while our planet is rotating and sleeping while beds are on fire, the band hammers home the simple logic while stressing the need for urgency. Similarly, the use of metaphors in the refrain implies that we need to reflect on how we can partake in pleasurable pastimes (like dancing and dreaming) when injustices are being committed around us, or perhaps when we should be worrying about crises looming on the horizon. The lyrics allow for multiple interpretations, and according to Hirst, the song is rather a celebration of the richness of the Aboriginal spirit:

> I thought we could write a song about [...] an ancient Australian community who had so much thrown at it but was still joyfully dancing in the desert, singing their songs and pushing back against all the shocking things that had been visited upon them ever since Europeans had arrived in this country.
>
> (Haskell 2019)

At another level, the lyrics reflect Garrett's personal trauma of having witnessed the house fire that claimed the life of his mother (Elder 2020). Another dimension lies in the idea of dreaming (or "sleep" in the song), which is generally perceived as a pleasurable activity for non-Indigenous people. For Indigenous people, "dreaming" is a cultural and spiritual lifeline. *Tjurrkupa*, as it is called in Central Australia, refers to the past, the present and the future at the same time and is an all-encompassing, sustainable tradition where people are in a custodial, not exploitative relationship to the land (Broome 2010).

Hirst and Moginie later rewrote the lyrics of "Beds are Burning" for a recording with 60 international musicians and celebrities for the 2009 UN Climate Change Conference in Copenhagen. In the recording, the refrain remains unchanged from the original version (Kofi Annan Foundation 2019).

With their white, urban, educated, middle-class backgrounds, the band has always been something of an anomaly as spokespeople for Aboriginal causes. They have also been criticised for cultural appropriation and for drowning out the voices of those for whom they attempted to speak. No more so than with the controversial release of "Truganini" (1993), when they erroneously claimed that she was the last of the Tasmanian Aborigines (Vellutini 2003). The complex relationships between colonialism and environmental destruction that the Tasmanian Aboriginals were subjected to is something Garrard (2012) describes as "a combination of genocide and ecocide" (194). This idea is something the band explores in the song "Tarkine" (2022), about the Tarkine rainforest in the northwest of Tasmania and the Aboriginal tribe of the same name that used to inhabit the forest.

Traditionally a tight-working unit, the band's music has been mostly *about* First Australians, and not so much *with*. After an 18-year hiatus from studio recording, 2020 finally saw the band return with the release of *The Makarrata Project*, a mini album inspired by the *Uluru Statement from the Heart* by the First Nations National Constitutional Convention (2017). The album featured collaborations with Indigenous artists and First Nations people from different walks of life. One of the most striking examples of a song addressing Aboriginal spirituality and Australia's landscape, and also combining lyrics in Indigenous language and English, is "Desert Man, Desert Woman", sung by an Indigenous voice, the Pitjantjatjara artist Frank Yamma.

While many of the song lyrics on the album can be interpreted as forward-looking and promoting reconciliation, "Gadigal Land" is a provocative recount of the fate of the Gadigal people, the traditional custodians of the land around present-day Sydney as well as the fates of other Aboriginal peoples in Australia. The lyrics play on the traditional Welcome to Country ritual or formal ceremony performed as a land acknowledgement at many events held in Australia. The song features lines sung by Gadigal poet Joel Davidson, who has been working on the revitalisation of his ancestors' tongue (Hocking 2020). The song addresses both the human and natural costs of European colonization, and after the opening lines repeatedly addressing the listener as "welcome to" the lands, the invitation is made provisional and inseparable from responsibility. Rhetorical repetition of utterances like "Don't' you ..." and "We don't need ..." allows for the listing of the wide range of violations and examples of destructive behaviour that have characterized the colonial project: from the use of poison or similarly lethal addictive substances to the introduction of pathogens, or the enforcing of an alien legal system and its framework of justice as a pretext of environmental destruction and institutionally sanctioned genocide. Similarly, the detrimental consequences of European colonization on nature and Aboriginal lands through the damming of rivers, tree felling, mining and overfishing are also listed. The song's addressing of the white, settler population in English is interrupted with lines in Davidson's ancestral language. This also implies a sense of another audience, a voice that reaches out to the Aboriginal community while talking to, or talking back, to those complicit with the ongoing effects of colonization.

In "Wind in My Head" (2020), featuring the legendary Aboriginal artists Kev Carmody and Sammy Butcher, the connection to the land and ancestors is strong. Having been entrusted with "a sacred land", the speakers can sense the old ones' love in the ground. Importantly, the lyrics also present the material landscape, ancestral presence and narrative tradition as one: the voice is "tracing circles" and says that from one specific location in the landscape, it is possible to reach "any place". "Footprints" underneath paved "city streets" and "songs" that can be read "in the stars" all indicate a method of mapping the environment through narrative memory. Again, the English language lyrics momentarily yield to lines in Aboriginal language, before resuming again. At the end of the song, the perspective widens from the Australian landscape to a planetary view, as the singers address climate change. Melting glaciers and dried-out land may be observable to us, but the long-term consequences of our "human footprints" for the universe are beyond our comprehension. The repetition of "footprints" here marks a shift in the temporal and the spatial perspectives: if the first reference was to footprints underneath the urban street (thus recognizing their origin earlier in time, and as embedded in the terrain rather than covering its surface), now they are a trace of human presence of any kind, diminished into insignificance in relation to planetary and cosmic scales. Not only is *all* human life threatened by climate change; it is the very significance of humanity as a measure of things when the perspective widens to consider the universe beyond the planet Earth.

Garrard (2012) sees the Australian outback as an interior wilderness space. Like in "Maralinga", the relationship between the land and Aboriginal Australians is a central theme in many of the songs on *Diesel and Dust*. The desert features prominently in songs like "Beds are Burning", "Bullroarer", "The Dead Heart" and "Warakurna". In "Bullroarer", the setting is a dry desert landscape before the outbreak of a thunderstorm, a metaphor for hope, change, regeneration and renewal. Likewise, the album cover of *Blue Sky Mining* shows parched earth, heavy clouds and lightning in the distance. Similar to "Maralinga", the final lines of "Bullroarer" stress the sense of place, belonging and home. As the speaker hears the bullroarers in the distance, the call of home, plans are altered as he decides head towards his "homeland".

For Jim Moginie, visiting the remote Aboriginal community of Warakurna in Western Australia on the Blackfella/Whitefella Tour was a real eye-opener. Feeling an outsider, and hearing for the first time the term "Europeans" used to describe the members of the band (Okie 2008), inspired him to write "Warakurna" (1987), a song which addresses political and economic injustices of white rule. Again, the sense of place is strong. It is a land of "diesel and dust" (drug abuse and infertile soil) that does not change or conform to Western ideals, but whose inhabitants have no intention of leaving.

The lyrics of "Warakurna" "attempted a synthesis of urban and outback landscape (both geographical and human) through a set of structural oppositions" (Steggles 1992, 147), where the band occupied a middle ground, "alienated from the 'logic' of contemporary society and unable to recapture the 'authenticity' of the past (or to enter fully into Aboriginal society either)" (Steggles 1992, 147). Instead, Midnight Oil, having sold over 12 million records worldwide, used their international success as a platform to inform their non-Indigenous audience about the sufferings of and injustices committed against Aboriginal Australians. Their transformed approach to Indigenous collaborations over the years further demonstrates the band's willingness to learn and adapt.

Concluding Remarks

The story of Midnight Oil is in many ways the story of the Australian environmental movement. Starting out in the 1970s as a protest against the general political stasis, the band chiselled out a clear anti-nuclear stance in the early 1980s. From the mid-1980s, the band's focus shifted towards questions of land, largely Aboriginal land rights, but also the effects of greenhouse emissions and pollution. Like the environmental movement's overall momentum (Hutton & Connors 1999, 4), the band's fortunes took a dip in the 1990s, before making a resurgence in the last decade as the reality of the climate crisis has become more serious and palpable. On their last two albums, *The Makarrata Project* and *Resist*, the band returned to the success formula of their commercially most successful albums, *Diesel and Dust* and *Blue Sky Mining*, focusing on raising awareness of the rights of Indigenous Australians and addressing environmental issues. The song lyrics on both albums issue clear didactic messages about the global climate crisis.

To return to Pedelty's (2012) observation, mentioned in the introduction, on popular music lyrics and their environmental concerns, the above discussion has sought to highlight the thematic and political reach of rock lyrics as socially and politically relevant. He argues that when it comes to topical rock, lyrics do matter, especially in recorded form. Fans listen to words over and over on musical recordings, picking up bits here and there until at least some message comes through (149). This he illustrates by demonstrating how political songs like "Beds are Burning" and "Blue Sky Mine" have impacted young activists in the USA; how they draw important information from songs and how musical knowledge can translate into action (61). In an educational context, such song lyrics thus have both formal and informal potential. In a classroom setting, the song lyrics could be used to promote awareness among learners of global challenges by, for example, connecting them to the UN's Sustainable Development Goals, with goals 13–16 being perhaps the most relevant: Climate Action, Life Below Water, Life on Land, and Peace, Justice and Strong Institutions (United Nations 2023). Outside the classroom, there is no limit to the upside of informal learning as the popularity of Midnight Oil's song lyrics influence current and future generations of rock fans and activists alike.

And such actions matter. "Nature affects our actions, and our actions affect nature" (Larsen, Mønster & Rustad 2017, p. 10, my translation). Activism helps. On his solo album *A Version of Now* (2016), Peter Garrett expresses a sincere hope that what still matters to him also matters to others. Only if we imagine that the planet has a future, are we likely to take responsibility for it. In the beautiful "Earth and Sun and Moon" (1993), the band looks fondly on the planet and closes with a hopeful note, not an apocalyptic one: "We will survive". *Resist*'s cover art is styled like a temperature graph, and while the songs deal with the climate emergency and environmental collapse, there is a sense of hope. There is no defeatism or abandonment in the songs, and the message of these lyrics is that it is not too late. On "At the Time of Writing" (2022), the lines in the present tense are set in the present, painting a dismal picture of the current situation where complacency rules with hardly anything growing "in the Garden of Eden". Yet, despite staring into darkness, the lyrics express hope for the future. The lines in the chorus are in the past tense, and are set in the future, looking back at the current crisis, at a time when "we were good as dead" and "fast asleep", but "still had time to think".

It was interesting to note that in his acceptance speech in May 2022, incoming Prime Minister Anthony Albanese mentioned the implementation of the Uluru Statement from the Heart and tackling climate change, the themes of Midnight Oil's last two albums, as his two top priorities. It shows that the band's music is still relevant, especially in educational contexts. (And in the case of Garrett, that he possibly still wields political influence.) The fact that both albums have been critically and commercially successful suggests that the band still reaches out to a broad audience. Moreover, many of the songs from the band's early years have found new relevance, as once again Australia is dominated by atomic superpowers – through the AUKUS security pact, all the while the Doomsday Clock is ticking ever faster down to midnight.

Works Cited

Aadland, Erling. 2013. "Sangen, stemmen og teksten – om sanglyrikk". In *Nordisk samtidspoesi: Særlig forholdet mellom musikk og lyrikk*, edited by Ole Karlsen. Vallset: Opplandske Bokforlag, pp. 241–255.

Blainey, Geoffrey. 2009. *A Shorter History of Australia*. New York: Vintage.

Bonastre, Roger. 2011. "Beyond Rock: Social Commitment and Political Conscience through Popular Music in Australia 1976–2002: The Case of Midnight Oil." *Coolabah* 5: 54–61.

Breen, Marcus. 2006. *Rock Dogs: Politics and the Australian Music Industry*. Lanham, MD: University Press of America.

Broome, Richard. 2010. *Aboriginal Australians: A History since 1788* (4th ed.). Crows Nest: Allen & Unwin.

Cuddon, John Anthony. 1992. *The Penguin Dictionary of Literary Terms and Literary Theory* (3rd ed.). London: Penguin.

Deutsch, Babette. 1974. *Poetry Handbook: A Dictionary of Terms* (4th ed.). New York: Funk and Wagnalls.

Diesen, Even Igland. 2018. "'Når vi svinger inn på Macern gjør vi det på ordentlig!': En studie i norsk raplyrikk". Doctoral thesis. Inland Norway University of Applied Sciences.

Eckstein, Lars. 2010. *Reading Song Lyrics*. Amsterdam/New York: Editions Rodopi B.V.

Elder, Catriona. 2020. *Being Australian: Narratives of National Identity*. London: Routledge.

Gadamer, Hans-Georg. 1980. "The Eminent Text and Its Truth". *Bulletin of the Midwest Modern Language Association* 13 (1): 3–10.

Garrard, Greg. 2012. *Ecocriticism* (2nd ed.). London: Routledge.

Garrett, Peter. 2016. *A Version of Now*. Sony Music 88985335372, Tidal.

Garrett, Peter. 2017. *Big Blue Sky: A Memoir*. Crows Nest: Allen & Unwin.

Gergis, Joëlle. 2018. *Sunburnt Country: The History and Future of Climate Change in Australia*. Carlton: Melbourne University Publishing.

Goldstein, Patrick. 1990. "Eco-pop Consciousness and Midnight Oil". *Los Angeles Times*, June 17, 1990. https://www.latimes.com/archives/la-xpm-1990-06-17-ca-75-story.html.

Gray, Martin. 1992. *A Dictionary of Literary Terms* (2nd rev. ed.). Harlow: Longman.

Haskell, Duncan. 2019. "How I Wrote 'Beds Are Burning' by Midnight Oil's Rob Hirst". *Songwriting Magazine*, May 5, 2019. https://www.songwritingmagazine.co.uk/how-i-wrote/beds-are-burning-midnight-oil

Hirst, Rob. 2012. *Willie's Bar and Grill*. Sydney: Momentum.

Hocking, Rachael. 2020. "The Story behind the Gadigal Poetry on Midnight Oil's Latest Track". *National Indigenous Television*, August 7, 2020. https://www.sbs.com.au/nitv/article/2020/08/07/story-behind-gadigal-poetry-midnight-oils-latest-track

Hutton, Drew & Connors, Libby. 2022. *A History of the Australian Environment Movement*. Cambridge: Cambridge University Press.

Karlsen, Ole (Ed.). 2013. *Nordisk samtidspoesi: Særlig forholdet mellom musikk og lyrikk*. Vallset: Opplandske Bokforlag.

Knightley, Phillip. 2001. *Australia: A Biography of a Nation*. New York: Vintage.

Kofi Annan Foundation. 2019. *Beds Are Burning – Tck tck tck Campaign*. Updated 12 November, 2019. https://www.kofiannanfoundation.org/videos/beds-are-burning-tck-tck-tck-campaign/

Larsen, Peter Stein, Mønster, Louise & Rustad, Hans Kristian. 2017. *Økopoesi*. Bergen: Alvheim & Eide.

Lawrence, Michael. 2016. *Midnight Oil: The Power and the Passion*. Melbourne: Melbourne Books.

McCredden, Lyn. 2007. "Postcolonial Displacements, Popular Music and the Sacred". *Journal of Postcolonial Writing* 43 (2): 216–231.

Midnight Oil. 1978. *Midnight Oil*. Powderworks/Sprint 233, Tidal.

Midnight Oil. 1979. *Head Injuries*. CBS 450903 4, Tidal.

Midnight Oil. 1981. *Place without a Postcard*. CBS 460897 2, Tidal.

Midnight Oil. 1982. *10, 9, 8, 7, 6, 5, 4, 3, 2, 1*. Columbia 38996, Tidal.

Midnight Oil. 1984. *Red Sails in the Sunset*. Columbia 39987, Tidal.

Midnight Oil. 1985. *Species Diseases*. Columbia 46135, Tidal.

Midnight Oil. 1987. *Diesel and Dust*. Columbia 40967, Tidal.

Midnight Oil. 1990. *Blue Sky Mining*. Columbia 45398, Tidal.

Midnight Oil. 1993. *Earth and Sun and Moon*. Columbia 473605, Tidal.

Midnight Oil. 1996. *Breathe*. Columbia 485402 2, Tidal.

Midnight Oil. 2002. *Capricornia*. Columbia 506203 4, Tidal.

Midnight Oil. 2020. *The Makarrata Project*. Sony Music 19439809981, Tidal.

Midnight Oil. 2022. *Resist*. Sony Music 19439905882, Tidal.

Mill, John Stuart. 1883. The Two Kinds of Poetry. *Monthly Repository, October*, 714–720. https://ncse.ac.uk/periodicals/mruc/issues/vm2-ncseproduct2624/.

Muldoon, Paul. 1998. *Hay*. London: Faber and Faber.

The Nobel Prize. 2016. *The Nobel Prize in Literature 2016*. https://www.nobelprize.org/prizes/literature/2016/summary/

Okie, Matt. 2008. "Oz Captain! My Captain!: An "Ode" to Midnight Oil & An Interview with Midnight Oil's Jim Moginie". *Identity Theory*, September 19, 2008. https://www.identitytheory.com/oz-captain-captain-ode-midnight-oil-interview-midnight-oils-jim-moginie/

Ong, Walter J. 1982. *Orality and Literacy: The Technologizing of the Word*. Milton: Taylor & Francis Group.

Pattison, Pat. 2012. "Similarities and Differences between Song Lyrics and Poetry". In *The Poetics of American Song Lyrics*, edited by Charlotte Pence. Jackson: University Press of Mississippi, pp. 122–133.

Pedelty, Mark. 2012. *Ecomusicology: Rock, Folk, and the Environment*. Philadelphia: Temple University Press.

Referendum Council. 2017. *Uluru Statement from the Heart*. https://www.referendumcouncil.org.au/sites/default/files/report_attachments/Referendum_Council_Final_Report.pdf

Steggles, Simon. 1992. "Nothing Ventured, Nothing Gained: Midnight Oil and the Politics of Rock". In *From Pop to Punk to Postmodernism: Popular Music and Australian Culture from the 1960s to the 1990s*, edited by Philip Hayward. Sydney: Allen & Unwin, pp. 139–148.

Stratton, Jon. 2004. "Pub Rock and the Ballad Tradition in Australian Popular Music". *Perfect Beat: The Pacific Journal of Research into Contemporary Music and Popular Culture* 6 (4): 28–54.

Stratton, Jon. 2006. "Nation Building and Australian Popular Music in the 1970s and 1980s". *Continuum* 20 (2): 243–252.

United Nations. 2023. *Sustainable Development Goals*. https://sdgs.un.org/goals

Vellutini, Laetitia. 2003. "Finding a Voice on Indigenous Issues: Midnight Oil's Inappropriate Appropriations". *Journal of Australian Studies* 27 (79): 127–133.

Warde, Paul, Robin, Libby & Sörlin, Sverker. 2018. *The Environment: A History of the Idea*. Baltimore: Johns Hopkins University Press.

Wolf, Werner. 2005. "The Lyrics: Problems of Definition and a Proposal for Reconceptualisation". In *Theory into Poetry: New Approaches to Poetry*, edited by Eva Müller-Zettelmann & Margarete Rubik. Amsterdam: BRILL, pp. 21–56.

Worster, Donald. 1994. *Nature's Economy: A History of Ecological Ideas*. Cambridge: Cambridge University Press.

Yeats, William Butler & Albright, Daniel. 1914/1994. *The Poems*. London: Everyman.

Zuel, Bernard. 2002. "The Sun Sets on Midnight Oil". *The Age*, December 4, 2002. http://www.theage.com.au/articles/2002/12/03/1038712934982.html

3   From Standing Rock to Flint, Michigan

How Indigenous Poets Contextualise the
Fight for Clean Water

Ronnie K. Stephens

Introduction: Poetry as Protest

The Dakota Access Pipeline, extending from North Dakota to Southern Illinois, is an underground network of pipes designed to deliver oil. Initial plans for the pipeline required that it cross the Missouri River near Bismarck, North Dakota, but those plans were rejected due to concerns about the potential impact to municipal water sources in the area. Revised plans required that the pipeline cross the river less than a mile from Standing Rock Sioux territory, prompting numerous environmental protection and government organisations to conduct research into the potential destruction associated with oil leaks. Despite dozens of petitions and warnings that an oil leak could impact as much as 800,000 square miles of Standing Rock Sioux territory, the United States government opted to continue with the plan. This prompted massive protests from Standing Rock Sioux youth and their supporters in 2016. The protests in opposition to the Dakota Pipeline quickly garnered international attention and reinvigorated conversations about whether or not access to clean water is a fundamental human right. At the centre of these debates is the increasing privatisation of and commodification of freshwater sources in the United States, as well as what responsibility, if any, government entities have to facilitate continued access to clean freshwater sources. I argue that Indigenous characterisations of water in poetry can work to reshape the conversation around access to clean drinking water in America and abroad, and that poems written in direct response to the Standing Rock protests may act as an access point for students to engage with the complex entanglement of New Materialism and Indigenous understandings of non-human agency.

One key feature during the Standing Rock protests was a disconnect between how Indigenous communities and Western communities think of water. In a break from the sometimes-charged rhetoric on the frontlines of the protests and the legalese put forth by government representatives, some Indigenous authors took to poetry in an effort to challenge the pollution of a sacred Lakota waterway. Demian DinéYazhi' responded vehemently in his poem, "Water is Life: A Poem For the Standing Rock," writing that "last year the gold king mine spill sent over 3,000,000 gallons of toxic wastewater down the/animas river in the four corners region of the united states/and you probably didn't even hear about it." The poem then descends into a litany about the history of the United States government polluting Indigenous water sources. One suite of poems, curated by poet Layli Long Soldier, features a number of Indigenous women writing in direct response to Standing Rock protests and water conservation. This suite offers an exceptional opportunity for educators and students to develop informed dialogue around human rights, environmental protection and our relationship to land outside Western frameworks.

Poetry has long been a popular medium for sociopolitical protest, especially within under-represented cultures, so it comes as no surprise that a number of Indigenous women wrote

DOI: 10.4324/9781003399988-5

poems in direct response to the Standing Rock protests. Author and activist Layli Long Soldier composed a series of poems invoking the language of former President Barack Obama's 2010 resolution apologising for the treatment of Indigenous lands by the United States government. In an interview about the series, Long Soldier stated,

> I didn't think of myself as a political writer. I still don't. I had never written overtly political subjects. Maybe it's because now I'm a parent. I want things to be different for my child. I want us, our people, to be seen. I want to be heard.
>
> (PBS Newshour)

This statement further signals the importance of climate activism and how the global climate crisis will affect future generations. The small suite of poems, "Long Soldier," written for *Orion Magazine* as a response to Standing Rock protests is an addition to her own work and brings Indigenous women's voices to a national readership. The suite features poems from seven Indigenous women alongside photographs from the Standing Rock protests which collectively seek to invert the Western understanding of water in a plea to protect the sacred domain at Standing Rock. These poems situate the construction of a pipeline through Indigenous lands as part of a larger attack on the planet. In the introduction to the suite "Long Soldier" describes the Navajo-Hopi Little Colorado River Water Rights Settlement Act of 2012 and its impact on the Diné community:

> The corporate interest in the water was not new or surprising, yet it heightened community outrage and protest...As a high-desert community that already lives with natural conditions of water scarcity, Diné people have developed traditional ways of honouring and conserving water. Yet they continue to be beleaguered by threats of contamination, waste, and legislative robbery of what little water they have.
>
> (Long Soldier 2017)

Solider speaks to the ongoing trauma of working to protect a vital aspect of Diné culture, but her words further invoke a troubled history of assault on Indigenous bodies. As Constanza Contreras explains in her talk, "'Some things cannot be charted': Land, Embodiment, and the Erotic in Natalie Diaz's Postcolonial Love Poem," Indigenous culture is imbued with a sense of transcorporeality that complicates the intra-action of body and land. This implies that, for some Indigenous people, land is not separate from the body but intricately connected to corporeal existence. Thus, an assault on sacred water sources is an assault on the body itself.

The poems included in the suite are, for the most part, free verse with few formal restrictions. The first poem, "Prayer of Prayers," offers a vivid description of the images that proliferated coverage of the Standing Rock protests: authorities with water cannons, eyes swollen shut, water protectors praying over the land and over those who assault them. The author, Deborah A. Miranda, focuses on transcorporeality, juxtaposing non-human entities with human beings. The poem opens with a pair of lines personifying an Earth that mourns its own destruction as Miranda writes, "The planet prays for us,/for itself" (Miranda 2017); She soon complicates this image further with the metaphor, "This planet *is* a prayer" (emphasis hers). Together, these images work to demonstrate that the Earth is simultaneously living and nonliving. The planet occupies a corporeal form insofar as it is capable of prayer, yet it also transcends physical form to become the prayer itself. Miranda juxtaposes this concept with a direct invocation of the reader: "You think prayer/cannot change this war?/Then redefine prayer" (Miranda 2017). These lines illustrate the author's focus on the need to find a common language in order to reach resolution over the conflict. Miranda assigns non-human agency to the planet, but her choice to end subsequent lines with "us" and "itself" emphasises the embodiment of the land. The following poem, "Women in the Fracklands" by Toni Jensen, blurs the lines between flash fiction and prose poetry. There are no line breaks and the poem is distinctly narrative, yet the combination of numbered sections and figurative wordplay strengthens its poetic quality. Jensen consistently references the names for collective nouns, such as how "a group of magpies [is] called a tiding, a gulp, a murder, a charm" and "a group of deer is called a herd; a group of roe deer, a bevy" (Jensen 2017). These collective nouns function as a parallel for the speaker's attempt to name and define the various threats of violence that permeate the poem. Ultimately, Jensen too emphasises the embodiment of trauma, closing the third section with the lines "How much brush can a body take before it becomes a violence, before it makes violence, or before it is remade—before it becomes something other than the body it was once, before it becomes a past-tense body?" (Jensen 2017).

Against the backdrop of Standing Rock protests, fracking and human trafficking, Jensen makes clear that land and bodily trauma are manifestly the same for Indigenous women's bodies.

Natalie Diaz' poem, "The First Water is the Body" is another included in the suite. The speaker opens with an attempt to define what water means to her people, explaining that "The Colorado River is the most endangered river in the United States—also, it is a part of my body./I carry a river. It is who I am: 'Aha Makav./This is not metaphor" (Diaz 2017). Diaz' explicit insistence that the water as body is not a metaphor signals her awareness of how many Western readers perceive water and its fundamental deviation from how Mojave culture treats water. Diaz continues with a lengthier explanation of the Mojave phrase and how it functions within her culture: "When a Mojave says, Inyech *'Aha Makavch ithuum*, we are saying our name. We are telling a story of our existence. *The river runs through the middle of my body*" (Diaz 2017). Diaz separates the poem into sections, each one addressing water from a different perspective. Every section offers an addendum to the initial assertion that water is not a substance separate from Mojave existence. These definitions disrupt traditional constructions of the animacy hierarchy described by Mel Chen and echo what Donna Haraway calls "becoming-with."

For these Indigenous people, it is impossible to separate water from the body, thus its liveness is inherently connected to the liveness of human beings. "This is not juxtaposition. Body and water are not *two unlike things*-they are more than *close together* or *side by side.* They are *same*-body, being, energy, prayer, current, motion, medicine" (Diaz 2017). Diaz is intentional in parsing out this disconnect throughout the poem. "*'Aha Makav*," she writes, "is the true name of our people, given to us by our Creator who loosed the river from the earth and built it into our living bodies" (Diaz 2017). Again, Diaz returns to the shortcomings inherent to translation, revisiting the image of the river running through the middle of the body. Diaz acknowledges, though, that "This is a poor translation, like all translations./In American minds, the logic of this image will lend itself to surrealism or magical realism—" (Diaz 2017). She further works to connect the Mojave word for tears and the Mojave word for river, describing the act of crying as "*A great weeping*." Even this translation, though, gives Diaz pause as she wonders,

> But who is this translation for? And will they come to my language's four-night funeral to grieve what has been lost in my efforts at translation? When they have drunk dry my river will they join the mourning procession across our bleached desert?
>
> (Diaz 2017)

Diaz draws on the act of translation a number of times in her poem, each time emphasising the strain of attempting to communicate the importance of water to a Western reader who is fundamentally unable to understand. Every attempt at translation is mired by the inability for Western language to describe the intra-action of land and body in Indigenous terms. Yet, Diaz is persistent in her effort to contextualise this transcorporeality. "A river is a body of water. It has a foot, an elbow, a mouth. It runs. It lies in a bed. It can make you good. It remembers everything" (Diaz 2017), she writes further into the poem. These lines, which Western literary critics may term personification, draw on a familiar poetic trope in an attempt to explain the Indigenous understanding of non-human agency for a Western audience. Again, though, Diaz seems keenly aware that the Western reader will read this image as figurative, as metaphor. She closes the poem with an allusion to Toni Morrison, who once wrote that water has memory, before leaving the reader with a haunting question: "Do you think the water will forget what we have done, what we continue to do?" (Diaz 2017).

The final poem in the suite is a reprint of Joy Harjo's poem, "This Morning I Pray for My Enemies." It is a brief poem, and one that mirrors several others in the suite, centring the idea of an enemy and the embodiment of trauma inherent to naming that enemy. Harjo, too, uses transcorporeal imagery to encapsulate this embodiment of trauma: "The heart is the smaller cousin of the sun./It sees and knows everything" (Harjo 2017). Here, Harjo trades on the concept of lineage with the word "cousin," implying that nature and the human body are physically connected. Like Diaz, Harjo seems to argue that we are the stars, and that this is not a metaphor. While this poem was not written in direct response to Standing Rock, it emphasises the ongoing struggle for Indigenous people to protect what is theirs. It also helps contextualise the non-violent protests at Standing Rock in that Harjo warns, "An enemy who gets in, risks the danger of becoming a friend" (Harjo). Thus, by embodying the enemy, water protectors risk becoming the enemy.

Though Long Soldier chooses not to include a poem of her own in the suite, her 2017 collection *Whereas* includes a section that borrows its name from the title of the book. This section begins with a series of statements beginning with the phrase "Whereas," employing both structure and language from the legalese in the Congressional Resolution of Apology to Native Americans. Long Soldier includes an epigraph before the section, asserting that her "response is directed to the Apology's delivery, as well as the language, crafting, and arrangement of the written document" (57). The epigraph further explains that as a dual citizen of both the United States and the Oglala Lakota Nation, Long Soldier must navigate the border between two distinct cultures. Each of the poems centres a specific experience, some of them are formative childhood memories and others are conversations Indigenous people. Each entry works to get closer to a language for Long Soldier's particular experience. "I walk out remembering that for millennia we have called ourselves Lakota meaning friend or ally. This relationship to the other," she recalls in one section (64). In another, Long Soldier describes a young girl holding in her tears. The speaker tells her, "*Stop, my girl. If you're hurting, cry,*" which prompts the girl to "let it out, a flood from living room to bathroom" (66). The speaker questions her part in teaching her daughter not to acknowledge pain, specifically in the way the speaker refuses to let out the pain she feels at the language of a "new chapter" for Indigenous people with the arrival of white settlers.

The second part of the series includes the subtitle "Resolutions," fashioning its style and language after the specific legal jargon of concrete actions in a suit. Long Soldier previously outlines the difference between the meaning of "whereas," a word with no concrete action or promise attached to it, and "resolution," which is a specific instruction or set of instructions included in a legally binding agreement. This part of the series is numbered just as a legal document would be, and Long Soldier employs the poetic method of erasure several times to create new meaning out of the specific phrases in former President Obama's official apology on behalf of the United States government. The seventh resolution is perhaps the most visually powerful. The poem begins with the phrase "I commend the inventive crafting of a national resolution so mindful of--" followed by a series of lines, each one adding a single word to the preceding line (Long Soldier 97). The first line contains just one word: boundaries. To the right of page is a slender box that extends from the first line to the last. As words are added, some gradually get pushed inside the box. At the beginning, no such words are inside the restricted zone of the box. By the end, the phrase "withIndiantribeslocatedintheirboundaries" is pushed inside the box. The text appears as a single word in notably small print, acting as a visual representation of the government's long history of piecing out and restricting Indigenous lands (97).

Long Soldier and the poets she highlights in her suite for *Orion Magazine* are a small subset of the Indigenous response to Standing Rock. Many other Indigenous poets wrote and published work during and after the protests, all offering context for opposition to the Dakota Pipeline and Indigenous connections to water as a sacred space. Mark Tilsen, an Oglala Lakota author and educator, recalls the number of times people recognised him following the protests in "I met you at Standing Rock." The poem describes a young woman and man together, sharing the summer night, yet the speaker is unable to discern whether or not the event was a dream or a memory. "This was before the water cannons and rubber/bullets snipers and mercenaries helicopter flyovers/humvees and mraps before the broken bones batons and mace," the speaker admits (Tilsen 2019). Tilsen's decision to weaponise water within the poem reflects the ways in which the government enforces its control over Indigenous bodies, shifting the sacred space from a connection to spiritual transcendence into a dangerous point of vulnerability for the speaker. Julian Talamantez Brolaski indicts spectators of Standing Rock for turning the protests into something trendy without recognising the spiritual importance of protecting water on Indigenous land. The speaker in the poem, "From Stonewall to Standing Rock," laments that "there's no sign of that struggle here but they are selling t-shirts commemorating/the other and the six days of riots…and now people are treating standing rock like burning man" (Brolaski 2011). Brolaski further describes the erasure of two-spirits and trans-women of colour at the protests before leaning into a metaphor about how water can hollow out stone. The dichotomous relationship with stone serves to assert the power of resistance and the inevitability of Indigenous survival against the cold, oppressive imposition of government expansion.

These poems are not meant to represent the entirety of Indigenous experience, nor should they be taken as wholly representative of Indigenous literature. I suggest, rather, that these poems offer a particularly effective entrypoint for students who are unfamiliar with ecopoetics, one that moves beyond the common pedagogical practice of framing Indigenous writing in terms of origin stories and myths. Though the origin stories of Indigenous tribes offer rich opportunities for students, they can also create a false sense that Indigenous culture is static and situated in the past. If students are to understand contemporary environmental issues, especially insofar as they relate to the governance of water sources in the United States, it is essential that they first engage Indigenous literature as a present and evolving body of work. Of course, to fully comprehend the complexities of water protection and the continued efforts of Indigenous people to protect their waterways, students also need to learn how to conceptualise transcorporeality in non-Western terms.

The Meaning of Water

Public education curricula have become increasingly politicised in America, particularly within southern states associated with conservatism. Several states have also passed legislation that prohibits discussion about topics ranging from reproductive rights to systemic racism in the

United States. Teacher libraries are under remarkable scrutiny. In November of 2021, Texas Governor Gregg Abbott went so far as to instruct the Texas Education Agency to conduct an investigation into violations of educational legislation and report these violations as criminal acts. American conservatives historically reject scientific consensus around climate change, the impact humans have on the environment and ecoactivism. Though not explicitly named in recent legislation, K-12 teachers are understandably wary of incorporating any politicised topic in their classrooms. This erasure is detrimental to students, ultimately perpetuating poor civic engagement and an inability to form critical opinions about the topics most pertinent to their future. These gaps are evident as students enter higher education spaces, where many encounter sociopolitical topics inside the classroom for the first time. As such, higher education instructors must actively engage students with relevant issues, including climate change and clean water access. With regard to water pollution and access to clean drinking water, the failure to acknowledge recent events from Standing Rock protests to the Flint, Michigan water crisis tacitly participates in the widespread erasure of contemporary issues directly affecting Black and Indigenous communities in America. It also risks graduating students who have little to no understanding about one of the most immediate crises of their generation.

Young people who do not have the opportunity to discuss important socio-cultural moments of their own lifetime are unlikely to engage critically with these events as adults. What information students do access, if any, is likely limited to brief coverage from media outlets and trending posts on social media. Compounding this relative dearth of information is a disconnect between colonial understandings of water as a resource and Indigenous understandings of water as a sacred space. This dichotomy is evident in texts across generations and cultures, as discussions of water proliferate everything from land surveys to legal treaties to literary work. Water is, after all, intrinsically linked to human civilisation throughout both nomadic and agrarian traditions. Its vitality is undisputed across eras and continents; in short, humanity has always understood the absolute necessity of access to freshwater. Despite its presence as a fundamental need, or perhaps because of it, Western notions of water deviate considerably from the conceptions held by many Indigenous poets. There is a distinctly capitalist mentality in Western thought, with water functioning not as a basic human right but as a commodity subject to governmental oversight. In contrast, Indigenous cultures frequently situate water as sacred, sometimes existing as an entirely separate world from the earth and sky.

Representations of water are, of course, more complex and nuanced than this in American literature. Contemporary poets Patricia Smith and Porsha Olayiwola, for instance, incorporate water as an imminent and permanent threat to the Black community, with Smith directly aligning Hurricane Katrina with the systemic oppression of people of colour embedded in white colonial systems in her award-winning collection, *Blood Dazzler*. "*Go,* he say. Pick up y'all black asses and run," Smith writes in "Man on the TV Say," recalling pleas for New Orleans residents to flee ahead of Katrina while the government failed to provide adequate resources for evacuation or protection for the historically Black communities across Southern Louisiana (18). Olayiwola unpacks a statistic that suggests 70 per cent of Black people do not know how to swim in "Water," tracing part of this historical phenomenon to segregation in the lines, "i heard a jim crow north and a ku kluxed south kept coloreds outta public/swimming pools and off public water fountains" (78). For Chicano poets like Marcelo Hernandez Castillo, who urges Chicanos to "continue this drowning/to remember what we look like" in "Origin of Drowning or Crossing the Rio Bravo," water is aligned with migration and generational trauma (17). Origin stories spanning continents and millenia feature massive floods as central elements. While these representations are equally viable and important discussions in the 21st century classroom, the limits of this essay require a focus specifically on the core separation between the way

Indigenous cultures understand water and how that understanding is vital to conversations about global conservation. Equally important, poetry in protest of the Dakota Pipeline by Indigenous women functions as an entrypoint for students, offering a tangible and engaging contrast to the colonial treatment of water as a resource for human consumption.

Water, insofar as we use the term in English, can function as both a noun and a transitive verb. As a noun, the Oxford English Dictionary traces its etymology to Germanic and Old English roots (uuaeter, water, wasser, et. al.) and categorises it first as a substance. Subsequent subcategories include reference to bodies of water, any liquid secreted from the body or liquids resembling water. In fact, the first and most prominent definition offered is "the substance (most commonly encountered as liquid) which is the principal constituent of seas, lakes, and rivers, and which falls in rain and other forms of precipitation" ("Water"). This immediately signals the Western use of the word water with something intrinsically separate from the human body. In fact, one has to look to the 7th entry, under figurative uses of water, before encountering any definition of water that does not centre water as a substance wholly independent of human life. The figurative definitions describe water as "refreshment to the soul" ("Water"), "referring to the loss of courage, strength, etc. Chiefly in *to turn to water*" ("Water"), and "something which quenches or extinguishes passion, enthusiasm, danger, etc." ("Water"). Even here, Western definitions of water are grounded in utilitarianism, centring how water functions in relation to humanity.

The etymological history is varied and dense, emphasising the importance of water and the many ways in which Western cultures reference water, almost all of them are utilitarian in nature. From baptism to business transactions, water and its cognates appear in writing from Old English forward with no distinct interruption. Shakespeare invokes water as cleansing when he writes "Go get some Water/And wash this filthy witness from your hand" (Shakespeare 2.2.60–61), while the Christian bible references drinking water and establishes water as a gateway into the kingdom of heaven through a spiritual rebirth. "Why are we taught that with water God doth purifie and cleanse his Church?" one citation on the intersection of religion and law reads ("Water"). Another from 1908 even equates water with reason, describing how "The fire that threatened to sweep over the West, seems to have been put out, by the simple application of the water of common-sense" ("Water"). The many etymological examples cited throughout the OED entry for water highlight its varied use but perpetuate a singular perspective of water as serving function for human beings.

Idiomatic phrases in English involving water echo the Western perception of water as utilitarian and, more often than not, as something that can be added to another substance to dilute or purify it. "Watered down," for example, refers both to the literal definition of water as a liquid which can dilute more potent substances and also, colloquially, to content or ideas that may be presented in a more understandable, less technical manner. Many idioms also situate water as a threat to human existence, as in "keep your head above water," or descriptions of those in trouble as "in hot water" or "treading water." Here, the idioms identify water as in direct opposition to life, indeed threatening to consume our liveness should we fail to overcome its power. Several idioms, in contrast, reference the "water of life," as in the Latin *Aquavitae*, the French *eau de vie*, and even the Irish *uisge bheatha* ("Aqua-Vitae"). Ironically, these references to the "water of life" are almost exclusively used in reference to various alcoholic beverages, perhaps stemming from the importance of wine in Roman culture and its correlation to both hydration and nutritional value. What remains evident throughout these definitions is that water, in the Western conception, is almost universally conceived as distinct from the human body and indeed as something which often threatens the human body, either literally or figuratively.

Many Indigenous words for water manifest in the names for landmarks, cities and regions. Mississippi and Ohio take their names from the Ojibwe words *michi ziibi* and the Iroquois word *Ohi-yo*, respectively (Lemay). Minnesota, for example, is derived from the Dakota word *mni-sota*, which translates roughly to "land where the water reflects the sky" (*Mni Sota Fund*). Many state names, in fact, derive from Indigenous words for the region; these words, like *mni-sota*, often describe land in proximity to water. Arizona may take its name from *Arizonac*, a Papagos word meaning "lack of water" or "land of the small springs;" Connecticut is derived from *Quonoktacut*, which could mean "river whose water is driven in waves by tides" or "long river;" the Algonquin word *Mishigamaw*, meaning "great water," inspired the name for Michigan while some attribute Wisconsin to the Indigenous word *Ouisconsin* or *Misconsing*, meaning "wild rushing channel" ("Origin of Names of US States"). As these examples illustrate, Indigenous communities situated geographical understanding in the intersection of land and water as both a practical necessity and a reflection of their veneration of water.

Indigenous categorisations of water often present water as wholly separate from human existence. Tiokasin Ghosthorse, for example, explains that the Lakota word for water rejects literal translation into English. "The fragmenting of *Mni* into simple English nouns would…lost most of the word's true meaning and essential idea of 'Water as a Being'" (Ghosthorse 2021). Rather than a static substance, the Lakota tradition categorises water as a "First Consciousness" that provides the Lakota people with a mirror of existence (Ghosthorse 2021). Here, water is not just a part of life but an active participant in creation. Ghosthorse explains it this way:

> Water is a cup of stars. When you put that cup of Water to your mouth and drink, you are drinking a cup of stars. You see the glimmering lights and reflections of the sun on the waters of the earth
>
> (2021)

The Lakota word for water, and its cultural understanding of water, is essential to understanding the protests at Standing Rock and the phrase many protesters coopted, "Mní wičhóni." Roughly translated as "water is life," this phrase appears on signage, apparel and other objects of protest directed at the construction of the Dakota Pipeline through Standing Rock Sioux territory. Rosalyn R. LaPier explains that, for the Lakota and other Indigenous cultures, water is sacred. "The Blackfeet viewed water as a distinct place - a sacred place. It was the home of divine beings…It can, in fact, be compared to Mount Sinai of the Old Testament," she writes. Like Ghosthorse, LaPier shows an immediate compulsion to draw comparison between Indigenous categorisations of water and Western ideology, highlighting the underlying disconnect that fuels the ongoing protests around Standing Rock.

In an official statement opposing the construction of the Dakota Pipeline, the Native American Rights Fund cites Lakota creation mythos to argue against the government's claim to eminent domain. According to Lakota tradition, the Creator specifically instructs the Lakota people to live in harmony with land, water and air. Failure to do so will result in the destruction not just of nature, but of humanity. That the organisation invokes this narrative in a formal and legal statement further illustrates the ways in which Indigenous people must operate within Western categorisations of water to defend their right to clean, unadulterated water.

Unfortunately, Barton H. Thompson Jr. explains in "Water as Public Commodity," the legal approach to water in America resists the understanding offered by Indigenous authors. "Three themes have dominated the principal debates over water law and policy during the last quarter century," he explains. "The first theme is water as a *public trust*…the second theme is water as an *economic commodity*…the final vision is water as a global *human right*" (17). Thompson delineates the ways in which these definitions often work in opposition to one another insofar as water as a human right is at odds with water as something that can be governed and/or traded. He argues that these three conceptions, though, "are potentially harmonious" and that together they help to define water as a "public commodity" that recognises water as essential to life but also assigns the responsibility of managing water to the government (18–19). Though Thompson comes close to bridging Western and Indigenous understandings of water, he ultimately fails to connect government oversight with the privatisation of natural resources. More importantly, he argues that Western government policies should dictate the management and distribution of water, which is at odds with Indigenous categorisations of water as sacred and waterways as inherently immutable because human interference pollutes their connection to the sacred.

Framing the Conversation for Students

Water is fundamentally connected to human existence but, in the midst of rapidly depleting freshwater sources and frequent ecological disasters along vital waterways, Americans must learn to bridge understandings of water, to combine the utilitarian ideology of the West with the sacred mythos of Indigenous peoples. The path toward sustainability lies in our ability to invert our categorisations of water and its connection to human liveness, to identify methods that ensure freshwater for all citizens while also preserving water sources. While legal definitions may not include water as sacred in explicit terms, it is possible to conceptualise water preservation in like terms, to consider waterways as inherently precious in the same way we preserve historical and natural landmarks through legal policy. An essential part of legislating water will be internalising the intra-action of humans and water, without which neither water nor humanity could survive.

Entering the conversation around water protection and ecopoetics requires a fundamental shift in thinking, subverting colonial categorisations of water as resource and reimagining the animacy hierarchy to accommodate Indigenous understandings of non-human agency. This shift mirrors New Materialist theory, but it would be both anachronistic and disingenuous to attribute Indigenous ideologies to contemporary Western theory. Indigenous literature reflects a robust history of engaging the landscape through terms of embodiment and non-human agency. Water has, for thousands of years, functioned as a sacred space that occupies the body and connects Indigenous people to the land. Thus, preparing students for more enriched understandings of ecopoetics does not require a deliberate framing of literature in theoretical terms, but the demythologising of Indigenous perceptions of non-human agency.

Constanza Contreras, speaking at the 2021 Pacific Ancient and Modern Language Association Conference, argued that Indigenous people have more complex relations to consider with regard to land and the body. She cites Natalie Diaz as one writer who centres that intra-action and alters our understanding of language, land and embodiment through verse. More importantly, Contreras stresses that the lack of translatability between Indigenous and Western conceptions of land and non-human agency inherently complicates discussions about land embodiment. Ultimately, Contreras notes, we must learn to approach Indigenous understandings of non-human agency and land embodiment outside the mythical, stripping away the metaphorical and centring Indigenous ideologies as sociopolitical configurations. During the same panel, Carmen Garcia-Navarro invoked Emily Dickinson to illustrate that Westerners "don't have words" to fully comprehend the Indigenous connection to land. She further quotes Joy Harjo, who says that "we need instructions on the language of the land" (García-Navarro 2021).

Ironically, some Western theorists are coming closer to the language of non-human agency through New Materialism, but this creates its own set of problems in that New Materialists have thus far resisted engaging with Indigenous scholars regarding theories of non-human agency. This was the subject of the panel discussion, "What's New About New Materialism?: Black and Indigenous Scholars on Science, Technology and Materiality." During the panel, three scholars illustrated the ways in which Indigenous Studies has long engaged with non-human agency and transcorporeality in more developed and nuanced ways than New Materialism presently allows. One of the panellists, Marcelo Garzo Montalvo, also sought to redefine poetry itself in Indigenous terms: "What is poetry as a time-space, as a state…in which poetic knowing happens, in which a form of knowledge is experienced in the body?" (13:30). Montalvo's characterisation of poetry as a transitive experience of embodying knowledge helps ground the poetics of protest as an exercise in understanding. The Indigenous women who wrote in response to Standing Rock, then, participate in a transcorporeal experience of both inhabiting and being inhabited by the language of ecopoetics as a direct response to the embodied trauma of Western contamination of sacred water sources.

According to Jerry Lee Rosiek et al., the continued reluctance of New Materialism to acknowledge the contributions of Indigenous scholars in theories of non-human agency perpetuates the erasure of Indigenous people in higher education spaces (332). In addition to acknowledging that Indigenous people have engaged with the concept of non-human agency for thousands of years, the authors assert that Indigenous people are presently better equipped to apply these theories, as New Materialism is relatively new and underdeveloped. One nuance that Rosiek et al. stress is that Indigenous relationships to spaces are not universal but particular (337). This particularity is evident in the protests at Standing Rock. According to the authors, Standing Rock Sioux resisted the Dakota Pipeline because it was a "disruption of the relation between the Sioux people and *[the] particular sites* found at the confluence of rivers in question" (339). Speaking to the commodification of the phrase "Water is Life" and its pervasiveness in mainstream coverage, Rosiek et al. explain that

> the understanding of the river or a particular confluence of rivers as the only place where particular insights become possible, as the only place where certain words and concepts can be understood…was filtered out by the extractive epistemic habits of public media discourse
>
> (339)

Conclusion

The nuances of New Materialism and Indigenous Studies are beyond the scope of most classrooms, but that does not preclude today's youth from engaging with perceptions that are fundamentally counter to their own. The Indigenous women poets presented herein provide an opportunity to process non-human agency and land embodiment in concrete ways. Poetry is also a particularly vital tool for the 21st-century educator in that it allows for discussions that may otherwise be discouraged by legislators working to restrict the content of public education spaces. The interpretative element of analysis centres students in the act of critical inquiry, thus allowing them to arrive at conclusions about the poems and the sociopolitical space they inhabit. This act of inquiry also helps prepare students to apply similar scrutiny to other matters of ecoactivism, such as the Flint, Michigan water crisis.

Like Standing Rock, government responses to the issues affecting communities of colour in Flint have been largely performative. One recalls, for example, former President Obama publicly taking a sip of tap water during a speech in the city. Though the optics were clearly meant to communicate a sense of solidarity, the public was immediately sceptical about whether or not real action would follow. I was new to the classroom at the time, and I remember that we were encouraged to discuss the event with our own students, many of whom lived in extreme poverty and experienced irregular access to water and electricity. Just over a decade later, educators face the impossible challenge of preparing students for a world that is increasingly politicised without overtly incorporating politics into the classroom. More importantly, students face the potential of exiting school without ever having meaningfully engaged issues of global climate crisis.

Without the language to engage with these issues, they cannot make conscious decisions about what are arguably the most immediate risks to their own longevity. Indigenous poets offer a tangible way to frame these conversations, and to help young people reimagine the animacy hierarchy to recognise non-human agency and land embodiment. Though we may not yet have the words to instruct, or even to process, the nuances of our relationship to water, Indigenous responses to Standing Rock offer a trajectory toward more informed, inclusive dialogue around one of the most important issues of our generation.

Works Cited

"aqua-vitae, n." *OED Online*, Oxford University Press, September 2021, www.oed.com/viewdictionaryentry/Entry/226109. Accessed 18 September 2021.

Brolaski, Julian Talamantez. "Stonewall to Standing Rock." *Poetry Foundation*, 2011. https://www.poetryfoundation.org/poems/147082/stonewall-to-standing-rock-5b1fea9b288ef. Accessed 13 April 2022.

Castillo, Marcel Hernandez. *Cenzontl.* Rochester, NY: BOA Editions, 2018.

Chen, Mel Y. *Animacies: Biopolitics, Racial Mattering, and Queer Affect.* Durham, NC: Duke University Press, 2012.

Diaz, Natalie. "The First Water Is the Body." *Orion Magazine*. 2017. https://orionmagazine.org/article/women-standing-rock/. Accessed 16 Sept 2021.

Diné Yazhi', Demian. "Water Is Life: A Poem For the Standing Rock." *Lithub*, 10 Oct 2016. https://lithub.com/water-is-life-a-poem-for-the-standing-rock/. Accessed 13 April 2022.

García-Navarro, Carmen. "Joy Harjo's Ecopoetics: Ethical Modes of Behavior to the Land." *Proceedings from the 118th Pacific Ancient and Modern Language Association Conference Nov. 11–14, 2021: Ecopoetics, 1960–2021.*

Ghosthorse, Tiokasin. "Living with Relativity." *Centers for Humans & Nature*. https://www.humansandnature.org/living-with-relativity. Accessed 16 Sept 2021.

Haraway, Donna J. *Staying with the Trouble: Making Kin in the Cthulucene.* Durham, NC: Duke University Press, 2016.

Harjo, Joy. "This Morning I Pray for My Enemies." *Orion Magazine*. 2017. https://orionmagazine.org/article/women-standing-rock/. Accessed 16 Sept 2021.

Jensen, Toni. "Women in the Fracklands: On Water, Land, Bodies, and Standing Rock." *Orion Magazine*. 2017. https://orionmagazine.org/article/women-standing-rock/. Accessed 16 Sept 2021.

LaPier, Rosalyn R. "Why Is Water Sacred to Native Americans?" *The Conversation*, 21 March 2017. https://theconversation.com/why-is-water-sacred-to-native-americans-74732. Accessed 16 Sept 2021.

Lemay, Konnie. "World Water Day: 12 Native Words for Water." *Indian Country Today*, 13 Sept. 2018. https://indiancountrytoday.com/archive/12-native-words-water. Accessed 22 Sept. 2021.

"Meet the Young Champions Protecting the World's Water." *UN Environment Programme*, 19 March 2021. https://www.unep.org/news-and-stories/story/meet-young-champions-protecting-worlds-water. Accessed 11 Nov 2021.

Miranda, Deborah A. "Prayer of Prayers." *Orion Magazine*. 2017. https://orionmagazine.org/article/women-standing-rock/. Accessed 16 Sept 2021.

Olayiwola, Porsha. *I Shimmer Sometimes, Too.* Minneapolis, MN: Button Poetry, 2019.

"Origin of Names of US States." *U.S. Department of the Interior Indian Affairs*. https://www.indianaffairs.gov/as-ia/opa/online-press-release/origin-names-us-states. Accessed 22 Sept. 2021.

"Our Name has Changed!" *Mni Sota Fund*. https://mnisotafund.org/namechange. Accessed 22 Sept. 2021.

Rosiek, Jerry Lee, et al. "The New Materialisms and Indigenous Theories of Non-Human Agency: Making the Case for Respectful Anti-Colonial Engagement." *Qualitative Inquiry* 26:3–4, Mar. 2020, pp. 331–346, doi:10.1177/1077800419830135.

Shakespeare. *Macbeth* from The Folger Shakespeare. Ed. Barbara Mowat, Paul Werstine, Michael Poston, and Rebecca Niles. Folger Shakespeare Library, November 19, 2022. https://shakespeare.folger.edu/shakespeares-works/macbeth/

Smith, Patricia. *Blooddazzler*. Minneapolis, MN: Coffeehouse Press, 2008.

Soldier, Layli Long. "Women and Standing Rock." *Orion Magazine*. https://orionmagazine.org/article/women-standing-rock/. Accessed 16 Sept 2021.

Thompson, Barton H. (Jr.). "Water as Public Commodity." *Marquette Law Review* 95:17, pp. 17–52

Tilsen, Mark. "I Met You at Standing Rock." *NDN Collective*, 14 Feb. 2019. https://ndncollective.org/a-poem-i-met-you-at-standing-rock/. Accessed 13 April 2022.

"water, n." *OED Online*, Oxford University Press, September 2021, www.oed.com/viewdictionaryentry/Entry/226109. Accessed 16 September 2021.

"We Are the Land, We Are the Air, We Are the Water." Native American Rights Fund. https://www.narf.org/we-are-the-land/. Accessed 16 Sept 2021.

"Young Climate Activists Demand Action and Inspire Hope." *UNICEF*. https://www.unicef.org/stories/young-climate-activists-demand-action-inspire-hope. Accessed 11 Nov 2021.

Part II

Perspectives on the More-than-Human

4   Last Migrations

The Poetry of Migratory Birds

Melanie Duckworth and Aidan Coleman

"For every bird there is this last migration" (Hope 2000, 27). So begins "The Death of the Bird" by Australian poet A.D. Hope (1907–2000). The poem imagines a migratory bird's emotional life as she is drawn back and forth across hemispheres, guided by a "whisper of love". Hope anthropomorphises the bird, describing her urge to migrate as fueled by passion – "exiled love" and "despair". She is a "speck", alone amongst her companions, and the adjectives "delicate", "small", and "tiny" reinforce this vulnerability. As her instinct fails, "the great earth, with neither grief nor malice/Receives the tiny burden of her death" (Hope 2000, 28). The poem, first published in 1955, can be read as an elegy for a specific bird, or the avian class, or by extension for the planet itself. The language and tone, and the poem's material objects, are haunted by ecological mourning in ways that come into sharper focus for a 21st-century reader.

Like Hope's bird, this chapter moves back and forth between hemispheres. Its three sections bring Scotland-based poets Kathleen Jamie, Don Paterson, and Jen Hadfield into conversation with Australian poets Judith Wright, Les Murray, and Jill Jones.[1] Birds, of course, do not recognise national borders, and while these poets may share nationalities, they inhabit, and write from, different bioregions. While birds rarely migrate directly between Scotland and Australia, we propose a primary focus on the poetry of the two nations partly because of the geographical distance between them, which resonates with the global remit of the collection, and partly because of their different but related postcolonial histories, which inflect the language and themes of the countries' ecopoetics. Our reading through an ecological lens often foregrounds the material world and science, while playing down those symbolist elements for which avian poetry is, perhaps, most famous. With reference to the literal birds the poems address – and drawing on zoopoetics (Moe 2014), extinction studies (van Dooren 2014), and ecocriticism (Buell 1995) – we argue that poetry about migratory birds presents unique opportunities for readers, teachers, and students to engage with questions of extinction, climate change, global belonging, and the precarity of survival in the Anthropocene.

Poets have long been fascinated with migratory birds, which appear in their works as markers of the seasons, and as symbols of freedom, mystery, and longing. Birds' migratory ability is a source of wonder, and poets attempt to capture the strangeness of their capacity to navigate vast distances and to decide when to leave. It is this leaving, however, that prefigures the possibility of permanent loss. In a time of climate emergency, the poetics of migratory birds has a new urgency. As global citizens, migratory birds are uniquely vulnerable to environmental disruption along their routes and the destinations where they breed. Migrating birds are images of change and continuity. Change, because they leave and arrive in time with the seasons, and continuity, because they have done it for millions of years. If seasons have traditionally been conceived of as reliable and cyclic, the arrivals and departures of migratory birds have been markers of this constancy. However, anthropogenic climate change has also disrupted migratory

DOI: 10.4324/9781003399988-7

paths and the timing, or "phenology", of bird migration.[2] Birds also face direct threats from humans such as hunting and habitat destruction.

Hope, a formalist poet with a classical bent, is an unlikely eco-poet, but his much-anthologised poem "The Death of the Bird" can be read in ecological terms. The poem concerns a specific bird but it is lacking in specific detail. Its concerns seem metaphysical and its mode symbolist. Yet, whatever the bird might stand for, the poem is beautifully realised and, we would argue, evokes sympathy in a way that focuses a reader on the bird itself, its sweeping journeys, and its reliance upon and connection with "the great earth". The Australian eco-poet John Kinsella captures this tension, when ruminating on how he might have written the poem differently:

> I would name the species, its precise migratory route, the flora and fauna of its "homes" … But let's not be fooled, this is a most specific description. ["The Death of the Bird"] is not (purely) symbolic, and not generic. It is its own centre, it is entire. It is so small and so large. Macro and micro – writing "nature" makes you aware it always has to contain both.
>
> (2008, 176)

Migratory birds invite this tension between the "micro" and the "macro", as diminutive birds can cover vast distances. One such bird, B95: a rufa red knot nick-named "moonbird", has, over cumulative migrations, surpassed the distance to the moon (Hoose 2012). The poetic moniker "moonbird" attests to the power of imagery and figurative language to create sympathy for and interest in birds. The poets we discuss in this chapter approach migratory birds from a number of perspectives, from elegiac to anthropomorphic, from scientific to surreal. In the first section, Scottish poet Kathleen Jamie and Australian poet Judith Wright observe migratory birds with longing and affection, while contemplating historical and future extinctions. They read the shapes the birds' bodies write on the sky as a kind of poetry in itself, a process of communication and interpretation that Aaron M. Moe calls "zoopoetics" (2014). In the second section, Australian Les Murray and Scotland-based Jen Hadfield attempt to express the birds' bodily perceptions, through linguistic dexterity and anthropomorphism. Finally, Jill Jones (Australia) and Don Paterson (Scotland), through formally and conceptually innovative poems, reflect on the entanglements of migratory birds, humans, commerce, and consumption.

The question remains, however, as to what exactly poems about migratory birds achieve in real terms – can they help the birds themselves, or the ways we might think about the climate crisis? We argue that poems are a potent way to tell stories about migratory birds, stories that witness, with wonder, both lives and deaths. Thom van Dooren asserts that "telling stories has consequences: one of which is that we will be inevitably drawn into new connections, and with them new accountabilities and obligations" (2014, 10). His book *Flight Ways* is "about birds and their relationships, about the webs of interaction in which living beings emerge, are held in the world, and eventually die" (2014, 4). Likewise, poetry about migratory birds also reflects and articulates these "webs of interaction": mourning, observing, and storying hope.

Kathleen Jamie and Judith Wright – Skywriting and Death Sentences

On an affective level, the arrival of migratory birds is reassuring, while the human observer often experiences their departure with sensations of longing and loss. Kathleen Jamie's "Skeins o Geese", written in Scots, is infused with longing and premised on indecipherability. Jamie (b. 1962), is an award-winning Scottish eco-poet and essayist whose "writing explores weighty issues – questions of nationhood, subjectivity … the health of the planet, what it means to be human … and the primacy of the human connection to other species" (Falconer 2015, 1). "Skeins o Geese" hinges on a word birds write on the sky: "Whit dae birds write on the dusk?/A word niver spoken or read" (Jamie 2007, 108). The word, formed by bodies of birds leaving together, is arresting but indecipherable. As this poem attempts to read the gestures and the bodies of birds, Moe's concept of "zoopoetics" offers a valuable perspective for approaching it.

Moe defines zoopoetics as "the process of discovering innovative breakthroughs in form through an attentiveness to another species' bodily poiesis" (2014, 6). In doing so, it embraces two main aspects: "First zoopoetics focuses on the process by which animals are makers. They make texts. They gesture. They vocalize" (Moe 2014, 18). The curves of birds' flight and the shapes their bodies make in the air can be read as forms of poetry. "The second focus of zoo-poetics emerges out of the first. It exposes how the gestures of animals – and the vocalisations embedded in their gestures – have shaped the makings of human poetry" (Moe 2014, 19). Moe reads Ray Gonzalez's poem "Rattlesnakes Hammered on the Wall" as an uncomfortable yet poignant example of zoopoetics, as the bodies of writhing, tortured snakes "form/twisted let-ters that spell a bloody/word I can't understand" (Gonzales 2005, 35, quoted in Moe 2014, 13). While the speaker claims the word is indecipherable, Moe argues the poem gives voice to the snakes' bodies. If flight formations and even birds' dead bodies eloquently gesture, then the long journeys and flight paths of migratory birds may also be understood as gestural and may perhaps be "read".

In Jamie's "Skeins o geese", the speaker reaches towards the word the birds form but can only define it in terms of what it is *not*: the past "which lies/strewn around", a lover, or "sudden death" (2007, 108). This list suggests intimacy and loss, but the word, and the experience of "reading" the birds in the sky, resides in between. The poem is a rich example of what Camille Manfredi terms "oikopoetics": "a spatial-ontological mapping of the point of contact between human and non-humans – but also material things – as fellow-transients of the liminal space of the 'neither…nor' and the 'almost'" (2019, 100). In this poem, the wind, a fence, and the sky also occupy this space. Even the poem's Scots language, for many readers, enhances the inti-macy and estrangement. As Crawford notes, Scots is often used in intimate forms such as nurs-ery rhymes and love songs, far from official contexts like schools, where its use is sometimes condemned. But for readers unfamiliar with Scots, it may also entail "in shifting proportions, an acoustic of strangeness and even estrangement" (Crawford 2015, 38).

The sound of the wind moans through the poem like the word itself – audible in the words "hame", "moan", and "soun". Repeated switches between visual and auditory imagery add to the sense of the liminal. The word written on the dusk is visual, but is described acoustically as "struck like a gong". Visual and aural images are further blended when "[T]he sky moves like cattle, lowing" (Jamie 2007, 108). The first image is of the movement of cattle, presumably representing wind-tossed clouds, but this shifts quickly to the sounds cattle make, which then circles back to the sound of the wind. If, as Moe points out, speech is essentially "breath moving amongst the myriad gestures of the mouth" (2014, 11), the wind moving amongst the myriad gestures of birds, sky, earth, cattle, human, and stone creates this poem's speech. Yet there is an excess of signification, and it cannot be fully interpreted, as "Wire twists lik archaic script/roon a gate" and "[t]he barbs/sign tae the wind as though/it was deef" (Jamie 2007, 108). There are words everywhere, but they are indecipherable.

The movements of birds also create words in the poetry of celebrated poet and environmen-talist Judith Wright (1915–2000). Wright's collection *Birds* was first published in 1962, but the sixtieth anniversary edition (2022) includes six additional poems about birds from Wright's other collections. In "Camping at Split Rock" (1971), Wright describes watching birds fly above a riverside cliff, their flight-lines hatching and cross-hatching the "patch/of vision" the speaker's tent offers. Each bird is distinguished by its pattern of flight: "Each curve has words;/each flight speaks its own bird" (Wright 2022, 70). Swallows, wrens, blue jays, and hawks fly distinctive paths and "we read each bird from its air-written scrawl" (Wright 2022, 70). Wright's poetry returns repeatedly to the rhyme of bird/word, reflecting both on the possibility of reading words that birds' gestures and bodies create, and the ways in which language conjures birds' beings: "The birds go by/but we can name and hold them, each a word/that crystals round a more than mortal bird" (2022, 70). Compared with Jamie (and writing 30 years earlier), Wright displays much greater confidence in her ability to read the birds' gestures.

In "Extinct Birds", Wright reflects on the power and limitations of language to evoke and sustain life (2022, 66). She responds in the poem to the journals of Australian poet Charles Harpur (1813–68), which recorded beautiful colourful birds he feared would soon be extinct due to white settlers damaging the forest and scattering Aboriginal people. Both Harpur and the birds are "vanished with the fallen forest", and the poem is a lament for the birds and Harpur himself "who helped with proud stained hands to fell the forest/and set those birds in love on unread pages" (Wright 2022, 66). As Wright's daughter Meredith McKinney puts it, the poem turns "a sorrowful and clear-sighted gaze … on the terrible damage we have done, and continue to do, to our world even as we love it" (2022, 6). In this case, words memorialise, but fail to protect, birds' lives.

Wright's most extensive engagement with extinction and migratory birds is "Lament for Passenger Pigeons", first published in *Alive*, 1973 (2022, 74). While Wright's poetry customarily engages with Australian birds, this poem mourns passenger pigeons, a migratory species endemic to North America. Passenger pigeons, which once migrated between the Great Lakes and as far south as Mexico, had a population of between three and five billion, but suffered a catastrophic decline in the 19th century due to over-hunting and habitat loss. The last known passenger pigeon, Martha, died in captivity at the Cincinnati Zoo in 1914. As van Dooren points out, however, "over the decades before Martha's death, the interspecies relationships that the Passenger Pigeon evolved and lived within would also have become increasingly fractured" (2014, 11).

Wright evokes the sound of the wind to posit how the loss of the passenger pigeon profoundly altered the world. The poem voices inanimate spaces and forces, but they are not invincible: "The voice of water as it flows and falls/the noise air makes against earth-surfaces/have changed; are changing to the tunes we choose" (Wright 2022, 74). Humanity stains, sullies, and alters the voices of air and sea, which have forever lost the voices of passenger pigeons. The poem reaches towards the birds' lost cries, asking how it can "reinvent" them:

> when we have lost the bird, the thing itself,
> the sheen of life on flashing long migrations?
> Might human music hold it, could we hear?
>   (Wright 2022, 74)

The voice of the extinct bird is lost, but Wright asks if poetry might have the power to recreate it. For most of the poem, the answer is a resounding no, as we only hear echoes of ourselves: "And it is man we eat and man we drink/and man who thickens round us like a stain,/Ice at the polar axis smells of me" (Wright 2022, 74). However, the final stanza changes tack, suggesting that poetry can, in some sense, "resurrect" the bird: "that bird-/siren-and-angel image we contain/essential in a constellating word" (Wright 2022, 75). This bold, hopeful, and not quite convincing claim should be understood in the context of Wright's romanticism and the philosophical writings of her partner, Jack McKinney (Hawke 2001; Rigby 2020, 137). However, Wright later rescinded these views and essentially gave up writing poetry in the 1980s and 1990s, concentrating instead on political activism for environmental and Indigenous rights

(Rigby 2020, 136). Poetry can recall and mourn a bird, and offer hope, but the eerie, "changed" voice of the wind still threatens.

As a post-romantic poet, Jamie is more circumspect about the relationship between birds and words, although like Wright she sees them as intertwined. While migratory birds appear in all Jamie's collections, they are particularly resonant in *The Bonniest Companie* (2015). In 2014, the year of the referendum for Scottish independence, Jamie wrote a poem a day. Following the course of the year, this collection meditates on the concepts of arrival, occupation, belonging, and ownership, echoing aspects of Scotland's fraught relationship with England and its contested identity as part of the United Kingdom. The presence of migratory birds in the collection underscores a notion of Scotland as Nordic, as many birds, such as the "Arctic-hatched, comfy-looking geese/occupying our fields" migrate to Scotland from further north during the winter months (Jamie 2015, 3). While in "Skeins o Geese", migratory birds leave, *The Bonniest Companie* repeatedly celebrates their arrival, commemorating the idea of home. The poems "Eyrie I" and "Eyrie II" re mark on the return of falcons and osprey: "What will the osprey do then, poor things/when they make it home?/...*big a new ane*" (Jamie 2015, 15). Not all is rosy, however. The "found poem" "Wings Over Scotland", a list of suspicious raptor deaths, documents the peril birds face from humans (Jamie 2015, 51).

"Migratory I" focusses on a dead whooper swan, its "neck slack on the turf, head pointing north/like a way sign" (Jamie 2015, 39). In "Migratory I", as in "Skeins o geese", there is excess signification. How should one read the body of a bird? As Jamie's companion opens the swan's wing, she pays little heed to the "naming of the parts: *coverts, ulna, primaries*":

– but this wing – this was a proclamation!
The wind-fit, quartz-bright power of the thing! A radiant gate
one could open and slip through…

(Jamie 2015, 39)

On one level, the swan is a sign, pointing the way, or pointing to an uncertain future. While "Migratory I" does not explicitly evoke the possibility of extinction, Jamie's essay "Wind", based on the same incident, muses on how the "sign" of the dead bird on the remote island, pummelled by wind, raises the possibility of extinction, not only for whooper swans but humanity: "The wind and the sea. Everything else is provisional. A wing's beat, and it's gone" (2012, 242). On another level, the wing parts can be named and categorised in scientific language. As Jamie puts it, "You could understand at once how these creatures make the journeys they do; its wing had been formed under the wind's tutelage, formed by and for the wind" (2012, 240). In the poem, however, the wing is a mysterious "proclamation", speaking of the wind it is formed to harness but also speaking something more: the "bodily semiosis" of the dead bird's wing is capable of almost transcendental speech. Jamie's insistence on the layered meanings and untranslatability of the bird's wing contrasts starkly with Wright's "constellating word" (2022, 75). However, in Wright's "Rainbow Bird", the cold, soft, colourful body of a dead parrot, killed by the winter as he "turned too late to find the spring", is a word requiring an undefined response: "He met me like a word/I needed–pity? love?–the rainbow bird" (2022, 48). Both poets approach migratory birds zoopoetically, as apprehended in poetry, but also as forming poetry themselves.

Les Murray and Jen Hadfield—Speaking For and To

The non-human natural environment is central to Les Murray's (1938–2019) multi award-winning collection *Translations from the Natural World* (1992). The collection, which is not limited to Australian flora and fauna, takes a significant risk in ecopoetic terms in that it seems ostensibly to "speak for" plant and animal life. However, few of the collection's subjects, which include DNA, mollusks, shellback tics, tree trunks, and grasses, are the usual fodder for anthropomorphism and, instead of portraying personality in the manner of a writer like Ted Hughes, Murray focuses on details: embryonic diapause in kangaroos, insects mating, or elephants' sounds. The poems are imaginative embodiments, which blend descriptive elements with the speech of invented (often arcane) languages. As Jonathan Bate notes, Murray's presentation of the poems as "translations" is in large part "a recognition that the poet's home in the logos is a different place from the natural world itself" (2000, 240). This difference – the natural world's untranslatability – is configured in the poems' difficulty – and much of it remains inscrutable. In many ways, these "translations" are meditations on "the limits of linguistic representations of nature" (Cone 2006, 122).

Compared to other poems in *Translations*, "Migratory" (52) employs simple diction and uncomplicated syntax but it is rich in alliteration and aural patterning. The poem's single stanza consists of four sentences, which due to Murray's use of anaphora – the "I am" statements – are reasonably easy to parse. The abstract noun "feeling" occurs four times in the poem and, in contrast to conventional lyric poems, the feelings under consideration are those of the animals rather than the poet's, though this "feeling" is something we would realise more as a sense or intuition that guides:

> I am the wrongness of here, when it
> is true to fly along the feeling
> the length of its great rightness, while days
> burn from vast to a gold gill in the dark
> to vast again, for many feeds
> [...]
>
> (Murray 1992, 52)

The voice of the poem (the "I") is difficult to locate, as are many of the voices in *Translations*. Because it speaks through physical objects in deceptively straightforward ways, it seems ostensibly free of metaphor but the speaking voice is itself a metaphor. Instead of reading the body of a bird, "Migratory", in terms of zoopoetics, imagines the body of a bird reading the world.

Although the science of climate change plays no direct role in "Migratory", the poem is undoubtedly ecological in its concerns. Lawrence Buell's *The Environmental Imagination: Thoreau, Nature Writing, and the Formation of American Culture*, a detailed consideration of environmental perception and the "place of nature in the history of Western thought" (Buell 1995, 1), is useful for considering how the natural world functions in writers' works beyond the immediate context of Thoreau's transcendentalism. In this study, Buell answers the question "What is an environmental text?" with four criteria, which challenge the prevailing anthropocentric orientation of western literature, metaphysics and ethics with a more ecocentric perspective, which is grounded in the physical world beyond the text. These definitive criteria for environmental writing are: that the nonhuman is not merely present as a framing device; that human interest is not understood to be the only legitimate interest; that the work conveys a sense of the environment as a process rather than as a constant or a given; and that the work has an ethical orientation that involves human accountability to the environment (Buell 1995, 6–8). In "Migratory" the physical environment is foregrounded. No humans are, in fact, present, nor is there the sense that humans or human qualities are symbolically represented, as they are in Hope's poem. While "Migratory" might speak for a single bird species, it also represents phenomena that have been occurring for millions of years – against which a human life, or even the lifespan of a species, appears infinitesimal. Most importantly, in terms of natural processes, the poem resists closure – ending not with a revelation but the "shade", "sand", and "sticks" of the poem's opening sentence. "Migratory" is cyclic rather than linear and so embodies an ongoing process.

Bate has noted the "biological accuracy" of Murray's work (2000, 239), a defining feature of *Translations*. Simple scientific details permeate "Migratory". The bird remembers extreme polar seasons – "while days burn from vast to a gold gill in the dark to vast again" – and equatorial crossings: "til the sun ahead becomes the sun behind". The poet's use of extremes and inversions alludes to the fine balance and precarity of the birds' existence, and images such as the "feedy sea", referring to diets of larger birds such as terns, who swoop and dive for small fish enroute, are grounded in the physical. Most birds that make inter-continental migrations to Australia are overwintering, spending the southern summer feeding to build energy reserves sufficient for the long return journey to their breeding sites, but a small percentage of birds, which include several tern species, spend the southern spring/summer breeding. Following an elaborate courtship display ("nests danced for") these birds scratch shallow dents in the gritty sand, decorated with pebbles, shells, sticks, and seaweed to create the "shade with sticks and the double kelp shade" (Murray 1992, 52).

"Migratory" invites readers to think locally and globally, through its emphasis on the bird's reliance on several local ecosystems as well as its far-distant habitats. This global ethic is reinforced through the poem's expressive typography. The right-hand margin alignment underlines the importance of the opposite hemisphere to global bird migration, but it serves at least two other purposes. The first is estrangement: we read in a subtly different way, which is more conscious of the materiality of the words themselves. Bird migration through most of human history has been largely inscrutable. The process is strange, even counterintuitive, and the typography of the poem embodies this. The second purpose seems to connect with migration's dynamic of presence/absence, or that of visible/invisible, captured in phrases such as "the nest that comes and goes", "the egg that isn't now", and "the wrongness of here" (Murray 1992, 52). The white space in "Migratory", which is the ghostly imprint of a more conventional poem, represents this absence (or invisibility) and so the poem's typography invites us to think both locally and globally, and to imagine what is not immediately present. The unfolding disaster of the climate emergency is, according to Buell, a crisis of imagination (Buell 1995, 2). "Migratory" enables readers to engage imaginatively with the intricacies of seasonal bird migration and so imagine how climate change might impact this complex process.

Jen Hadfield (b. 1978) grew up in England but has spent her adult life in Scotland. She has lived for the last two decades in the Shetlands and writes about the local ecology. Her work employs a wide English lexicon, together with words from Scots and Shetlands dialects. Murray seems an influence on Hadfield, in whose poetry flora and fauna are central. The poets share a talent for vivid imagery, which is the fruit of close observation. They both engage with forms of life that have remained obscure to poetry until relatively recently. Hadfield has written poems on lichen, limpets, and puffballs. The title of her third book, *Byssus* (2014), describes the sticky fibers that enable bivalve mollusks to attach themselves to rocks and other surfaces.

Like Murray's, Hadfield's work often risks anthropomorphism, and her writing speaks for, and to, animals. In reviewing the award-winning *Nigh-No-Place*, Ali Alizadeh, who characterises Hadfield's style as "energetic" and "resourceful", decries the absence of anything in Hadfield's "treatment of the ecological world that could be called progressive or ecopoetic" (2010, np). Alizadeh is particularly critical of Hadfield's tendency towards anthropomorphism, noting "the poet's desire to capture, own and control the wildlife for her, and her reader's, amusement"

(2010, np). However, Moe argues that "[A]nthropomorphism is only a fallacy when one is a staunch humanist who does not see continuity between ANIMAL ↔ HUMAN spheres" (2014, 23). In fact, many ecocritical and environmental theorists, including Val Plumwood (2009), Jane Bennet (2010), Timothy Clarke (2011), and Greg Garrard (2012), have defended anthropomorphism as a valid tool to understand and connect with the non-human. The interests of the non-human world often overshadow human concerns in Hadfield's oeuvre, and her poems show an awareness of ecological processes and the pre-history of the Shetlands. Hadfield's work is not overtly political or formally radical, but it converses with a tradition of British nature writing, deploying a degree of scientific knowledge that the poet wears lightly.

In "The Moult", from the collection *Byssus* (2014, 66), Hadfield addresses a group of birds. Waterfowl and seabirds migrate to breed and moult on The Shetlands, where the long summer days provide these temporarily flightless birds with fast-growing nitrogen-rich food to replenish their plumage. Oddly, for a poem of such specificity, the particular species of bird addressed in the 'you' plural is uncertain. "[W]haups", or curlews, are mentioned in third person. The poem focuses on the birds' vulnerability, manifested in the contrast between their awkward, flightless fragile quality, and the scale and violence of the elements: "the wind", "the blinding sea" and even "the sun" that "freeze[s]" when it "hits" (2014, 66). The poem's concrete form, in which single-line stanzas break a pattern of tercets for phrases concerning the extremity of the elements, emphasises the birds' exposure. The moulting itself is figured as if the birds are shedding armor: "Scratch off // your dreamcoat of silver money" but this vulnerability can also be inferred through the speaker's protectiveness:

> Stay out of the sun:
> we can all see you. Stop picking fights
> above your weight. [...]
> (Hadfield 2014, 66)

All but one sentence begins with an imperative ("Stay", "Stop", "Shelter", "Freeze", "Scratch" "Run") and these act, in a similar manner to Murray's "I am" statements, as a formal binding. There is a move from admonition to description, which by the final lines becomes a release – "[R]un/double-jointed when the valley dims". The exception is the third sentence, which begins:

> [...] We've this high
>
> golden bowl of heather and moss
> company of whaups and cries [...]
> (Hadfield 2014, 66)

This gesture, while admitting an observer's intrusion, strikes a pact of peaceful co-existence between human and non-human. Hadfield writes from a position that Neal Alexander and David Cooper describe as an insider-outsider dialectic in which she "witnesses the landscape" (2013, 9), and this is evident in "The Moult" where the poem's address holds otherness in tension with cross-species commonality.

A radical ecopoetics would dismiss such poetry as romantic and would characterise the speaker's protective impulse as patronising. But we would argue that these qualities display an ecocentric ethic and that an understanding of the fragility of ecosystems, and the vulnerability of the animals that inhabit them, needs to be cultivated, as does the instinct to protect and preserve. "The Moult" exhibits a tension between the visible and invisible, but what the poem makes visible is most important from an environmental standpoint. Most of the effects of global warming are invisible to most people most of the time, and many endangered bird species – and their habitats – are not in the public eye. The unique bioregion of the Shetlands, as a chain of islands, is particularly vulnerable to climate change through rising sea levels, but they are remote and invisible to most.

Hadfield's use of literal and figurative language (including anthropomorphism) renders the non-human world strange, which calls for reader's attention. As Hadfield explains, "I certainly don't think of nature as a microcosm of the human world. But we may meet it as we do people from other cultures. We ask each other about our likenesses and our differences" (2010). In their poems about migratory birds, Hadfield and Murray "bear witness" to the intricacies of other-than-human ways of life (van Dooren and Rose 2017). Their poetry aligns with van Dooren and Rose's approach to storytelling:

> The intention here is not to slip into the hubris of claiming to tell another's stories but, rather, to develop and tell our own stories in ways that are open to other ways of constituting, or responding to and in a living world
>
> (2016, 85)

This attentiveness can inspire not only wonder but an ethic of care.

Jill Jones and Don Paterson – Domestic Economy

The ecological often occurs alongside the quotidian in the work of Adelaide-based poet Jill Jones (b. 1951), conveying a sense of mutual complicity for environmental destruction between speaker and reader. Ecological crisis is sometimes foregrounded in *A History of What I'll Become* (2020), but it is usually interwoven with other themes. Timothy Morton asserts in *Ecology Without Nature* (2007) that environmental writing in the romantic tradition – that is, most conventional nature writing up until the present – has tended to separate nature from the human and elevate it, with disastrous consequences for the environment. "Putting something called Nature on a pedestal and admiring it from afar", Morton wryly remarks, "does for the environment what patriarchy does for the figure of Woman. It is a paradoxical act of sadistic admiration" (2007, 4). In contrast to this tradition of environmental writing, Morton insists that "we are 'embedded' in nature" (2007, 4). The refrain "the thick weave" occurs a number of times in Jones's *History*. The phrase resonates with "mesh", Morton's term for the "interconnectedness of all living and nonliving things" (2010, 28), emphasising as it does the entanglements between nature, politics, and culture, and even within nature, most poignantly between the human and non-human.

Migratory birds are an overt presence in two poems in *History*. Set in summer, the short lyric "Step Shadow" largely concerns "the shorebirds" that "will soon fly north" but also includes "[h]oney eaters" clinging "onto wires". These images are juxtaposed with human migrations, for business and leisure, represented by a "jet's underside" that "pushes into the west" (Jones 2020, 102). The poem's title is a play on carbon footprints and the shadow industrialisation casts in the form of global warming and environmental destruction. Hinting at a more sinister migration, the poem ends: "Concrete slowly flakes as/if it's also going somewhere" (Jones 2020, 102). This image, which suggests humankind's intrusion on the non-human world, also implies that our species' time is running out.

"As If The Large Magellanic Cloud Looks Over Us" reads as an unpunctuated journal of summer days, set against the backdrop of Australia's cataclysmic 2019–20 bushfires that burned more than 18 million hectares across four states and destroyed habitats of numerous endangered species (Readfearn 2020). The poem is delivered in a stream-of-consciousness monologue that moves by formal and free association. The setting is appropriately domestic, and the immediate context for the speaker's meditation on migratory birds involves cooking, an act which blends creation and consumption, and the local and global. The speaker is cooking, while drinking *Red Knot* Shiraz from South Australia's McLaren Vale region, and this brings thoughts of bird migrations:

> Some shorebirds will leave soon Ruddy Turnstone
> Red Knot, Sanderling you have to drive an hour or so
> to see them someone tags them then they go
> along the East Asian-Australasian Flyway
>
> I wonder if they smell the grape harvest this summer
> long and dry that will make acidic whites rich shiraz
> will bushfire smoke affect some pickings
>
> (Jones, 86)

The poem engages with science and is grounded in specificity. The passage names a migration route and three bird species, including the endangered Red Knot. Climate change presents a significant threat for these shorebirds. Rising sea levels degrade shoreline habitats (Iwamura et al. 2013), but results from long-term tracking studies have also shown the increasingly advanced phenology of migration for Ruddy Turnstones from Australia (Zhao 2016).[3] Due to changing temperatures, they are leaving their overwintering sites two days earlier each year, creating potential mismatches between northern hemisphere arrival times and food resources.

Of their suite of navigational senses, olfactory memory perhaps most strongly guides birds' return to specific nesting sites each year (Holland et al. 2009). The speaker asks whether these birds sense the subtle changes in the weather and moves associatively to a more immediate and visible environmental catastrophe. This meditation on migratory birds is embedded within – or bracketed by – human consumption.[4] Life's brevity is juxtaposed with a vast time-scale, and the ecological is ubiquitous in the complex inter-relations between time, identity, and language (English and the Kaurna language); and the domestic and "nature" (Jones, 86–87). The possum (native to South Australia) landing on the roof could equally be a cat (an introduced species). Humans, in Jones's terms, are enmeshed within 'the thick weave' of nature. The poem concludes with the speaker "wak[ing] from dreams of profit and loss in the warm breath of morning" (Jones, 87).

We began this chapter by considering a last migration, so it seems apt to close with another dream of "profit and loss", which centres on anthropogenic extinction. "St Brides: Sea Mail" by Scottish poet Don Paterson (b. 1963) is a parable of environmental exploitation and a metaphor for our present predicament. While St Bride is not an actual place, the name associatively invokes St Kilda, home to more than a million seabirds, and the description of harvesting, "milking", and drying the birds resembles practices that took place on St Kilda (Fleming 2000, 353). Until the 1930s, when they were evacuated, the remote island of St Kilda was home to a small human community that relied on seabirds, particularly the fulmar, for food and oil: "The northern fulmar was a mainstay of the St Kildan's economy, supplying 'oil for their lamps, down for their beds, a delicacy for their table, a balm for their wounds, and a medicine for their distempers' " (Warham 1977, 84). The oil was also exported: "In some years the St Kildans exported part of their oil harvest, as the Australian mutton-birders still do with oil from the chicks of *P. tenuirostris*". (Warham 1977, 84). While the pelagic fulmar is not migratory, it seems a fitting emblem for all life if we continue on our current trajectory.

Paterson's poems are frequently voiced by dramatis personae, and "their weird specificity seems confidently pitched to suggest deeper significance, but this often remains unfixed, lurking below, or beyond, or within, their alternatively supple and gnarled textures" (Gillis 2009, 177). "St Brides: Sea Mail" is voiced by an islander, who explains the work undertaken to kill and milk seabirds to retrieve their highly flammable oil: "our sole export/our currency/and catholicon" (Paterson 2003, 2). The process is driven by "rumour of their infinite/supply and the blunt fact/of our demand". Once the oil is extracted, the islanders hang the birds up to dry. The brittle bodies are then hurled from the cliffs in an irreverent approximation of flight. The image, after the day's "sport", is one of moral bankruptcy:

> […] Whatever our luck,
> by sunset, they'd fill the bay
> like burnt moths.
> (Paterson 2002, 3)

The poem sits elegantly on the page, its seven-line stanzas tapered to points, so that each resembles an arrow, or a wing, and this typographical representation of the bird's grace and elegance belies the sordid use to which the birds are put.

The poem ends with the bird's disappearance, which is not so much elegy as a flat statement of loss. The speaker is disappointed not by the disappearance of the birds themselves, but by the income that they represent. The close attention to the birds' bodies as merely a resource is unsettling, as is the poem's pessimistic resolution:

> The wind has been so weak all year
> I post this more in testament
> than in hope or warning.
> (Paterson 2003, 3)

As per the title, the poem is "posted", but this act seems as futile as the launching of the birds' dead, dried bodies, which now fill the bay. Even the wind has lost its power, seemingly transformed by human wastage. "In ecological thinking," Morton notes, "the fear is that we will go on living, while the environment disappears around us" (2010, 253), and Paterson presents readers with this indelible and permanent loss. In "St Brides: Sea Mail" a reader might see a grotesque embodiment of the complacent ecocide in which we are all enmeshed.

Conclusion: "What difference does it make?"

In Hope's "The Death of the Bird", the bewildered bird is buffeted by the winds' "hungry breath" (2020, 28), but in Wright's "Lament for Passenger Pigeons" the wind itself is "changed", it "has no angel, no migrating cry" (2022, 75). Jamie's "Skeins o geese" "turn hame,/on the wind's dull moan" (2007, 108), but for Paterson, the wind itself is "weak", hope is lost (2003, 3). Our earth is wrapped in wind, and the wind is threaded still with the paths and cries of birds who journey there. The poems discussed in this chapter bear witness to the "wind-fit, quartz bright" (Jamie 2015, 39) bodies of birds, to the wonder not only of their flight but of their journeys and their belonging to sky, to rock, to sea, to the "East Asian-Australasian Flyway" (Jones 2020, 86) and to "this high/golden bowl of heather and moss" (Hadfield 2014, 66).

In *Nerves and Numbers: Information, Emotion, and Meaning* (2015), Paul and Scott Slovic consider why humanity is emotionally numb to statistics. They augment their research with reflections from ecologists, political activists, journalists, artists, creative writers, and psychologists, who consider how different communication forms might bridge the gap between harsh statistical realities and humanity's emotional response. One contributor, Nicholas D.

Kristof, who reported on the Darfur genocide, expressed his disbelief at the public's impassioned campaign to save the nest of a red-tailed hawk, Pale Male, who resided within the façade of a Fifth Avenue apartment building in New York, compared to their relative indifference over two million homeless Sudanese (Slovic & Slovic 2015, 85–86). This incongruity underlines the emotional efficacy of writers favouring showing (images) over telling (abstraction). The central importance of the image in poetry is a reason why this ancient art form can bridge the gap between alarming statistical data on the climate emergency and individuals' emotional responses. We need poets to bear witness to what is not immediately present. We need images not only of catastrophe, such as the fulmer filling "the bay/like burnt moths" (Paterson 2003, 3), but also images of joy: moulting birds "run[ning]/double-jointed when the valley dims" (Hadfield 2014, 74); hope: "the egg that isn't now" (Murray 1992, 52); and wonder: "Whit dae birds write on the dusk?/A word niver spoken or read" (Jamie 2007, 108). We need an imaginative ecological vision that focuses on the full range of emotions to engender engagement and compel action.

That so many memorable poems concern birds is testament to the wonder they stimulate. They continue to capture our imaginations and can offer students access to a world they might not otherwise imagine. Birds can move people to take political action – as in the successful campaign to preserve the nesting site of Pale Male – but their migratory habits can also cause us to think as global citizens. Such stories, as told through poetry, cut across the disciplines in powerful ways and can engage students of any age. In a time when political polarisation in many Western nations can lead to inaction, birds' welfare might bring consensus. Rebecca Huntley, in her book *How to Talk About Climate Change in a Way that Makes a Difference* (2020), describes how conservative-leaning members of the Ohio Audubon Society, a bird appreciation and protection group, were transformed from ambivalence to action on climate change through their participation in a citizen science project that tracked declining bird populations. As the project's lead researcher Lynsey Smithson-Stanley noted:

> People could disagree with the extent of human involvement in climate change but they could agree on the solution because we connected it to the protection of birds… Birds were the gateway drug to get them interested in climate change.
>
> (Huntley 2020, 229–230)

Poetry cannot be a substitute for statistics and it cannot, in terms of education, replace nature documentaries; it cannot – as more than one anthology has claimed – "save the planet". But in the emotional engagement it engenders, avian poetry can be a part of the solution: a chink in the armour of the way things are.

Notes

1 Excerpts from "Migratory" from *New Selected Poems* by Les Murray. Copyright © 2007, 2012, 2014 by Les Murray. Reprinted by permission of Farrar, Straus and Giroux. All Rights Reserved. Australia and New Zealand rights for "Migratory" are provided by Margaret Connolly and Associates, and UK rights for "Migratory" are provided by Carcanet Press. Jill Jones has provided permission to quote seven continuous lines from "As If The Large Magellanic Cloud Looks Over Us".

2 That climate change is influencing the phenology of bird migration has been widely documented (Chmura et al. 2018). Research based on historic US weather radar imaging, for example, has revealed earlier spring migration for nocturnal Northern American populations by up to 1.5 days per decade, associated with higher temperatures, and with the strongest shifts observed for higher latitude populations (Horton et al. 2020).

3 An Australian study that tracked Ruddy Turnstone migrations over seven years showed they departed their non-breeding grounds in south-eastern Australia two days earlier and advanced their arrival at their breeding grounds in the high Arctic by a day each year (Zhao 2016, 75).

4 Australia has the world's highest per capita emissions of greenhouse gas, so the individual in these moments is implicated in the precipitation of climate change and the birds' demise.

Works Cited

Alexander, Neal and David Cooper. 2013. "Introduction: Poetry & Geography." In *Poetry & Geography: Space and Place in Postwar Poetry*, edited by Neal Alexander and David Cooper, 1–18. Liverpool: Liverpool University Press.

Alizadeh, Ali. 2010. "Ali Alizadeh Reviews Jen Hadfield', *Cordite Poetry Review*, 11 January 2010. Accessed 9 June 2022. http://cordite.org.au/reviews/alizadeh-hadfield/

Bate, Jonathan. 2000. *The Song of the Earth*. Cambridge: Harvard University Press.

Bennet, Jane. 2010. *Vibrant Matter: A Political Ecology of Things*. Durham, NC: Duke University Press.

Buell, Lawrence. 1995. *The Environmental Imagination: Thoreau, Nature Writing, and the Formation of American Culture*. Cambridge: Belknap Press of Harvard University Press.

Chmura, H.E., Kharouba, H.M., Ashander, J., Ehlman, et al. 2018. "The Mechanisms of Phenology: The Patterns and Processes of Phenological Shifts." *Ecological Monographs* 89(1): e01337–n/a. https://doi.org/10.1002/ecm.1337

Cone, Temple. 2006. "Murray's Presence: Translations from the Natural World." *Explicator* 64: 131–133.

Crawford, Robert. 2015. "Kathleen's Scots." In *Kathleen Jamie: Essays and Poems on her Work*, edited by Rachel Falconer, 33–41. Edinburgh: Edinburgh University Press.

Falconer, Rachel. 2015. "Introduction." In *Kathleen Jamie: Essays and Poems on her Work*, edited by Rachel Falconer, 1–8. Edinburgh: Edinburgh University Press.

Fleming, Andrew. 2000. "St Kilda: Family, Community, and the Wider World." *Journal of Anthropological Archaeology* 19: 348–368.

Garrard, Greg. 2012. *Ecocriticism*, 2nd edition. New York: Routledge.

Gillis, Alan. 2009. "Don Paterson." In *The Edinburgh Companion to Contemporary Scottish Poetry*, edited by Matt McGuire and Colin Nicholson, 172–186. Edinburgh: Edinburgh University Press.

Gonzales, Ray. 2005. *Considerations of the Guitar: New and Selected Poems 1986–2005*. Rochester: BOA Editions.

Hadfield, Jen. 2008. *Nigh-No-Place*. Hexham: Bloodaxe.

——. 2010. Interview with Zoë Brigley, Warwick September 6, 2010. Accessed 10 June, 2022. https://blogs.warwick.ac.uk/zoebrigley/entry/interview_with_the/

——. 2014. *Byssus*. Sydney: Picador.

Hawke, John. 2001. "The Moving Image: Judith Wright's Symbolist Language." *Southerly* 61 (1): 160–178.

Holland, R.A., Thorup, K., Gagliardo, A., Bisson, I.A. et al. 2009. "Testing the Role of Sensory Systems in the Migratory Heading of a Songbird." *Journal of Experimental Biology* 212 (24): 4065–4071. https://doi.org/10.1242/jeb.034504

Hoose, Phillip. 2012. *Moonbird: A Year on the Wing with the Great Survivor B95*. New York: Farrar, Straus and Giroux.

Hope, A.D. 2000. *Selected Poetry & Prose*. Rushcutters Bay: Halstead Press.

Horton, K.G., La Sorte, F.A., Sheldon, D. et al. 2020. "Phenology of Nocturnal Avian Migration has Shifted at the Continental Scale." *Nature Climate Change* 10 (1): 63–68. https://doi.org/10.1038/s41558-019-0648-9

Huntley, Rebecca. 2020. *How to Talk About Climate Change in a Way That Makes a Difference*. Sydney: Murdoch Books.

Iwamura, T., Possingham, H.P., Chadès, I. et al. 2013. "Migratory Connectivity Magnifies the Consequences of Habitat Loss from Sea-Level Rise for Shorebird Populations." *Proceedings of the Royal Society B, Biological Sciences* 280 (1761): 20130325–20130325.

Jamie, Kathleen. 2007. *Waterlight: Selected Poems*. Saint Paul, Minnesota: Gray Wolf Press.

——. 2012. *Sightlines*. London: Sort of Books.

——. 2015. *The Bonniest Companie*. London: Picador.

Jones, Jill. 2020. *A History of What I'll Become*. Crawley: University of Western Australia Publishing.

Kinsella, John. 2008. "An Uncanny Reading of A.D. Hope's 'The Death of the Bird.'" *Southerly* 68 (3): 172–187.

Kristof, Nicholas D. 2015. "'The Power of One' in *Numbers and Nerves Information, Emotion, and Meaning in a World of Data*." In *Numbers and Nerves Information, Emotion, and Meaning in a World of Data*, edited by Paul Slovic and Scott Slovic, 85–88. Corvallis: Oregon State University Press.

Manfredi, Camille. 2019. *Nature and Space in Contemporary Scottish Nature Writing and Art*. Cham, Switzerland: Palgrave Macmillan.

McKinney, Meredith. 2022. "Introduction." In Judith Wright, *Birds: Poems by Judith Wright: 60th Anniversary Edition Introduced by Meredith McKinney*, 2–7. Canberra: NLA Publishing.

Moe, Aaron M. 2014. *Zoopoetics: Animals and the Making of Poetry*. Lanham, MD: Lexington Books.

Morton, Timothy. 2007. *Ecology Without Nature: Rethinking Environmental Aesthetics*. Cambridge: Harvard University Press.

——. 2010. *The Ecological Thought*. Cambridge: Harvard University Press.

Murray, Les. 1992. *Translations from the Natural World*. Sydney: Isabella Press.

Paterson, Don. 2003. *Landing Light*. London: Faber and Faber, 2003.

Plumwood, Val. 2009. "Nature in the Active Voice." *Australian Humanities Review* 46: 113–129.

Readfearn, Graham. 2020. "'Silent death': Australia's Bushfires Push Countless Species Towards Extinction." *The Guardian*, 4 January 2020. https://www.theguardian.com/environment/2020/jan/04/ecologists-warn-silent-death-australia-bushfires-endangered-species-extinction

Rigby, Kate. 2020. *Reclaiming Romanticism: Towards and Ecopoetics of Decolonisation*. London: Bloomsbury Academic.

Slovic, Paul and Scott Slovic (Eds.). 2015. *Numbers and Nerves Information, Emotion, and Meaning in a World of Data*. Eugene: Oregon State University Press.

van Dooren, Thom. 2014. *Flight Ways: Life and Loss at the Edge of Extinction*. New York: Columbia University Press.

van Dooren, Thom and Deborah Bird Rose. 2016. "Lively Ethnography: Storying Animist Worlds." *Environmental Humanities* 8 (1): 77–94.

——. 2017. "Encountering a More-than-Human World: Ethos and the Arts of Witness." In *The Routledge Companion to the Environmental Humanities*, edited by Ursula Heise, Jon Cristensen and Michelle Niemann, 120–128. London: Routledge.

Warham, John. 1977. "The Incidence, Functions and Ecological Significance of Petrel Stomach Oils." *Proceedings of the New Zealand Ecological Society* 24: 84–93.

Wright, Judith. 2022. *Birds: Poems by Judith Wright: 60th Anniversary Edition Introduced by Meredith McKinney*. Canberra: NLA Publishing.

Zhao, Meijuan. 2016. *Constraints and Strategies of Long-Distance Migratory Shorebirds along the East Asian-Australasian Flyway*. PhD Thesis, Deakin University.

5 Animal Politics and Ecological Haiku

Dean Anthony Brink

This chapter argues that ecological themes in poetry need not be overt to promote change in the human dimension of biomes at various scales. Since being too direct may indeed reduce a poem's multivalence – steering it toward a superficial didacticism that fails to realize its affective potential – it is important to note that environmental issues are rarely explicit and not even necessarily taken for granted in these examples. Rather, this essay traces the introduction of ecological issues by way of semantic elements or even ways of phrasing that invoke attention to environmental issues or consciousness of other species. These subtle strategies invite readers, teachers, and students to analyze the impact of human behaviors that, although they are not obviously related to danger to the planet, must nevertheless change as the planet develops an ecological ethos.

Season Words in English Language Haiku

Flora, fauna, seasonal patterns, and meteorological phenomena sometimes, but not always, appear in haiku. The season words and poetic lexicon in classical haiku are *conventionalized* in terms of semantic range as well as associations and tenable usages. Indeed, focusing on classical Japanese poetry alone can be counterproductive to engaging current ecological problems, in that it may amount to encouraging a superficial idealizing of poetic practices of premodern others as if one could be transported to a preindustrial time.[1] Isolated from contemporary poetry and experimentation is akin to following Wordsworth and turning to nature as a source of solace. Environmental engagement requires that readers and writers face today's issues, rather than escaping into romanticized emotions. Thus, this essay focuses on what might be called "posthuman" haiku as a subgenre that marks ecological measures of human impacts and envisions alternative practices and cultures to stave off climate change.

What are the ecosophical possibilities raised by haiku and related forms? In English language haiku, which lacks the conventionalization of Japanese haiku or senryu, poets may invent seasonal references loosely modeled on Japanese examples, which can include any living organism or meteorological phenomenon of interest. Local manifestations are generally preferable to the Japanese season-word lexicon; instead, writers will ideally draw on ecosystems with which they are familiar. Though it is a matter of taste and aesthetic aims, the use of season words alone does not necessarily make haiku ecologically engaged. Just as clichés in English Romantic poetry (idealizing memories of places and endangered or lost species) subjectively fog the present ecological dimensions while reassuring superficially that form itself has enabled an appearance of ecological concern,[2] season words may become the icing on a conventionalized cake, "nature poetry" at its worst.[3] Alternatives can emerge, however, and can be found among a wide diversity of poets composing haiku and senryu today.

DOI: 10.4324/9781003399988-8

Transportation and Living Conventions

The *human footprint* is a term that predates the Anthropocene and invokes both local and global scales, rather than assuming a global scale and working backward to the local. To generalize might be helpful in eliciting recognition of common problems – for instance, the release of methane or carbon monoxide contributing to climate change – but addressing even large-scale problems will involve local solutions. Practices derived from Enlightenment humanism, Eurocentric colonial assumptions, or more general ethnocentric assumptions about how humans, flora, and fauna coexist in one biome are often mirrored in such global schema, but this worldview obscures various cultures of engagement: the poetic language we use and abuse, and stories we tell. I would thus like to focus on how smaller-scale *living practices* affect the kinds of attention paid to species and ecosystems. To put it in Deleuzian terms, I wish to explore with readers how poetry in Japanese verse forms, especially haiku and senryu, opportune new models for poetic engagement in English. To borrow from Alain Badiou, these forms offer an entirely different sense of how language *appears* in aesthetic configurations to expose emergent worlds. The worlds do not exist before the poetic formulation, and any words that do not recombine with other words to form something new are not significant poetry, in an approach continuing to build on the suggestions of Badiou. Haiku and senryu do not reflect or represent so much as invoke and present artifacts of attention that, through their brevity, construe affiliations through their intertextual reach into other discourses.

This essay argues from the assumption that simple declarative statements without inter-discursive intertextual complication are seldom effective conduits for ecological reading and writing. Rather, what is required are referentially sustained representational stagings that rebuild intertextual and interspecies connections. The difference between many of the haiku chosen for this essay and run-of-the-mill ecologically-themed haiku can be defined in ecological terms as a difference between declarations of intentionality and embodiments of somatically inculcated learned practices and habitual behavior that exemplify being human. The fourth wall in theater preserves a safe distance, as does the transparent language of conventional poetry; this distance can be overcome, however, through experimentation and self-reflexivity. One approach would have even clichéd language be mixed, as Ashbery exemplifies in his haiku:

Too low for nettles but it is exactly the way people think and feel[4]

among his "37 Haiku." Read ecologically, the poem situates humans objectively, describing them spatially in relation to a plant. Ashbery can be read two ways: as using nettles to reflect how humans "think and feel" and as establishing "the human" in relation to nonhuman nettles. The ambiguity focuses attention on absent details concerning the relationship while avoiding nouns that might function as categorical abstractions. At the same time, the poem announces that it is: "Too low for…" which connotes folk knowledge about nettles and related interspecies growth and interdependencies. Further, Ashbery's phrase "it is exactly the way" spends seven syllables emphasizing a generalizing gesture about people; however, these appear as a form of misdirection that point to a relation, albeit one left up in the air, for the reader to sort out.

By contrast, a representative premodern haiku would handle language, ambiguity, and novelty differently. For instances, Bashō wrote about the relation of loneliness and moths and an action, here in David L. Barnhill's translation, including Basho's introductory remarks:
Autumn, the 60th year of Genroku: wearied of people, I locked my gate.

morning glories—
locked during daytime,

my fence gate[5]
asagao ya/hiru wa jō orosu/mon no kaki

Here, the species is a plant that acts in concert not with the poet's loneliness but rather expresses a need for relief from streams of visitors. The complications are entirely social, the plant merely coincidentally assisting in making an excuse to shut oneself away. Ecological readings would be farfetched, it would seem, although one could argue that Bashō dramatises the interaction with the morning glory as a form of alliance-making or even taking solace by siding with the vegetal against the human.

The following haiku by Kyle Sullivan exemplifies the emplacement of human technology and modern interiority, as a young person riding a train identifies with the rice sprouting up in the fields:

unknown words
of a train conductor...
wind over young rice[6]

The image suggests a complex parallel between the words announced by the train conductor walking down the aisle or through the overhead speakers. His voice demands submission even though his words are not provided (implying travel or a move overseas). This, combined with classical Japanese expectations, in which wind crosses the rice by implication in waves (or it would not be visible), suggests the speaker sitting in the train feels affinity with the young rice, which in turn suggests budding adventure and hope. Ecologically, such an entanglement cannot be reduced to simple metaphors but rather displays a collaboration across scales of human life and cycles that require both rice and hope, even when a traveler must trust an unknown voice for instructions. It also, unlike classical Japanese haiku, includes trains, a technology instrumental to human colonization of lands and also nostalgically imbued (perhaps problematically) with politico-cultural associations indifferent to its intrusion on ecosystems. As such, one could even say that the poem reflects a naiveté that is both charming and frightening in its capitulation to human processes leading historically from rice cultivation to railroad expansion.

In poetry, weaving together discourses draws attention to what we have not yet realized as possible. In *Interdependence: Biology and Beyond*, Kriti Sharma draws distinctions between physical and psychological phenomena in ways that cut through many assumptions while pointing to new directions for poetic exploration. She writes, "the idea of matter, or of physical phenomena, is itself a metaphor whose resonance and power derives from its contrast with life and mind. There is nothing intrinsic to matter that makes it passive, dull, cold, and determined."[7] Even in plant life, as Sharma writes, the concept of non-sentient vs. sentient is problematic, in the ways it can privilege the sentient and the human. Haiku, as I have begun to argue, can move readers into the speculative world of interspecies sympathy and help them imagine a less anthropocentric world.

English Language Haiku and Senryu

English language haiku has de facto begun to fuse with senryu even as senryu aficionados also champion the form independently of haiku. Unfortunately, as the forms continue to assimilate into English language tradition(s), poets often give in to the impulse to use pseudo-literary conceits of sustained "deep" moments. That said, some poets do successfully draw language into ecologically and socially engaged expressions that operate more subtly. One may note numerous haiku poets are even writing the short forms in one line, which follows the Japanese model which also works very well in English, where line breaks have been conventionally used in translations of haiku and tanka since Victorian times, yet can also seem heavy-handed, indeed, three-line haiku a bit awkward or even comical by default, though at times also a useful option.

One element of all Japanese short-form poetry is the absence of a title. There are many precedents for not titling poems or lines within English publishing formats, including long poems with lines or stanzas standing alone on pages or a page, or using numbers. The most famous haiku in English leans into a title for support – Ezra Pound's "A Station in the Metro" ("The apparition of these faces in the crowd:/Petals on a wet, black bough."). However, using titles can blur the difference between a haiku, senryu, or tanka (also usually printed as one line) and a monostich (titled one-line poem).

So, how does an untitled poem differ, and what makes this form of Japanese poetry potentially ecological? Does the lack of a title connote the lack of a concept (as in some visual art)? Or does an untitled poem undermine the illusion of mastery by refusing to limit the world of the poem? In an ecopoetic context, I would say that titles in these Japanese forms of poetry are unnecessary, and that having no titles can productively draw otherwise-invisible connections. A poem without a title demands an earnest accounting of all the words in relation to what is exposed and what remains invisible, unsaid: supportive, aligning, linked intertexts. What remains unsaid is an implication in the world of words, but it is a containment from the perspective of an expressive poet writer. The brevity of a haiku is like the sharp waves of a conductor's baton, with the entire language as its orchestra.

Poetry can reset how we mediate through natural languages (English, Japanese, Arabic, Finnish, Indonesian) the appearance of the world, the world existence shows us and the world which can appear through its exposure by way of language. This is *unlike* Heidegger's formulation because many local forms of engagement do *not* necessarily align with nations and nationalism. Short verse modeled on Japanese can form a model of not only poetic form but a crucible of transcultural (and transnational or even post-national) experimentality that cuts across national borders and rethinks the way we physically intrude with our "human footprints" on other species' territories in our own expansiveness. In exploring the borrowing from Japanese short-form verse, then, I wish to turn from formalism toward an evaluation of more experimental work that engages the complexities of our living ecosystems in colloquial language. Indeed, I will suggest that transcultural poetics can enact multiple forms of recursivity to emulate biological functions of input and output, revealing interconnections between disparate autopoietic living systems.

Poetry, with its intertextual and interdiscursive tools, can both engage with intertexts within a given language, such as Japanese, while also changing and expanding the reader's experience through multiple discourses crossing disciplinary and national boundaries. Interdiscursivity as a practice might be more important than naming locales mapped to endangered species, at least in the literary realm. The actual invocation of disparate discourses within poetry can enable writers and readers to think differently about questions of borders, systems, bodies, and (perhaps especially) scale.[8]

Stitching Patchwork Discourses

One of the takeaways from the study of senryu and tanka in Japanese is that these short forms become more interesting when they do more than simply echo some mix or pastiche of established conventions. Rather than leaning exclusively on the poetic lexicon (or *saijiki*), these poems, at their best, introduce non-conventional discourses *as if* they were a key element of a yet-unincorporated conventional poetics. This implies an urgent need for new forms of expression. Thus, short-form poetry – especially senryu but others as well – concentrates attention on the relation between two elements (as in the Ashbery example above), usually invoking irony either from the recognition of the "all too human" or from the juxtaposition of observations or statements at odds with each other. Short-form poetry is adept at drawing attention to uncomfortable situations such as ecological contradictions within human behavior. By combining disparate discourses and forming intertextual metaphors – rather than metaphors scaled to the human alone as the measure of all life – a poem can maintain its aesthetic idea or model while inviting new configurations.[9] Such work can be especially effective if it integrates interdisciplinary media, such as visual art, music, electronic interfaces, and interactive gallery spaces.

Before I discuss contemporary experimental presentations of short verse online, it is helpful to mention that English-language senryu from the 1980s already includes, even in more reserved poetry conforming to literary conventions, elements of inquiry into other species and invocations of disparate discourses. For instance, the bilingual senryu poet John Michio Ohno, known by the pen name Shūhō, includes in his guide to writing senryu in English a poem by Tōmei:

Even to catch only one
Tiny flea, I needed to
Use my brain somehow[10]

Through a simple snapshot of humorous human-insect relations, students and readers with a background in ecological studies will be primed to read into such poems a complex web of interdependencies, so that even fleas seem part of the web of life. Similarly, Shūhō includes a senryu by Yoshiko,

Weeds grown by themselves
Made us busy
Weeding them out[11]

This poem depicts the recursive competing needs of species – weeds need to reproduce and humans wish to keep them away so as to cultivate preferred species (of vegetables or flowers), but this business caused by needing to weed is a pleasurable practice in its own right. The weeds act on the humans. Some haiku in English by Kyle Sullivan also exhibit a sense of interdependency, interspecies care, and concern along with shades of lonely moments, as the "you" can be the moths or a lover who is missed:

winter moths…
still I keep the room
warm for you[12]

This verse exemplifies an ethos of sharing spaces with other species, turning what many might term an inconvenience into vital mutual benefit.

Peg Byrd's one-line haiku, which turns the very scales of attention to both minute ozone molecules and the grand hyperobjects of storms, invents a fresh use for personification:

ozones breath thunderstorms or worse[13]

Byrd's poem conjoins in eight syllables a discourse on atmospheric science that is part of climate change studies ("ozone"); meteorology and mythic images of animated clouds ("thunderstorms or worse"); and also, by way of "breath," invokes a double-personification of both the ozones and storms on two competing scales, thus arguably satirizing the limited scope of human knowledge of the sublime hyperobjects.[14]

Another poet, Michele Tennison, depicts a human mind racing to find the words and concepts to contain – in vain – a word or thought pinning meaning to fireflies in the following haiku:

thoughts escape the matrix fireflies[15]

The discourses invoked (in eight syllables and five words, no less) include the taxonomy of insects, the limits of human comprehension in observing dynamic relational systems, and a sort of logical positivist procedural approach to defining functions among living creatures such as fireflies.

Less obviously related to ecological poetics is John Stevenson's poem,

more automatic words about weapons[16]

Stevenson mixes a critique of how the fascination with weapons technologies may morph into war, or into a growing military industrial complex (depending on how one reads the verse), while also invoking the "weapon" of Surrealist automatic writing. More generally, the poem suggests how easily we focus on one technological fetish at the expense of the larger ecological picture.

Scott Mason provides an example of how light humor can turn a grave ecological observation into a somewhat tongue-and-cheek and very visual (usually slow-motion) image. Evoking a National Geographic special on melting icebergs, he uses the discourse-specific verb "calve" to describe something in one's hand:

microclimate change
my popsicle
calves[17]

Thus scale becomes, through humor, more anthropocentric, but in a way that reminds readers of the larger issue of melting icecaps. As a theme taken to an absurd extreme, the poem asks if holding a popsicle might stop the warming.

The Onus of Ecological Pastiche

In *On Infertile Ground*,[18] Jane Sasser has analyzed certain environmental activists, noting how they have used reproductive rights issues to expedite fundraising. This, in turn, can reproduce racializing policies and make universal assumptions based on United States politics that are not appropriate for other continents, such as sub-Saharan Africa. Inspired by Sasser to mix discourses in a senryu or haiku, I wrote the following working draft:

only love,
vegan condoms
reign in the Anthropocene[19]

This haiku or senryu reduces the American discourse on free love without reproduction to a sacrifice for the environment while also involving a strict vegetarian interspecies nonviolent ethos (vegan condoms do exist). At the same time, I play with scale, punning on the need to "reign in" and "rein in" the Anthropocene. This implies riding the Anthropocene like a horse, suggests a degree of sexual energy, and – for readers of a certain age and background–might also conjure the memorable closing scene of Stanley Kubrick's *Dr. Strangelove or: How I Learned to Stop Worrying and Love the Bomb* (1964), in which the bomb is likewise mounted by a human being.

A more mundane example derives from an experience near where I lived in Old Town Tacoma, Washington, in the Pacific Northwest of the United States. Gradually, the entire hillside became mostly bare, as first an old apple tree in a backyard was removed to build a garage. Then a tall, old but very healthy horse chestnut, as well as several pine trees lining the street, was likewise taken down. The landscape suddenly felt empty, with old houses on vacant lots. The ecosystem had been converted in service of human desire – not to integrate with diverse species, but to convert life into capital. Cutting the horse chestnut tree was gratuitous; however, to the investor, it was apparently necessary: it would open a grand view to the Puget Sound and the Olympic Mountains, adding to the dollar value of both dwellings. Many other trees disappeared in direct correlation with the rising house prices and popularity of the neighborhood, as it entered into a gentrification pattern:

> the house flipper
> traded apple and pine
> for a bay view

This sort of senryu or haiku exemplifies how ordinary observations can nudge readers and writers into a critical consciousness of anthropocentric or profit-based decisions and processes. People might appreciate a "water view," as a manifestation of sublime nature, but in fact many trees, that could have alleviated global warming and provided fresh air for all the neighbors, were lost. Moreover, trees are one of safest places for tree-nesting birds to reproduce. Though legally the investors have the right to cut trees, their investment was not *in* the local neighborhood. Its ecological efficacy was compromised for the benefit of the value of the lot and associated transactions alone. There was in fact no investment in the neighborhood except for a series of transactions that could be taxed. My poem, though perhaps insignificant given the scope of the problem, helped me focus on the trees and why they mattered – to me, but also to the ecosystem. A short poem can plant the seeds for building a broader consciousness of how we make decisions as we build local and global communities.

In polishing these English haiku and senryu, one can try variations, whereas in Japanese there might be preordained, as it were, specific "best words" for specific emotions. Thus, perhaps one could get the point across in a symbolically satisfying rendering that is nevertheless unfaithful to the original "political" or ecological battle being waged, a situation that called for critical engagement with some ecological issue involving community decision-making. This is a process that students at all levels can try, as they think through what is important to them as the future citizens of a changing world.

Scifaiku as Minimalist Ecological thought Experiments

Scifaiku is a new subgenre of English haiku, roughly a quarter century old, that draws on recent developments in popular culture. The xenobiological imagination in the science fiction documentary TV miniseries *Alien Worlds* (2020) offers an example of how science fiction can

through extrapolation based on melding properties attune us better to the ecological sensitivi-
ties of species and their intricate interdependencies, along the lines that Aldo Leopold's *A Sand
County Almanac* outlined decades ago. Leopold detailed how human activities – even with
good intentions – create interspecies consequences at scales of influence that are difficult to
analyze and reduce to actionable policies, suggesting the need for sustained observation and an
appreciation for the contingent nature of nature always in flux. "Alien Worlds" takes such an
empirical approach and extrapolates from examples on earth what exoplanets with ascertained
masses and atmospheric compositions. Scifaiku engages in similar speculation, drawing on the
plausible science more than actual science.

Tom Brinck, one of the founders of scifaiku, exemplifies a sort of discursive pastiche as he
seeks to raise ecological awareness. One tongue-in-cheek poem mixes discourses, referring to
the traditional American misinterpretation of haiku as a Zen practice, rather than a poetry practice, by invoking a young Monk. At the same time, the poem also includes the current discourse
on neural implants which is part of the cyberpunk science fiction tradition. Brinck writes:

> neuronal stimulation:
> young monk trades minds
> with a sparrow

It should be noted that even back in 1998 when this was published, discourses on transhuman-
ized posthumanism existed, although not in their current form. In any case, the suggestion here
is that uploading one's mind to become a bird is akin to fantasy, but with a Zen twist. This poem
suggests a monk, presumably Buddhist (if the European association of haiku with Buddhism
holds), is attempting to empty his mind in order to attain Nirvana. But, in the process, he takes
a science-fictional shortcut by trading minds with a sparrow. Thus, Brinck presents a humorous
take on the Western association of Zen and haiku, but – exemplifying the best use of contemporary haiku and senryu – integrates multiple discourses. In terms of measuring ecological impact,
broadening our understanding of the cultures surrounding interspecies and self/environment
organization, this haiku demonstrates how the form is equipped to pose complicated ecological
problems: what would it mean to trade minds with a sparrow?

An example of the journal *Scifaikuest's* haibun – that is, prose with haiku interspersed, often
as a concluding verse – shows how prose may be used to frame haiku ecologically. The following example, just one short paragraph followed by one haiku, shows how science fictional
English language haiku can engage in poetic speculations with ecological implications. In this
case, readers are forced to rethink the world as not given wilds and urban spaces, but rather
a constant terraforming-like conscious engagement even on earth, our place of reference for
terraforming itself. Terri Leigh Relf writes:

> Remembering the taste of fresh water… How the darkened skies once released torrent
>   after torrent. But now, in this world with desert all around, how we dare to hope as
>   the first mist alights on our skin.
> the greenhouse heavy
> with succulent fruit
> species unknown[20]

The prose here is repetitive, emphasizing a change in climate as water goes from abundant to
scarce. The haiku itself and the opening prose image are linked by the senses of taste and also
thirst since both water and succulent fruit are prized for quenching dryness. But what makes this
worthy of discussion is that the prose sets up some undefined drastic change with torrent after

torrent of rain in the desert, perhaps suggesting some sort of war, as is typical in post-apocalyptic science fiction scenarios. The last line, "species unknown," drives home the implication that there was some sort of a nuclear event, since radiation might make fruit mutate into "something unknown." Thus, this poem provides an example of how science fiction haiku can draw on speculative motifs to raise awareness of ecological dangers to the planet. Since science fiction and fantasy are popular genres, especially with young people, the scifaiku offers many possibilities for teachers, in particular, to spark the poetic imaginations of their students.

The following simple poem by Kiersta Recktenwald epitomizes the "flow chart" planning common in capitalist bureaucracies, where economics is pegged to future expectations:

robot forgot
to remember
to forget[21]

In this poem, the robot forgot to remember to forget to purge something from its memory – something that might embarrass, irritate a human. This poem works as an actual speech-act denoting a specific speculative story. At the same time, it performs what, in science fiction, is often referred to as a mapping of the science fictional world onto our contemporary world. The robot does something that humans cannot do, namely, plan to forget something. We can only enter into a traumatic state of attempting to overwrite through various forms of distraction, symptoms, cathexes, or other strategies including drugs and alcohol, talking cures and creative writing in order to remember as we forget. This little multi-discursive gem thus uses science fictional motifs to stage a very real human problem that has become acute in our current era.

Conclusion

There is no fixed formula for English language haiku or current events senryu; rather, one may discern and deploy multiple generic options within a changing tradition. If one approaches poetry as a synthesis of multiple discourses, as described by Mikhail Bakhtin, then Japanese forms offer a rich field of relations, intertextualities, and competing cultural and individual voices. Material acts of enunciation or configurations of words that become, through affiliation linked to multiple discourses, do not exist in a vacuum but rather are enabled by people who make these discourses, however objective and autonomous they may seem. As haiku poetry becomes "entangled," across cultures and across multiple large-scale problems and small-scale landscapes, it demonstrates that poetry is never autonomous, and that even poetry that is not about nature can have ecological dimensions.

In relation to expanding awareness of ecological justice issues, the integration and transformation of haiku genres across languages and cultures destabilizes rigid ways of thinking that stem from unexamined conventions and stereotypes. Through haiku, the "others" of the ecosystem can speak to the human unconscious and change it, making new articulations possible. Small-scale poetic ecologies – configurations presenting interdiscursive paradoxes that upset established forms of discursive power – can reframe large-scale ecosystems and allow readers to speculatively imagine new possible worlds.

Notes

1 For a broad argument for using classical haiku to promote "environmental education," with no sense of how to bridge modern issues in poetry today, there is Deborah H. Williams, and Gerhard Shipley, "Japanese Poems with Strong Nature Themes as a Tool for Environmental Education," *Creative*

Education, 10 (2019), 2457–2472. DOI:10.4236/ce.2019.1011174. It seems to exemplify the tendency to simplify Japanese poetry due to its brevity, which may be on the contrary read as forcing more attention to intertexts inclusive of current events.

2   See Dean Anthony Brink, *Poetics and Justice in America, Japan, and Taiwan: Configuring Change and Entitlement* (Lanham: Lexington Books, 2021), Ch. 1, which questions contemporary limitations to ecological poetic engagements due precisely to the ongoing idealisation in Anglo-American poetry of a certain limited reading of Wordsworth.

3   In addition to the general conventionality of the various short-form genres, it is helpful to recall that haiku and senryu are popularised derivatives of comic or anyways less pretentious linked poetry (*haikai no renga*), an already vulgarised form of linked verse (*renga*) that had been a court practice. Senryu were originally satirical lampoons, often bawdy, but in the twentieth century divided into literary senryu (*bungei senryū*) and current events senryu (*jiji senryū*). Haiku were the opening verses for linked poetry sessions (the *hokku*), but took on a life of their own, including forming new genres modelled roughly on *uta-nikki* (poetic diaries including waka), haibun, prose with haiku interspersed. English haiku associations now include haibun and less often linked poetry. One of the major haiku and Japanese short-form literary journals, *Frogpond*, now blurs haiku and senryu in the main opening section of poems in each issue. For a more detailed introduction to Japanese senryu, see Brink, *Poetics and Justice*, Part II.

4   See John Ashbery, "37 Haiku," *A Wave* (New York: Viking, 1984 (also appears in *Sulfur* #5 [1981]). See for more examples Dean Brink, "John Ashbery's '37 Haiku' and the American Haiku Orthodoxy," in *Globalization and Cultural Identity*/Translation, Pengxiang Chen and Terence Russell, eds. Occasional Papers Series 1, Fo Guang University and University of Manitoba, 2010: 157–165; reprinted at: https://www.academia.edu/3318916/John_Ashbery_s_37_Haiku_and_the_American_Haiku_Orthodoxy

5   Matsuo Bashō, and David L. Barnhill, *Bashō's haiku: Selected Poems by Matsuo Basho* (Albany: State University of New York Press, 2004), 139.

6   Kyle Sullivan, *Frogpond* 39.3 (Autumn 2016), 15.

7   Kriti Sharma, *Interdependence: Biology and Beyond* (New York: Fordham University Press, 2015), 64.

8   See Brink, *Poetics and Justice*, 20–22, 49–50.

9   Brink, *Poetics and Justice*, Ch. 2, esp. 72–80.

10   Shuho Ohno (John Michio Ohno), *Modern Senryu in English* (Seattle: Hokubei International, 1987), 243.

11   Ohno, *Modern Senryu in English*, 115.

12   Kyle Sullivan, *World Haiku Review*, June 2016, Haiku page 1, Neo-classical.

13   Peg Byrd, *Frogpond: Journal of the Haiku Society of America* 39:2 (Spring/Summer 2016), 7.

14   See Brink, *Poetics and Justice*, 52, 108.

15   Michele Tennison, *Frogpond* 39.3 (Autumn 2016), 17.

16   John Stevenson, *Frogpond* 41.2 (Summer 2018), 16.

17   Scott Mason, *Frogpond* 40.3 (Autumn 2017), 15.

18   Jade Sasser, *On Infertile Ground: Population Control and Women's Rights in the Era of Climate Change* (New York: New York University Press, 2018).

19   Many thanks to Kyle Sullivan for workshopping this with me.

20   Terri Leigh Relf, *Scifaikuest*, 18th Anniversary Issue (August 2021), 60.

21   Kiersta Recktenwald, *Scifaikuest* (August 2021), 20.

Works Cited

Ashbery, John. "37 Haiku." *A Wave*. New York: Viking, 1984.

Bashō, Matsuo, and David L. Barnhill. *Bashō's haiku: Selected Poems by Matsuo Basho*. Albany: State University of New York Press, 2004.

Brink, Dean Anthony. *Poetics and Justice in America, Japan, and Taiwan: Configuring Change and Entitlement*. Lanham: Lexington Books, 2021.

Brink, Dean. "John Ashbery's '37 Haiku' and the American Haiku Orthodoxy," in *Globalization and Cultural Identity/Translation*, Pengxiang Chen and Terence Russell, eds. Occasional Papers Series 1, Fo Guang University and University of Manitoba, 2010: 157–165; reprinted at: https://www.academia.edu/3318916/John_Ashbery_s_37_Haiku_and_the_American_Haiku_Orthodoxy.

Frogpond. The Journal of the Haiku Society of America. Vancouver, WA: Haiku Society of America.

Sasser, Jade. *On Infertile Ground: Population Control and Women's Rights in the Era of Climate Change.* New York: New York University Press, 2018.

Scifaikuest. Hiraeth Publishing. https://www.hiraethsffh.com

Sharma, Kriti. *Interdependence: Biology and Beyond.* New York: Fordham University Press, 2015.

Sullivan, Kyle. *World Haiku Review*, June 2016, Haiku page 1, Neo-classical.

Williams, Deborah H. and Gerhard Shipley. "Japanese Poems with Strong Nature Themes as a Tool for Environmental Education." *Creative Education*, 10 (2019), 2457–2472. DOI:10.4236/ce.2019.1011174.

6 Greeting a Ginkgo

How Anthropomorphism in Poetry Can Inspire Eco-Empathy

Christina Thatcher

Introduction

...They're feeding on contaminated insects,
wild seeds glistening with acid rain.
'Birdsong from my Patio'[1]

(Ellen Bass 2012)

Like many people, I have been conscious of the climate crisis for years. However, it wasn't until I read the poem 'Birdsong from My Patio' by Ellen Bass that I felt the full emotional impact of climate change. In particular, the image of the birds' 'porous, thin-shelled eggs...lying doomed in each/intricate nest' sparked in me an urgent desire to take action. Since 2020, the UN has considered climate change to be the biggest threat that modern humans have ever faced. As climate change worsens, communities across the globe can expect more extreme weather conditions as well as increased wildfires, droughts and ocean temperatures which threaten animals' survival and people's livelihoods. In the next 50 years, nearly one-third of all animal and plant species on Earth could face extinction.[2] Despite these sobering predictions, the current global response has been insufficient even as the UN's 2019 Climate Action Summit calls for 'transformative changes' in order to restore and protect our planet. The poet Jorie Graham (2012) notes that people 'know' all this information about climate change already but do not 'feel it' and therefore they do little to combat the issue. So, environmental activists have begun asking for help communicating the impact of the climate crisis: 'help it be felt, help it be imagined.'[3] Illingworth (2019) notes that poets are uniquely positioned to communicate the science of climate change in language that is not only 'felt' but which also 'has the potential to stimulate accountability and inspire action' (p. 1).

As I discuss in an article for *The Conversation*, since reading Bass's poem (and many more after it), I have researched ways to mitigate the effects of climate change, donated to environmental campaigns and have started writing my own ecopoetry.[4] The poet Helen Moore (2012) states that poetry has the unique ability to (re)connect us with nature, witness the losses of flora and fauna, resist the capitalist commodification of our ecologies and create visions of both utopian and dystopian futures influenced by our response to climate change. Through context and concrete imagery, poetry can also localise a global problem for readers[5] and can put a 'human face and emotional experience' on the abstract and complex issues which make up the climate crises'.[6] Poetry, I believe, can promote climate action by allowing people of all ages – particularly nonscientists – to engage with the natural environment effectively, the way we engage with other humans.

It is this notion of 'putting a human face' on climate change that has occupied me as a poet and researcher throughout the pandemic years. These thoughts gave rise to a series of questions,

DOI: 10.4324/9781003399988-9

including: how might poetry inspire climate change empathy? What tools, in particular, can poets use to invoke empathy? These questions led me to read poetry as well as academic articles, chapters and books across a wide range of disciplines, including psychology, medicine, social science and more. This research created a huge amount of data which I needed to interpret and synthesise. For this, I turned to poetic inquiry.

Discovering (and Debating) through Poetic Inquiry

Prendergast (2009) states that poetic inquiry is the 'attempt to work in fruitful interdisciplinary ways between the humanities [literature/aesthetic philosophy], fine arts (creative writing), and the social sciences' (p. xxxvi). The sources and inspiration for many poets' projects 'resemble arts-based researchers' use and considerations for poetry, breaking down the false separation between humanities and social sciences' (p. 213). Rather than conducting a thematic analysis on collected data, for instance, poetic inquiry allows researchers to use poetry, academic texts, archival material, newspaper articles and interviews, as well as personal experience, to represent their findings (Faulkner 2019; Poindexter 1998). Walsh (2012) describes her 'poetic inquiry process as being present and dwelling with particular artifacts rather than analyzing or interpreting them' (p. 273). She says this involves 'listening to the text, asking what it wants her to do' (p. 274).

This is similar to my process – listening to the texts and identifying what sounds the loudest, what needs poetic attention. It soon became clear in my research that, although debated as a concept, something important was happening with anthropomorphism and poetry. Anthropomorphism is the act of attributing human motivation, behaviours and/or psychological characteristics to nonhuman entities.[7] Humans seem hardwired to consider organisms 'as bodies ruled by unobservable forces. No matter if the target entity is really endowed with these features, or not' (p. 2). This can be seen in the way that 'anthropomorphism is built into common expressions…in the way human characteristics are automatically, even unthinkingly, ascribed to inanimate objects (e.g. "table leg or chair arm")' (p. 8). However, despite its common usage, anthropomorphism has been hotly debated by poets, scientists, biologists, conservationists and literary eco-critics.

The anthropomorphic attitude has long been considered a 'cardinal crime'[8] or a 'dangerous pit'.[9] Anthropomorphism is often seen as 'anthrocentric' because it suggests that humans are 'central or of most importance' when compared to the nonhuman organisms their characteristics are being ascribed to (p. 4). This can be seen when an animal is described 'as human-like (as happens in most anthropomorphisms) [which then] elevates that animal's status, or at least compliments it' when, in contrast, 'describing a human as animal-like is almost always a disparagement or an insult' (p. 68).

This 'anthrocentric' attitude is also linked to 'speciesism (the belief that humans have a moral status superior to nonhumans)' which Chan (2012) states is 'still common among the public' (p. 1891). Some animal rights activists see anthropomorphism as 'internal to speciesism, which tends to neglect the genuine features of animal species, conflating them in relation to humans only' (p. 4). With these debates in mind, Arbilly and Lotem (2017) state that 'constructive anthropomorphism' may be the best way forward (p. 2). They explain that our natural tendency to apply human motivations and characteristics to the nonhuman 'can actually be harnessed productively' (p. 2). One of the many ways that anthropomorphism can be harnessed productively is by using it to promote empathy in humans which can then lead to positive behaviour change, such as campaigning for more effective climate change policies.

This poetic inquiry into the anthropomorphism debate – as well as the discovery of 'constructive anthropomorphism' and its ability to invoke empathy – led me to raise and refine my own research questions: how can anthropomorphism be used in poetry, in particular, to inspire empathy? And, more specifically, how can it be used in poetry to inspire eco-empathy?

In this self-reflexive chapter, I will explore how writing poetry which 'puts a human face' on trees and waterways – or 'anthropomorphises' them – might help readers to *feel* the consequences of climate change. To this end, I will discuss the debates surrounding anthropomorphism and empathy. Then, using two poems from my collection-in-progress, *Breaking a Mare*, I will consider the ways in which poetry can use anthropomorphism to invoke empathy in readers. At the centre of this chapter is an attempt to understand what it means to write anthropomorphic poems during a global climate crisis and how poetry written in this way might inspire empathy, and a desire to act, in those who read it.

Anthropomorphism and Poetry

In Thomas Nagel's (1974) essential essay, 'What is it like to be a bat?' he poses an unanswerable question. The attempt to '"enter the animal's world" is undoubtedly praiseworthy, but it is an effort intrinsically limited by our human cognitive status' (p. 7). We will never truly understand what it is like to be a bat, although we can think it and imagine it. According to Westling (2014), literature and poetry offer us the possibility of:

bridging the gap between others—be they of a different species or not—and ourselves. It [literature] functions as one of our species' ways of singing the world to ourselves, in concert with the songs and artistic creations of many other creatures, from birds and primates to dogs and dolphins.

(p. 103)

She notes that when we see animals and ourselves as:

psychophysical wholes in interweaving landscapes it is not a question of being alike enough to establish empathy. It is rather a question of how to train the senses to be able to see this wholeness. In finding a route to accomplish this, poets can serve as a guide.

(p. 13)

And many poets like Denise Levertov, Wisława Szymborska and Alice Fulton do just this, using their work to 'demand a free play of language, knowledge, and power, all purposed to emphasise participatory engagement with and empathy for other-than-human others' (p. 148). According to Kelen and Chengcheng (2019), these poets and others like them, share:

a common ground in using anthropomorphism to imagine a space for encountering nonhumans and in taking us beyond the normative language and ethical assumptions of mainstream anthropocentric society and culture.

(p. 148)

Although truly understanding what it is like to be a nonhuman organism is impossible, poets can attempt to 'imagine their way into nonhuman subjectivities in order to see the world from another's perspective' (p. 216). And, because we are limited by our own humanness, anthropomorphism gives us, as poets, an opportunity to do this. This allows us to understand the nonhuman *as humanlike* and therefore we can relate to them and empathise with them.[10]

Anthropomorphism and Empathy

Empathy is difficult to define. Cuff et al. (2014) uncovered 43 discreet definitions in scientific, medical and psychological literature but, for the purposes of this chapter, I will use the definition of empathy put forward by Pease (1995):

> [Empathy is] the action of understanding, being aware of, being sensitive to, and vicariously experiencing the feelings, thoughts and experience of another of either the past or present without having the feelings, thoughts and experience fully communicated in an objectively explicit manner.
>
> (p. 202)

Cuff et al. (2016) note that an important step in understanding empathy is contrasting it with another emotion, usually sympathy. According to Brüggemann (2017), 'empathy, then, is described as 'feeling with', whereas sympathy is described as 'feeling for' (p. 2). It seems the link between most definitions of empathy is the idea of recognising the emotions of others and experiencing these feelings too, either cognitively or emotionally.[11]

Airenti (2015) states that 'relatedness is a precondition for human empathy' (p. 123). She notes that empathy towards human beings means 'being affected by the positive or negative things which happen to them, feeling what they feel, [and] being disposed to help or console them when they are in distress' (p. 123). But how can we 'relate' and feel empathy for nonhuman organisms? According to Bruni et al. (2018), anthropomorphism allows us to empathise with the 'humanness' of nonhuman others which creates a sense of relatedness. For instance, humans are already inclined to feel empathy for:

> 'vertebrates, especially mammals, as they have similar physical features to human ones, like eyes, mouth, and biological motion. Human empathy toward these animals does not depend on any prior scientific knowledge on other animals' psychological skills, but simply on the link between anthropomorphism and empathy.
>
> (p. 4)

When animals show emotions like sadness or happiness (Bekoff 2000) or demonstrate high cognitive reasoning (Blaisdell et al. 2006) then humans can 'see themselves' in the animals and empathise with them (p. 1889). But this does not only happen with animals. Chen et al. (2021), demonstrates how anthropomorphising 'unattractive' produce in the grocery store led people to purchase more of it 'because the unattractive appearance makes them feel empathy for the produce that is generally rejected' (p. 3). Anthropomorphism of plants, waterways and geographical features has also been shown to inspire empathy which can lead people to increase their sustainable behaviours (Ketron and Naletelich 2019) by creating a 'higher conservation awareness' and encouraging individuals to 'connect with nature' (Maguire et al. 2020, p. 116).

Empathy can be broad or it can be targeted and specific. Within this chapter, I am interested in both: the empathy which, broadly, invokes human feelings of loneliness, loss, guilt etc. as well as 'eco-empathy' which, specifically, invokes empathy for the 'planet and other species' which may cause anxiety as well as a desire to act in a way which can help our ecosystems (Hickman 2020, p. 416).

Meet Ginkgo

When it's time, she sounds

nothing like an owl, nothing
like the lowest note of a trumpet.
You can't compare her to swishes
of taffeta or the crack of confetti
canons. She could never be mistaken
for the hush of a slow stream.
There is nothing
that sounds quite like a ginkgo
in the forest, in October, releasing
her stinking fruit like a Changuan robe,
nothing like that soft *pfft*
as her flesh and seeds separate, hit
the woodland floor with no him
to hear for miles and miles.

This poem, from my collection-in-progress *Breaking a Mare,* explores the impact of climate change on the ginkgo tree. Gibbons (2020) states that ginkgo trees have existed in their 'current form for 60 million years' and have 'genetically similar ancestors dating back 170 million years to the Jurassic Period'.[12] However, according to the International Union for the Conservation of Nature, ginkgoes are now endangered in the wild.[13] Even though these trees are highly resistant to damage from pollution, fungi or pests,[14] climate change is now threatening their survival.

Unlike most other trees, ginkgoes are dioecious which means that 'the male and female reproductive organs are found on different trees' (p. 230). The female gingko holds fruit-like seeds which drop to the ground while the male ginkgo has sperm, which is transported inside a pollen grain by the wind, to fertilise the seeds (p. 231). According to Meyer (2017) the day that the female ginkgo releases her seeds (sometimes called 'ginkgo-dump day' or 'leaf-drop day') has been 'sliding forward over the ensuing decades. Every decade, the ginkgo tree loses its leaves an average of three days later than it had 10 years prior' due to climate change.[15]

According to Grabar (2018), climate change is stretching and compressing seasons which alters 'the fragile balance of phenology, or biological timing'. That is, these trees:

unfold their leaves earlier and lose them later, sometimes dramatically so. It's easy to brush off a few days as not mattering much, but these changes mean co-dependent species are decoupling in time, threatening the survival of one or both.

My poem, 'When it's time, she sounds', considers what it means when these timings are off and when the ginkgoes' sperm and seeds are no longer able to reach each other. Here, the gingko tree – also known as the maidenhair tree – is anthropomorphised as a female woman, dropping her lingerie to the floor in preparation for lovemaking. The pronoun 'she' is used to remind readers that the tree is not an 'it' or an 'object', but a living thing and female too. The repetition of 'nothing' resists anthropomorphism since it suggests that the ginkgo dropping her seeds sounds 'nothing like taffeta or the crack of confetti /canons', nothing like any human thing. It also identifies the uniqueness of the tree within nature, since her sound is also 'nothing' like an 'owl' or a 'stream'.

The use of enjambment creates a sense of expectation, of turning the corner again and again to find out what she *does* sound like, all the while the lines keep turning back to 'nothing'. The repetition of 'nothing' also acts as a foreshadowing – that in the wake of climate change and the dwindling population of ginkgoes around the world, soon, there will be nothing left: no more ginkgoes.

The 'nothings' and enjambment in the poem create a tension, reminding the reader that the tree is *humanlike* in her motivations and desires but doesn't have the same autonomy as humans. She cannot go to her lover, she cannot be close to him. There is 'no him/to hear for miles and miles' and there is nothing she can do. The tree is rooted to her spot and she is now at the mercy of climate change which has shifted the seasons and, therefore, her opportunity to procreate. Despite her efforts, she will not be able to have children, her legacy will stop with her. This might invoke a sense of loneliness or lovelessness within readers. According to the empathy-helping two-stage model put forward by Coke et al. (1978), identifying others' – human or nonhuman – in a needy situation generates empathy, which in turn increases helping behaviour.

In the poem, I have attempted to position the ginkgo as 'needy', as an organism which cannot 'save' herself but, instead, needs to be saved and united with her lover. Perhaps the reader will relate to, or feel a connection to, her plight and decide to read more about the ginkgo, donate to a conservation charity, or even begin exploring what they can do – individually and politically – to slow the effects of climate change.

Meet Creek

How sad the creek was

when the girl drowned, no one could see it
because the creek is always wet but she was *very* sad.
It is her nature to be wet, it is her nature to bulge
with rain, it is her nature to be swift, her rapids
rushing the rocks and yet it is not natural
to rise this high, to drown, and certainly not her,
this little girl in the creek who was swept up, unsteady
from the edge. If only the creek had arms,
if only she had the power to slow and go dry,
offer this girl a safe place to stand.
The creek can do other things, sure.
She gives home to the smallmouth bass.
She gives water to the waterfowl.
She gives root to the alder shrubs on her banks.
The dogwood blooms, thanks to her, and yet
this girl is all she thinks about. If only the creek
were different, if only the creek were more
humane but she isn't, she wasn't, and now
miles away, upstream, there is a funeral
happening and the creek has no good mouth
to say *I'm sorry.*

I grew up on a farm in eastern Pennsylvania and, running through the property, was Tohickon Creek. Fed by the Delaware River, and at nearly 30 miles long, this is the second-largest stream in the county.[16] According to surveys conducted by the Bucks County Audubon Society, this creek 'houses 82 bird species, including 4 species of rare concern and 10 rare breeders.'[17] Since the early 1900s, the Delaware River Basin Commission has tracked the impact of climate change on the Delaware River and the creeks, streams and estuaries it feeds.[18] It is clear that climate change has already begun impacting the Delaware River, leading to 'increased temperature, changes in precipitation patterns, and sea level rise, all of which affect water supply and water quality'.[19]

In particular, the Commission notes that 'precipitation is predicted to occur in the form of fewer, more intense storms occurring in the winter months. This means a potential increase in flood events coupled with extended drought cycles'.[20] In 2021, Hurricane Ida hit Pennsylvania and the Delaware River overflowed and flooded huge areas. The Tohickon Creek burst its banks too, flooding much of the farm where I grew up. This caused me to consider the creek and how, if it were human, it would feel turning into a destructive force. Many people drowned across the East Coast during Hurricane Ida,[21] so I used this as a fictional starting point in my poem, 'How sad the creek was'.

Chan (2012) states that 'anthropomorphism will be most useful to garner empathy toward species that are perceived to be non-charismatic'; this includes geographical features which are further away from humanness (p. 1891). Although creeks are something humans enjoy – thanks to pastimes like swimming and fishing – waterways such as these are less prone to anthropomorphism than, say, an animal. Conservation biologists believe that anthropomorphism is most effective when highlighting specific human features, such as: '1) high cognitive ability, 2) ability to suffer or experience pain, and 3) prosocial behaviour' (p. 1889). According to Chan (2012), anthropomorphism 'through these three traits will likely draw empathetic attention' towards the target species or organism (p. 1890). In this poem, I attempted to demonstrate that the creek has all three of these features.

In the opening lines, the creek's 'high cognitive ability' can be seen through language which indicates her self-awareness. The creek understands her nature (i.e. 'to be wet', 'to bulge with rain', 'to be swift') as well as her role (i.e. to 'give home to the smallmouth bass', 'water to the waterfowl', 'root to the alder shrubs'). She recognises these key aspects of herself but also states that it is 'not natural/to rise this high' and certainly it is not 'natural' for her to drown a little girl. The creek is clearly aware of what is happening to her but is unable to stop it.

The creek also demonstrates 'an ability to suffer and experience pain' throughout the poem (p. 1889). For instance, the second line states 'she was *very* sad' and suggests that because she is 'always wet' (as creeks are) no one can see her crying or her tears. Later in the poem, it is clear that the death of the girl is plaguing the creek: 'this girl is all she thinks about'. Basil et al. (2008) state that 'guilt is often related to empathic concern' and that 'both empathy and guilt enhance prosocial behavior' (p. 2). The creek demonstrates this 'prosocial behavior' throughout the poem as well. She notes that 'no one could see' her sadness and that she has 'no good mouth/ to say *I'm sorry*'. This suggests that the creek wants others to understand her pain and she wants others to know that it was not her, not the 'natural' her, that caused this drowning. Her rising water was too much and she wants to say that she's sorry but cannot.

The creek also wishes that she could be more humanlike, noting that this might have helped her save the girl. Lines like 'If only the creek had arms' and 'If only the creek/were different' emphasise the creek's desire to be more humanlike. She also states that she wishes she were more 'humane' which, in the context of the poem, is ironic. The creek is doing nothing but showing compassion and benevolence to the girl and is blaming herself for what happened even though she knows it wasn't her 'natural' state. The humans who are existing outside of the poem, and holding the funeral for the girl, are arguably the ones who should be apologising as it was their species' actions – not the creek's actions – which caused climate change, including the rising water levels which claimed the girl's life.

According to Lethem et al. (1983), humans are strongly psychologically affected by emotional and physical pain. This allows us to relate to situations that cause others 'pain and project how we would feel unto them' (p. 1889). As a result, the empathy we feel can allow us to 'assess a situation as if it were affecting us rather than someone else' (p. 4). What must it feel like to carry guilt and grief? What would it be like to be the creek, plagued by this young girl's death? Basil et al. (2008) suggest that positioning ourselves in others' shoes can result in a difference in 'perspective or a reduction in perceived social distance' (p. 4). The empathy-altruism hypothesis proposes 'that empathy motivates individuals to help others through altruism, focusing on the welfare of the needy others (p. 4). Again, the creek has been positioned as 'needy' and has been given a voice which may even flatter readers since the creek believes being *humanlike* and more *humane* would make her better. This may encourage readers to think of creeks – or other waterways – as something which they can relate to and help.

Looking Ahead – From Empathy to Action

Although speciesism and anthrocentric attitudes are problematic, it is important to recognise that many members of the public still hold these views, and to understand that even with such a worldview, there can be room for empathy.[22] With this in mind, encouraging the 'public to anthropomorphise threatened organisms' gives people a way to relate to them.[23] In this chapter, I have considered how anthropomorphism can be used in poetry to invoke empathy in readers and highlight how nonhuman others need our help to combat climate change. In school settings, instructors can take the lead by framing anthropomorphism, not as a forbidden impulse, but as one tool among many that readers and poets can access as they seek to embrace the world.

In my two poems, 'When it's time, she sounds' and 'How sad the creek was', I introduced readers to a ginkgo tree and a creek who have been impacted by the climate crisis and are struggling. Both of these are anthropomorphised as females since studies show that women in difficult situations invoke more empathy than men.[24] Through the use of repetition, enjambment and word choices like 'nothing' and 'if only', both the creek and the tree can be viewed as 'needy'[25] and unable to save themselves. In line with the 'empathy-helping two-stage model'[26] and the 'empathy-altruism hypothesis',[27] positioning the tree and creek as needing help will inspire empathy in readers and may even motivate them to take positive action[28] to slow, or stop, the effects of things like global warming and rising sea levels.

According to Anabaraonye et al. (2018) poetry is a 'vital and effective tool which can be used in the global response to climate change' (p. 82). This is because poetry has the capacity to help people 'easily understand the impact of climate change', invoke empathy and encourage changes in their attitudes and behaviours (p. 82). In short, empathy can lead to action. Very young children are often given anthropomorphic texts in school, but later they are often taught that anthropomorphism is unsophisticated or even ecologically destructive. As my own work suggests, however, it is possible to embrace anthropomorphic thinking without necessarily "othering" the natural world. I hope that the poems I have shared, which imagine trees and creeks as (a-)kin to humans, will help readers to *feel* and imagine the consequences of climate change and motivate them to take positive action.

Notes

1 "Verse Daily: Birdsong from My Patio by Ellen Bass". n.d. www.versedaily.org. Accessed June 11, 2022. http://www.versedaily.org/2007/birdsongpatio.shtml.
2 Cristian, Román-Palacios, and Wiens, John J. "Recent Responses to Climate Change Reveal the Drivers of Species Extinction and Survival". *Proceedings of the National Academy of Sciences* 117, no. 8 (2020): 201913007. DOI: 10.1073/pnas.1913007117
3 Graham, Jorie. *Place*. Manchester: Carcanet. 2012.

4 Thatcher, Christina. 2021. "How Poetry Can Help Us Understand the Urgency of the Climate Crisis". *The Conversation*. https://theconversation.com/how-poetry-can-help-us-understand-the-urgency-of-the-climate-crisis-170971.

5 Illingworth, Sam. A Change of Climate - How Poetry Can Help Localise a Global Problem. Abstract. In the *20th EGU General Assembly*, EGU2018. Vol. 20. 2018.

6 Santos Perez, Craig. "Teaching Ecopoetry in a Time of Climate Change – the Georgia Review". 2020. Thegeorgiareview.com. Accessed April 10, 2022. https://thegeorgiareview.com/posts/teaching-ecopoetry-in-a-time-of-climate-change/

7 Chan, Alvin A.Y. "Anthropomorphism as a Conservation Tool". *Biodiversity and Conservation* 21, no. 7. (2012): 1889–1892

8 p. 12 of Broadhurst, P. *The Science of Animal Behaviour*. Baltimore, MD: Penguin Books. 1963.

9 p. 3 of Breland, Keller and Breland, Marian. *Animal Behavior*. Toronto, ON: MacMillan. 1966.

10 Airenti, Gabriella. "The Cognitive Bases of Anthropomorphism: From Relatedness to Empathy". *International Journal of Social Robotics* 7, no. 1 (2015): 117–127.

11 Cuff, Benjamin M.P., Sarah J. Brown, Laura Taylor, and Douglas J. Howat. "Empathy: A Review of the Concept". *Emotion Review* 8, no. 2 (April 2016): 144–53. https://doi.org/10.1177/1754073914558466.

12 Gibbons, Sarah. 2020. "Ginkgo Trees Nearly Went Extinct. Here's How We Saved These 'Living Fossils.'" *Environment*. 2020, https://www.nationalgeographic.com/environment/article/ginkgo-trees-nearly-went-extinct-how-we-saved-these-living-fossils.

13 Gibbons, Sarah. 2020. "Ginkgo Trees Nearly Went Extinct. Here's How We Saved These 'Living Fossils.'" *Environment*. 2020, https://www.nationalgeographic.com/environment/article/ginkgo-trees-nearly-went-extinct-how-we-saved-these-living-fossils.

14 Dallimore, W. *A Handbook of Coniferae and Ginkgoaceae*, St. Martin's Press, New York, 1967, pp. 229–233.

15 Meyer, Robinson. "The Great Ginkgo-Tree Leaf Dump Is Here." *The Atlantic*. November 10, 2017. https://www.theatlantic.com/science/archive/2017/11/the-great-gingko-dump-climate-change-autumn/545585/.

16 U.S. Geological Survey. National Hydrography Dataset High-Resolution Flowline Data. The National Map, accessed April 1, 2011: https://www.usgs.gov/national-hydrography

17 "Tohickon Valley Park". 2022. Bucks County, PA. Accessed April 11, 2022. https://www.buckscounty.gov/Facilities/Facility/Details/Tohickon-Valley-Park-8.

18 "Delaware River Basin Commission|Climate Change". 2022. www.nj.gov. Accessed May 11, 2022. https://www.nj.gov/drbc/programs/flow/climate-change.html#:~:text=Local%20climate%20change%20impacts%20for.

19 "Delaware River Basin Commission|Climate Change". 2022. www.nj.gov. Accessed May 11, 2022. https://www.nj.gov/drbc/programs/flow/climate-change.html#:~:text=Local%20climate%20change%20impacts%20for.

20 "Delaware River Basin Commission|Climate Change". 2022. www.nj.gov. Accessed May 11, 2022. https://www.nj.gov/drbc/programs/flow/climate-change.html#:~:text=Local%20climate%20change%20impacts%20for.

21 Ensor, Josie. 2021. "Hurricane Ida: At Least 46 Dead in the US after Drowning in Their Homes and Cars". *The Telegraph*, September 2, 2021. https://www.telegraph.co.uk/world-news/2021/09/02/hurricane-ida-northeastern-us-battered-rain-flooding-tornadoes/

22 Chan, Alvin A.Y. "Anthropomorphism as a Conservation Tool". *Biodiversity and Conservation* 21, no. 7 (2012): 1889–1892

23 Chan, Alvin A.Y. "Anthropomorphism as a Conservation Tool". *Biodiversity and Conservation* 21, no. 7 (2012): 1889–1892

24 Malin Angantyr, Jakob Eklund, and Eric M. Hansen. "A Comparison of Empathy for Humans and Empathy for Animals". *Anthrozoös* 24, no. 4 (2011): 369-377, DOI: 10.2752/175303711X13159027359764

25 Coke, Jay S., Batson, C. Daniel., and McDavis, Katherine. "Empathic Mediation of Helping: A Two-Stage Model". *Journal of Personality and Social Psychology* 36, no. 7 (1978): 752–766.

26 Coke, Jay S., Batson, C. Daniel., and McDavis, Katherine. "Empathic Mediation of Helping: A Two-Stage Model". *Journal of Personality and Social Psychology* 36, no. 7 (1978): 752–766.

27 Basil, Debra Z., Ridgway, Nancy M., and Basil, Michael D. "Guilt and Giving: A Process Model of Empathy and Efficacy". *Psychology & Marketing* 25, no. 1 (2008): 1–23.

28 Basil, Debra Z., Ridgway, Nancy M., and Basil, Michael D. "Guilt and Giving: A Process Model of Empathy and Efficacy". *Psychology & Marketing* 25, no. 1 (2008): 1–23.

Works Cited

"2019 Climate Action Summit." United Nations, 2019. https://www.un.org/en/climatechange/2019-climate-action-summit.

Airenti, Gabriella. "The Cognitive Bases of Anthropomorphism: From Relatedness to Empathy." *International Journal of Social Robotics* 7, no. 1 (2015): 117–127.

Anabaraonye, Benjamin, Nji, Ifeyinwa, and Hope, James. "Poetry as a Valuable Tool for Climate Change Education for Global Sustainability." *International Journal of Scientific and Engineering Research* 9 (2018): 81–85.

Arbilly, Michal and Lotem, Arnon. "Constructive Anthropomorphism: A Functional Evolutionary Approach to the Study of Human-Like Cognitive Mechanisms in Animals." *The Royal Society Publishing*: *Proceedings of the Royal Society B*284 (2017). https://doi.org/10.1098/rspb.2017.1616

Basil, Debra Z., Ridgway, Nancy M., and Basil, Michael D. "Guilt and Giving: A Process Model of Empathy and Efficacy." *Psychology & Marketing* 25, no. 1 (2008): 1–23.

Bass, E. *The Human Lines*. Copper Canyon Press, 2012.

Bekoff, Marc. "Animal Emotions: Exploring Passionate Natures." *Bioscience* 50 (2000): 861–870.

Blaisdell, Aaron P., Sawa, Kosuke, Leising, Kenneth J., and Waldmann, Michael R. "Causal Reasoning in Rats." *Science* 311 (2006): 1020–1022.

Breland, Keller and Breland, Marian. *Animal Behavior*. Toronto, ON: MacMillan, 1966.

Broadhurst, P. *The Science of Animal Behaviour*. Baltimore, MD: Penguin Books, 1963.

Brüggemann, Tirza. "Animal Poetry and Empathy." *Humanities (Basel)* 6, no. 2 (2017): 1–14.

Bruni, Domenica, Pietro, Perconti, and Alessio, Plebe. "Anti-Anthropomorphism and Its Limits." *Frontiers in Psychology* 9 (2018). https://doi.org/10.3389/fpsyg.2018.02205.

Chan, Alvin A.Y. "Anthropomorphism as a Conservation Tool." *Biodiversity and Conservation* 21, no. 7 (2012): 1889–1892.

Chen, Tong, Razzaq, Amar, Qing, Ping, and Cao, Binbin. "Do You Bear to Reject Them? The Effect of Anthropomorphism on Empathy and Consumer Preference for Unattractive Produce." *Journal of Retailing and Consumer Services* 61 (2021): 102556.

Coke, Jay S., Daniel, Batson C., and Katherine, McDavis. "Empathic Mediation of Helping: A Two-Stage Model." *Journal of Personality and Social Psychology* 36, no. 7 (1978): 752–766.

Cristian, Román-Palacios, and Wiens, John J. "Recent Responses to Climate Change Reveal the Drivers of Species Extinction and Survival." *Proceedings of the National Academy of Sciences* 117, no. 8 (2020): 201913007. https://doi.org/10.1073/pnas.1913007117

Cuff, Benjamin M.P., Brown, Sarah J., Taylor, Laura, and Howat, Douglas J. "Empathy: A Review of the Concept." *Emotion Review* 8, no. 2 (April 2014): 144–153. https://doi.org/10.1177/1754073914558466.

Dallimore, W. *A Handbook of Coniferae and Ginkgoaceae*. New York: St. Martin's Press, 1967, pp. 229–233.

"Delaware River Basin Commission|Climate Change." 2022. www.nj.gov. Accessed May 11, 2022. https://www.nj.gov/drbc/programs/flow/climate-change.html#:~:text=Local%20climate%20change%20impacts%20for.

Faulkner, Sandra. *Poetic Inquiry: Craft, Method and Practice*, 2nd ed. Routledge, 2019.

Gibbons, Sarah. 2020. "Ginkgo Trees Nearly Went Extinct. Here's How We Saved These 'Living Fossils.'" *Environment*, 2020. https://www.nationalgeographic.com/environment/article/ginkgo-trees-nearly-went-extinct-how-we-saved-these-living-fossils.

Grabar, Henry. "The Night of the Gingko Lets Us Watch Climate Change in Real Time." *Slate Magazine*, 2018. https://slate.com/technology/2018/11/gingko-trees-climate-change-leaves-fall.html.

Graham, Jorie. *Place*. Manchester: Carcanet, 2012.

Hickman, Caroline. "We Need To (Find a Way To) Talk About … Eco-Anxiety." *Journal of Social Work Practice* 34, no. 4 (2020): 411–424. https://doi.org/10.1080/02650533.2020.1844166

Illingworth, Sam. Review of For What We Can Hope to Afford – What Poetry Tells Us about the Perception of Climate Change. Abstract. In *EGU General Assembly 2019*. Vol. 21 (2019).

Illingworth, Sam. A Change of Climate - How Poetry Can Help Localise a Global Problem. Abstract. In *20th EGU General Assembly*, EGU2018. Vol. 20 (2018).

Kelen, Christopher, and You, Chengcheng. "Liminal Encounters: Ethics of Anthropomorphism in the Poetry of Levertov, Szymborska, and Fulton." *Mosaic* (Winnipeg) 52, no. 2 (2019): 147–165.

Ketron, Seth, and Naletelich, Kelly. "Victim or Beggar? Anthropomorphic Messengers and the Savior Effect in Consumer Sustainability Behavior." *Journal of Business Research* 96, no. March (2019): 73–84. https://doi.org/10.1016/j.jbusres.2018.11.004.

Lethem, J., Slade, P.D., Troup, J.D.G., and Bentley, G. "Outline of a Fear-Avoidance Model of Exaggerated Pain Perception." *Behaviour Research and Therapy* 21 (1983): 401–408.

Malin, Angantyr, Jakob, Eklund and Hansen, Eric M. "A Comparison of Empathy for Humans and Empathy for Animals." *Anthrozoös* 24, no. 4 (2011): 369–377. https://doi.org/10.2752/1753037 11X13159027359764

Maguire, Peta, Kannis-Dymand, Lee, Mulgrew, Kate E., Schaffer, Vikki, and Peake, Sheila. "Empathy and Experience: Understanding Tourists' Swim with Whale Encounters." *Human Dimensions of Wildlife* 25, no. 2 (2020): 105–120.

Meyer, Robinson. "The Great Ginkgo-Tree Leaf Dump Is Here." *The Atlantic*. November 10, 2017. https://www.theatlantic.com/science/archive/2017/11/the-great-gingko-dump-climate-change-autumn/545585/.

Moore, Helen. "What Is Ecopoetry? | IT." 2012. Internationaltimes.it. Accessed May 7, 2022. https://internationaltimes.it/what-is-ecopoetry/

Nagel, Thomas. "What Is It like to Be a Bat?" *The Philosophical Review* 83, no. 4 (1974): 435–450. https://doi.org/10.2307/2183914.

Pease, R. W. (Ed.). *Merriam-Webster's Medical Dictionary*. Springfield, MA: Merriam-Webster, 1995.

Poindexter, C.C. "Poetry as Data Analysis: Honoring the Words of Research Participants." *Reflections* (Long Beach, Calif.) 4, no. 3 (1998): 22–25.

Prendergast, M. "Poem is what?" Poetic Inquiry in Qualitative Social Science Research. In M. Prendergast, C. Leggo, and P. Sameshima (Eds.), *Poetic Inquiry: Vibrant Voices in the Social Sciences*. Rotterdam, The Netherlands: Sense, 2009, pp. xix–xlii

Santos Perez, Craig. "Teaching Ecopoetry in a Time of Climate Change – the Georgia Review." Thegeorgiareview.com, 2020. Accessed April 10, 2022. https://thegeorgiareview.com/posts/teaching-ecopoetry-in-a-time-of-climate-change/

Thatcher, Christina. 2021. "How Poetry Can Help Us Understand the Urgency of the Climate Crisis." *The Conversation*. https://theconversation.com/how-poetry-can-help-us-understand-the-urgency-of-the-climate-crisis-170971.

"Tohickon Valley Park." 2022. Bucks County, PA. Accessed April 11, 2022. https://www.buckscounty.gov/Facilities/Facility/Details/Tohickon-Valley-Park-8.

U.S. Geological Survey. National Hydrography Dataset High-Resolution Flowline Data. The National Map. Accessed April 1, 2011. https://www.usgs.gov/national-hydrography

Walsh, Susan. "Contemplation, Artful Writing. Research with Internationally Educated Female Teachers." *Qualitative Inquiry* 18, no. 3 (2012): 273–285

Westling, Louise. *The Logos of the Living World. Merleau-Ponty, Animals and Language*. New York: Fordham University Press, 2014.

7 Of Jellyfish, Lichen, and Other More-than-Human Matter

Ecopoethical Writing Research as Transformative Politics

Katharina Maria Kalinowski and Rosanne van der Voet

Poethics of Lichen

i. What if
ii. The opposite of yes/no
iii. Go back to the how not the what
iv. Single drop of water
v. What good a key to a uni
                verse
vi. Lie next to the fallen language
vii. This is the shell that survived
viii. Life is not safe
ix. We remain neutral ised
x. Go back to the what not the how
xi. Cultural brokers for ideology and ecospeak
xii. High flowability/low flowability
xiii. Made of dust and sunburst
xiv. It won't sell
xv. The world is a collage of major and minor interests
xvi. AGAINST [crisis]
xvii. We swim through the end times, temporally emergent
xviii. You think this is for joy(ou) only, look at the possibility
xix. Not all harm can be measured
xx. Slow slow slow grow lichen-ethics through doub#
xxi. "developing is a matter of interspecies communication"
xxii. Atomise discourse to bumper stickers
xxiii. We need to understand where we're going before
                we can
                      question where we're coming from
xxiv. Any movement of the pointers requires movement of other pointers
xxv. Grow and look, think into all directions; there's beauty every
where

DOI: 10.4324/9781003399988-10

Numbing a Jellyfish I

circle of gentle sensations buoys a translucent body softly on a current always displacing this self of pulsations organ of roundness articulates suggestion of direction balancing out a wave a drop in temperature an increase in sound vibration inertia smoothening movement into softness and swim-like trembles of watery limbs this body always attuned to a synthesis of nearby occur-rences ever a crossing between things fused into sense of multiple selves extending no singular beliefs into this sea of words and saltwater a sense so plurally formed of minute larval selves that anemone-like jelly-trees branch out in layers of thoughts and a free-swimming body learns to situate its truth never just in one location in one body in one story

that tells of this buoyant spherical bell a culmination of dazzlingly colourful body fooling percep-tion into a notion of too separate and too human head a term which becomes meaningless to this body's concentric symmetry and orbicular perception encircling, body-center held in whitely glow above marginal lappets of gelatinous skin and eight arms strongly extending into myriad of blue- and white-speckled tentacles animal hovering just beneath the surface of a deep blue and temperate sea no coastline is in sight as plankton cloud floats by a shell tumbles many, metres down across the sand a pale green light illuminates algal growth envelops this body as does this sea saturating a permeable form with blurry edges yet somehow presenting as an entity a word which is displaced as so many are sucked away by never-ceasing current dissipating their meaning and widening the gap between a nearly liquid jellyfish and a terrestrial animal held up by calcareous skeleton with language-making brain still watery in black letters words emerge on a white screen representing one of a million modes of narration yet these words can be limitless they can flow gently suggest-ing direction and unfold towards stories written in translucent tissue in the small movement of a bifurcated moutharm, harbouring new generations within this language lies the larva of another form of writing narration-trees closing in on the abyss of alienation nudging a human-jellyfish relationship slowly surfacing and world-facade of a screen's white-blue radiance melts into liquid blueness with human and jellyfish watery bodies drifting in a nebulous glow without exterior

Introduction

An alliance of algae, bacteria, and fungi grows into a new being, forming lichen. A transpar-ent animal, more water than skin, eliminates its own individuality by forming multiple selves from one larval beginning. A human types on a plastic keyboard, her body held up by cal-careous bones and a language-making brain. These are just three examples of current earthly diversity, all forming part of vast networks of material interconnection, "a mosaic of open-ended assemblages of entangled ways of life" (Lowenhaupt Tsing, 2015, 4). As forests are felled, drills bore into the earth in search of oil, and warming seas are rising, the connections that constitute all life become precarious, causing collaborations and entanglements to disin-tegrate. As Anna Lowenhaupt Tsing argues, the "patchy unpredictability" (5) of the current global condition demonstrates that the world can never be understood in any singular way. This highlights the necessity to critique and decentre ideologies that have been dominant so far, such as capitalism and anthropocentrism. This moment of crisis is therefore a time to "re-open our imaginations" (5) to different ways of thinking and living together in a contaminated world. In a similar vein, Joan Retallack asserts that life – which we here define as both human and nonhuman – is subject to constant swerves, change, and risk. She argues for the need of a poetics of the swerve, which emerges as a "poetics of responsibility" (Retallack, 2003, 3), a creative method that takes on an ethical project in the face of the environmental crisis. She identifies this as a "poethical attitude" (Retallack, 2003, 3), a form of poetical inquiry which speaks to the human responsibility for living in interrelation and intimate proximity to others. Seeking to pursue such an inquiry in this essay, we conceive the creative writing process as a mode of research in itself. Through practice as research, our essay thus explores the politically transformative potential of an emerging hybrid, creative-critical, ecopoethical writing mode. Such practices have strong potential for pedagogical applications, moving students away from formulaic thesis-driven essays. Instead, students can be urged to take riskier, more creative – and ultimately, we would argue, more rigorous – approaches to reading and writing about the climate crisis.

The current global predicament – consisting among other things of environmental pollution, global warming, and widespread extractivism of people and planet – presents us with such an enormous problem it becomes difficult to imagine as a whole. Timothy Clark points out that at a certain threshold, the sum of many seemingly meaningless human actions, such as driving to work, forms "a new, imponderable physical event, altering the basic ecological cycles of the planet" (Clark, 2015, 72). The vast scale of the problem and the abstract terminology used to describe it preclude a more emotional and imaginative response to the crisis, thus constituting important factors in preventing change. Therefore, scientific knowledge on these issues is simply not enough to mobilise a change of approach – we need conversations between different disciplines, some of which provide better tools for nudging the imagination (Retallack, 2018, 229). Following Retallack's argument, we explore the politically transformative potential of what she identifies as the most important work of poets: "to transgress what appear to be the limits of imagination – to exceed the apathetically probable" (Retallack, 2018, 233).

In this essay, we combine a practical and theoretical poethical method with the lens of material ecocriticism. For in a world where the material intimacy between all things becomes increasingly evident, we recognise that language co-constructs the world and is thus able to make material interventions. We assert, therefore, that all matter is "storied matter", and that storytelling and poetics are not exclusively human practices (Iovino and Oppermann, 2014, 1). A story emerges in the letters on this page, but another lies in the growth of a lichen and the gentle pulsations of a jellyfish. To further the conversation between disciplines and this inclusive definition of poetics, we specifically explore a creative-critical poethics, which challenges genre conventions and emphasises language as an unresting practice that constantly (re)connects us to the ever-changing conditions of the global present. In this context, we explore how we can use language in analytically inquisitive, argumentative, and experimental ways that disrupt its complicity in destructive systems and raise a tangible environmental concern. Extending poethics into ecopoethics, we take on the project of an experimental ecological writing mode to poethically confront the limits of the imagination by putting insights from material ecocriticism into practice. Through such a hybrid critical and practice-based creative inquiry, we explore how a developing ecopoethical writing mode forms new human-nonhuman relationships that have the potential to articulate a transformative politics. In so doing, we explore the potential of Retallack's notion of the "poethical wager", which enacts an open-ended courageous "swerve" through the writing process as a potentially transformative action itself (Retallack, 2003, 3).

Numbing a Jellyfish II

when something emerges
      holding words that sway and balance
           statocyst-like
                as a drill bores itself into the earth held by this sea

and soundwaves ripple

       gelatinous body

              inertia holding

         words cling onto meaning

            cells apart

     kinocilia missed

              stereocilia flaccid

                sensory epithelium begins featurelessness

ultrastructurally

          a hairy chaos

holes in seafloor

             tentacled skin-cracks

      speckle

                senseless void
     erasing

            unhearing
     yellow bell

laden

        disintegrating

               responsibility

Poetry as Wager: Towards an Experimental and Material Ecopoethics

Ecopoethics and the Wager

"If you're to embrace complex life on earth", writes Joan Retallack, "if you can no longer pretend that all things are fundamentally simple or elegant, a poetics thickened by an *h* launches an exploration of art's significance *as*, not just *about*, a form of living in the real world" (2003, 26). As Rosanne's prose-poetic stream of a jellyfish dissolves into the open sea, attention is created through disorientation. Are the minimalistic lines part of one "gelatinous body"? Who and how many of the multiple selves are speaking; who is "unhearing" the eerie "senseless void" enacted by the extended blank spaces on the page? Syntax is disrupted, language de-automised from its expected behaviour, moving across registers that include what could be described as scientific, lyrical, and academic. The strangeness often associated with the translucent, boneless, faceless organism and its jelly-tentacles creates jellyfish-text as an equally ongoing estrangement. Free from any punctuation, it is propelled by language-making as relation-making, extended towards the reader who is invited to follow the pulsating words from the drilling into the seabed to the final word "responsibility". Embracing the "hairy chaos" of a jellyfish's sensory tissue inspires a form of writing equally bent towards "chaos". We argue that this explorative form stretches a conversation between poetics, poiesis, politics, aesthetics, and ethics towards an ecological interaction with the more-than-human to express an ecopoethics of the present moment. Embedded in this moment, the page we write on is disclosed as a place of human-nonhuman encounters, where new transformative relationships are formed in textually material ways that have the potential to extend beyond the page.

Jellyfish are fascinatingly resilient, extremely ancient organisms, although humans encounter them predominantly as edible objects, aquarium decor, or stinging intruders. They are inhabitants of the even more ancient sea, an intersection of known and unknown, a vast archive of times, lives, and stories that has given our home planet the figurative name "Blue Planet". Originating in tandem with the first aerial photograph of the planet Earth, the narrative of a distant, isolated, harmonious, and finite blue global environment has substantially shaped the cultural imagination of the Earth in Europe and North-America (cf. Heise, 2008, 22–24; Jasanoff, 2001). While it arguably reduces the complexity of the "pulsing, detailed vitality of terrestrial life" (Garb, 1985, 19) and renders Earth as a static object, the so-called God's eye view on the Blue Planet points to the difficulty of escaping a totalising singular view and registering the "patchy unpredictability" in the face of the incomprehensible size, scale, age, and many layers of the Earth. This task, however, is at the heart of poethics as it launches its critical-creative exploration of life as "complex realism" (Retallack, 2003, 13). Poethics acknowledges that the present globalised moment in which we are embedded as writers trying to respond to changing climates is composed of multiple places, perspectives, languages, and stories, "a convergence of infinite relationships, past and future, real or possible" (Calvino, 1988, 107) and thus permeated by "radical unknowability" (Retallack, 2003, 22). To do justice to these complexities, poethical writing needs to accept unknowability and changeability as the only constants and weave them into its structure. Critical research can tell us that the jellyfish's sensory epithelium disintegrates when exposed to high levels of sound. The creative task is to poethically imagine how that feels, how language functions as part of this endeavour, how it can translate the imaginative act into a textual intimacy, let human and jellyfish bodies collide on the page, with words shaped by a human mind as well as a jellyfish's body. At the same time, the poethical implication is to frame this human-nonhuman collision as tentative in its assumptions and uncertain in its outcomes. Poethical writing meets ecological attentiveness in this sense, defying a singular point of view and beginning to shape an open ecopoethical form that is enmeshed in an acknowledgement of complex realism.

As Retallack phrases it: "We can't really know where we are going and that is precisely why we must experientially, experimentally *make* (poesis) our way by means of considered poethical wagers" (Retallack, 2018, 234). "[W]ords can be limitless" as they are born out of a moment of limitless possibilities and relations that only light up temporary paths while remaining indefinite as a whole. Explicitly founded on not-knowing, the project of the poethical wager presents a radical disruption to any claim of being in full knowledge and control; to gauge, quantify, and dissect life, put a price tag on it, measure it in figures and productivity, press it into categories, and stratify its "man-made" geology. In this vein, a poethical recognition of life runs counter to a hubristic narrative of the geochronologic Anthropocene that envisions the universalised human "God Species" (cf. Lynas, 2011) as a maker and shaper of weather and history.[1] Instead, poethics is fully embedded in the inevitable complexity and indeterminacy of life, seeking to generate attentiveness and responsibility towards constantly changing, unsettling conditions. Acknowledging language as a co-shaper of complex realism, an open and reflective poethical approach opposes totalising visions, making space for polylogues instead of monologues. Herein lies its potential to compose an ecologically-aware response to the crisis without reproducing stories of mastery, exploitative relations of power, and legitimations of objectifications that sustain the current environmental degradation and that have arguably led to it in the first place. As it charges poetics with an h, poethics veers away from questions of pre-determined style and genre, from an assumed separation of art and politics, language and the physical world, "towards the making of language into a complex form that has the character (ethos) of living in the contemporary experience" (Retallack, 2003, 35–36). It thus articulates an ongoing negotiation of one's own, constantly shifting embodied location in the world in relation to everything else, including lichen, jellyfish, and the political, ecological, economic, socio-historical systems in which they are, we are, entangled at all times.

Poethics, the making of language in this spirit, turns into an investigative negotiation, necessarily confronting change and indeterminacy. It needs to be ready to "swerve", as Retallack puts it (2003, 1–3; 56), break out of predetermined patterns and thoughts and centrisms, and precisely "learn to situate its truths never just in one location in one body in one story". To ponder the connection to the jellyfish as more than food or object by registering it in relation to drilling into seabeds can thus be understood as such a swerve, towards an ecological point of view that imagines how we live together as participants of a vital ecosystem. The experimental openness of "Numbing a Jellyfish", its lack of coherent narrative, voice, and perspective refute any ready-made assumptions or easy conclusions. Who, again, is speaking, who is experiencing "this animal hovering just underneath the surface of a deep blue and temperate sea"? Swerving from an anthropocentric mindset towards the possibility of an unfolding human-jellyfish relationship, the text brings into view a realm that may not be necessarily part of human everyday life but that is part of the complex realism of the ecosystem earth. We, as readers, do not see this Earth as an object from aerial distance in this case but are interacting with it. Introducing an unexpected relationship that speaks to the imagination, the ambiguity of the text invites us to become active co-producers of its unfurling more-than-human stories, and thus of the ecosystems it interacts with. We are likewise invited to become actively involved in the generation of a wager that stretches from unknowingness to the materially transformative potential of ecological attention. It is here that poethical and ecological discourse converge, "through a shared concern for establishing human relationships to the natural world that remain vigilant, urgent, and subject to, even welcoming, change arising through contact with indeterminacy" (Burnett, 2016). An ecopoethics arises, orienting language's potential to shape attentive, eco-ethical responses to continuously changing contemporary issues, thus taking on a form of transformative politics.

This acknowledgement refuses a clear-cut separation between writing and action, a much debated relation that continues to play an influential role in the developing field of environmental studies. In fact, the interaction between the two seems to touch upon the very architecture and function of this young (inter-)discipline, including its methodologies, theoretical paradigms, and epistemological assumptions. The formation of ecological poetry itself is couched in ongoing debates as to whether or not it should be judged based on its presumed effectiveness in raising environmental awareness (cf. Skinner, 2005; Hume and Osborne, 2018). Within a poethical framework embracing the eco-prefix to emphasise more-than-human cohabitation, it becomes evident that any presumed political impact of poetry cannot be regarded independent of its making, its form, its ecopoethics. This is, perhaps, the only potentially evident condition, as we adapt an angle of indeterminacy, not-knowing, potentially never knowing. Acknowledging complex realism, we simply cannot know the outcome of any of our actions; we cannot presume any straightforward causal relations between events and actions that are all intertwined, in interaction with the physical world and furthermore tied together by language. Ecopoethics acknowledges that our makings are inevitably part of the fabrication of the chaotic, intertwined transcorporeal material world that the self-contained Blue Planet turns out to be once we put ourselves in its unfolding patchy midst. Writing is already an action, in that sense, an ecopoethic making expressing the courage to swerve away from the familiar and comfortable in its commitment to responsibly attend to ecologies that sometimes escape everyday life. Arising from responsible attention to the convergence of relationships between nonhumans and humans, language, perspectives, events, and developments, both possible and real, the project of the wager, as Retallack writes,

> is just that we do our utmost to understand our contemporary position and then act on the chance that our work may be at least as effective as any other initial condition in the intertwining trajectories of pattern and chance.
>
> (2003, 46)

Before we can fully move on to explore this "act" then, we will do our utmost to understand that as "we" make poetry in a time of climate crisis, we are embedded as symbiotic subjects and "our" ecopoethics include the physical-material more-than-human realm.

Poetic Matter and Textual Materiality

With its celebration of not-knowing, the ecopoethical wager not only takes up an eco-ethical project in writing but also makes the page into a space for open-ended human-nonhuman encounters. The poetry that emerges from this experimental space still originates in a human perspective, but not without significant, more-than-human movements and interests flowing into the language, altering its structure, as it wagers on the notion that anthropocentrism is not an inevitable condition but a mindset that can be pushed against to disclose the emerging new perspectives. As Katharina contemplates lichen from her inevitably human and embodied perspective, the patchiness and multiplicity of lichen encroach on her words, breaking up the structure and forging strange, unexpected connections between lichen and language, between a bumper sticker and ecological discourse. Lichens slowly grow into the words, questioning any clear-cut sense of individuality, seamlessly shifting from the scale of a droplet to that of the universe, reflecting its patchy manifoldness. The poem that is the result of this process, though written by a human being, emerges forever altered by the unfamiliar and irreducible complexity of the life of lichen. It is this element of the wager that is ecologically significant. For the idea of human-nonhuman intimacy is not only theorised but also emerges materially on the page. It is this direct application of insights from material ecocriticism, forging a synthesis of scholarly and creative writing modes, that characterises our methodology in this essay. Building on Retallack's definition of poethics, this element of textual materiality, as we will outline further below, is an important tool in seeking to make tangible connections to an environmental crisis that is frighteningly material in its effects though often seemingly abstract in its sheer scope.

As argued by prominent material ecocritics such as Serpil Oppermann, Serenella Iovino, and Stacy Alaimo, the current environmental emergency is a material process which is connected to other material and meaning-making practices, such as societal, economic, political, and cultural processes, including the writing of poetry. In this context and in contrast to the Blue Planet gaze, nature is no longer conceived of as an object separated from human activity but is viewed instead from an ecological stance of more-than-human interconnectedness. A material ecocritical perspective thus presents an alternative to traditional binary views in Western thought, presenting a challenge to ideas of human mastery, anthropocentrism, and scientism. This perspective highlights that the materiality of all things – whether the body of a fish killed in an oil spill, human relationships to oil and oil extraction, or a poem inhabiting the body of a fish – is not individual and separate, but rather connected to other materialities. Questioning the idea that storytelling is an exclusively human practice, Serpil Oppermann asserts that nonhuman animals have their own narrative agency, expressed in their interactions with their surroundings (Oppermann, 2019, 453). In the context of the poethical wager, which relies on an intimacy with and ethical responsibility to its subject matter, the textual, human-written story thus becomes interwoven with nonhuman storied potential embedded in a jellyfish's pulsations or the slow crusting of lichen over rock. The resulting ecopoethics can take on many different forms; in this essay, we focus on poetry as one of these forms of expression. In our own poems included in this essay, this human-nonhuman intimacy embedded in the lyrical writing process erodes not only the expected syntactical coherence of language, but also the category of the human. Viewing humanity as a homogenous force, as the concept of the Anthropocene can make it seem, is problematic as it obscures social inequalities and the complexities of the current crisis. As argued by Stacy Alaimo, a more transcorporeal definition of the human – as inextricably interconnected with nonhumans and other matter – is needed to forge collective ways out of this predicament (Alaimo, 2016, 155). Given environmental issues exhibit the enmeshment of earthly processes, it is no longer viable to hold on to traditional subject-object binaries – even human bodies have always been much more nonhuman than assumed, as will be explored further in part 2 of this chapter. This lack of human control over material processes that erode the boundaries of individual bodies invites the ecopoethical wager's exploration of unknowability. Against this background, our poetry emerges from open-ended questions. How might we translate the concept of transcorporeality into a lyrical style? How do we creatively represent the reality of human-nonhuman intimacies? And how may this emerge materially on the page, forging a tangible representation of a complex issue?

Within a poethical framework, there can be no final answers to these questions; rather, the writing of poetry turns into an explorative process that begins with an interest that transgresses the self and stretches towards ecological connectedness. An experimental transcorporeal approach thus embraces a human-more-than-human intimacy prior to the writing process. Moreover, it employs poetic writing itself as a form of research, exploring the potential of ecopoethics to push the limits of the imagination as it explores juxtapositions between different registers running breathlessly into each other, such as in the following example: "harboring new generations within this language lies the larva of another form of writing". By developing experimental and hybrid poetic styles and forms, this ecologically-aware lyrical approach forges a synthesis between material ecocritical insight – such as the concept of transcorporeality – and a poethical project inspired by the perseverance of lichen in a contaminated world or a jellyfish's disintegrating body. The issue of tangibility, of writing the environmental crisis in any concrete, graspable way, becomes all the more challenging when it is coupled with an awareness of the incredible amount of material connections at its heart, all of which make up the poethical wager at hand. As expressed in our jellyfish and lichen poems, we believe there is potential for such tangibility in a specificity of subject matter, as well as in a crisscrossing through traditionally separated writing styles and forms (Retallack, 2003, 39) that blend lyrical language with scientific insights. We further this potential by a creative use of page space, with words slowly dripping off the corners of a page through the extended use of white space, or interrupting each other, allowing multiple voices to speak simultaneously. This allows for the bodies of the nonhuman subject matter to emerge materially on the page. Fluidity and tentacular nature come to the fore in the unpunctuated and dissipating structure of "Numbing a Jellyfish I" and "II", while the composite nature of lichen is reflected in the stacked structure of "Poethics of Lichen". Diving into radical unknowability, our ecopoethical-materialist approach and focus on textual materiality make it possible to shift scales freely, concretely representing an element of a very vast and global problem, thus wagering on making tangible a shred of the environmental crisis and the nonhuman experience of it.

The synthesis of ecopoethics and material ecocriticism thus anchors a tangible interdependency between language and the physical-material world, allowing for poetry to become politically transformative beyond its traditional page space. As outlined in the context of material ecocriticism, poems as expressions of textual stories are material, but so is storied matter beyond text, which includes environmental processes as well as animals and other matter. These connections have ramifications for a relationship beyond the story told here – a poem can be a starting point for forming connections with non-charismatic animals we do not interact with on a regular basis. For without any relationship, how will we fully register how human practices affect their lives, let alone take action on this knowledge? The lack of a cultural, emotional relationship with other beings is connected to the large-scale and often unrecognised ecological decline of the present moment. Our hybrid ecopoethical and experimental wager therefore attempts to make the creative voices heard more diverse and to cultivate a relationship that stimulates a societal change of approach to the natural world beyond the reach of a lichen's minute branches growing over this page. This wager thus emerges as a relationally transformative practice, with its sticky tentacles rippling out into this discourse, beyond this text, entangling itself with other meaning-making practices. Demonstrating that poems can write stories of change, this approach creatively asserts and performs the potential of ecopoethical language – beginning in text and expanding beyond – to act as transformative politics.

Reflections, Relations, and Recompositions

Watery Intimacies

A green-blue globe, with oceans cradling continents. A temperate sea, harbouring gelatinous and watery bodies. This human body, holding its own seas of blood and bile, of spinal fluids and urine. The material connections between these watery bodies are difficult to imagine due to the scale-shifting that this requires. However, as the human authors of this essay, we are as much participants in watery flows as a jellyfish adrift in salty seas. As Astrida Neimanis asserts in her landmark study *Bodies of Water: Posthuman Feminist Phenomenology*, all living beings on the Earth, including human bodies, are bodies of water (Neimanis, 2016, 1). Though water presents differently in each body, it is a defining characteristic of earthly life. Exploring watery flows beyond our own human scale by stimulating the imagination through a visually and textually innovative form can therefore be helpful in establishing a tangible sense of how our own human bodies are implicated in the world. As emphasised in the previous section, we can never fully escape our human perspective or even the embodied experience of our own specific bodies. However, as explored above, we are already more-than-human in our transcorporeal entanglements with the physical-material world. Following Neimanis, we can thus use a variety of art forms, such as poetry and storytelling, as amplifiers of watery flows beyond our own bodies (55). This has the potential to make connections and relationships that usually elude us tangible and material. This is the starting point for "Numbing a Jellyfish I" and "II", and this endeavour is complemented by the material and ecopoethical pursuits of this hybrid prose poem which are further explored in this section.

In "Numbing a Jellyfish I", the watery body of the jellyfish drifts into the words from the beginning of the text, at first forming a contrast with the grounded, terrestrial orientation of the human writer and her language. A tentative balancing of words reflects the gentle pulsating of a body that is composed almost entirely of water, slowly floating through another body of water. The plural nature of the jellyfish's life cycle, which allows multiple adult jellyfish to develop from a single larva, unsettles any notion of individual bodies and selves. This invites a textual consideration of a multiple and dispersed embodied sense of the world. Enacting an ecopoethics, it influences the form of the text, removing punctuation and destabilising the syntax. As the poem progresses, the words dive ever further into the world of the jellyfish's experience, flowing into its "orbicular perception", "whitely glow", and "blue- and white-speckled tentacles". Composing the words from the jellyfish's concentric symmetry, the writer becomes immersed in its watery world, dragging the reader along into "algal growth" and "plankton cloud". This adopting of jellyfish nature in the poem creates an opening for a human-jellyfish intimacy, a textual sinking of human perspectives into salty seas. This is further elaborated in the poem as it progresses into a reflection on language, emphasising its potential to explore uncertainty, to gently drift in a direction like the body of a jellyfish. Asserting the joint storied potential of the jellyfish and the human, the writing seeks an intimacy with its nonhuman subject matter, suggesting a literary adaptation of the jellyfish's strange life cycle through "narration-trees closing in on the abyss of alienation". This ecopoethical venture invites the language to serve more than just human interests. Driven by research on the jellyfish prior to the writing process, it nudges writer and reader towards a consideration of human-jellyfish relationships. The reflection on the use of language thus occurs through form and content – not only does the poem suggest the experimental potential of language to illuminate human-jellyfish relationships, it also puts this pursuit into practice with its unpunctuated and hybrid style. Evoking the image of the blue radiance of a computer screen slowly dissolving into the liquid blueness of the sea, a kinship of watery bodies afloat in the ocean is presented as a way of exploring human-jellyfish intimacy.

These ecopoethics come to the fore more strongly in "Numbing a Jellyfish II", which explores the far-flung negative outcomes of offshore oil drilling. Jellyfish are not usually viewed as victims of the oceanic environmental crisis – instead they are often represented as thriving in warming seas and taking over Anthropocene oceans with excessive blooms. With its focus on the numbing of jellyfish sensory tissue due to acoustic pollution, this poem illuminates a different story. The erratic structure and the use of extended white space in the poem not only represent the disintegration of jellyfish body and perception, they also materially enact the necessary loss of the story itself that is the result of this process. For it is not just the jellyfish who is numbed – it is also its storied nature and a potential human-jellyfish textual relationship that are lost through its decomposition. While the first part of the poem thus establishes a sense of textual human-jellyfish intimacy through a transcorporeal and watery exploration of writer, jellyfish, and ocean, "Numbing a Jellyfish II" demonstrates the fragility of such a relationship. Bringing into view more-than-human stories, these poems thus serve as amplifiers of human-jellyfish relationships, materiality of text, and of environmental loss at sea. The fact that the physical nature of the jellyfish – its fluidity and strange life cycle – shaped the form of the text from the beginning makes this sense of loss even more tangible, with the words not just describing but also poethically enacting this sentiment. The fragile and tentative human-jellyfish intimacy that surfaces from the text therefore presents a relationally transformative experience, rippling out beyond its page space into the minds of readers and the material and cultural practices of which they are part. The hybridity of this wager, incorporating scientific insight as well as lyrical language, allows for a synthesis of an ecopoethics on these various levels.

This hybrid, experimental wager takes on an ethical project in the face of the environmental crisis, focusing on the materiality of bodily experience. Informed by research into the nature of the jellyfish prior to the writing process, the poem becomes an eco-ethical project, interweaving the nonhuman experience of its subject matter with reflections on the use of language. Composing an inquisitive ecopoethics, it invites a collaboration between science and a creatively adapted posthuman, material ecocritical phenomenology. As Neimanis emphasises, science and phenomenology are not necessarily in conflict with each other, even though their respective outlooks differ, given scientific inquiry does not usually involve studying bodies as they are experienced. However, she notes that bodily experience needs scientific devices such as theories and measuring instruments to be interpretable. Moreover, scientific knowledge is never disembodied – any kind of knowledge is conceived of through embodied experience (Neimanis, 2016, 55–56). Echoing Retallack, the endeavour to understand how our watery bodies are implicated in the world calls once again for cross-disciplinary collaborations. While scientific inquiry is thus an important element of the ecopoethical wager, it should not be seen as the only way to produce knowledge, nor as a way to produce absolute truths. Such a scientistic approach would oppose critical awareness of the limitations of human perspectives while exaggerating the objectivity of scientific methods and forgetting that no unmediated – and thus no objective – knowledge of the world exists (Neimanis, 2016, 61). The material ecopoethics as developed in this essay – through a synthesis of creative-experimental and academic approaches – are therefore a way for science and creative phenomenological approaches to complement each other. Bundling imaginative and critical thinking, this proposes a diverse assemblage of knowledge that does justice to the fundamental uncertainty of the ecopoethical wager and the unknowability of its subject.

As the jellyfish drifts on, lopsided, a halo of numbness slowly drifts around its head. Entering the watery body of the text, an ecopoethical awareness bathes these pages in its salty inner sea, remembers its once concentric symmetry, its tentacles coiling into sea, into text, entangling a human hand. Slowly,   a fusing   soaked   sense

     heralds

         hears

              watery trickle

    calcareous-fluid

        oceanic-terrestrial

            body of

   watery story

            and text

      as water

We Are All Lichens

Poet(h)ics of Lichen: The makings of lichen, their stories. Exploring the lives of lichen, our experiencing of their lives meeting our lives. Registering lichenous occurrences in the physical-material world, trying to translate something of their form, their character into text. Turning observations pertaining to representations of lichen into questions opening up a meeting space for lichen, language, everyday life. What happens, is "temporally emergent", embedded and embodied in complex realism, connected to critical notions and developments across time and space; materialism, Haraway, Enzensberger, neoliberalism, climate crisis growing through the text, shaping various modes of research coming together ecopoethically, symbiotically, perhaps sympoietically; made with one another.

Arguing that "we have never been individuals", the biologist Scott Gilbert (2012, 336) endorses a paradigm that foregrounds symbiotic relationships among the different creatures living on this Earth. Neither from the viewpoint of developmental biology, nor from a physiological, anatomical, genetical, immunological, or evolutionary perspective does it make sense, he argues, to view organisms as isolated, self-contained entities. Rather, they can be regarded as "composites of many species living, developing, and evolving together" (326), thus blurring the boundaries of an individual self that is assembled through intimate interactions and exchanges with other organisms. Lichens, for instance, one of the examples cited by Gilbert, emerge from a reciprocal ecological relationship between at least two organisms, fungi and algae (or cyanobacteria). While the former provides protection, the latter produces nutrition via photosynthesis, making the lichen in Lynn Margulis' term a "holobiont" that is composed of more than one individual. As more and more insights reveal the omnipresence of symbiotic relationships in plants and animals, Gilbert's concluding contention that "[W]e are all lichens" (336) not only throws up a new set of questions and frameworks in biology and related natural sciences. Fostering a symbiotic angle on life as a whole, it has also posed and continues to pose challenges when taken into the (post)humanities, when paired with ecocriticism, shared materialities, and a substantiated transcorporeality that affects how we perceive ourselves as collaborative, materially embedded language-makers. Donna Haraway, citing Gilbert, draws attention to the ways our linked stories, knowledges, and knowledge practices must be "relentlessly relational" (Haraway, 2016, 49); sympoietical (made with): no thing makes itself (cf. 58). Echoing the previously explored material connection between language and "things", a sympoietic perspective necessarily extends to language as well. With this in mind, Gilbert's call turns into an open invitation to think through and about and with lichen to map a materially transformative ecopoethics in contingent, unexpected, and endangered more-than-human ecologies.

> The language of one's own contemporary moment is a complex barometer of all sorts of crosscurrents that are affecting us, that we are sensing, that fill us with energy and breath, anxiety and terror, but that we cannot yet bring into discernible form,
>
> writes Retallack (2003, 39).

The language that we experience in this contemporary moment is *made with* machines and shaped by marketable catchphrases, spectacle-driven headlines, instagrammable information, and the rhetoric of multinational corporations whose unconditional "dedication to profit and growth" feels unstoppable. A poetics of greed, of delusional grandeur. Environmental concerns are increasingly subsumed by a pervasive neoliberal system whose aggressive promotion of competition in every realm of life seems to be directly opposed to values of ecological kinship. Within the logic of this system, sustainability discussions are decoupled from their underlying social and anticapitalist critique and sold in the form of sustainable lifestyles and green bumper stickers. In its most controversial shades, the notion of the Anthropocene, too, seems to lack an attentiveness to the violently unjust distribution of capital and power. Instead, it once again perpetuates imperial dreams recentring the Western (hu)man (did he ever really leave the stage?) as the epoqual winner of an inflated human vs. earth fight: We, problematically homogenised humanity, have apparently become a global geological force and are now called to use our enlightened rationality and technological expertise to step up, "'optimize' climate" (Crutzen, 2002, 23), and properly tend our global Anthropocenic garden (cf. Marris, 2011). Meanwhile, in this garden, lichens grow, anywhere, everywhere; in the fissures of power, in the fissures of walls, gravestones, roofs, tree bark, and animal skin. Unabashed, unperturbed, uneconomically slow, in more forms and ways and colours than are recorded or understood. What if. We become part of a mutualistic relationship that changes all of us. We may grow, harmlessly, 1–2 mm per year, in complex shapes not fully discernible, revealing all our complexity, our connectedness through differences.

I/We trace lichen through complex networks and encounter the German poet Hans-Magnus Enzensberger's "Flechtenkunde" (lichenology) in 1967: "sie ist der erde/langsamstes telegramm/ein telegramm, das nie ankommt: überall ist es schon da, [...]" (71) ("they [lichens, our comment] are/the slowest telegram of the earth / a telegram never delivered: it's already everywhere" [translation by K. M. Kalinowski]). Written at a time when environmental concerns increasingly gained public attention, Enzensberger's ecopolitical poem contrasts social competition and post-war economic acceleration with the vision of a peaceful symbiotic lichen community. It does so by enacting a communal poetics that includes references to Woyzeck, Barbarossa, Linné, the Bible, and the Brockhaus Encyclopaedia. Enzensberger's ecopolitical list of Roman numerals turns into a substrate for the much more condensed "Poethics of Lichen", a partial ecotranslation. I trace texts trying to understand the crises of the present, of the presents. I make an attempt at the plural. Have "we" been living in crisis since the 1970s? Have we ever *not* lived in the end times? This is a polylogue; developing becomes a matter of interspecies communication (cf. Gilbert, 2012, 328). This is a negotiation, between myself and others and other selves and other Others. This is language trying to stay in motion, measuring the contemporary moment, seeking to make reconnections with the complex reality. This is making ecopoethics with collected fragments from conversations, the feeling of sunburst lichen on our hands, with documentaries on symbiosis, with snippets from critical theory. Language, storied matter, like lichen, exists in all spaces, in unexpected shapes, in fissures and cracks. If you know, you cannot unsee it. Our theories and concepts shape our perceptions, our texts echo other texts, connect across space and time, wager on future paths lit up by colourful relationships. Enzensberger's lichen, again; bluntly stating that "we" did neither work out in the past nor do we work out now, yet in the same breath leaving no doubt that "wie es mit uns sein wird / wird es vortrefflich sein, / ganz ohne zweifel" (74) ("it will work with us / it will be extraordinary, / no doubt" [translation by K. M. Kalinowski]).

We embrace poetry's capacity to express more than one point of view, to hold contradictions, to continue, and to push against old stories. The ecopoethic orientation maximises this capacity, anchoring a relational approach to language that defies totality and thus dives into the "patchy unpredictability" (Lowenhaupt Tsing, 2015, 5) of the current complex global condition. "Poethics of Lichen" begins every stanza from a new angle, in a different register that fosters reflection on its use in everyday life. In place of a stable voice or narrative, its governing principle is a form of connectivity and interdependency between, across, and beyond the snippets each stanza presents, seeking to forge transformative new relations. This is language propelled by elusiveness, gaps, and leaps, language that can no longer be consumed easily and thus – this is the wagering hope – not as easily assimilated by the systems it tries to disrupt. A lichenous ecopoethics seeks to draw attention to language and the material impact arising from the ways in which we perceive, categorise, label, and respond to embodied experiences in the contemporary moment. Slogans, hashtags, short and performative capture-phrases seem to be the flagships of an economy based on fast consumption, fast profit, and fast-growing injustices left in its wake. Time is money, language is money. In contrast, "slow slow slow" ecopoethics reflects on and swerves away from ecospeak, taking on indeterminacy and doubtfulness as a potential ethics to grow new, transformative connections with the "beauty everywhere". Through its explorative, open-ended form, ecopoethics makes space for complex realism, for issues reduced to yes/no decisions to be tested against critical consciousness. The ambiguous fabric inspires different, multiple readings that challenge absolute truths and that emerge sympoietically, between page and reader and echoes of old and new connections with the physical-material, textual, and extra-textual ecologies we are part of. To alter the violences and destructive elements within these constellations, it seems crucial to be able to imagine that they actually could be different, meaning the popular neoliberal "no alternative" rhetoric is countered with a critically informed empowering imaginative wager. *What if.* It will be extraordinary. We are interconnected subjects inhabiting a multiverse. We are the single drop of water and the ripples it can generate.

Conclusion

Throughout this hybrid essay, we have explored the potential of a conversation between methods and disciplines to come together through the project of the poethical wager thickened with material ecological concerns. Incorporating academic, critical, scientific, and poetic insights and writing forms, this essay swerved, focused, and re-oriented itself, as unpredictable in form as its subject matter. Our practice-based, creative-critical method explored a jellyfish's experience of the effects of human actions and the quiet resistance of a lichen's slow and persistent survival. Moreover, it allowed for an open-ended exploration, an ecopoethical investigation of the politically transformative potential of our hybrid poetic process. Through this process, ecopoethics and storied matter came together in the exploration of the unknowability of the full effects of the environmental crisis and its ramifications for nonhuman experience.

Shifting between various forms of research and emerging from the collaboration between two authors, we formulate a tentative conclusion of the politically transformative potential of a material ecopoethical writing project as conducted in this essay. In times of emergency, we need questioning, experimenting, connecting, and reconnecting to constantly changing conditions. We need unmooring from the above-discussed illusion of separation between human and nonhuman realms. Researching this creatively, we swerved through poetry, empty page space, broken words, stacked sentences, dense jelly-words, the voice of disintegrating bodies, two human writers, lichen-growth, a single drop of water, dust. In doing so, we theorised and enacted the potential of language to form unexpected human-nonhuman relationships. Exploring the politically transformative potential of our own poetry, we investigated its ability to resist and reframe environmentally destructive practices and discourses in which it is implicated. We examined the human and nonhuman embodied experience of this potential through a kinship between watery bodies, before connecting again to global neoliberal economies, consumerist rhetoric, and the commodification of sustainable lifestyles.

The patchy and explorative structure of this essay reflects the complexity of its subject matter, expressing a complex, open-ended, and never-final response to a complex global issue. Emerging from an ongoing conversation, our essay itself defies a singular point of view and highlights the necessity to meet the continuous challenges of the present world with responsive and responsible relations. This necessity shapes our insistence on an approach that not only explains but enacts an explorative relational structure, composing an ecopoethics of its own. As we acknowledge that language is intertwined with material processes, that it is sympoietically more-than-human and thus implicated in the cause of ecological decline, we acknowledge that our language may need to enter different, transformative relations as well. Instead of claiming any absolute truths, the responses we provide as poets and researchers embedded in a vibrant, ecologically inter-connected world then need to incorporate the indeterminacies resulting from this ever-shifting position of entanglement. Instead of claiming unconditional objectivity, not only the themes, but also structures, forms, and methodological conceptualisations of our texts may need rethinking.

Using an overlapping creative-critical poetic approach that blends declarative with explora-tive modes, we sought to draw attention to this challenge, which likewise points to the peda-gogical value of research-based creative writing. Decentring scholarly norms and assumptions, materially-oriented ecopoethics poses a disruption to human control over language. Ecopoethi-cal poetry, through reinvention, self-reflection, formal openness, and reliance on interpretation, allows other perspectives to shine through. Reflecting on, subverting, and making new relations, it is dedicated to generating imaginative spaces to re-organise harmful power structures and to cultivate attentiveness to vulnerable earthly transcorporealities. It thus provides an empower-ing and hopeful approach to the role of poetry in times of climate crisis, one that nevertheless always remains uncertain in its certainty of expressing a transformative politics. As Camus put it, responding to a different crisis: "We have nothing to lose except everything. So let's go ahead". (1961, 246). Informed by radical unknowability, critical attentiveness to material entan-glements, and a willingness to experiment, ecopoethical poetry wagers on the imaginative pos-sibility of eco-ethical relationships, making new, less destructive ways of ecological coexistence imaginable for students, teachers, readers, and writers.

Note

1 Such an aggrandised notion of the Anthropocene has been widely criticised, see for instance Malm and Hornborg, 2014; Lepori, 2015; Yusoff, 2016.

Works Cited

Alaimo, S. *Exposed: Environmental Politics and Pleasures in Posthuman Times*. Minnesota: University of Minnesota Press, 2016.

Burnett, E.-J. "Cynthia Hogue's The Incognito Body as Ecopoethics." *Readings: Response and Reactions to Poetries* 5 (2016). http://www.bbk.ac.uk/readings/issues/issue5/ElizabethJaneBurnett_on_cynthiahogue (accessed June 10, 2019).

Calvino, I. *Six Memos for the Next Millennium: The Charles Eliot Norton Lectures, 1985–86*. Cambridge, MA: Harvard University Press, 1988.

Camus, A. "The Wager of Our Generation." In *Resistance, Rebellion and Death*, translated by Justin O'Brian, 237–248. New York: Alfred A. Knopf, 1961.

Clark, T. *Ecocriticism on the Edge*. London: Bloomsbury Academic, 2015.

Crutzen, P. J. "Geology of Mankind." *Nature* 415 (2002): 23.

Enzensberger, H. M. "Flechtenkunde." *Blindenschrift* (1967): 71–75.

Garb, Y. J. "The Use and Misuse of the Whole Earth Image." *Whole Earth Review* 45 (March 1985): 18–25.

Gilbert, S. "A Symbiotic View of Life: We Have Never Been Individuals." *The Quarterly Review of Biology* 87, no. 4 (2012): 325–341.

Haraway, D. *Staying With the Trouble. Making Kin in the Chthulucene*. Durham and London: Duke University Press, 2016.

Heise, U. *Sense of Place, Sense of Planet*. Oxford: Oxford University Press, 2008.

Hume, A. and Osborne, G. "Ecopoetics as Expanded Critical Practice. An Introduction." In *Ecopoetics. Essays in the Field*, edited by A. Hume and G. Osborne, 1–18. Iowa City: Iowa University Press, 2018.

Iovino, S. and Oppermann, S. "Introduction: Stories Come to Matter." In *Material Ecocriticism*, edited by S. Iovino and S. Oppermann, 1–17. Bloomington: Indiana University Press, 2014.

Jasanoff, Sheila. "Image and Imagination: The Formation of Global Environmental Consciousness." In *Changing the Atmosphere: Expert Knowledge and Environmental Governance*, edited by C. A. Miller and P. N. Edwards, 309–337. Cambridge, MA: MIT Press, 2001.

Lepori, M. "There Is No Anthropocene: Climate Change, Species-Talk, and Political Economy." *Telos* 172 (2015): 103–124.

Lowenhaupt Tsing, A. *The Mushroom at the End of the World: On the Possibility of Life in Capitalist Ruins*. Princeton: Princeton University Press, 2015.

Lynas, M. *The God Species: Saving the Planet in the Age of Humans*. London: Fourth Estate, 2011.

Malm, A. and Hornborg, A. "The Geology of Mankind? A Critique of the Anthropocene Narrative." *The Anthropocene Review* 1, no. 1 (2014): 62–69.

Marris, Emma. "Ecology Without Wilderness: Tending the Global Garden We Call 'Nature'." *The Atlantic* (2011). https://www.theatlantic.com/technology/archive/2011/09/ecology-without-wilderness-tending-the-global-garden-we-call-nature/245170/ (accessed April 5 2022).

Neimanis, A. *Bodies of Water: Posthuman Feminist Phenomenology*. London: Bloomsbury Academic, 2016.

Oppermann, S. "Storied Seas and Living Metaphors in the Blue Humanities." *Configurations* 27 (2019): 443–461.

Retallack, J. *The Poethical Wager*. Berkeley and Los Angeles: University of California Press, 2003.

Retallack, J. "Hard Days Nights in the Anthropocene." In *Ecopoetics: Essays in the Field*, edited by A. Hume and G. Osborne, 228–248. Iowa: University of Iowa Press, 2018.

Skinner, J. "Statement on 'New Nature Writing'." In *Ecopoetics 04/05*, edited by J. Skinner, 127–129. Lewiston, ME: Periplum, 2005.

Yusoff, K. *A Billion Black Anthropocenes - Or None,* Minneapolis, MN: University of Minnesota Press, 2016.

8 Using Poetry to Learn from the Animals We Brought to Antarctica

Caitlin Scarano

Can it be that the dog has not understood its master? Or is it the master who has not understood the dog?
—Roald Amundsen, *The South Pole: An Account of the Norwegian Expedition in the Fram, 1910–12*

In October 2018, I flew from Seattle, Washington to Christchurch, New Zealand, which was the gateway to my ultimate destination—McMurdo Station, one of two United States research bases in Antarctica. I lived and worked there for the month of November 2018 as a participant in the National Science Foundation-funded Antarctic Artist and Writer's program. Having long been fascinated by the circumpolar regions, the goal of my time was to use poetry as a lens to examine intersections of humanity and landscape in the Antarctic region. After my time in Antarctica, I completed a poetic project titled *Dogs of a Never-ending Winter: The Animals We Took to Antarctica,* which takes a historical and archival approach to examining the impacts of colonialism and exploration in Antarctica on non-human beings, specifically, the domestic animals brought to the continent. These poems will be of interest to general readers, but more specifically, for the current context, they offer students an unusually accessible lens through which to consider the broader cultural, political, and climatic forces at work in Antarctica.

The roots of this project originated in Christchurch. Before leaving New Zealand for McMurdo, I visited the Canterbury Museum, which focuses on New Zealand's cultural and natural heritage. On the second floor of the museum lived an exhibit titled *Dogs in Antarctica,* a temporary exhibition which ran from 21 September 2018 to 28 April 2019, framed by this description: "Stories about Antarctica usually focus on the heroic humans who explored the continent, but none of their feats could have been accomplished without the work and sacrifice of the dogs that accompanied them."

Antarctica was first sighted in January 1820. During the Heroic Age of Antarctic Exploration (late 1800s–1917), ten countries launched a total of 17 major Antarctic expeditions, the majority of which were from the United Kingdom. Almost as soon as human beings began exploring the continent, they brought other animals with them, mainly beasts of burden—ponies, mules and dogs, a few cows, and even a cat (Mrs. Chippy of Ernest Shackleton's 1914–17 Imperial Trans-Antarctic Expedition). The colonisation of Antarctica was distinctly masculine; the history of dogs in Antarctica is really a story of men. The first woman to step foot on the continent—Caroline Mikkelsen, the wife of a Norwegian whaler—didn't do so until 1935. During the Heroic Age of Antarctic Exploration, none of the 17 expeditions included women. The prevailing attitude was that women could not handle the harsh conditions of the continent. Women didn't enter McMurdo Station until 1957. They were Ruth Kelley and Pat Heppinstall, airline stewardesses who were visiting the American base. The first women to overwinter at

DOI: 10.4324/9781003399988-11

McMurdo, Mary Alice McWhinnie and Mary Odile Cahoon, did so in 1974, only 44 years before my own arrival.

The family-friendly "Dogs in Antarctica" exhibit included stories and artefacts—journal entries, photos, film footage, and material objects, like harnesses, whips, and collars. I was struck by how the meticulousness and sentimental tone of the curation juxtaposed with an undercurrent of violence hinted at but left largely unaddressed. The exhibit framed the dogs as consenting heroes and fellow explorers. Yet, as I would discover in my years-long archival research journey that began that day in the museum, much of what humans did to the dogs brought to Antarctica was strange and disastrous—dogs shoved from airplanes by the U.S. Navy to test parachutes; whole dog teams and sledges disappearing into crevasses of ice hundreds of feet deep; dogs marching until their hearts gave out; dogs starving alongside humans; dogs tied to ship decks in years of wind and rain; dogs with dead penguins tied to their collars to discourage them from wiping out whole sections of rookeries; dogs watching from their chains as men abandoned bases, leaving them behind; puppies shot; dogs fed to other dogs; and dogs eaten by humans.

When I flew to McMurdo the day after my museum visit, my mind was swirling with questions of history, exploration, and why humans feel so compelled to exert their power over non-human beings and landscapes.

Since first discovering HAS in 2012 while in graduate school at the University of Alaska Fairbanks, I have been fascinated by the field and its possibilities when in relationship with poetry. HAS is an emerging, transdisciplinary field that considers interactions between humans and non-human animals and draws on various methodologies and disciplines, from history to animal law to anthropology. As Susan McHugh describes, HAS "researchers are united by a commitment not so much to common methods or politics as to the broader goal of bringing the intellectual histories and values of species under scrutiny."

Similar to queer studies' relationship to LGBTQIA+ rights, HAS is entwined with the cause of animal rights, and, by extension, broader ecological justice. Michael O'Shaughnessy posits this well in a summary of a study by Kenneth Shapiro,

> Historically, animals have been used as a foil for humans, presented less in terms of their own capabilities and traits than as beings deficient in some fundamentally human features. [...HAS] has endeavoured to change this by exploring the relationships between humans and (nonhuman) animals, and by challenging our construction, understanding, and treatment of them.

HAS takes critical aim at the problematic dualities of culture/nature and human/animal, which enable the construct of human exceptionalism. One of my project's primary goals is to question human exceptionalism and anthropocentrism embedded in acts and narratives of exploration, specifically in the Antarctic context.

During my time in Antarctica, I began what would become a years-long, and still ongoing, research immersion into the history and archives of Antarctic explorations, specifically focusing on the roles of domestic animals, mainly the dogs. After leaving Antarctica, I tried writing critical and creative essays about what I uncovered in this research but these mediums did not offer the emotional resonance and imaginative flexibility the project called for. Often when I am grappling with something particularly heavy or complex, I turn to poetry. When I wrote my first poem about the dog skeleton at Cape Evans (more on that soon) my project took a transformative and compelling turn. The poems, fuelled by hundreds of hours of research and notes, poured out of me.

The time frame covered in these poems ranges from the 19th century, when humans first landed in Antarctica, through the early 1990s, when all non-native species, *except* humans, were banned from the continent via the Protocol on Environmental Protection to the Antarctic Treaty (otherwise known as the Madrid Protocol). The Madrid Protocol was signed in 1991 and entered into force in 1998. Each poem in the project draws from and engages with a different account involving human and animal interactions in Antarctic history. In this essay, I will show how I employ poetry to story the relationships between humans and animals, as well as the complex networks of relationships between humans, animals, technology, and the Antarctic landscape.

The human drive for exploration is innate, and the consequences, both positive and negative, of exploration are manifold. One of the purposes of art is to question, chart, and chronicle these consequences. In *Dogs of a Never-ending Winter*, I attempt to frame the complexity of how we got from that initial sighting in 1820 to Antarctica as it stands now—an international continent, comprising 70 permanent research stations representing 29 countries, dedicated to scientific discovery. In the project's opening poem, "And in the act of naming, we became less afraid, we created," I am particularly interested in how the acts of naming and designation are used to construct meaning amidst the risks and violence inherent to conquest. The poem opens:

Origins. Points I chart on a map to meaning,
wayfinding. Trace back, unbraid the tangled
tongue, infinite threads, architecture of the Heroic
Age of Polar Exploration.

If I am disciplined, steady with the sextant reading
of star sight and angle, count the number of knots
that go over the stern, faithful in how I log
each nightmare, if I follow a lodestone, if I name
each landmark for king and country,

I will find my way back to you.

Through a speaker on his way to the Antarctic continent, I explore the motivations and discipline of a captain or navigator, while also framing the journey the reader of the poems is about to undertake. Here, the reader can see the captain's dedication to naming, charting, and keeping logs, as if these acts are talismans against what danger may lie ahead of their expedition. The idea that if we can control something, we can conquer it, is at the centre of colonisation. In the poem, I list possible external forces governing his quest, a catalogue of justifications of colonisation:

All of this navigation
in the name of (   )
              adventure
              knowledge
              glory
              man
              immortality.

I end the poem by returning to the question and power of naming (in this case, the roots of the names for Antarctica) and the true subject of the manuscript, the animals:

Antarctic, *antarktikos*, anti-arctic,
opposite to the north, unnorth, not north.
Originally called *terra australis incognita*,
as in, unknown southern land.

Each man had a name.
Each ship, expedition, and base.
                          Each dog.

In this opening poem, I frame the project with a set of questions: in the aftermath of masculine exploration, who is remembered? Who is left out? What is altered?

So far in this essay, I've described the dogs of Antarctica *generally*, but part of the transformative power of developing a posthumanist ethic derives from the radical care, questioning, and imagined futures that emerge when we give deep attention to the *individual* lives and agency of non-human beings. Four expedition bases built during the Heroic Age of Antarctic Exploration (late 1800s–1922) remain intact near McMurdo, around the Ross Sea region of Antarctica. Through the archival research I conducted in McMurdo, I learned there was a carcass of a dog near Cape Evans. This dog was left behind, still chained up with a leather collar around its neck, outside of Scott's Hut (the Terra Nova Hut) sometime during the Heroic Age. This particular dog, both anonymous and tangible, is often photographed, so its phases of mummification and decomposition are publicly chronicled.

While in Antarctica, I had the privilege of visiting these historic huts, which are currently maintained by the Antarctic Heritage Trust, a New Zealand nonprofit whose mission is to conserve, share, and encourage the spirit of exploration. Meeting this dog, or what remained of this dog, interacting with its materiality *and* the idea of it, was a catalyst for my project, described in the poem "Cape Evans Dog":

What is gone and what is still here—this is what I catalog.

Eyes? Gone. The sockets are deep
and void though not without
expression.

Tongue? Gone. I imagine a human hand, a man's hand, the last one
it might have nervously licked.

But the teeth—most of the teeth remain, fitting together
by design. The mouth, remnant of maw, softly closed.

The jaw? Intact. Shoulder blade and ribs, intracts. Vertebrae disconnected
halfway down what would have been the back.

I want to take one of those ribs for myself. Possession,
always a human undercurrent.

Even in the Antarctic environment, which serves somewhat as a freezer, the dog is decomposing, albeit slowly. There is less dog left now than in photographs of it from the 1950s and 1990s. My poetic impulse is to catalogue the pieces that remain, and, in their assemblage, imagine moments of this dog's life. For me, the couplet form, my favourite form and one that I use selectively, indicates a feeling of intimacy between the speaker and the subject.

In the context of this poem, the poet and the speaker are one. Yet, there is distance here; the speaker does not address the dog but *refers* to it. This stems from the cognitive dissonance of possession. I feel close to this being or thing, or the idea of what it was while alive, therefore

I want to claim or take a part of it. These sentiments, usually projected onto a landscape, are echoed in chronicles and justifications of conquest and exploration. The dog is the landscape, what was acted upon, and the viewer is the explorer, the actor. However, I would like to point out that the dog, like the landscape, is never without agency, though we may try to control, diminish, or dismiss that agency. I am changed by this dog; it acts upon me. I imagine and create from my encounter with its remains. This actual dog was an individual being brought to and abandoned in this landscape. It exists in this landscape today in an altered form.

In the conclusion of the poem, I wonder about this dog's history and return to the desire to name it in order to know it:

> He sleeps on bits of hay. A collar still around the bones
> of his neck. A chain still attached to the collar to keep him
> home, even after every man he knew is gone. Was he one of Shackleton's
> dogs? Did he get left behind? Shot? What was his name?
>
> His pelvis—so small,
> delicate architecture, curve
> of socket—seems
> to crawl away. There is so much
> we can never put back
> together, so many holes
> in all of these stories.

In the first stanza of the concluding section quoted above, the speaker is closer to the dog, now imagined as "he" instead of referred to as "it." The speaker cannot know the answers to the questions they raise ("Did he get left behind? Shot? What was his name?"), but there is empathy in simply bringing attention to the dog, what it is, and what it might have been. Yet, the dog resists the speaker, "seems to crawl away," as the poem evolves into a reflection on the fragmentary and selective nature of human history, and the intractability of *acting upon*. Despite my attention to this dog in retrospect, it died because of the humans that left it chained there.

What I encountered in the vast amount of archival material, including journals, photographs, and even film footage, about the animals we took to Antarctica is surreal. Along with human-animal relationships, these poems also consider animal-animal entanglements. In his diary, Henry Bowers describes a particularly strange and violent entanglement in March of 1911. Members of Robert Falcon Scott's Terra Nova Expedition and several ponies were camped on sea ice, which typically melts away in the austral summer, in McMurdo Sound. During the night, they woke to the sounds of the ice breaking up as chronicled in my poem "When the Ponies Met the Orcas." Italicised passages are from Edward Adrian Wilson's *Diary of the Terra Nova Expedition* and Henry Robertson Bowers' personal journal sent to his mother, the transcript of which can be found in the Scott Polar Research Institute. This is the first section of the poem:

> That morning, Wilson notices thread-like cracks
> in the sea ice *every 30 paces which could only mean*
> *they were caused by a swell.* Bowers,
> Cherry-Garrard, Crean and four ponies are miles behind, crossing
> the fracturing expanse. By nightfall,
> they've not made it. The three men and the ponies camp

on unstable ice, the unseen
sea swelling beneath them. Rhythm of a noxious lullaby.

Outside the tent, Bowers sees: *we were in the middle
of a floating pack of broken-up
ice* flushing toward the open ocean. *As far as the eye
could see* nothing solid, the whole
world wavering. Shouting for Cherry-Garrard
and Crean, he scrabbles. *Long black tongues
of water were everywhere.*

(Bowers doesn't know it yet but he will survive this
only to die
a year later next to Scott and Wilson
in a human-soiled tent. 11 miles from the One-Ton
Depot they could not reach.) Guts

the pony is already gone, *a black streak
of water* where he'd been standing. Bowers insists
they try to save the remaining ponies. *I never
for one moment considered
the abandonment of anything.* The men
and ponies jump from floe to rocking floe for hours.

Then, the orcas arrive, *snorting and blowing*,
churning the ice and the floes. Perhaps
already having consumed Guts. *The huge black
and yellow heads
with sickening pig eyes* watching them. The men finally see
the base of the Barrier but cannot cross a last, wide
gap of water. Using sledges as ladders, the men
climb on top of an iceberg to reach the edge of the Barrier.

They abandon the three remaining ponies, watch
as they drift on a floe toward the Ross Sea.

Bowers' and Wilson's accounts of this incident, the strange clash of ponies, sea ice, and orcas,
are nightmarish. Only one of the ponies on this particular trek across the sea ice survived. His
name was Nobby. In the poem, I pull the focus from the encounter between the orcas and ponies
to my own encounter with photos of Nobby:

In my research, over a century later, I find
a picture of Nobby right after.
Two of the men tilt his head
upward and back. A third man grips
the pony's lower jaw, pries open his mouth
to pour whiskey down his throat. To warm him, to erase
what could not be erased
from his animal mind.

In the final stanzas of the poem, I try to bring Nobby's terror to the surface and scrutinise the human responses to this tragedy. For example, this gesture of memorialisation that *hints* at culpability: "Later, in 2010, eleven of the airway navigation waypoints / on air route A338 between Christchurch and McMurdo Station / will be renamed for some of the dogs and the ponies, / including Nobby." The poem ends with a close reading of another image from that day, returning to the theme of intractability: "In the image, another man holds a fistful / of hay in his right hand. It hangs / limp at his side, as if he's finally seen the futility / of his offering."

Finding new narratives that resist human exceptionalism is at the heart of the poems in *Dogs of a Never-ending Winter.* But *kinship* also drives this project—the complex networks of relationships between humans, animals, and technology, what Barbara Herrnstein-Smith describes as "increasingly rich and operative appreciation of our [...] infinitely reconfigurable relations with other animals, including each other" (15–16). For example, my poem "The Cat and the Carpenter" illustrates the connections between the crew of Sir Ernest Henry Shackleton's Imperial Trans-Antarctic Expedition (1914–17) and the ship's cat, Mrs. Chippy, who travelled with them to Antarctica. In particular, I am drawn to the relationship between Mrs. Chippy, who was male, and the ship's carpenter and namesake, Henry "Chippy" McNish:

> The other men said Mrs. Chippy followed McNish
> around like a worried housewife. One night, the cat
> jumped out one of the cabin portholes straight into
> the sea. The officer on watch happened to hear his cries
>
> and turned the ship around. The expedition's biologist
> pulled Mrs. Chippy, very much alive, from the icy waters
> with one of his sample nets.

McNish, who Shackleton did not recommend for the Polar Medal because of an interpersonal falling out, died alone and destitute in Wellington Hospital in 1930. But, almost 30 years later, he was symbolically united with Mrs. Chippy: "In 2004, / the New Zealand Antarctic Society added a simple statue to McNish's grave—a life / size bronze sculpture of a tabby cat. / The object lies / as if in a warm square of summer sunlight."

In the reverberating effects of colonialism, memory and memorialisation become central to meaning-making, as demonstrated in the addition of the cat sculpture to McNish's grave. In the poem, "Each Mule Had a Man," I come back to a central question of the manuscript:

> Trained for sledge work at high altitudes in Landour, seven mules
> leave New Zealand on December 1, 1911. A gift
> from the Indian government to Captain Scott.
>
> Who deserves to be remembered?

The answer, in the context of this poem, is the mules themselves: Lal Khan, Khan Sahib, Pyaree, Gulab, Begum, Abdullah, and Ranee. Before the mules even departed for their journey, they were fashioned into mascots for Scott's Terra Nova Expedition:

> In the newspaper photos, the mules are beautiful—sleek,
> well-fed, muscular from the months of training Lieutenant G. Pulleyn
> of the Indian Supply and Transport Corps. Lined up
> in companionable little rows. Evidence of God-

willed British imperialism. Locked in time, in snapshot, they have no idea
what waits for them.

In "Each Mule Had a Man," I am also interested in the power of *details* in chronicling, how the
mules "came to the continent equipped with mule snow shoes, leg / wraps, shades to protect
their eyes from snow blindness, felt-lined / rug covers, and tethering chains." In my research,
I found photographs of these mules and the men they were paired with ("Each mule was given a
man / assigned to exercise him each day"). Relationships formed between them:

> In the images, the animals are alert, ears perked, heavy lashes
> over doe-eyes, manes ruffled by unseen wind, their coats thick
> and snow-dusted. The men
> wear funny hats, awkward mitts, and grip halters
> of animals that have nowhere to escape to. Abdullah looks to Hopper's
> pocket as if he knows there might be a sugar cube. Pyaree
> rests his head in the crook of Wright's arm. The Antarctic sea ice
> lays flat behind them, blurs the background to white.
>
> They fed them oats mixed with oil cake until the mules refused
> to eat what the men offered, as if in protest. Instead, they snacked
> on ropes, tobacco ash, hats, and leather straps—anything
> they were not supposed to.

The humour at the stubbornness of the mules hints at the suffering to come:

> Of course, they all died. No mule made it back.
>
> In the stalls at Scott's Hut, I find Khan Sahib's name—the mule
> who yawned so much the men joked that he had
> polar ennui, the mule it took five bullets to kill—so carefully
> stenciled into the wall across from his designated
> stall. I want to trace my fingers over the letters
> but I'm not supposed to touch anything
> for fear
> of what I might erase.

The ending of this poem ("for fear of what I might erase") illustrates my inner conflict at the
unavoidably anthropomorphic aspect of the project—a human writing poems about these animals, in some ways, attempting to "give voice" to them. It is challenging, paradoxical even, to
account for the actual experience of animals in Antarctica, due to the distance of space and time,
but also the inherent unknowability of the non-human beings we share the planet with; as Kari
Weil explains, "there is another consciousness there, a consciousness we desperately desire to
know through language, but that may remain impenetrable" (7). Acknowledging the risk of
anthropomorphisation, through poetic techniques and historical research, I believe it is possible,
and worthwhile, to at least imagine this space.

One approach to imagining animals is what Kenneth Shapiro refers to as "the animal turn with
the 'animal turn,'" which shifts from a too "exclusive focus on the social construction of other animals to attempts to get at 'animals as such,' animals as they actually experience the world, while

giving due weight to the degree that our social constructions actually inform that experience." One of my poems, "Taro to Jiro," focuses primarily on the harrowing experience of two dogs. The men are pushed to the periphery of the poem. In February 1958, the members of the Japanese research expedition at Showa Station, Antarctica had to make an emergency evacuation. They left fifteen sled dogs chained up outside with a week's supply of food, thinking the incoming expedition team would reach the dogs soon. But the incoming team's ship was trapped in the ice and was rescued by an American icebreaker. No one returned to Showa Station for 11 months. When they arrived in January 1959, they found two of the dogs, brothers Taro and Jiro, had survived.

In "Taro to Jiro," one dog speaks to another, his brother, after they've survived alone in Antarctica for nearly a year. Through questions and sensory details, I try to bring language to the suffering and confusion they might have experienced:

Brother, somehow, we got out

of those chains. Still, the tangled mess
of history. What did I know

in those days? What comprised
them? The unyielding smell

of rock. Hint of fish. Your feces
I chewed and rechewed. A howl

for the sake of sound. No one
answered us.

The couplet form of this poem mirrors the intimacy and isolation of the two black dogs alone against the white landscape. The poem ends with the return of the Japanese researchers but the perspective of the poem stays with the dogs. In these stanzas, the reader considers the men through the gaze of the dogs, who wonder at what the men may have wondered:

And then there was a day when we were not
alone. Brother, we heard the men

before we saw them. Your eyes startled
with recognition. We watched them

with patient caution from a hill
near the Station. Did we stand like wraiths

against the snow? Did the humans
think they were dreaming?

I tackle the question of anthropomorphising more directly in the manuscript's final poem, "A Dog Speaks." By the 1960s, with the introduction of snow machines, airplanes, and other motorised vehicles ("tin dogs"), the sled dogs were viewed as no longer necessary. Because of the Madrid Protocol, the last dogs were removed from Antarctica in February 1994. In "A Dog Speaks," I try to embody, through the perspective of one of the last dogs on the continent, the complexity of the end of this era, as well as the potential richness of the dogs' lives there. After all, most of these dogs were types of huskies, bred to haul, and thrive in harsh winter conditions. Certainly, suffering, kinship, and pleasure were enmeshed. Here is the poem in its entirety:

And if I had to do it again—
    night
       howl
          ice
all stretching, all extending—

yes, I would still be
what I was made to be.

I would still be beast, I would sing
from gangline, scoop snow
with my mouth as we run
beneath the star-spiraled sky. Slow,
sweet erosion of cartilage pads
in my hips.

If I had to, I'd still try not to
    tangle
    fall
    freeze.

I'd try not to disappoint.

Back to sledge-bound, back to the driving
white. Landscape-silence enveloping
our working bodies. He said *pull,* he said
    whoa
    haw
    gee.

Pleasure spotted my days, his hand
below my chin. He said *hike*, he said

my name. If I had to do it again, I could
smell blood on the ice. Eat the hunks
of seal meat from a freshly opened
body. Blubber and skin. Pemmican
and blocks of butter. Collared
in heavy leather, a box to sleep in,
some hay. Pace at the end

of my chain. This sliver moon
path worn in and reburied by snow
again and again, his voice

every bright or ink-dark morning.
We had a purpose, even if
it was their purpose.

In dreams years later, I run,
bark below my breath, twitch
at the memory
of all that weight
always behind me.

The binary of animals/technology in Antarctica, as well as the idea that dogs were suddenly and simply replaced by different transportation technologies, is inaccurate. These three forces—humans, non-human animals, and technology—are very much entangled, compromising what Donna Haraway refers to as "an interweaving triad." Dogs helped establish human habitation in Antarctica. As Francis Spufford describes in his introduction to *The Ends of the Earth: An Anthology of the Finest Writing on the Arctic and the Antarctic,* this "barbarous beginning is the foundation of the human sense we've made of the continent" (3). This barbarous beginning is also the foundation to the scientific advances and discoveries, including the discovery of the hole in the ozone, that enables the National Science Foundation to secure taxpayer funding in order to send artists and writers to Antarctica.

I was, and remain, conflicted about my own presence there in 2018. It is the only place on Earth without indigenous human inhabitants. We cannot survive the environment without extensive interventions. The research bases are small diesel cities. As Michael Lucibella explains,

Each season more than 450,000 gallons is either flown in by ski-equipped LC-130s or delivered by the South Pole Traverse, fleets of tractors that together haul it more than 1,000 miles from McMurdo Station to the South Pole. Once it arrives, the fuel operators, or "fuelies" as they're known, unload and distribute the station's lifeblood. […] Just about everything there runs on fuel in some way or another.

The Antarctic landscape is changing. Micro plastics are present in freshly fallen show. The ever-expanding Antarctic tourism-industrial complex continues to take a toll on the landscape's flora and fauna. Weather in Antarctica grows increasingly extreme. Greenhouse gasses continue to rise. Through the Antarctic Treaty System, the continent is currently owned by no nation, protected from mineral exploitation and conflict, and understood as a place dedicated to peace and science. But the Treaty becomes modifiable in 2048. As geopolitical tensions worsen, particularly between the United States, China, and Russia, will these nations honour the Treaty? As energy reserves and fishing resources dry up elsewhere, will nations turn to the Antarctic region?

What will happen to Antarctica?

HAS and poetry can help us make decisions to live differently and imagine different futures. Imagining different futures is a first, tentative step toward their realisation. My interest in the history of the dogs in Antarctica has always been tied to my investment in the future of the continent itself and all that comprises it. We look back to look forward; this is why educating students about this romanticised (and yet–or therefore–exploited) landmass is important.

A few months after I returned to the United States, I read a passage in *The Methow Naturalist*:

We have to conclude that the world isn't supposed to be like anything in particular. It is always changing. The evolution of species and ecosystems goes on constantly, blindly, always adapting to the interplay of other species changing the environment. Species and ecosystems are defined by a continuous process, not a fixed state.

Antarctica is the most dynamic environment I have ever encountered. Our continued human presence there is all but certain. The central question of our time remains: in what ways will we choose to be in relation?

Works Cited

Herrnstein-Smith, Barbara. "Animal Relatives, Difficult Relations." *differences: A Journal of Feminist Cultural Studies* 15, no. 1 (Spring 2004): 1–23. https://www.sas.upenn.edu/~cavitch/pdf-library/Smith_AnimalRelatives.pdf.

Lucibella, Michael. "Powering the South Pole." *The Antarctic Sun.* September 18, 2019. https://antarcticsun.usap.gov/`features/4405/

Shapiro, Ken. "Human-Animal Studies: Remembering the Past, Celebrating the Present, Troubling the Future." *Society and Animals* (2020): 1–37. https://pdfs.semanticscholar.org/8c7c/ddf2fccb07a15718c2958d-9d2e56e76f41fd.pdf?_ga=2.227767386.671181896.1666717059-907813318.1666717059.

Shapiro, Ken. "Series: 'Why Animal Studies?' with Ken Shapiro." *Animals in Society: Animal Studies Scholar Advocacy,* May 23, 2016. https://animalsinsocietygroup.wordpress.com/2016/05/23/series-why-animal-studies-with-ken-shapiro/.

Spufford, Francis. "Introduction." In *The Ends of the Earth: An Anthology of the Finest Writing on the Arctic and the Antarctic,* edited by Elizabeth Kolbert, 1–11. New York: Bloomsbury USA, 2007. *The Methow Naturalist.* 2019.

Weil, Kari. *Thinking Animals: Why Animal Studies Now?* New York: Columbia University Press, 2012.

Part III

Critical and Theoretical Perspectives

9 Imaging the Real in Times of Crisis

Empowerment and Ecosophy in Shaun Tan's *Tales from the Inner City*

Heidi Silje Moen

Introduction

I had seen it before, and even fed it, once.
Now I had mauled its unobtrusive world
Unmendably.

(Philip Larkin, "The Mower" [1979] 2003)

On the night of August 14, 2022, the beloved 1.300lb international celebrity walrus, Freya, was euthanised and removed from the highly frequented Oslo Fjord. The decision had been made in secret by the Norwegian Directorate of Fisheries due to the potential harm she could have caused to curious onlookers. Her secretive and swift execution and removal created national and international outrage. Members of the public were criticised for not heeding repeated warnings from wildlife experts and the police to stay away from endangered Freya; in encounters with humans, wild animals might get stressed and behave unpredictably. Yet, the press, wildlife enthusiasts, and sun-hungry members of the public kept insisting on their right to watch, bathe, photograph, film, and interact with the walrus. The shock and grief many experienced when learning about Freya's death could only be surpassed by the shameful realisation that it was our curiosity, fascination with, and desire to encounter and interact with a wild animal (in real life, on YouTube, through live feeds) that proved fatal for her.

According to the United Nations, "preserving nature is the essence of the Sustainable Development Goals (SDGs) and … indivisible from the rest of the United Nations' agenda" (The UN System Chief Executive Board of Coordination 2021). The decision to euthanise a walrus for the safety of curious onlookers tells us that the Norwegian Directorate of Fisheries deemed Freya's life less worth than the life of a human being. The fact that at the end of an ephemeral Norwegian bathing season, spectators and bathing tourists refused to sacrifice their recreational wants and curiosity for the sake of a walrus says something about how easily and unthinkingly humans may resort to anthropocentrism when the interests of wild animals conflict with human interests, no matter how banal.

As the quote at the beginning of the chapter illustrates, the case of Freya reflects a dynamic that has also been explored in poetry. In Philip Larkin's "The Mower," for instance, interaction with humans is described as dangerous. In the poem, the speaker has tried to befriend a hedgehog by giving it food before he accidentally "mauls" it with his mower – "It had hidden in the long grass" (Larkin 2003). The accidental murder of the hedgehog and the calculated execution of Freya suggest that unless we change our attitude to what constitutes a life worth preserving, wild animals like the walrus and the hedgehog – both species officially classified as vulnerable to extinction – are better off without us.[1] Hence, our moral responsibility would be to leave wild

DOI: 10.4324/9781003399988-13

animals' worlds be, whether, as in the case of the hedgehog, it is "unobtrusive," or, as in the case of Freya, it has gone viral. But in the poem the speaker also realises that he has not merely killed a hedgehog: he has taken a life. By describing the emotional impact and death of a wild animal in terms normally used on fellow human beings, the main realisation in "The Mower" may be that the death of a hedgehog represents the loss of a valuable life, as does the death of Freya – "Next morning I got up and [she] did not" (Larkin 2003) – and both casualties take place in spaces humans have appropriated as their own. In this chapter, I will focus on *Tales from the Inner City* (2018), a picture book by Australian-born artist Shaun Tan of Malaysian-Chinese and Anglo-Irish descent, to explore how readers and learners, including children, might use visual-verbal poetry to re-frame their relationship with nature in an urban context.

Tales from the Inner City consists of 25 individual prose poems, poems, and short stories in which the visual artwork "carr[ies] unique and independent narrative information," which means that the illustrations are integral to the picture book's total aesthetic expression (Stafford 2011, 28). The first part of this chapter examines how two of Tan's visual-verbal poems, "The Rhino was on the Freeway Again" and "We took the Orca from the Sea," and the visual artwork in the collection as a whole can help create epistemic self-doubt. Epistemic self-doubt is here understood as the ability to "adjust one's beliefs about the way things are" based on the acknowledgement that we are "fallible" (Roush 2017, para 1 and 4). As such, the collection can help readers unlearn their reflexive (as in habitual, unthinking) anthropocentrism and aid in developing a willingness to embrace *ecosophy* as beneficial to all life.

By making learners realise the extent and consequences of our interference with the non-human, Tan's poem "Once we were Strangers" poses a dilemma explored in Arne Næss' *Ecology, Community and Lifestyle* (1989), namely that "the flourishing of human life and cultures" may not be compatible with the flourishing of non-human life (29). The second part of this chapter uses Sofia Ahlberg's idea that instigating change in times of environmental crisis requires a pedagogy of empowerment which includes making learners resilient to and able to accept interpretive openness, dilemma, and self-doubt (*Teaching Literature in Times of Crisis*, 2021).[2] But creating a desire in individuals to make necessary changes in lifestyle on behalf of the other also requires the development of a holistic sense of connectedness, humility, and responsibility. The reading of "Once we were Strangers" connects the development of a "sympathetic imagination" (Nussbaum, *Cultivating Humanity* 1997, 85) and ICC to Næss' idea of *biospheric egalitarianism* through *Self-realisation*. Thus, through imaging and imagining our essential dependence on and interconnectedness with the non-human as intrinsic to the self and, by simultaneously enabling learners to read critically and empathetically, poetry can empower learners to take responsible action on behalf of the living earth.

Ecosophy as Ethical Obligation

Already in 2001, and as a response to the 1987 Brundtland Report *Our Common Future*, Stephen Sterling urged that creating a sustainable society requires a transformative change in epistemology and worldview (*Sustainable Education: Re-visioning Learning and Change* 2001, 13). Since 2001, the urgency to empower learners to deal with the climate crisis and instigate individual and collective action has frequently been reiterated in climate reports and research as well as in Sterling's own work.[3] One example of the former is the 2014 *UNESCO Roadmap on Education for Sustainable Development* (ESD):

> To create a world that is more just, peaceful and sustainable … require[s] a wholesale change in the way we think and the way we act – a rethink of how we relate to one another and how we interact with the ecosystems that support our lives. … [A]ll individuals and

societies must be equipped and empowered by knowledge, skills and values as well as be instilled with a heightened awareness to drive … [informed and responsible] change.

(8)

Two of Tan's poems that can instil awareness of human fallibility and as such "drive …change" in the way we think, act, relate to, and interact with ecosystems, are introduced with pictograms of an orca and a rhinoceros.

In Tan's prose poem, "We took the Orca from the Sea," humans place an orca in the sky for its "inspiring" beauty (147). Immediately after, the penetrating calls from its grieving mother make them realise what they have done: "From a cold and foreign sea, her subsonic wavelength penetrated all concrete, steel and urban clamour, reverberated through pipes and sewers, kept us awake all night and broke our hearts" (147). In the poem, Tan makes use of the collective "we" to indicate that the speaker expresses the perspective of the onlookers rather than that of one individual. Once the poem's speaker realises that they have separated a child from its mother, it is already too late: "We knew we had done something unforgivable … But so many years have passed, and the orca is still in the sky" (147). The poem is made even more upsetting, our actions even more unforgivable, by the fact that the reason for causing years and years of grief for mother and child was the onlookers' instant gratification, the novelty of the spectacle. On the diegetic level, the end of the poem offers no relief as the consequence of this inconsequential and ignorant act is permanent: "We just don't know how to get it down" (147).

Like in the real-life example of Freya who inconvenienced bathing tourists and boat-owners, the detrimental consequences for animals of humans' myopic dealings with the non-human based on a lack of informed decisions and concern are also addressed and criticised in the poem introduced by a stencilled rhinoceros and the line, "The rhino was on the freeway again." Already in the poem's second line, "Men came, shot it dead" (95). Based on the inconvenient delay the rhinoceros causes to traffic, the decision to shoot it to clear the way is instant but also prosaic, something which is also mimicked in the poem's efficient rhetoric; two four-line stanzas offer brief matter-of-fact statements. Yet even though the crowd is quick to rejoice in the death of the rhinoceros, "We blew our horns in gratitude" (95), in the poem's last (and second) stanza, the collective speaker repents belatedly:

But that [shooting the rhinoceros] was yesterday.
Today we all feel terrible.
How could we know it was the last one?

(95)

However, both poems' conclusions consist of double spreads with the respective animals drawn in gigantic proportions hovering over blurry backgrounds representing a cityscape bathed in artificial light and a crowded freeway, respectively. By centring on and foregrounding an individual orca, and an individual rhinoceros, the visual artwork, as opposed to the poems' hurried rhetoric, commemorates and individualises them as it keeps them indefinitely suspended on the page for the reader to contemplate. Whereas some species of rhinoceros are extinct, five still remain.[4] The orca is known to live in tightly knit family groups where the bond between mother and child is particularly strong, and their life span is usually between fifty to eighty years.[5] Combined, the poems' visual-verbal rhetorics clearly state what the reader's priorities should be: there is still time to make informed decisions and act accordingly. Importantly, and in the light of the real-life story of Freya, these tragic displays of myopic self-centredness in the form of instant gratification combined with human intellectual and moral deficiencies ("We just don't know how to"/"How could we know") also show the necessity of embracing *ecosophy* as ethical direction to effect a transformative change in epistemology and worldview necessary to protect all life.

Arne Næss' "Yay" to the Living Earth

To use books such as *Tales from the Inner City* to reframe one's relationship to the non-human, it is helpful to have a broader framework rooted in environmental ethics. Arne Næss' ontological *ecosophy*, also called deep ecology, is a radical branch of said ethics. Central to *ecosophy*, as with environmental ethics, is the ethical obligation for humans to reconsider human chauvinistic – or anthropocentric – perspectives. It is, however, important to note that when Næss argues for creating a sustainable future for "the richness and diversity of life forms," he is defining life in a "comprehensive, non-technical way to refer also to things biologists may classify as non-living: rivers (watersheds), landscapes, cultures, ecosystems, 'the living earth'" (*Ecology, Community and Lifestyle*, 29). Because Næss endorses the idea that "all [life forms] whatsoever [have] a similar right to live and flourish," his position has also been termed *biospheric egalitarianism* (Brennan and Lo 2022, Section 3.1, para 2).

The main idea underpinning *biospheric egalitarianism* is that the well-being, life, and rights of everything inhabiting the biosphere – non-human animals, plants, nature – should be considered as having equal importance. Thus, with *biosphere egalitarianism* comes the responsibility to contribute to the richness and diversity of all life forms which, according to Næss, requires a reduction of human interference with the non-human world and a large-scale change in lifestyle. Both the extent of human interference and lifestyle were termed "excessive" at the time of writing (1976 and 1989).[6]

David Rothenberg, translator and editor of *Ecology, Community and Lifestyle*, explains that Næss' *ecosophy* could, above all, be termed a series of "motivations" calling for individual as well as local and global responsibility and action on behalf of the living earth (8). To motivate a transition towards this new ontology, or to "make the link from ethical principles to decisions," Næss proposes a holistic reconceptualisation of humans' place in nature through *Self-realisation* (8). This term, Rothenberg admits, is "vague," and is more a "process, a way to live one's life" than a rigid definition; it is a "direction" which one, in Næss' words, "can say *yes* to ethically" (9). One way of understanding the term is to "expand oneself to include other people and species" (9). That is, instead of conceptualising "our species and the Earth" as separated by an "abyss," *Self-realisation* "connect[s] the individual to the principles of interconnectedness in Nature" (8). Or, as Brennan and Lo put it, "'Self-realization' is … the realization of a wider ecological Self" (Brennan and Lo, Section 3.1, para. 4). The motivation to embrace this ethical direction can be found in "the deep satisfaction that we receive from identification with nature and close partnership with other forms of life in nature [which, according to Næss,] contributes significantly to our life quality" (Næss in Brennan and Lo, Section 3.1, para. 4). Thus, the concept of *Self-realisation* connects life quality to the concept of *interconnectedness*, the idea that "[t]he identity of a living thing is essentially constituted by its relations to other things in the world" (Brennan and Lo, 3.1, para. 3). Consequently, if our well-being were both dependent on and inseparable from the life quality and well-being of "the living earth," *Self-realisation* would make it impossible for humans to achieve satisfaction in isolation. As Rothenberg writes,

> If this ontology is fully understood, it will no longer be possible for us to injure nature wantonly, as this would injure an integral part of ourselves. From this ontological beginning, ethics and practical action are to fall into place.
>
> (*Ecology, Community and Lifestyle*, 2)

In other words, if our physical and mental well-being were dependent on the physical and mental well-being of orcas and rhinoceroses, which Tan's poems in fact suggest that they are, embracing *ecosophy* as ethical direction would be beneficial and empowering for all.

Imaging the Real in Times of Crisis: Biospheric Egalitarianism in *The Inner City*

In *Tales from the Inner City*, both the non-human and human have been forced to adapt to rapid change as cityscapes have displaced the natural environment; deer and crocodiles occupy skyscraper apartments and floors, "the eighty-seventh floor," to be precise (1),[7] eagles hunt in airport terminals, and the mighty tiger appearing on the book's back endpapers uses black and orange caution lines as camouflage (and warning). As we have seen in the tragic destinies of Freya and Tan's orca and rhinoceros, positing the relation between human and the non-human as egalitarian and through *ecosophic* lenses is essential for the preservation of biodiversity. *Tales from the Inner City* images and imagines this potentiality as possibility.

In the volume, Tan argues for the centrality and primacy of non-human experiences and perspectives by offering readers ways of "stepping back from a rather narrow anthropocentric mindset, trapped as [they are] in contemporary human concerns and self-obsession" (Shaun Tan, "*Tales from the Inner City*," Shauntan.net). Both the collection's visual-verbal poems and prose stories as well as its peritextual elements offer the reader humbling perspectives on the human animal's so-called moral superiority and the fallacious nature of epistemic certainties concerning our significance and place within different ecosystems.

Already the double spread introducing the book's table of contents contributes to dethroning the human animal's self-appointed centrality in the narratives. On these pages, all stories except one are introduced by animals or insects drawn in stylised silhouettes reminiscent of stencil street art. Non-human animals, insects – and one outnumbered member of the human species – appear similar in size but in random order. By visually deconstructing established species hierarchies and instead positing the non-human and human in random numerical order, the book's peritextual elements contribute to making a statement about the book's relational and egalitarian approach to biological diversity. It is also worth noting how Tan signals the importance and ever-presence of insects, animals, and nature in the collection, and in our lives, by visually foregrounding them on the collection's front and back covers, and on the title pages (there are two) and endpapers.

Tan's stories and illustrations are often imaginatively surrealistic, yet realistic when it comes to the scenarios dramatised, which in the poems of the rhinoceros and the orca would be humans prioritising their own convenience, desires, and wants over the non-human. However, through the use of rhetorical devices such as size, perspective, colour, contrast, and positioning, the visual art in these poems also creates counter discourses to these verbal narratives. Sometimes centred, sometimes occupying the space on the right-hand page so as not to disappear in the book's middle fold, throughout the collection, Tan always makes sure the reader's gaze is drawn to the non-human through its placement on the page and use of contrast. If humans are present in the visual artwork at all, they often appear as shadowy near-monochrome silhouettes with indistinguishable faces – in some cases, they are even drawn with their backs to the reader. Positioned behind or beneath strongly outlined animal representations, humans are more often than not portrayed as unremarkable and unidentifiable members of a crowd in contrast to unnaturally large and vividly coloured animals hovering over or in front of humans who in comparison are dwarfed in size and significance. In the prose story introduced by a stencilled pictogram of a cat celebrating and illustrating the disproportionate significance of cats in our lives, for instance, humans are represented as small miniatures positioned atop a gigantic cat's head in a dark tumultuous sea where the image visualises cats' ability to convey and support humans through emotional tempests.

In "The Monster of our Nightmares," on the other hand, disproportionate size, perspective, style, and colour are used to condemn our reflexive anthropocentrism and create doubt concerning our moral capacity to tend to the living earth through reversing the trope of the carnivorous animal as monstrous. In the prose story, a shark is hunted down and killed for its monstrosity. However, on the concluding double spread, the representation of the suffering shark directly confronts the reader. Drawn in gigantic proportions, the shark is suspended on hooks above a crowd, its jaws wide open in pain. The blurry spectators facing the shark with their backs to the reader are dotted with red. The impressionistic red dots may represent the flags of the victorious shark-hunters *and* the hacked-up pieces of shark babies described in the prose narrative. Both readings confirm the crowd's – and reader's – fall from grace reflected in "the fishermen's" refusal to look them in the eye: "The Fishermen didn't look at any of us, not once, just kept cutting, even after they turned off the floodlights" (57). Depicting the result of the shark hunt as a hellish carnage in dark colours reminiscent of Hieronymus Bosch's scenes of hell in "The Last Judgment," Tan turns the trope of the open shark jaw as monstrous (popularised in *Jaws*, the 1975 movie and franchise) into a representation of abject suffering, simultaneously reconceptualising acts commonly termed "commercial" or "recreational" ("shark hunting," "fishing") into a scenario of torture with "sights and smells" foul enough to invert the stomachs of the shadowy spectators (56–59).

Size, perspective, positioning, and contrasting use of colours contribute to drawing the reader's gaze to representations of animals and nature. Consequently, even though, with one exception (the mystifyingly narrated "I am fox! I go wherever I go!"), the collection's speakers and narrators are always human, the rhetoric of Tan's drawings more often than not decentres the importance of human perspectives and concerns. In addition, by reconceptualising and reversing the trope of the carnivorous animal as a threat to human survival, Tan creates doubt concerning our moral propensity to dominate the non-human. Through challenging the primacy and supremacy of human experience, knowledge, and morality both visually and verbally, the collection poignantly suggests that the human animal's place in nature should (at best) be relational.

However, by foregrounding the abject suffering of a mother and child irrevocably separated, of a shark and its shark babies being massacred en masse, and the shooting of the last rhinoceros as utterly unnecessary and, as such, cause for shame and regret, the ultimate realisation these visual-verbal poems and prose narratives offer the reader in light of Næss' *ecosophy* is the acknowledgement that we are all connected; in these examples, the connection is made through the discomfort experienced by humans (the collective "we" in the poems as well as the reader). By dramatising Næss' proposition that "our well-being is both dependent on and inseparable from the life quality and well-being of 'the living earth'," these narratives require us to extend our moral responsibilities and obligations to include the non-human, since what we do to life, we do to the self.

Yet another effect of foregrounding the tragic consequences of humanity's reflexive anthropocentric actions brought on by empathetic and epistemic deficiencies is to offer the realisation that bio-egalitarianism is as yet only a poignant "simulation" in the Baudrillardian sense, a "generation by models of a real without origin or reality," models which, one should add, could become reality (*Simulacra and Simulation* 1995, 1). Consequently, the collection cries for action.

Living with Climate Crisis: Poetry, Empowerment and Ecosophy

A number of UNESCO sustainability reports on education argue that halting the loss of biodiversity requires collective as well as individual action.[8] This, according to Sofia Ahlberg (2021), requires a pedagogy of empowerment as well as a reconceptualisation of the term "crisis." If one envisions crisis in the Greek sense, as krinō (a transliteration of κρίνω), "which has meanings including decision, discernment and judgment" (Ahlberg 1), it is not conceptualised as a "diagnosis with only a fatal outcome," "synonymous with disaster or calamity ... even referring to a situation that is beyond control," but rather as "a decisive stage where change must occur" (ibid. 1). The latter sense invites action and personal accountability rather than despair. Ahlberg uses *Alice in Wonderland* and the coming-of-age story as examples of narratives with characters that need to, and do, manage to successfully overcome adversity by being able to adapt to rapid change. As such, as Meaghan Morris in Bruner writes, "once we have a simulacrum, 'the true (like the real) begins to be reproduced in the image of the pseudo, which begins to become the true' (*Culture on Tour: Ethnographies on Travel* 1988, 5)" (145). Or, put differently, like *ecosophic* principles, literary models (representations), can be emulated and guide by example.

Still according to Ahlberg, in times of crisis, a pedagogy of empowerment must enable learners to become resilient as they contemplate "dilemmas and paradoxes" (5). Learners must be aided in developing the ability to both navigate and "accept doubt and uncertainty" because, she writes, the problems of and solutions to the climate crisis are simply too complex for consensus – "the conformity of consensus [and blind acceptance of received 'truths'] may even constrain learning and change" (Reinertsen in Ahlberg, 5). Most importantly, however, since "[t]he possibility of social transformation lies in the relation with and responsibility towards others" (4), learners must be able to connect because "[w]ithout the power to connect ... we won't have the power to rebuild a fractured community" (8). Nor, should we add, can we rebuild fractured ecosystems.

Visual-verbal poetry cannot in itself halt the loss of biodiversity, but it can help learners connect through developing what Martha Nussbaum terms a "sympathetic imagination" (*Cultivating Humanity* 1997, 85). Such an imagination is necessary "to comprehend the motives and choices of people different from ourselves, seeing them not as forbiddingly alien and other, but as sharing many problems and possibilities with us" (85). And, according to Nussbaum in Carlsen, the arts play a vital role in cultivating the powers to develop such an imagination because "when we read, we enter into a 'third space' in which we try to make sense of the narrative, make an effort to understand the values and attitudes communicated, and reflect on our own standpoint in the process" (Christian Carlsen, "Reading Literature" 2020, 210). Including the development of attitudes such as openness and willingness to understand that which is other, respect, tolerance, and flexibility; skills such as the ability to listen to, observe, analyse, relate to; and, importantly, the ability to empathise with that which in not self (Dypedahl and Bøhn, "Intercultural Competence and Culture" 2020, 85), Nussbaum's "sympathetic imagination" finds correspondences and elaborations in the attitudes and skills constituting ICC.[9]

Through cultivating readers' "sympathetic imagination" and ICC, poetry can help learners take on the perspectives of, understand, empathise with, and, ultimately, connect to that which initially seemed different from the self. As such, it can remind us of the *Self-realisation* that our identity and physical and mental well-being are constituted by and inevitably connected to the physical and mental well-being of the other (whether that other is human or non-human). Finally, due to the interpretive openness of the medium, critical encounters with textual and visual dilemmas and paradoxes in hermeneutically ambiguous works can not only help learners develop resilience to doubt, dilemma, and paradox, it may also, as we have already seen in Tan's work, help learners realise that epistemic self-doubt may in fact be a prerequisite for change.

Self-Realisation and Self-Doubt in Tan's "Once We Were Strangers"

One poem that explores a particularly recognisable sense of *Self-realisation* through dramatising "the deep satisfaction that we receive from identification with nature and close partnership with other forms of life in nature" (Brennan and Lo, Section 3.1, para. 4), is the poem introduced with the stylised pictogram of a dog, "Once we were Strangers." At the same time, through questioning the possibility for animals to exert agency in post-industrialised society, it also shows how

> social, political and economic structures, originally created to promote human interests [which via *ecosophic* extension would also include the interests of the natural environment and its non-human contents] and with genuinely good intentions, can … end up being very dehumanizing and counterproductive.
>
> (Tan, "Cicada," Shauntan.net)

Hence, by addressing the centrality of non-humans as aids in alleviating alienation and spiritual, existential, and emotional disconnectedness and, at the same time, suggesting the catastrophic consequences choices made on behalf of the human species may have for the non-human, it makes the dilemma it poses in the context of *biospheric egalitarianism* even more paradoxical. Due to the narrative techniques utilised (his animals never really speak) and the nature of visual artworks (visual artwork conveys meaning non-verbally), it also offers interpretive uncertainty, an uncertainty which, in this poem, reminds the reader that in matters of the environment, even though not immediately accessible, there will always be more than one perspective to take into consideration.

"Once we were Strangers" unfolds through centuries and across continents. In the first double spread human and dog meet eyes across a black gulf representing the emotional void of the time "before," when they were strangers: "every tooth and claw and stick a weapon" (13). But, "one day" the beginning of an interspecies friendship transcending time, place, and death is initiated by the throwing of a stick (16). Following the initiation of this friendship, in the second double spread, human and dog are centred on a savannah, dog first, human after. The golden warm colours enveloping them clearly indicate the mutually beneficial warmth generated between dog and human, a togetherness strong enough to ward off existential dread even:

> Together we chased away all loneliness and fear
> And saw everything happen that was ever going to happen,
> Every beauty and terror, rise and fall.
>
> (20)

However, as needs happen, the dog dies. The enormous emotional impact of this death spans eight successive wordless double spreads.

In the double spreads illustrating separation, human and dog are drawn in landscapes that are not identified, yet still recognisable as Asian rice fields, African savannah, a railway line in a war-torn field, an aqueduct in a landscape reminiscent of South-East Europe. The colour palettes used evoke the seasons as well as night and death, suggesting the passing of time. In each double spread, human and dog are positioned on separate sides of a diagonally drawn railway line, a field, a road, or a waterway. The dog in the lower right corner and the human to the upper left on the verso page are looking away from each other into a black void diagonally framing each illustration. Yet even though location and colour palette change, and even though the dog is represented by different breeds and the human appears in different attires, genders, and ethnicities, in each double spread, dog and human are drawn in the same style and position, so that even though separate, they still appear "side by side" (16). If the reader flips quickly through the pages (as one would do with flip books), they will also see that in all drawings the width of the field, road, or waterway is constant, the distance between human and dog is the same. Consequently, the variation in depiction combined with the constancy in positioning and the continuity of the verbal narrative suggest that we are to understand the relation between human and dog as universal and unbroken. The visual narrative of unbroken connectedness across time, space, death, and species is confirmed in the following lines:

> And when I died
> you waited for me by the shore
> So it was that time passed between us.
>
> (21)

The use of "us" in the last line suggests that both human and dog are connected in waiting with the same aim: to be "together again" (39). The fact that, as opposed to other animal-human representations in the collection, in this poem, both human and dog are depicted as equal in size, makes the argument in favour of mutual connectedness even stronger.

In the three illustrations concluding the poem, the dog and human are again shown to seek eye contact before they meet in a heartfelt embrace after centuries of waiting close but apart. On the last two double spreads, human and dog are, like in the second double spread, centred. Together on a road which no longer symbolises emotional and physical separation, the dog is again leading the way, its tail up high. Visually, the body language of the dog and human suggests that they are both rejoicing in the companionship of a long-sought friend. This is also confirmed verbally:

> You … push your nose into the back of my knee,
> and cry out to me as you always do,
> *The world is ours!*
>
> (Italics in the original, 47)

All these visual and verbal elements seem to confirm the narrative humans have created about their relationship to dogs, of a mutual *interconnectedness* strong enough to close the "abyss" separating species (Næss, 8).

Ecosophic Pedagogy: Student Empowerment and Responsibility

As a teacher, I introduced "Once we were Strangers" to the tertiary classroom due to its philosophical, imaginative, and emotional ways of celebrating a seemingly egalitarian human-animal relation. I wanted students to see how, aided by the universal appeal of the visual artwork, the poem could remind readers in a very recognisable form of the *Self-realisation* that the human self is incomplete without its "wider ecological Self" (Brennan and Lo, Section 3.1, para. 4), or, in other words, their essential connection to, and dependence on, the non-human for their well-being emotionally, physically, and existentially.

To empower and enable the students to read the poem critically while at the same time opening up for *ecosophic* readings and reflections, I first introduced concepts and ideas central to Næss' ethics with a particular focus on *Self-realisation* and *biospheric egalitarianism*, and we also discussed the consequences, not only for the non-human, but also for us as moral human beings, of seeing human – non-human relations through anthropocentric lenses on the one hand, and through the lenses of *biospheric egalitarianism* on the other. My second step was to adapt the pedagogic approach suggested by Sylvia Pantaleo on how to develop "personal, appreciative and critical interpretations" of visual artwork ("Exploring Grade 7 Students' Responses to Shaun Tan's *The Red Tree*," 67). Pantaleo's approach includes giving students a metalanguage for reading visual artwork. Hence, in addition to reminding them of how to close read poetry, I encouraged the class to respond to Tan's use of colour, perspective, point of view, size, and how the different elements in the artworks are positioned in relation to each other (Where are the human and dog positioned in relation to each other, are they interacting, where are they looking, where are they positioned in relation to their surroundings?). I also asked them to consider the location of the double spreads in the poem as a whole, and the relation between the visual and verbal aspects in the poem within the framework of the ethics of *ecosophy*.

After having close read the poem critically, the students reported that at the same time as they recognised themselves, their emotional link to, and relationship with, dogs (live, dead, or imagined) in the poem, they were also left with conflicting emotions brought out by textual and visual clues. One student who had noticed slight differences between the first and last double spread celebrating the interspecies friendship between human and dog, perceptively asked, "Why is the dog on a leash in the concluding but not the first double-spread? What has happened to their relationship?" Another student asked, "Isn't the poem written from the perspective of the human? How, then, can we know what the dog thinks and wants?"

The dogs in the poem are certainly portrayed as loyal companions who want to be with us. But in order to know for certain what dogs think and want, it is essential to understand how and what they communicate. The advantage of anthropomorphic representations would be that, albeit imaginative, readers are left with confirmation, a certainty regarding what animals are communicating to us. But, as Tan writes on his website,

> Importantly, my animals never really speak, and their natures remain inscrutable. They are beings that move in and out of each story as if trying to tell us something about our own successes and failures as a species, the meaning of our imagination and our true place in the world, albeit unclearly.
>
> ("Tales from the Inner City," Shauntan.net)

What the students noticed was that even though Tan does offer a stunning and emotionally recognisable dramatisation of the interconnectedness between human and non-human animal through the impossibility for both human and dog of achieving satisfaction in isolation, in the poem there is also the issue of narrative perspective (who speaks) and the leash. When it comes to narrative perspective, there is verbal confirmation of mutuality in the use of "we," but at the same time the students held that, logically, the speaker must be the human. This alerted them as they were unable to get access to the dog's wants, needs, and thoughts. It is also important to notice that if we accept that the speaker must be human, even though the use of "we" (as well as other visual-verbal aspects explored above) signals a mutual, inclusive, and egalitarian approach to difference, it is also possible to find indications of an asymmetric relationship between human and dog. When they first meet, it is the human that throws the stick whereas the dog fetches, "One day I threw a stick at you./You brought it back" (16); when they are together, the speaker runs first, the dog follows, "When I ran, you ran" (20). There is also a verbal focus on the dog, not the speaker, as loyal companion: "when I [the speaker] died," "you [the dog] waited for me by the shore" (21). This focus is further emphasised in the poem's visual rhetoric. The fact that on the eight double spreads illustrating waiting, different versions of the dog are consistently positioned in the lower right-hand corner (the human to the upper right on the verso page) means that when the reader turns the pages, the gaze will immediately be drawn to the dog. In addition, dogs and humans are looking in opposite directions. This means that whereas the dogs are turned towards us, the differently portrayed humans, backs bent, are facing away from the dogs, but also the reader. Consequently, visually as well as verbally, it is the dog's patient loyalty that attracts the main attention.

The students also found the last double spread to conflict with the idea of human-animal egalitarianism since, even though the dog leads, and even though there is no sign of discomfort in the dog (the tail is up), it is, undeniably, on a leash. In addition, in the last double spreads, bricks and concrete have replaced the fields and open spaces in the previous double spreads. This significant change is also signalled in the poem's penultimate stanza:

> But now everything is different,
> the river flows wrongly,
> the plains are gone ...
>
> (43)

The last illustrations, human and dog excepted, are completely devoid of anything resembling nature or animal life. And even though, proportionally, both human and dog are depicted as equal in size, they are both smaller in comparison to their surroundings than the other illustrated animals in the collection: instead of hovering over the landscape, human and dog seem dwarfed by it. Completely enclosed in and by bricks and concrete, the dog appears entirely dependent on aid for sustenance, and it is, as noticed by the students, kept on a leash.

The poem's ending suggests that a possible outcome of replacing nature with "civilization" (houses, skyscrapers, cars, freeways) is to turn a seemingly voluntary and egalitarian human-animal relationship into one of dependence. As such, the leash can be read as a symbol of lost animal agency and mutuality. Consequently, the bent backs of the shadowy human figures could not only signify sorrow but also regret. The end of the poem thus offers a grim view of the possibility of mutual coexistence in the catastrophe humans have brought on entire ecosystems. Paradoxically, but not unsurprisingly, the poem also upsets what we thought we knew about ourselves as humans in relation to those which we love, and, even more importantly, those who improve our lives by loving us back. And, if this is what we offer those that we love, what about those we do not?

Even though anecdotal, the questions posed by the students suggest that learning and understanding how to read poetry and visual artwork aesthetically and critically can in itself feel empowering for learners. Their engagement with the poem through *ecosophic* lenses also suggests how in encounters with poetic and visual representations of non-human animals, learners are usually quick to invest emotionally (with the dog in particular) and connect the fictional to the real. Thus, approaching poetry and visual arts aesthetically, critically, and empathetically can not only help train readers to contemplate dilemmas and paradoxes in the safe space of literary encounters but also help identify real-life examples and consequences.

Drawing attention to the importance of interpretive dissensus alerted the students to a central dilemma in *ecosophic* ethics that the threat of ecocatastrophe forces us to deal with holistically: How to coexist without causing damage to the emotional, mental, and physical needs and well-being of another? As such it creates the self-doubt necessary to find (new) solutions to this question. Consequently, the poem may not only enable readers to connect with the non-human as fellow beings equal in worth and value, by envisioning the non-human not as separate from, but as part of the self, the poem also urges us to extend our moral responsibilities and obligations to encompass the emotional, physical, and mental well-being of all life forms when finding sustainable solutions to the climate crisis.

Conclusion

"With uncertainty comes a greater need for care," Ahlberg writes (5). The fact that Tan gives primacy to non-human experience at the same time as he refrains from anthropomorphising creates ample room for interpretative openness and epistemic self-doubt. As such, he invites the reader to take on a humble perspective on the significance of the human-animal within eco-logical systems and on what we think we know. This is why interpretive openness, self-doubt, modesty, and humility are essential prerequisites for change.

Of equal importance is individual responsibility. In poems that offer strong critiques of human myopic ways of being-in-the world, Tan is thematising how time and again our falla-cious and often irrational priorities have proven disastrous for the other. One way in which such poems may empower is through making learners realise how much power they have in their relation to the non-human and, as seen in the tragic decision to euthanise Freya, how with power comes responsibility.

Embracing a "new ontology which posits humanity as inseparable from nature" (Rothenberg in Næss 1989, 2), requires that one unlearns received human chauvinistic perspectives and hierarchical patterns of thinking and speaking about the other, but it also requires the abil-ity to sympathetically imagine and empathise with other perspectives, ways of being, sensing, and knowing. Through refusing to let that which may seem unobtrusive and inconspicuous – whether hedgehog or dog-leash – pass in silence, poetry can help give primacy to the experi-ences, perspectives, and the plight of that which is not human and, if necessary, it can also help us commemorate the non-human as kin. Another consequence of displaying hedgehogs, orcas, rhinoceroses, sharks, and dogs as the central aesthetic subject is to individualise them and, as such, make the reader able to identify and empathise with wordless yet expressive non-human representations.

Through imaging and imagining perspectives, needs and ways of being-in-the-world that are not only different from, but that may in fact directly conflict with human perspectives, wants, and needs, Tan makes the reader acutely aware of the impossibility of finding emotional, mental, and physical satisfaction in isolation. Consequently, Tan's *Tales from the Inner City* can be seen as a work of *ecosophic* literature that strives to create a desire in individuals to act, to forego short-term pleasures, and adjust individual needs and comforts for the sake of the emotional, physical, and mental well-being of the extended self, which in *ecosophy* simply means life.

Notes

1 According to the IUCN Red List of Threatened Species, some, not all, hedgehog species have been assessed for the red list of threatened species. The walrus was assessed for the red list in 2016.
2 Ahlberg addresses "crisis" in plural. Climate change, systemic racism and the global pandemic are used as examples of crises affecting students' ability and motivation to learn as well as their emotional wellbeing.
3 See Stephen Sterling's "Concern, Conception, and Consequence: Re-thinking the Paradigm of Higher Education in Dangerous Times," *Frontiers in Sustainability* 2, 2021: 1–13.
4 "About Rhinos," International Rhino Foundation, Rhinos.org.
5 "Orca," National Geographic, Nationalgeographic.com.
6 In the preface, David Rothenberg explains that *Ecology, Community and Lifestyle* (1986) should be considered a revised and rewritten "new work" based on Arne Næss' 1976 publication Økologi, Samfunn og Livsstil. "Excesses" in lifestyle choices that have detrimental effects on biodiversity and must be reined in (referred to in the English edition on p. 29 and outlined in the Norwegian edition on pp. 11–20) include population growth, economic growth, the exponential increase in manufactured products and consumer demands (i.e., the global spread of consumer ideology and praxis).
7 "Crocodiles Live on the Eighty-Seventh Floor," *Tales from the Inner City*, 2018, p. 1.
8 See especially *UNESCO Roadmap for Implementing the Global Action Programme on Education for Sustainable Development*, UNESCO Report, 2014; *Issues and Trends in Education for Sustain-able Development*, Alexander Leicht, Julia Heiss, and Won Jung Byun (eds.), UNESCO, 2018; and *Getting Every School Climate-Ready: How Countries are Integrating Climate Changes in Education*, UNESCO Report, 2021.

9   These attitudes and skills are also essential in the promotion of "collaborative competency" which in *Issues and Trends in Education for Sustainable Development* is defined as "being in the service of participatory problem solving, including the ability to learn from others and to understand and respect their needs, perspectives, and actions" (In Ahlberg, 2021, 5).

Works Cited

Ahlberg, Sofia. *Teaching Literature in Times of Crisis*. London and New York: Routledge Taylor & Francis Group, 2021.

Baudrillard, Jean. *Simulacra and Simulation*. Trans. Sheila Glaser. Michigan: University of Michigan Press, 1995.

Brennan, Andrew, and Lo, Yeuk Sze. "Environmental Ethics." In *Stanford Encyclopedia of Philosophy.* Edward N. Zalta (ed.). Summer 2022 Edition. Accessed June 20, 2022. https://plato.stanford.edu/archives/sum2020/entries/ethics-environmental/

Bruner, Edward M. *Culture on Tour: Ethnographies on Travel*. Chicago: University of Chicago Press, 2004.

Carlsen, Christian. "Reading Literature." In *Teaching and Learning English* (2nd ed.). Christian Carlsen, Magne Dypedahl, and Sarah Hoem Iversen (eds.). Oslo: Cappelen Damm Akademisk, 2020, 209–225.

Dypedahl, Magne, and Bøhn, Henrik. "Intercultural Competence and Culture." In *Teaching and Learning English* (2nd ed.). Christian Carlsen, Magne Dypedahl, and Sarah Hoem Iversen (eds.). Oslo: Cappelen Damm Akademisk, 2020, 81–97.

International Rhino Foundation. "About Rhinos." Rhinos.org., n.d. Accessed July 12, 2022. https://rhinos.org/our-work/the-crisis/.

The IUCN Red List of Threatened Species. "Hedgehog" and "Walrus." Version 2022-1. Accessed September 26, 2022. https://www.iucnredlist.org/.

Larkin, Philip. "The Mower." In *Collected Poems*. Anthony Twaite (ed.). London: Faber & Faber, 2003, 162.

Næss, Arne. *Ecology, Community and Lifestyle: Outline of an Ecosophy*. Trans. & ed. David Rothenberg. Cambridge: Cambridge University Press, 1989.

National Geographic. "Orca." Nationalgeographic.com., n.d. Accessed June 12, 2022. https://www.nationalgeographic.com/animals/mammals/facts/orca/.

Nussbaum, Martha Cynthia. *Cultivating Humanity: A Classical Defense of Reform in Liberal Education*. Cambridge, MA: Harvard University Press, 1997.

Pantaleo, Sylvia. "Exploring Grade 7 Students' Responses to Shaun Tan's *The Red Tree*." *Children's Literature in Education* 43 (2012): 51–71.

Roush, Sherrilyn. "Epistemic Self-Doubt." In *The Stanford Encyclopedia of Philosophy*. Edward N. Zalta (ed.). Winter 2017 Edition. Accessed June 3, 2022. https://plato.stanford.edu/archives/win2017/entries/epistemic-self-doubt/.

Stafford, Tim. *Teaching Visual Literacy in the Primary Classroom: Comic Books, Film, Television and Picture Narratives*. London and New York: Taylor & Francis Group, 2011.

Sterling, Stephen. *Sustainable Education: Re-visioning Learning and Change*. Totnes: Green Books for the Schumacher Society, 2001.

Tan, Shaun. *Tales from the Inner City*. Sydney, Melbourne, Auckland, London: Allen & Unwin, 2018.

——. "Cikada." Shauntan, n.d. Accessed November 11, 2021. https://www.shauntan.net/cicada-book.

——. "Tales from the Inner City." Shauntan, n.d. Accessed November 11, 2021. https://www.shauntan.net/tales-from-inner-city-2.

UNESCO. *UNESCO Roadmap for Implementing the Global Action Programme on Education for Sustainable Development*. UNESCO Report, 2014.

The UN System Chief Executive Board of Coordination. "Biodiversity." May 2021. Accessed September 28, 2022. https://unsceb.org/topics/biodiversity.

10 Vegetal Relationality

Three Australian [Eco]poets

Anne Buchanan Stuart

> I believe that the tree sustained me, for almost from the first day the tree and I entered into a relationship of looking.[1]
>
> —Amanda Lohrey

Can poetry help readers, teachers, and students think in new ways about climate change? In this chapter, I engage with the transformative potential of what I call vegetal poetry to further an open-ended "dialogue" with matter, resisting "the arrogance of certainty"[2] to "bring forth" and create in poiesis, an argument that non-human life is not passive nor unable to convey meaningful expression.[3] The Australian poems "The Municipal Gum" by Oodgeroo Noonuccal, "The Red Gum" and "Winter Trees" by Martin Harrison, and "The Cycads" by Judith Wright (1915–2000) challenge common assumptions that posit trees and plants as passive natural resources. These poems are informed by a biocentric perspective of ecological interrelatedness which, as Fisher-Wirth acknowledges, expresses the agency and integrity within and of the other-than-human world (xxiv & xxviii).[4]

Andrew McMurry has posited four types of ecosocial literary texts: ecophobic, ecophatic, ecoliterate, and ecophilic.[5] The ecophobic text is disinterested in the non-human world and the ecophatic text draws on the non-human to metaphorize human self-understanding. On the other hand, ecoliterate and ecophilic texts register and reflect on the interplay of the human and non-human and speak with/toward the non-human. In my readings of work by Noonuccal, Harrison, and Wright, I will show that in such ecoliterate/ecophilic texts, there is a language/translation which moves toward/[in]to decentering the human, which, as McMurray notes, counters the "ideological dispositions embedded in the [current] ecosocial [dis]order." [6] The poems reveal several things. First, they suggest that through a fixed position, anthropocentrism locks humans into a certain worldview and a privileged role in existence. Second, they consider how poetry can break and disrupt this thinking, thereby encouraging reflection and even bringing the not-yet-seen into appearance. Finally, they show how a different style of thinking toward/ [in]to can reveal how the human is constituted by and symbiotically related to things such as trees and other plants. To teach these texts is thus to invite students into a community that reaches beyond the human species.

All three poets bring distinctive perspectives to bear. The poetry of Oodgeroo, of the Noonuccal tribe of Minjerribah on North Stradbroke Island, reveals the unbroken connection between First Nations people and Country. For Oodgeroo (which means paperbark), trees are part of Indigenous kinship networks, where shared kinship with humans and plants is genealogical. For Australian Aboriginal cultures, Matthew Hall writes, Dreaming beings who walked the earth and created the local landscapes are ancestral to all components of the natural world.[7]

DOI: 10.4324/9781003399988-14

The work of poet Martin Harrison reflects his thinking as a philosopher and keen observer of natural phenomena, particularly the locales in which he lived. Judith Wright also reflects deeply on the human relationship to the natural world, and as Katie Holmes acknowledges, her poetry conveys "a sense of the land, frequently giving expression to the deepest, often unacknowledged concerns not only of Australian society but of the planet as a whole." [8] As non-indigenous poets both Harrison and Wright express an acute interest in Country and Indigenous Australia. Read together, these three extraordinary poets have helped shape thinking about the human relation to the natural environment and Australian society and are well situated to reach a wider global readership, particularly in climate-conscious classroom settings.

Australia offers a compelling backdrop for vegetal poetry because its flora and fauna have been so visibly affected by climate change. The devastating Australian firestorms of 2019–2020 completely outstripped projections for early 21st-century climate scenarios. In New South Wales alone, it is estimated that more than 70 per cent of endangered plants, animals, and habitats in the state are currently threatened due to the fires and their aftermath and that the bushfires left 62 per cent of the state's vegetation communities under threat.[9] During 2022 unprecedented floods, the result of record ocean temperatures surrounding Australia greatly exceeded historical records, inundating entire eastern coastal towns and swathes of inland food-producing farmland. In such times, as Dipesh Chakrabarty incisively observes, we are all "reduce[d] ... to our creaturely lives."[10] Collectively, now more than ever, humans shape the terrestrial landscape and its ecology. There is no longer a "natural" background against which humans can differentiate themselves – and this new, more integrated worldview must be incorporated into our cultural institutions, including our educational practices.

Climate change is often referred to as a "super" wicked problem, in that it resists attempts to understand it through a single disciplinary perspective. That said, poetry as a genre can embrace the "wickedness" or many-sidedness of climate change because poetry is such a flexible medium. Poetry reading can help students and teachers think toward/[in]to the environment by suggesting that material forces and the non-human have agencies of their own. Rather than reading poems that tackle the broad problem of climate change, in this chapter, I examine work that stages local encounters with the vegetal world, showing that through the generative force of the poetic idiom, it is possible for humans to imagine a greater sense of kinship with all life forms.

Rather than a text's linguistic core revealing the primacy of human agents through human-centric construction, these poems recast language as a thinking [in]to other relations. Pushing back against reductionist, instrumental, and anthropocentric approaches, I interrogate the thinking behind our encounters with the vegetal world arguing that non-human life is, following Opperman, neither passive nor unable to convey meaningful expression.[11] I suggest that the potential of each of the poems lies in their capacity to creatively instantiate ecological relation, taking imagination to the edge of human perception so that it enters into a becoming with that of which we are a part.[12]

The Figure of the Tree in Oodgeroo Noonuccal's "Municipal Gum"

Oodgeroo Noonuccal's "The Municipal Gum" resists instrumental readings of nature that see "others" (such as trees) only as objects for human use or as metaphors for human experiences. An instrumentalized object, such as a tree in a poem, could be seen as a symbol of something else, abstracted, detached from its referential context, detached from its intra-relation, its co-constitutionality. Isolated, it becomes the product of our imposed, subjective meaning. This way of thinking has consequences for the non-human-other. Do we see trees and plants in their bewildering diversity as raw material to serve our purposes, or do we treat them as autonomous agents with purposes of their own and worthy of respect? By contrast, Noonuccal invites readers to see a tree differently (not the object for our subject); it becomes inseparable from its context, inseparable from the common ground we share with it, and holds its own proper meaning. For the tree to appear, we need to step back from daily habits into another attitude, to co-respond as openly as possible to what might come into presence. Ultimately, poetry is not reducible to content and information. Poietic understanding culminates in less signification and more of an entangled semantic structure: leading to an analogous configuration of nature/life itself. In and through the poem, we open ourselves to ourselves and our relation to the world, in a way that is not instrumental. Instead of judging whether a poem could be instrumental in delivering an argument about the challenge of climate change, can a poem demand a reading which requires an engagement, even a degree of critical distance with which to exercise a certain amount of critical thought, toward understanding that humans are not surrounded by passive matter but are embedded in a web of relationships with planetary deep history and vegetal time?

To experience the thing-tree on its own vegetal terms requires an enormous transformation in our sensibility and perception. In an attempt to break [in]to this thinking, the poem "Municipal Gum"[13] offers a way to move [in]to both worlds: the world of the shared community tree and the familial tree itself. In his essay "All the Trees," Peter Minter thinks about the "figure of the tree … and how trees in Aboriginal poetry and poetics resist certain kinds of western figurings of the tree."[14] Unlike western thinking, where the tree is an exemplar of an object, Minter writes that "tree stories" and "family trees" are part of a rich genealogy of trees in the work of Aboriginal poets such as Noonuccal.

In "Municipal Gum," the gumtree in the city street, bitumen around its feet, strapped and buckled in hopelessness, is for the poet a "fellow citizen." It is not an abstracted symbol of Aboriginal subjugation, "a thing wronged." As Minter points out "Noonuccal also tropes trees as haunting specters of recently lost and alienated connections to family and culture."[15] The loss of trees for Indigenous people becomes an existential crisis, a loss of connection to Country and kin.

Before the voice of reason, there is the voice of pathos. In our earliest experiences, we recognize our relation to the being of things, where our eyes are moved by pathos, the sympathetic relation to the world. The everyday has not escaped the eye of the poet. In addressing the tree with pronouns, you, your, and us, the tree is infolded, and brought forth into its singular agentic presence gathered into an intimate, familiar community of co-responding familial relations. Whether verbal, gestural, or internal thought, the discourse with/address to the tree is how the other (of the tree) and the poet in the Aboriginal tradition, are "essential, complex, embedded, and immanent, a relation."[16] The tree and the poet are related. The poet is moved to actively listen to the presence of the tree, taking thought from her exposure to the tree as a way to ask: why has this happened that together, in the world, they are (both) so [dis]placed.

The municipal gumtree is lost to its natural fellowship, listless, dispossessed, misplaced, bereft of its primal elementality in a "cool world of leafy forest halls/And wild bird calls." The poet weeps through intense pathos for the hell of the tree, the "thing wronged" dolorous in relation to the tree, letting its vegetal figure emerge into its "sentient, percipient, responsive, autonomous"[17] agentic presence amid the bitumen cityscape, asking lamentably: what have they done to us? The pronoun "us" is key here, because it implies that we are one with the tree, on a familial level. We share roots that make us one, reorienting our autonomous objectivity toward inter-subjectivity.

Minter hopes that Australian onto-poetics can move beyond the "colonial matrix of power"[18] to nourish the sovereignty of Aboriginal thought and being. Indigenous peoples have inhabited the biosphere in Australia, for over 50,000 years,[19] but their insights have been at best, marginalized. From a western perspective, Minter argues that the object of the tree by virtue of its conceptual privilege has become distant and detached, alienated from its common ground.[20] When trees are familial relations, a symbol of a life, the seeing, and the relation become one, as "The Municipal Gum" suggests. To learn from Aboriginal thought is not necessarily to appropriate Aboriginal culture; rather, as Noonuccal implies, it is to enter into a more respectful relationship with all beings beyond the self.

Poietic Thinking Toward/[in]to Vegetal Relationality

Plant life constitutes 90 per cent of all living matter. Plants have supported humans with medicinal remedies, food, and shelter throughout history but are seldom granted the ontological and ethical status of animals. Animals are sometimes afforded rights and forms of selfhood. Plants, on the other hand, are often posited as non-beings, beyond the reach of ethical consideration. They sadly miss out on important forms of human attention, resulting in an impoverished appreciation for their mysterious intricacies, their ontological status, and their ethical situation.[21] According to a rapidly-expanding body of research, John Charles Ryan concludes vegetal life "exhibits a multitude of behaviors congruous with intelligence."[22] What are these "others" telling us by way of their relationship with climate change? Do we have the eyes to actively see, ears to keenly listen, and minds to calmly wait? Can poets and readers cultivate an open and receptive manner, entering into an interplay of relations where the potential for reflection becomes not just performative but authentic? Like "The Municipal Gum," the other poems considered in this chapter question whether we must remain oblivious to our relation and phenomenological experience with the vegetal. Plants, as Ryan suggests, can literally be understood as "growing, suffering, competing, and aspiring." [23] Ryan cites research that concludes that plants learn by association, act spontaneously, recognize the self, decide among options, correct errors in judgment, communicate with kin through chemical vocabularies, and remember past interactions with animals.[24] While biology will continue to explore these insights scientifically, poetry can help readers experience vegetal agency and power on a more visceral level.

Given that trees are wood-makers, trees are, in a sense poietic, they bring forth and inscribe in their wood, chronologies of the past, stories of place, and genealogies. When they burn, they return carbon to the soil, enlivening and nourishing future generations: human and non-human. Michael Marder and Patricia Vieira argue that the vegetal (as such) will elude us as long as our human-sense perception is mediated exclusively by scientific knowledge and by cultural histories of human-vegetal interaction informed by exploitive practices. [25] Nevertheless, they conclude that we should not relinquish attempts to relate and even learn from vegetal modes of existence. To this end, the task of the poet is to imaginatively break the strictures of human thought and language, wresting the palpable forces of our inter-dependence from the un-imaginable into the imaginable, and enabling moments of ontopoetic intra-genera recognition.

The Perception of a Tree in Martin Harrison's "The Red Gum"

The hallmark of Australian poet-philosopher Martin Harrison is his power to evoke and enliven each agentic element in his work, his poetic thickness. Poetic thickness, according to Rafe McGregor, is to experience a work of poetry such that neither form nor content can be isolated without loss of work identity, a demand which is satisfied by the work itself rather than being a property of the text. [26] This is exemplar in "The Red Gum." [27] The reader is witness to the poet watching a red gumtree through a window. The tree is thrashed by dry westerly winds against a clear blue-water day, framed against Sydney Harbour. The elements of wind, light, and red corporeal blood: "blood-red new leaves" as the "… reds of the red tree" are set against human mundanities like "thinking of the washing," where the tree itself finally "burns its way into the mind/under thought and reference." The value of the poem lies in the agentic nature of the gumtree as it is observed, singularized, and scribed [in]to ink. Even as the poem unfolds, the tree continues "making words impossible." The consequence for us is to experience the tree as "a premonition you can't tease out," a relationship framed by language that goes *beyond* language.

Such encounters are not wholly outside of western intellectual history, although their importance has often been minimized in favor of instrumental thinking. Martin Heidegger, for example, once found himself looking at a tree and began to ruminate on how

> …the tree stands before us. The tree faces us. The tree and we meet one another, as the tree stands there and we stand face to face with it. As we are in this *relation* (emphasis added) of one to the other and before the other, the tree and we are.[28]

Likewise in Harrison's poem, the speaker cultivates his perceptual capacities, his response-abilities to the tree, while questioning how these responses are constituted. Did the tree first present its "cochineal stain" to the eye of the poet or was it the sound of the "shake [of] the branches/into horse-heads neighing and rearing into shoals of silver."? This occasions a question of meaning in the poetic encounter: "what becomes of the face-to-face, the meeting, the seeing, the forming of the idea, in which the tree presents itself and [the poet] comes to stand face-to-face with the tree?"[29] Inspired by Heidegger, a reader might say that the tree *trees,* inserting itself into the (peripheral) vision of the all too distracted poet. As our limitations are revealed, we also come to see our potential for more intersubjective relationships with vegetal life.

"The Red Gum" is made compelling by the concatenation of nature's elemental events: "October's first dry wind, blowing across the Harbour,"; memory, "back of mind" where a "Spring wind blasts…/[crackling] the leaves like a fire that's burning up too fast, too dry," culminating in the eerie event of the tree "looming at the window" like the "ghost's rattling" in its "own forest of sun-lit fire." The sensation is of apprehension, a vertiginous tension, and thinkable foreboding. Something strange has arrived, something eerie, uncanny. Something which is the subject of a life, the red gumtree in its corporeality, is in play with shifting ecological forces – now in the presence of the present. The poem compels the tree and its surroundings to become part of it. And yet, the gumtree is neither silent nor passive: its agency has brought forth an organic poem.

The poem, like the tree, is not simply a representation but, as Timothy Morton puts it, a "non-human agent."[30] It is as though we are caught within the mind chatter of the poet, as the imminence of the tree presses against the window, intersecting with the mind of the speaker-poet. As Angus Fletcher proposes: the poem should share a coextension in our lives.[31] The red gumtree has been brought into a dialectically permanent open relationship with the poet, sharing the same intrusion into space, coexisting with the poet through the window, enjoining a back-and-forth attentive response, in thinking toward/[in]to, through acute imagination. The tree and the poet (through attention) are always becoming, slowly. Through the window, the tree changes imperceptibly, as does the poet in relation to both tree and window. As an act, to "attend" has many meanings, but its etymology (Latin) ad +tendere: means to reach or stretch toward something. To attend to is to direct the mind to the whole conception of the thing one is attending to. To attend is to reach out through the senses toward something, to be open and available to seeing, and in doing so generate answers which, however, may change over time and location. The tree stimulates and contributes to the process of poetization, lingering with corporeal residue in a poietic bringing-forth. The tree's becoming is bound with the attentive imaginative material of the poet, thereby becoming coextensive with the (different) responses of the reader.

In his critical writing, Harrison has argued that a poem or other creative piece needs to fulfill "some order of ecological requirement, to [be] operative in its structure as a formal work and experientially operative within its aesthetic range (response, feeling, affect, and judgment)." Equally, to respond to climate change, he claims that "we must listen to what is other-than-human and how it is speaking to us, and that the act of attention between self and the environment is intertwined and interdependent and completely mutual."[32] In setting out his proposals for environmental writing, Harrison calls for the work to "carry a truth value, be observational and expressive." Additionally, he insists that it shows "an understanding of interconnectedness with natural and biological systems…forming and defining new structures [and finally] that the work… does not predispose us to think that we [humans] are only those who speak." Furthermore, Harrison writes that

[i]n the current moment it is clear that we must listen to what is other than human and how it is speaking to us and that the act of attention between self and the environment is intertwined and interdependent and completely mutual. [33]

"The Red Gum" begins with the simple line, "A camera could catch it." The poet is drawn to movement, drawn like a lens to light and a lens to detail. The detached opening, belies his relationship with the tree, as a way to perhaps distance himself from the event. It is though no words could capture what he wanted to say, only a camera might, or a video. However, "A painter can't." We are left with mechanisms for the eye. Harrison alludes to Maurice Merleau Ponty, who, in deconstructing his earlier conception of the subject-object structure observes that "…the look envelops, palpates, espouses visible things. It is though our looking were in a relation of pre-established harmony with them, as though it knew them before knowing them." [34] Brian Reed considers that during 1997, Harrison's phenomenological approach was on the cusp of what we might now call ecological or ecopoetic. Reed says that Harrison's approach to place was a way an individual perceives, as something created through the act of perception, a way that shapes and transforms the perceiver.[35] Stuart Cooke, fascinated by Harrison's work, notes the immediacy "within the moment of perception" that the poet "in a self-reflexive sense" was keenly aware of the moment in time and space, a thinking through language that gently probes and contemplates.[36]

The tree catches the eye of the poet, at the edge of his awareness. The tree moves into his presencing orbit, transforming the poet. Harrison discloses no prior serious pre-re-cognition of the tree until this point, revealing the ambiguity of its presencing, the now present presencing of this tree which was in some way [un]concealed from the poet's knowing. To be sure, the tree does not move (in our sense of moving): it is static, so we think. "I'm stuck with this red tree," ("and, then, again the tree,") the poet laments, as he would rather like to "make coffee, think of the washing …[or] an hour at the pool." These lines are emblematic of the notion of ecopoetry as a way of thinking intersubjectively rather than anthropocentrically. The tree, rendered through the poet's linguistic images and cadences, has lodged itself in the mind of the poet. The tree disrupts the poet's pedestrian thinking, calling him to reflect and make plain what has always been before him: the tree as a being-in-itself. This articulation releases the tree into its full agentic power, its uncanny embodiment in place: its locus. The poet has thought [in]to the relation with the red gum, transforming the way he sees the tree, as "For all the time, this storm-tossed red gum/burns its way into the mind .../taking over everything around it." The gumtree has decentered the human in its contiguity, it is now animated, no longer faceless, and can be apprehended and noticed as an agental being.

The red gum too has been altered by human observation, as it now takes over everything in the visible (and thinking) field of the poet: "whether neighboring roofs/or the gulls battling to the Heads,/with rain-storms of flowers hanging out, dryly, for heat and bees." The dialectic relationship between the poet and the tree gathers thinking toward all beings we share with the world, who are subjects of a life. The poet observes himself observing the tree and this sharpened focus changes him. As a result, he finds that "Just for a second, ... static under cloudless light, golden as a haystack," the tree has momentarily paused its material life-world of energy, light, and blood-red color.

I want to briefly return to the lines "its tentacle flowers" and "rain-storms of flowers, hanging out, drily, for heat and bees." These lines are significant even though the poet mentions the red gum's staggeringly beautiful flowers and their relation to bees just once. The most remarkable thing about the red gum is its capacity to bring forth "outstanding ... masses of conspicuous flowers of red or vermillion-orange."[37] Has the poet missed the natural fecundity of the tree in its growing and blossoming, its vigorous drive to reproduce, in relation with the bees, the wind and the heat? The poet's macrocosm comes up against the tree's microcosm. We are all distracted with thoughts of washing, lunch, and "maybe an hour at the pool" – yet this poet is deeply mindful that "All the while, the red tree flickers and threshes..."

The conclusion of the poem suggests that the event of the tree has interrupted the poet's way of thinking. The fluidity of both the subject (poet) and thing (tree) is such that the expressive articulation of the liveliness of the tree enacts both its entelechy (for itself) and its otherness (to us) in an iterative circular (non-linear) movement. The tree, in "its own forest of sun-lit fire, taking over everything around it" fully enacts its "golden" presence. The tree's unremitting "images will never be finished, never held..." For the poet, the generative but initially tangential engagement with the red gumtree is now part of his (self-) awareness and his (self-) perception, fusing sensual/perceptual experience with semantic/denotational understanding to generate poiesis. At the same time, the "poem [itself] in a corporeal-semiotic sense–functions as "the thing itself.""[38] The text intervenes in reality with its own vibrant materiality that is central to its capacity to perform (read/interpret/feel/question) in changeable ways. Poem, poet, and red gumtree thus all shape and co-create their shared world. These moments in the poem reflect Harrison's criteria for an ecoliterate text as the non-human environment does not just frame the human narrative but is fully implicated in relation.

In another Harrison poem, "Winter Trees," [39] the poet draws attention to our unquestioned familiarity ("So how oblivious do you/have to be") with the inconspicuous backdrop of a tree in the glare of the afternoon. Harrison is again captivated by the relation between trees and the mind. The winter trees in their otherness shift our thinking toward the "outlined hills," through the "rippling walls of time." Here the trees of the mind's eye wrap their net into relation; they are described as

... masks over glimmer
which is creamy stucco glare
from afternoon's warm stone [.]
The trees then create "a net" in the poet's mind,
so that it can, clear-eyed, shepherd
rippling walls of time
down laden valleys, on outlined hills.

One way to meet plants in their own time, to make them conspicuous and clear to us, is to let them be and recognize this letting be, in its undeniable relation to our temporal existence. As we shape the trees and their environment, the trees also shape, or "net" us.

The Question of Deep Time in Judith Wright's "The Cycads"

Judith Wright's poem, "The Cycads" echoes Harrison's "rippling strings of time" as she imagines the storylines of these ancient seed plants. During the Jurassic period, Cycads were so common that it is sometimes called The Age of Cycads.[40] Cycads have come down from the remote past with little change. If we were transported back a hundred million years, we would recognize this "living fossil" as numerous and widely distributed, yet only a single family and about a hundred species now survive, confined to tropical and subtropical regions. [41] Cycads are restricted to certain warm regions, with two of the nine genera living only in Australia. Charles Chamberlain observes that their "great antiquity"[42] serves as a reminder of their vulnerability to sudden changes in the climate because they seem prone to adapt very slowly. The long-term impact of scorching fire on the few remaining species of cycads remains to be seen.

In reading Wright's poem, it is important to note her sensitivity to the concept of deep time. "The Cycads" is as much a poem about deep time as it is about a newfound relation to a coexisting vegetal life form. I will thus begin by reading Wright's poem as engagement with plant time as it enfolds Aboriginal temporalities along with time consciousness, before turning to a discussion of vegetal relationality.[43]

Wright sees time as both productive and problematic. Her sympathetic approach to botanical conservation depicts Australian plants through her response to the temporal. The problem with time for Wright is that it is not linear or sequential. Time weaves around and comes to be understood as part of the being of the land and its rhythms. This poem offers a "complex relation of past and present to present and future readers."[44] Harrison insightfully reads the operations of time in Wright's poetry via Octavio Paz, wherein Paz writes that poetry can be "pure time" and a "heartbeat of presence in the moment of its appearance/disappearance."[45]

Wright begins the poem with a lyrical description of the cycad: "Their smooth dark flames flicker at time's own root." Wright illuminates time: time evinced, fire evinced, and earth evinced. Here is the elemental genesis, here an "integrative conception of time" [46] as it weaves:

> Round them the rising forests of the years
> alter the climates of forgotten earth
> and silt with leaves the strata of first birth.

From the interrelatedness of plant to climate, the progress of geological epochs as layers of silt cover eons of time where "Only the antique cycads sullenly/keep the old bargain life has long since broken;" that of a surly acceptance of temporality "cursed by age" as

> they watch the shrunken moon, but never die,
> for time forgets the promise he once made
> and change forgets that they are left alone.

Without imposing a human translation of vegetal temporality, Wright accedes to the linguistic otherness to time. Time for "brilliant birds/that cry in air one moment, and are gone" is not the time of cycads as "they seem a generation carved in stone." Wright is saying that animal life is fugacious, compared to the deep time of forgotten climates, where cycads once thrived. Yet today the cycads are in peril; they

> ... cling on the last ledge
> over the unthinkable, unfathomed edge
> beyond which man remembers only sleep.

Eerily prescient, the unthinkable edge of the emergence of humans from the primordial and our emergence into a new epoch, the Anthropocene, is irrelevant to the brilliant bird and the antique cycad. Embedded in this line is the vivid insight that there are two conceptual timelines: the world as a cultural/humanocentric construction and the cosmic planet, or primordial earth-time. By "earth" Wright does not mean the planet as seen from space, "but its very superficial pellicle, the shallow layer of earth in which we live, ... transformed into a habitable milieu by the aeons-long labor of evolution" [47] and the cultural constructs of "world" which layer our thought like "silt with leaves." Wright's poetic aim is to move our fossilized thinking toward thinking which opens up [in]to. "The Cycads," both the poem and the species, are not to be seen as or in a simple fixed state, but rather as vibrant and dynamic: that which as Kleinberg-Levin observes, draws together, engages all perception, all-seeing, and all-hearing.[48]

Wright does not just stop at forgotten time, momentary presence, and broken bargains; she asks us to: "Take their cold seed and set it in the mind,/and its slow root will lengthen deep and deep." This is a call to the imagination: to "quicken" through relational embeddedness. Wright calls for a thinking to poetically extend vegetal thought [in]to us, to irrupt another type of being into our being. Irrupt is derived from the Latin *irrumpere*, which means to break into, the word erupt is derived from the Latin *erumpere* means to break out. Yet the word that encompasses both irrupt and erupt is *physis*: beings as dynamic, nature as growth and outgrowth, emerging-appearing, and as bringing-forth in relation.

The implications in the Greek word *physis* can be a way to think about reducing our domineering relationship with the vegetal other and to recuperate the relational. Wright uses her poetic activity in the highest sense, as *physis*: bringing forth as a striving toward emergence. Like "The Municipal Gum" and "The Red Gum," "The Cycads" brings into focus (through its irruptive expression) vegetal matter understood on its terms, illuminating the possibility of co-existence, or even co-creation, with the vegetal. This is the thinking "over the unthinkable, unfathomed edge" which we need to come to terms with, to survive along with the "temporal otherness of vegetality ... to imagine plants across vast biopaleontological scales ... through a myriad of events that corporeally trace the rhythms of our co-constituted lives..."[49]

Conclusion

The world of our senses is not unchanging. In the work of all three poets, we see changes in their everyday looking and thinking about trees and other plants. We witness changes to their modes of perception which shape their intimate relation with vegetal materiality. The changing pattern of the poets' perceptual experiences nudges us into reading ecocentrically rather than anthropocentrically and discloses the interplay of the human and non-human.

The becoming of the thing-tree is not dependent on the poet or the reader, but both are bound to the tree in ecological space and planetary time. Poems can change how readers – and students in particular – understand themselves: not as dominating subjects, but as part of an interrelated and ever-changing web. As Eugen Wassiliwizky has argued, poetry represents an ancient cross-cultural, and emotionally powerful force within the human expressive repertoire.

[50] As students learn to read poems, they can learn to read trees, and to understand the vegetal world as important.

The essence of our relationship with the world is the need to take response-ability toward/[in] to the endangered, toward/[in]to an ecological relation to the world. Michael Marder writes that we can only experience relationality from within, that is, by inhabiting a relation, by dwelling in that relation in its energetic fullness.[51] If we briefly think about the etymology of the word "relation," it means to: "bring back, bear back" from re- "back, again" "borne, carried."[52] Hence, in the act of relation one is borne back in thought, borne back to the dis-remembered relation with the earth, its elements, its great time, fragility and our co-constitutionality. The desire to be open to relation is what separates the ecophilic/ecoliterate text from the ecophobic/ecophatic.

The poems in this chapter strive for an engagement with the vegetal, illustrating that plants can have agency. Noonuccal, Harrison, and Wright use poetry to move towards other-than-human relations that do not privilege human time, space, and perception as unique. Because poems are experiential and might be seen as agents in themselves, they offer readers, and students in particular, ways to imagine cross-ontological alliances with the non-human. As we come to understand our existence on earth as relational, we can learn to feel a kinship with all our non-human relations.

Acknowledgments

I am grateful to Stuart Cooke and Angela Sorby for their valuable comments on earlier drafts of this chapter.

Notes

1 Amanda Lohrey, *The Labyrinth, A Pastoral* (Melbourne: Text Publishing, 2020), 52.
2 Stuart Cooke, "The Ecological Poetics of Deborah Bird Rose: Analysis and Application," Association for the Study of Literature, Environment & Culture, Australia – New Zealand, ASLEC-ANZ, *Swamphen* 7 (2020): 1–17.
3 Serpil Opperman, "How the Natural World Communicates, Insights from Material Ecocriticism," in *Routledge Handbook of Ecocriticism and Environmental Education,* ed. Scott Slovicz, Swarnalatha Rangarajan and Vidya Sarveswaran (London and New York: Routledge, 2019), 109.
4 Ann Fisher-Wirth and Laura-Gray Street, eds., *The Ecopoetry Anthology* (Texas: Trinity University Press, 2013), xxiv and xxviii.
5 Andrew McMurry, "Ecocriticism and Discourse," in *The Routledge Handbook of Ecocriticism and Environmental Education,* ed. Scott Slovic, Swarnalatha Rangarajan, and Vidya Sarveswaran (London and New York: Routledge, 2019), 18.
6 Andrew McMurry, "Ecocriticism and Discourse," 16–18.
7 Matthew Hall, "Talk among the Trees; Animist Plant Ontologies and Ethics," in *The Handbook of Contemporary Animism,* ed. Graham Harvey (London and New York: Routledge, 2014), 388.
8 Katie Holmes, "Gardening at the 'Edge'": Judith Wright's "Desert Garden, Mongarlowe, New South Wales." *Australian Humanities Review, Eco-humanities Corner* 36 (July 2005): n.p. <http://www.lib.latrobe.edu.au/AHR/archive/Issue-July-2005/08Holmes.html>
9 *Australia, New South Wales, State of the Environment Report* (New South Wales: Environment Protection Agency, 2021). Accessed 01 February 2022. <https://www.soe.epa.nsw.gov.au/>
10 Dipesh Chakrabarty, *The Climate of History in a Planetary Age* (Chicago: University of Chicago Press, 2021), 198.
11 Opperman, "How the Natural World Communicates," 109.
12 Donna Haraway, *When Species Meet* (Minneapolis: University of Minnesota Press, 2008), 289.
13 Oodgeroo Noonuccal, "Municipal Gum," in *My People,* 5th ed. (Milton: John Wiley & Sons Australia Ltd., 2020), 49.
14 Peter Minter, "All the Trees," in *New Directions in Contemporary Australian Poetry*, ed. Dan Disney and Mathew Hall (Switzerland: Springer 2021), 67.

15 Minter, "All the Trees," 62.
16 Minter, "All the Trees," 61.
17 John Charles Ryan, "Botanical Wilderness Narratives, Plant Intelligence and Shifting Perceptions of the Botanical World," in *Rethinking Wilderness and the Wild, Conflict, Conservation and Co-existence*, ed. Robyn Bartel, Marty Branagan, Fiona Utley, and Stephen Harris (London and New York: Routledge, 2021), 167.
18 Minter, "All the Trees," 57.
19 <https://publications.csiro.au/rpr/download?pid=csiro:EP124759&dsid=DS5>
20 Minter, "All the Trees," 59.
21 Gagliano Monica, John C. Ryan, and Patricia Vieira, "Introduction," in *The Language of Plants: Science, Philosophy, Literature*, ed. Gagliano, Monica, John C. Ryan, and Patricia Vieira (Minneapolis: University of Minnesota, 2017), viii–x; Peter Wohlleben, *The Hidden Life of Trees* (Vancouver: Greystone Books, 2015); Michael Marder, "Plant Intentionality and the Phenomenological Framework of Plant Intelligence," *Plant Signaling & Behavior* 7:11 (2012): 1365–1372. <https://doi.org/10.4161/psb.21954>; Michael Marder, "Plant Intelligence and Attention." *Plant Signaling & Behavior* 8:5 (2013). <https://doi.org/10.4161/psb.23902>; Richard Karban, "Plant Communication," *Annual Review of Ecology, Evolution, and Systematics* 52:1 (2021): 1–24. <https://doi.org/10.1146/annurev-ecolsys-010421-020045>; Anthony Trewavas, *Plant Behaviour and Intelligence* (Oxford: Oxford University Press, 2014); Suzanne Simard, "Mycorrhizal Networks Facilitate Tree Communication, Learning and Memory," in *Memory and Learning in Plants*, ed. Monica Gagliano, Guenther Witzany, and Frantisek Baluska (Cham, Switzerland: Springer International Publishing, 2018), 191–213; Monika Gorzelak, Amanda Asay, Brian Pickles, and Suzanne Simard, "Inter-Plant Communication Through Mycorrhizal Networks Mediates Complex Adaptive Behaviour in Plant Communities." *AoB Plants* 7 (2015): 1–13.
22 Ryan, "Botanical Wilderness Narratives," 166.
23 John Charles Ryan, "Writing the Lives of Plants: Phytography and the Botanical Imagination." *a/b: Auto/Biography Studies* 35:1 (January 2020): 103.
24 Ryan, "Botanical Wilderness Narratives," 166.
25 Michael Marder and Patricia Vieira, "Writing Phytophilia: Philosophers and Poets as Lovers of Plants." *Frame* 26:2 (2013): 44.
26 Rafe McGregor, "Poetic Thickness." *British Journal of Aesthetics* 54:1 (January 2014): 56.
27 Martin Harrison, *The Kangaroo Farm* (Brooklyn: Paper Bark Press, 1997).
28 Martin Heidegger, *What Is Called Thinking?* Trans. J.G. Gray (New York: Harper Perennial, 1968), 4.
29 Heidegger, *What Is Called Thinking?*, 42.
30 Timothy Morton, "An Object-Oriented Defense of Poetry." *New Literary History* 43:2 (2012): 205–224:215. <http://www.jstor.org/stable/23259372>
31 Angus Fletcher, *A New Theory for American Poetry, Democracy, the Environment and the Future of Imagination* (Cambridge: Harvard University Press, 2004), 227.
32 Martin Harrison, "The Act of Writing and the Act of Attention." *TEXT*, special issue 20 (2013): 10–11. <http://www.textjournal.com.au/speciss/issue20/Harrison.pdf>.
33 Harrison, "The Act of Writing and the Act of Attention," 10.
34 Maurice Merleau Ponty, *The Visible and the Invisible*, ed. Claude Leforte, trans. Alphonso Lingis (Evanston: Northwestern University Press, 1968), 133.
35 Brian Reed, "Martin Harrison's "Red Gum,"" *Journal of the Association for the Study of Australian Literature* 18:2 (2018): 2.
36 Stuart Cooke, Liminal Narratives. Review of *Music: Prose and Poems* by Martin Harrison. Jacket 28 (October 2005). <http://jacketmagazine.com/28/cooke-harrison.html> Retrieved 18 April 2022.
37 <https://www.bgpa.wa.gov.au/about-us/information/our-plants/plants-in-focus/corymbia-ficifolia>
38 Marder, "Plant Intentionality," 5.
39 Martin Harrison, *Happiness* (Western Australia: UWAP Publishing, 2015), 37.
40 <https://hort.extension.wisc.edu/articles/cycads>
41 Charles Joseph Chamberlain, *Gymnosperms, Structure and Evolution* (Illinois: University of Chicago Press, 1935), 61.
42 Charles Joseph Chamberlain, *The Living Cycads* (Chicago: University of Chicago Press, 1919), ix, 3 and 6.
43 John Charles Ryan, *Plants in Contemporary Poetry Ecocriticism and the Botanical Imagination* (New York and Oxon: Routledge, 2020), 163–185.

44 Elizabeth McMahon, "Judith Wright and the Temporality of Composition." *Australian Literary Studies* 23:2 (2007): 25.

45 Martin Harrison, "The Myth of Origins." *Southerly* 60:2 (2000): 156.

46 Ryan, *Plants in Contemporary Poetry*, 167.

47 Bruno Latour, "The Pandemic Is a Warning: We Must Take Care of the Earth, Our Only Home," *The Australian Guardian Weekly*, 2021. <https://www.theguardian.com/commentisfree/2021/dec/24/pandemic-earth-lockdowns-climate-crisis-environment?> Viewed 25 December 2021.

48 David Kleinberg-Levin, *Heidegger's Phenomenology of Perception, Learning to See and Hear Hermeneutically, Volume II* (London and New York: Rowman and Littlefield, 2021), 154–155.

49 Ryan, *Plants in Contemporary Poetry*, 163.

50 Eugen Wassiliwizky, Stefan Koelsch, et al., "The Emotional Power of poetry: Neural Circuitry, Psychophysiology and Compositional Principles." *Social Cognitive and Affective Neuroscience* 12:8 (August 2017): 1239. <https://doi.org/10.1093/scan/nsx069>

51 Michael Marder, "Philosophy's Homecoming," in *The Task of Philosophy in the Anthropocene, Axial Echoes in Global Space*, ed. Richard Polt and Jon Wittrock (Maryland: Rowman & Littlefield, 2018), 126.

52 <https://www.etymonline.com/word/relate?ref=etymonline_crossreference> Viewed 26 April 2020.

Works Cited

Chakrabarty, Dipesh. *The Climate of History in a Planetary Age* (Chicago: University of Chicago Press, 2021).

Chamberlain, Charles Joseph. *Gymnosperms, Structure and Evolution* (Illinois: University of Chicago Press, 1935).

Chamberlain, Charles Joseph. *The Living Cycads* (Chicago: University of Chicago Press, 1919).

Cooke, Stuart. "The Ecological Poetics of Deborah Bird Rose: Analysis and Application." Association for the Study of Literature, Environment & Culture, Australia – New Zealand, ASLEC-ANZ, *Swamphen*, 7 (2020), 1–18.

Cooke, Stuart. "Liminal Narratives." Review of *Music: Prose and Poems* by Martin Harrison. Jacket 28 (October 2005). <http://jacketmagazine.com/28/cooke-harrison.html> Retrieved 18 April 2022.

Fisher-Wirth, Ann and Laura-Gray Street, eds. *The Ecopoetry Anthology* (Texas: Trinity University Press, 2013).

Fletcher, Angus. *A New Theory for American Poetry, Democracy, the Environment and the Future of Imagination* (Cambridge: Harvard University Press, 2004).

Gagliano, Monica, John C. Ryan, and Patricia Vieira. "Introduction," in *The Language of Plants: Science, Philosophy, Literature*, ed. Gagliano, Monica, John C. Ryan, and Patricia Vieira (Minneapolis: University of Minnesota, 2017), 1–26.

Gorzelak, Monika, Amanda Asay, Brian Pickles, and Suzanne Simard. "Inter-Plant Communication Through Mycorrhizal Networks Mediates Complex Adaptive Behaviour in Plant Communities." *AoB Plants,* 7 (2015), 1–13.

Hall, Matthew. "Talk among the Trees; Animist Plant Ontologies and Ethics," in *The Handbook of Contemporary Animism*, ed. Graham Harvey (London and New York: Routledge, 2014), 385–395.

Haraway, Donna. *When Species Meet* (Minneapolis: University of Minnesota Press, 2008).

Harrison, Martin. *Happiness* (Western Australia: UWAP Publishing, 2015).

Harrison, Martin. "The Act of Writing and the Act of Attention." *TEXT*, special issue 20, (2013). <http://www.textjournal.com.au/speciss/issue20/Harrison.pdf>.

Harrison, Martin. *The Kangaroo Farm* (Brooklyn, NSW: Paper Bark Press, 1997).

Harrison, Martin. "The Myth of Origins." *Southerly*, 60, no 2, (2000), 148–162.

Heidegger, Martin. *What Is Called Thinking?* Trans. J.G. Gray (New York: Harper Perennial, 1968).

Holmes, Katie. "Gardening at the 'Edge': Judith Wright's desert garden, Mongarlowe, New South Wales." *Australian Humanities Review, Eco-humanities Corner* 36 (July 2005). <http://www.lib.latrobe.edu.au/AHR/archive/Issue-July-2005/08Holmes.html>

Kleinberg-Levin, David. *Heidegger's Phenomenology of Perception, Learning to See and Hear Hermeneutically, Volume II* (London and New York: Rowman and Littlefield, 2021).

Latour, Bruno. "The Pandemic Is a Warning: We Must Take Care of the Earth, Our Only Home." *The Australian Guardian Weekly,* 2021. <https://www.theguardian.com/commentisfree/2021/dec/24/pandemic-earth-lockdowns-climate-crisis-environment?> Viewed 25 December 2021.

Lohrey, Amanda. *The Labyrinth, A Pastoral* (Melbourne: Text Publishing, 2020).

Marder, Michael. "Philosophy's Homecoming," in *The Task of Philosophy in the Anthropocene, Axial Echoes in Global Space,* ed. Richard Polt and Jon Wittrock (Maryland, MD: Rowman & Littlefield, 2018), 119–135.

Marder, Michael. "Plant Intelligence and Attention." *Plant Signaling & Behavior* 8 (2013): 5. <https://doi.org/10.4161/psb.23902>

Marder, Michael. "Plant Intentionality and the Phenomenological Framework of Plant Intelligence." *Plant Signaling & Behavior* 7 (2012): 11. <https://doi.org/10.4161/psb.21954>

Marder, Michael and Patricia Vieira. "Writing Phytophilia: Philosophers and Poets as Lovers of Plants." *Frame* 26, no. 2 (2013), 37–53.

McGregor, Rafe. "Poetic Thickness." *British Journal of Aesthetics* 54, no. 1 (January 2014), 49–64.

McMahon, Elizabeth. "Judith Wright and the Temporality of Composition." *Australian Literary Studies* 23, no. 2 (2007), 15–26.

McMurry, Andrew. "Ecocriticism and Discourse," in *The Routledge Handbook of Ecocriticism and Environmental Education,* ed. Scott Slovic, Swarnalatha Rangarajan, Vidya Sarveswaran (London and New York: Routledge, 2019), 15–26.

Minter, Peter. "All the Trees," in *New Directions in Contemporary Australian Poetry*, ed. Dan Disney and Mathew Hall (Switzerland: Springer 2021), 55–69.

Morton, Timothy. "An Object-Oriented Defense of Poetry." *New Literary History* 43, no. 2 (2012). <http://www.jstor.org/stable/23259372>

Noonuccal, Oodgeroo. "Municipal Gum." *My People,* 5th ed. (Milton: John Wiley & Sons Australia Ltd., 2020).

Opperman, Serpil. "How the Natural World Communicates, Insights from Material Ecocriticism," in *Routledge Handbook of Ecocriticism and Environmental Education,* ed. Scott Slovicz, Swarnalatha Rangarajan and Vidya Sarveswaran (London and New York: Routledge, 2019), 108–117.

Ponty, Maurice Merleau. *The Visible and the Invisible,* ed. Claude Leforte, trans. Alphonso Lingis (Evanston: Northwestern University Press, 1968).

Reed, Brian. "Martin Harrison's "Red Gum"." *Journal of the Association for the Study of Australian Literature* 18, no. 2 (2018), 1–11.

Ryan, John Charles. "Botanical Wilderness Narratives, Plant Intelligence and Shifting Perceptions of the Botanical World," in *Rethinking Wilderness and the Wild, Conflict, Conservation and Co-existence,* ed. Robyn Bartel, Marty Branagan, Fiona Utley, and Stephen Harris (London and New York: Routledge, 2021), 165–179.

Ryan, John Charles. "Writing the Lives of Plants: Phytography and the Botanical Imagination." *a/b: Auto/Biography Studies* 35, no 1 (January 2020a), 97–122.

Ryan, John Charles. *Plants in Contemporary Poetry Ecocriticism and the Botanical Imagination* (New York and Oxon: Routledge, 2020b).

Simard, Suzanne. "Mycorrhizal Networks Facilitate Tree Communication, Learning and Memory," in *Memory and Learning in Plants*, ed. Monica Gagliano, Guenther Witzany and Frantisek Baluska (Cham, Switzerland: Springer International Publishing, 2018), 191–213.

Trewavas, Anthony. *Plant Behaviour and Intelligence* (Oxford: Oxford University Press, 2014).

Wassiliwizky, Eugen, Stefan Koelsch, et al. "The Emotional Power of Poetry: Neural Circuitry, Psychophysiology and Compositional Principles." *Social Cognitive and Affective Neuroscience* 12, no. 8, (August 2017). <https://doi.org/10.1093/scan/nsx069>

Wohlleben, Peter. *The Hidden Life of Trees* (Vancouver: Greystone Books, 2015).

11 Carceral Climates

Poetry, Ecology, and the U.S. Prison System

Angela Sorby

Etheridge Knight ends his landmark collection *Poems from Prison* (1968) with an allusion to the carceral environment: "Songs, like birds, die in poisonous air/So my song cannot now be candy" (Knight, 30). To frame prison air as poisonous is a powerful metaphor, but it is not just a metaphor; as a special report sponsored by the Earth Island Institute notes:

> the toxic impact of prisons extends far beyond any individual prison, or any specific region in the United States. Though some prisons provide particularly egregious examples, mass incarceration in the US impacts the health of prisoners, prison-adjacent communities, and local ecosystems from coast to coast
>
> (Berndt et al., n.p.)

The problems of climate change and mass incarceration are enmeshed, as public health research S.J. Prins observes:

> [T]he climate movement has mainstreamed the idea that we cannot avoid environmental catastrophe without fundamentally transforming our economy and society. Prison abolitionists and public health advocates have long made analogous arguments when they describe the fundamental causes of mass incarceration and health disparities as systems of extraction, exploitation, domination, racism, and heteropatriarchy. But mass incarceration, health inequity, and the climate emergency are all intertwined, in more than an analogy and in ways that no single field can address on its own.
>
> (Prins and Story, 235)

As Hank Black has pointed out, George Floyd's phrase "I can't breathe" eloquently "joins the environment and the racial justice movements (2020). Although poetry workshops are a popular feature of prison education programs, poets, critics, and teachers have only recently begun to consider how humanities fields – and poetry in particular – can address the deeply enmeshed problems of mass incarceration and climate change.

This chapter, then, uses current work by system-impacted poets to ask: what happens – what *might* happen – if we understand prison poetry as eco-poetry? First, it offers ecological readings of five poems, all of which appeared in a special issue of *Poetry* magazine: T.L. Perez's "Fog Count: Inmates Walk from Chow," Janine Solursh's "Forgotten Portraits," Spoon Jackson's "At Night I Fly," David A. Pickett's "Disaster Is In the Eye of the Beholder," and Kirk Nesset's "One Place is As Good As Another." Second, it outlines the troubled reception of Nesset's poem to explore how the ecological functions of prison poetry can be complicated in a social climate that stresses individual punishment over systemic healing. Third, it draws on my own experiences

DOI: 10.4324/9781003399988-15

teaching in carceral spaces to argue that, when it is carefully framed, prison poetry can foster connections within and beyond the human world. Ultimately, I conclude that prison poetry can help all writers and readers practice what the ecocritic, Donna Haraway, calls "intentional kin making across deep damage and significant difference" (Haraway, 138).

Carceral Ecologies

Poetry magazine, a visible and prestigious outlet for new poetry in the United States, devoted its February 2021 issue to writers affected by the American prison system. I will focus on this document for several reasons: first, it is freely available, in its entirety, both online and in a pdf format; second, the poems are exceptionally accomplished (although this means they are exemplary rather than strictly representative); and third, the editors frame the entire issue as specifically "ecological." In a supporting prose piece, co-editor Joshua Bennett asserts:

> The vision we seek to extend is one in which the prison is shown to be an *ecological* problem, one that damages not only individual lives but entire life-worlds, entire communities and landscapes and alternative forms of knowledge. The semiotic is a battleground. Our struggle against the prison state must also be waged at the level of the aesthetic, and it is my sense that the poetry produced by the world's captive is an absolutely critical space in which to engage in that struggle.
>
> (Bennet, 557)

Bennet's emphasis invites readers to understand *all* of the selected poems, not just those that are specifically "nature" poems, as ecological; that is, as implicitly connected to the life-world(s) of multiple forces and communities beyond prison walls. In this way, the poems are figured as spaces in which new relationships – new "states" of nature – can be imagined. Bennet concludes that the prison-industrial complex (and its dire ecological effects) requires "the creation of new language, new approaches, new visions for the symbolic order beyond the one we have inherited" (Bennet, 557).

In the field of cultural criticism, Donna Haraway has been especially focused on the need for new language and new visions in response to climate change. Haraway and Anna Tsing (and now others) use the term *Plantationocene* to describe our current symbolic order. Meant to supplement the broader label of the Anthropocene, the Plantationocene highlights specific forms of (often colonial) domination based on reducing complex social and environmental systems into manageable, surveillable, interchangeable units. Plantationocene economies rely on "radical simplification; substitution of peoples, crops, microbes, and life forms; forced labor; and, crucially, the disordering of times of generation across species, including human beings" (Haraway and Tsing, 2020).

Incarcerated Americans occupy severely nature-deprived environments, conditions that affect their mental and physical well-being; for instance, one study showed that "Michigan prisoners whose cells faced a prison courtyard had 24 percent more illnesses than those whose cells had a view of farmland" (Louv, 46). In the Plantationocene, times of generation – the organic productive cycles of bioregions and rooted communities – are disrupted by rigid, linear, exogenous systems. Incarcerated people are deprived of what Bennett calls "entire life-worlds, entire communities and landscapes, and alternative forms of knowledge." Nevertheless, Sarah Nolan has argued that precisely because prisoners lack "multidimensional environmental experiences," writing practices can help them become "more conscious of the complex and often invisible ways in which environments manifest themselves." This very deprivation, she proposes, generates "an ecopoetics of the prison poetry genre that results from the inmate's hyper-awareness of the environmental encounter and the various unexpected and non-traditional forms in which that can arrive" (Nolan, 313). In other words, while all poets make imaginative leaps, incarcerated poets in particular, must consciously, or even subversively, imagine "multi-dimensional environmental experiences" from inside of institutions that deliberately suppress the non-linear complexities of (human and more-than-human) nature. To read ecologically is to realise that there is never just one story.

The first poem in *Poetry's* special issue, "Fog Count: Inmates Walk from Chow," by T.L. Perez, draws on imagist techniques to disrupt a (literally) linear and confined experience. In a few stark lines, Perez captures the transitional moment when inmates pass single file between buildings. Crows descend through the fog, looking for crumbs "from the generous." Some of the men, it seems, have established a relationship with the crows by feeding them. Crumbs are small things in the human world, but in the more-than-human world they loom large and make a meal. Moreover, at the moment the crows descend, the men are not murderers, burglars, or rapists; they are defined (from an avian perspective) as *generous*. As an ecopoem, "Fog Count" does not strain towards a pristine vision of nature. Rather, it imagines a reciprocal scene in which crows "fog" the "count": when they feed the birds, prisoners become agents; they are nodes in an ecosystemic matrix, rather than objects of numeric surveillance.

The moment is fleeting, however; as the yard fills "with extra guards./ Birdsongs interlace/ their scraggly gaits" (Perez, 428). Because the title refers to walking inmates, it's not clear if the "gaits" in the last line belong to the guards or the prisoners; all are enclosed, and all are "inter-laced" with birdsong. Eschewing the common pastoral move of using birds to connote freedom, Perez imagines the crows as bound up with the "gaits" of the people (prisoners and guards) caught in the system as well as the gates of the yard itself. The birds are ultimately an image, not of individual freedom, but of collective entanglement: crows, prisoners, and guards are all part of a life-world that is marked by the tension between reductive carceral narratives and the complexity of an ecosystem that does not stop at the gates of the prison.

In Perez's poem, the inmates, the crows, and even the guards are interlaced in ways that resist the dehumanisation of prison life by implicitly connecting *all* life. Donna Haraway calls this process "making kin." In her book *Staying with the Trouble,* she proposes that kin-making "is making persons, not necessarily as individuals or as humans." Echoing the lyrical, juxta-positioning logic of poetry, Haraway suggests that "kin" "is an assembling sort of word. All critters share a common "flesh," laterally, semiotically, and genealogically. Ancestors turn out to be very interesting strangers; kin are unfamiliar (outside what we thought was family or genes), uncanny, haunting, active" (Haraway, 106). For Haraway, the more-than-human world is not just a recreational site of escape for humans; it is (like most families) a matrix of desire, competing interests, and generative tension.

Janine Solursh's poem "Forgotten Portraits" outlines the ways that prison blocks kin-making, beginning at the moment "you" enter a carceral space with shorn of all complexity. Her poem opens with a shock: "Suddenly, nobody knows where you are./You're just a memory,/ An echo…" When prisoners are sentenced to "do time," their time is measured in calendrical years: manmade, uniform, and countable. By the end of the poem, Solursh describes herself as "dead," concluding: "I am not apart from you for long,/ except for breath,/except for eve-rything." Solursh's poem captures the uncanniness of carceral extinction: on the one hand, incarcerated people are tracked and surveilled, so in this sense, their location is known to the institution. But organic everyday exchanges – with family, friends, strangers, animals, plants, or even fresh air – halts, dislocating the speaker from any sense of place and making her part of a radically de-natured prison-industrial complex. While much research has shown that prison weakens family ties, Solursh's poem goes further: her sentences trace a death, both eternal and absolute, unbinding her from others at the molecular level of oxygen. The "you" that the speaker addresses is herself and not herself; she is human, but damaged. She feels uncannily split, as if she no longer breathes the same air as other creatures.

The idea of prison as social death has a long history. The concept was first advanced by the Jamaican sociologist Orlando Patterson to differentiate plantation slavery from other forms of historical oppression. According to Patterson, enslaved people were "natally alienated and ceased to belong to any formal recognised community" (Patterson, 6). More recently, Joshua Price and others have extended the term "social death" to system-impacted people – a link that makes sense historically, especially if both plantations and prisons are seen as part of the Plantationocene. Thus, in Solursh's poem, time in prison stops her biological clock; the sentence that she must serve cuts her off from "times of generation."

At the same time, the acts of poetry-reading and writing can re-affirm the complex networks that prison systems simplify or extinguish. In "Toward a Prison Poetics," the critic Doran Larson proposes a useful "dissociative/associative" model for reading prison poems: "The prison writer returns herself to language, and thus necessarily into an identity separate from that which power seeks at once to impose, to know, and to destroy." Through "dissociate/associative" moves, the writer uses the poem to separate from the imposed identity that prison attempts to impose, associating instead with another assemblage of images that imagines the possibility of kinship (Larson, 147). In "Forgotten Portraits," Solursh deploys the "you" pronoun to bridge the gap between herself and the reader. Throughout most of the poem, up until the last few lines, the second person essentially functions as an "I," but then the "I" appears as "apart from you…" Ironically, even as the "I" and "you" come apart in the end, the ambiguity of the "you" pronoun (as first a stand-in for the speaker and later a stand-in for the reader) is generative. Literary sentences *reduce* the dehumanising distances Solursh's institutional "sentence" imposes. The poem makes space for a tentative assemblage of kin because its pronouns play with "you" and "I," implying that intersubjective convergence is at least theoretically possible.

In the *Poetry* magazine poems, writers frequently perform dissociative/associative gestures to connect with the human and more-than-human world; this life-world functions, not as a pastoral backdrop but as a generative force for kin-making that goes beyond what usually counts as family. That said, associative moves towards nature are seldom easy and always partial in carceral contexts. Spoon Jackson's "At Night I Fly" maps the many ways that prison enforces forms of personal, creative, and ecological sterility from which it is impossible to completely dissociate. Jackson's poem begins with a dream; at night, he writes, "I soar with the red-tailed hawk." However–like Perez's crows–Jackson's hawk is not an unfettered romantic "freedom" trope. The speaker's nocturnal association with a hawk is framed as a fantasy that ultimately underscores his diurnal prison identity. By day he views the "real" world through a "narrow slit" in a cell wall that he calls "my window theater…" The tiny aperture makes everything outside of the cell remote: "buzzards, turkeys, geese,/Deer, wild dogs, coyotes, snakes,/And rock doves." The same window-theatre also forces him to see and re-see the homicide he committed 40 years prior, as if no time has passed. The speaker asserts a profound remorse for his crime, but because he is socially dead, there is little he can do to repair the harm. Snakes and rock doves, predators and prey, destruction and restoration: all of these complex life cycles remain beyond his grasp, framed by the little window-theatre.

Only towards the end of the poem does the speaker attempt to make a real (as opposed to dreamlike) connection with the outside world. He cannot physically move, but he can make a rhetorical move. He asks an unspecified "you": "Isn't it enough that you keep me away/ From people I could surely help,/From clean water, nutritious food?" Unlike in the Solursh poem, Jackson's "you" is very much an "other": he addresses the reader, not as a person, but as the representative of a punitive outside society. In keeping with the theatre metaphor, his speaker breaks the fourth wall, shifting out of the solipsistic dreamtime to seek some reciprocity from the world. And yet, the world cannot respond in kind; true reciprocity is impossible, just as in a theatrical performance. A degree of stuckness emerges as the speaker repeats "isn't it enough?" as he pictures the women he might have loved, and the "rivers, trees, and seas" he might have seen if he were not incarcerated. Poetry-writing is a creative act that pushes back against social death, allowing the speaker to expand his sense of self to incorporate other birds, animals, landscapes, and people, but the reader ("you") remains an abstract and silent figure, more of an obstacle than a fully realised human being. Neither the "I" nor the "you" can fully dissociate from the defining fact of the prison.

David A. Pickett's "Disaster is in the Eye of the Beholder," another poem in the *Poetry* issue, performs a more dramatic act of dissociation/association, this time spurred by a climate event, in an effort to imagine authentic connections beyond prison. The first stanza begins with a memory, viewed from the outside: "I used to live in a single-/wide, tilted on blocks ...." The trailer is an enclosed, industrial space, while the word "block" evokes a cell block in a prison. Even before the speaker was in prison, it seems, he inhabited – like many economically-disadvantaged Americans – a denatured, quasi-carceral space. When the speaker in the second stanza zooms in on the mobile home itself, however, he focuses not on the humans living inside but on insects: "Thin pressboard panels/hid a million roachy lives ...." Rather than serving as objects of human disgust, the roaches are tiny, sympathetic creatures; their feet patter "like rain/showers in retreat from the sun." Playing with scale, Pickett then envisions a natural disaster, the "dark, twisted arm" of a tornado reaching down to pick up all the trailers in the park. He watches the twister "crush them in a cloudy fist/and scatter them like seeds/across a plowed and fertile land." As the poem's title implies, climate catastrophes affect "beholders" differently and unevenly; in this poem, a storm is necessary to re-seed the plowed land. The "radically simplified" modular trailer park is destroyed by chaos, but chaos is productive. The surrounding land is not "wild" – it has been plowed by human hands – but it teems with possibilities that the trailer park, with its manufactured uniformity, does not. Instead, an unsettled mix of human dreams, roaches, and funnel clouds makes new forms of growth imaginable on an environmental rather than an individual level. The dreamer's "time of generation" is intimately linked to the seeds in the eye of the storm. For Pickett, terrestrial images (a funnel cloud, an open field) allow him to dissociate from the simplified "monocrop" logic of the Plantationocene. A new beginning is possible, but at a tremendous cost: the individual must dissociate from the built environment and surrender to large-scale disruptions if he is to find any sense of belonging in the world.

Kirk Nesset's "One Place is As Good as the Next," also from *Poetry,* takes the opposite tack, seeking renewal through association with small-scale natural phenomena. This, too, is difficult in the context of prison and re-entry. The poem starts mid-sentence as it seeks places: "...to begin. The bobwhite's nest. Redstarts on branches/in birches, phoebes peeping from rotting eves./Begin with an unfinished page..." The nest, the budding branches, and the blank page co-exist as potentially generative spaces, but they are not analogous spaces: the connected, organic life-world unfolds spontaneously, while the blank page requires deliberate human agency. Beginning is difficult for the "you," a speaker who is "unhooked/ and detached. Shattered." The speaker reassures himself that "the morning will answer itself ...," but can such a conversation include a detached person, as well as bobwhites and phoebes? In Nesset's poem, hierarchies are unsettled – every place is equally good – and human language is not privileged over the more-than-human utterances of a spring morning. As a rhetorical act, the poem associates with natural images, but the story it tells is one of near-social death. "One Place is As Good as the Next" ends with images of kinship rooted in biological diversity: "the shovel-nosed snake and the oriole's aerial cradle,/mud daubers daubing by the meandering river," but the speaker's own place in the world remains unclear.

Jackson, Pickett, and Nesset all use more-than-human images to re-situate their speakers in imagined communities other than prison, while implicitly acknowledging the always-partial success, and the high costs, of such moves. As I have shown, natural imagery carries additional resonances in a carceral context because prisons deliberately "unhook" (to use Nesset's verb) people from complex ecosystems. To make a poem is to create a kind of therapeutic "window-theater" through which otherwise-inaccessible images can be viewed. Even second-hand experiences of the natural world can be restorative to people deprived of sensory stimulation. In one study, a "nature imagery intervention," in the form of a forest-scenes video, was offered to men in a maximum-security setting. Prisoners reported that nature imagery helped them sustain feelings of well-being, control their anger, and relate better to the prison staff. One participant wrote, "The nature project help's [sic] me think clearer to know there is so much more beauty in this world then this prison" (Nadkarni, 399). When I taught poetry-writing in prison, the students let me know that they did not want their poems to simply re-hash their experiences "inside." Rather, they longed to transport themselves *outside,* to make associative leaps to reconnect with the wider life-world. For that subset of the incarcerated population who are able and willing to write poetry, a "nature imagery intervention" can be accessed independently, and more actively, using pencil and paper.

In addition to benefiting prison writers as individuals, prison poems can also, potentially, help non-incarcerated readers empathise with incarcerated populations. In one sociological study, "The Effect of Reading Prisoner Poetry on Stigma and Public Attitudes," a team led by Christopher P. Dum found that stigmatising attitudes towards prisoners could be reduced through poetry. The effects were genre-specific; reportorial prose texts did not have the same effect. Interestingly, the subject-matter was important also; non-incarcerated readers who were given poems written by prisoners became more sympathetic and open to education and re-entry programs, but *only when those poems were not about prison.* The researchers note: "One way that individuals rationalise punitive attitudes is through dehumanisation, 'whereby targets of punitive attitudes are linguistically and euphemistically stripped of their personhood.' Narrative humanisation acts as a counterforce to dehumanisation by creating an empathetic picture of an individual" (Dum et al., 16). Poems that rhetorically dissociated their writers from prison, re-situating them in a larger life-world, made non-incarcerated readers "see" them as kin, as human like themselves, rather than as socially dead criminals. In her preface to the *Poetry* issue, co-editor Tara Betts notes:

> The contributors, who are often no longer perceived as people in the non-incarcerated world, are indeed human. Many of them have partners, families, friends, and try to help other people. Some of them have made mistakes. Some have faced cycles of violence and abuse themselves. I hope that people come to this issue with open minds, and I'd like to underscore that openness by saying that poets are not members of the jury. No one undertook this project to declare a verdict on any of the contributors therein.

(425)

Readers of prison poems – like writers – can, ideally, learn to dissociate from the terms set by the prison-industrial complex, and to seek complexity (rather than morals or "verdicts") in poems. This is both a reading practice and an ecologically-regenerative mindset predicated on what Haraway calls "kin-making across deep damage."

Troubling Kinship

Who *wouldn't* want to imagine a more inclusive life-world, a collective planetary consciousness rooted in beauty and kin-making and freedom and generativity? The very attractiveness of this vision also betrays its potential pitfalls. Indeed, soon after the *Poetry* issue was released, a controversy erupted over the inclusion of Kirk Nesset's poem. Nesset, a former college professor, had been arrested for possessing child pornography. A petition, begun on Change.org, garnered over 2,000 signatures:

> This petition calls for *Poetry* Magazine to remove Nesset's work from their pages and their website. That such an established publication would use their widely-read and highly selective platform to further the work and career of a predator cannot be labeled an oversight, nor defended. It is an offensive and a destructive misuse of power.

From an ecocritical perspective, the Plantationocene is indeed sustained by gross imbalances of human power – imbalances that privilege white men like Nesset. On the other hand, crime-and-punishment narratives also follow the logic of the Plantationocene: they simplify people, conflating offenders ("predators") with their crimes and enforcing the sentence of social death. The terms of the dispute index real problems that arise when we seek to balance, even on the very small scale of a lyric poem, the value of all human and more-than-human life-forms. The novelist Dan Kios summed it up thusly in *Slate*:

> In this particular imbroglio, it seems clear to me that two cultural waves are crashing against each other: from one direction, the growing visibility and acceptance of the prison abolition movement, and from the other, the rising understanding of how damaging sexual abuse is and how often privileged abusers escape punishment. Nesset—white, educated, repugnant, directly connected to the academic English community that makes up much of *Poetry*'s audience—becomes the perfect nexus for those two issues.
>
> (Kios, online)

If, as Bennet suggests, we read "One Place is as Good as Another" ecologically, then the questions get even more vexed. The petition posted on Change.org calls Nesset a "predator," while simplifying the term "predator" to connote negative, and implicitly non-human, qualities.[1] Nesset's poem in Poetry, by contrast, speaks from a distinctly non-predatory perch, celebrating (but not disturbing) nesting birds. The question becomes: must two versions of a single author *compete* for cultural primacy, or can they co-exist as facets of one (flawed, or even "repugnant") person? Moreover, what is the relationship between the person and the poem?

   To move towards potential co-existence requires sensitive framing. An open letter from the interim editors, in response to the uproar, began with expressions of respect and empathy:

> We, the interim co editors of *Poetry* magazine, understand that many people are disturbed by our editorial decisions in the February 2021 issue, "The Practice of Freedom." We condemn all acts of violence and recognise its life-shattering impact. We acknowledge the trauma of those who have been harmed.
>
> (*Poetry*, online.)

The editors then affirmed that they would nonetheless keep the issue as-is, stressing that "weighing people's convictions in editorial decisions for this issue would be antithetical to the discourse around the practices of freedom we are seeking to facilitate." In addition, they argued, choosing to publish (or not) based on specific crimes "would be exercising individual punishments for systemic problems." As Betts pointed out in the introduction quoted earlier, readers are not jury members. At the same time, the team concluded that they should have been "more transparent" about their principles of selection: "The response to this issue has led us to consider the ways in which we should be more thoughtful and proactive about sharing the editorial principles that guide our future work." The *Poetry* editors had experience teaching and writing in prison, but most of the magazine's readers did not. Suspension of judgement is a best practice in prison education, but – as the *Poetry* editors belatedly realised – readers new to prison poetry needed more "thoughtful and proactive" frameworks for reading.

To write, read, or publish prison poetry is not to celebrate crime; it is rather to "stay with the trouble," as Donna Haraway would put it. Haraway argues, in her inimitable style:

> We—all of us on Terra—live in disturbing times, mixed-up times, troubling and turbid times. The task is to become capable, with each other in all of our bumptious kinds, of response. Mixed-up times are overflowing with both pain and joy—with vastly unjust patterns of pain and joy, with unnecessary killing of ongoingness but also with necessary resurgence. The task is to make kin in lines of inventive connection as a practice of learning to live and die well with each other in a thick present (1).

Our "thick present" is a place, not of innocent or Edenic nature, but of trouble that implicates everyone in ways that none are fully equipped to judge. One task of ecological prison poetry might be to help readers become more capable of living with, and in, moral complexity, rather than mining poems for didactic messages. An ecological lens is ideally composed (to extend the metaphor) of multiple lenses that take many competing human and more-than-human interests – including prison abolition and victim advocacy – into account. To "come to this issue with open minds," as Betts suggests, does not entail suspending all judgements permanently; rather, it entails making a space (not *all spaces,* but *a space*) for the carceral imagination to flourish across boundaries.

Towards Ecopoetic Kinship: One Model

As the reader backlash to the *Poetry* issue suggests, kin-making across boundaries can be hard to picture and even harder to practice, especially when stigmatised populations are involved. In closing, then, I will offer one example of how such work might safely and productively proceed. In 2019, I began working with the Educational Preparedness Program (EPP) at my home institution, Marquette University, to design a poetry-writing course that incarcerated and non-incarcerated students could take together. Professors teaching in the EPP program receive intensive training from a national organisation, "Inside/Out," that approaches prison pedagogy as a chance to strengthen community ties. As the Inside/Out website states, its model "is unique because incarcerated students and traditional campus-based students are in class together as peers, learning collaboratively, through a dialogic process." Such a dialogic process requires guardrails; in keeping with Inside/Out best practices, my course was taught using first names only. My "outside" (traditional college) students were carefully prepped to treat the "inside" students as peers, not curiosities or objects of pity. In addition, no one's past criminal offenses were to be discussed or taken as writing topics. Although we convened on the grounds of a men's federal prison, the class was not "about prison. Instead, it was structured to facilitate dissociation/association: during class time, students detached from their institutional status as 'prisoners' or 'Marquette undergraduates.'" Instead, they all adopted the identity of poets and were set up to associate with one another in a "thick present" that was defined by the work they produced and shared.

Like most prisons, the facility where I taught was a cluster of utilitarian buildings that deprived inmates of contact with complex natural systems: the walls were cinder block, the exercise yard was mono-cropped grass, and all physical movement was highly regulated. In response, I tried to design assignments that facilitated dissociation with the prison environment and with crime-and-punishment narratives, steering the poets (inside and outside) to focus on the life-worlds they had in common: animals, childhood, landscapes. One particularly generative assignment revolved around water – a resource that is both inside and outside every human body.

Water has been central to the human ecopoetic imagination since (at least) *The Odyssey,* when Homer saw a "wine-dark sea" that reflected both wild waves and an intoxicating, adulterated substance. To begin a poem with water is to begin a poem at the origin-point of all life, but not necessarily in Eden. I set up the assignment by distributing images of water from around the world, cut out of magazines; there were irrigation ditches, pristine alpine lakes, river baptisms, catastrophic floods, and crowded swimming beaches. Together, the images offered students multiple lenses – different ways of understanding the beautiful and dangerous and necessary power of water. Everyone picked an image to keep, and I encouraged them to sit with the images for a few days before writing about them. This was the first assignment I gave when our class met in person, after we had to begin via Zoom because of Covid. Students were just getting to know one another, and the process of haggling over specific photos got them talking (to one another) about which images they preferred and why. Their preferences were idiosyncratic and – crucially – not directly related to their social status as incarcerated or non-incarcerated people.

As a sample poem, I provided Juan Filipe Herrara's "Water Water Water Wind Water," from the Poetry Foundation website, a meditation on Gulf Coast hurricanes. Herrera's poem is an accessible and yet complex model of ecological thinking. As the wind hits, mothers go underwater, "casinos in biloxi become carnations," new algae and planktons emerge, and stars appear under stairs. Herrara acknowledges natural and political power imbalances without simplifying the problem: "again and again a new land edge emerges/a new people emerges where race and class and death/and life and water and tears and loss …" Asking students to read Herrara's poem carefully was important to the success of the assignment because it prompted them to think of water as a medium for assemblage – a unifying force that can bring together, without "reconciling," disparate images and ideas.

The resulting student poems, like the poems in the *Poetry* issue, dissociate their speakers from their institutional environment and allow them to connect with more generative forms of life.[2] One incarcerated poet, Lord, writes in "Like Life Flowing":

The water flows down river,
washing over rocks, boulders,
rinsing them of all uncleanliness,
while at the same time the river that flows downriver
provides protection for the life underneath,
and maybe a nutritious
meal not provided by the embankment.
As the river flows ever so freely downward
it makes a gurgling sound
as if water could gurgle
but as with everything in nature

or the wide world over
just maybe the river has its own language…

Lord's poem does not just describe a photograph; it makes the photograph "come alive," creating a space of movement and transformation. The water in "Like Life Flowing" embodies, not prison life, but human and more-than-human life writ large. Analogously, when Lord presented his draft to the class for feedback, we were able to have a reciprocal conversation based on elemental experiences that we had all shared, co-creating a common language.

Another incarcerated student poet, Martise, begins his poem, "Life is Water," with a stanza that counters the work of the Plantationocene (simplification, sterilisation) at every turn:

> Land dry and full of dust,
> last year's crop scattered about throughout
> the open flat mowed down fields of great harvest.
> Seeds self-planting await natural fertilization.
> A drink of refreshing water, cool and soothing
> to the stalk's esophagus. Growth, as the draught
> of despair will soon disappear.

Martise's poem brings the life-giving power of water inside the body, through the esophagus, and outside, onto the open field. The changes he charts are also internal and external (inside/outside) as growth begins.

Conclusion

Poetry can be an exceptionally effective medium for the ecological work of complex community-building because most good poetry is willing to suspend judgement, embrace contradictions, and "stay with the trouble." The carceral state and much of the general public defines people like Lord and Martise (or Spoon Jackson, or Kirk Nesset) simply in terms of their crimes; Jackson is a "murderer," Nesset is a "predator." Our classroom practices sought, not to deny the gravity of a given crime, but to affirm the human complexity of every student – an ongoing struggle made possible through the sensitive preparatory education of all participants. Mass incarceration is a kind of poison, as Ethridge Knight understood: its toxins affect even those who never go to prison. Poetry can be a vehicle for environmental justice precisely because it is not a didactic blunt instrument; instead, it offers us a way to make oblique and unexpected – and sometimes even beautiful – connections.

Acknowledgements

Special thanks to Mr. Dan Derler, Dr. Theresa Tobin, Ms. Alex Gamabacorta, and the poets at Racine Correctional Institute.

Notes

1 The trouble with "predators" also extends to the conservation world. See, for example, Christian C. Young's *In the Absence of Predators: Conservation and Controversy on the Kaibab Plateau*. Wolves inflict real harm on livestock and debates continue about how, and whether, to live with them.
2 The two poems cited here are quoted with permission from their authors, Lord and Martise, who are identified by their first names for privacy and *per* DOC regulations. Thanks to these authors and thanks also to Mr. Dan Derler, Director of Education, for granting institutional approval and for making our class possible.

Works Cited

Bennett, Joshua. "In Pursuit of the Practice of Freedom." *Poetry* 217:5 (February 2021): 555–557.

Berndt, Candice, Maureen Nandini-Mitra, and Zoe Loftus-Ferren. "America's Toxic Prisons: Earth Island Journal: Earth Island Institute." America's Toxic Prisons | Earth Island Journal | Earth Island Institute. Earth Island Institute, 2017. https://earthisland.org/journal/americas-toxic-prisons/.

Betts, Tara. "To Keep a Green Branch from Snapping." *Poetry* 217:5 (February 2021): 425–427.

Black, Hank. "'I Can't Breathe': Connecting the Green and Black Movements." *BirminghamWatch. Alabama Initiate for Independent Journalism*, July 2, 2020. https://birminghamwatch.org/cant-breathe-connecting-green-black-movements/.

Dum, Christopher P., Kelly M. Socia, Bengt George, and Halle M. Neiderman. "The Effect of Reading Prisoner Poetry on Stigma and Public Attitudes: Results from a Multigroup Survey Experiment." *The Prison Journal* 102:1 (January 2022): 3–24. https://doi.org/10.1177/00328855211069127.

Graham, Melanie. "Support the Removal of Convicted Pedophile Kirk Nesset's Work from Poetry Magazine." https://www.change.org/p/poetry-magazine-support-the-removal-of-convicted-pedophile-kirk-nesset-s-work-from-poetry-magazine?recruiter=847401&utm_source=share_petition&utm_medium=facebook&utm_campaign=psf_combo_share_initial&utm_term=share_petition&recruited_by_id=fec1c1b0-c2fc-012f-b5e3-404067ca6a7a&utm_content=fht-27160820-en-us%3A6. Accessed 7 July 2022.

Haraway, Donna J. *Staying with the Trouble*. Experimental Futures. Durham, NC: Duke University Press, 2016.

Haraway, Donna, and Anna Tsing. "Reflections on the Plantationocene." Moderated by Greg Mittman. Edge Effects. University of Wisconsin, 2019. https://edgeeffects.net/wp-content/uploads/2019/06/PlantationoceneReflections_Haraway_Tsing.pdf. Accessed 7 July 2022.

Herrera, Juan Filipe. "Water Water Water Wind Water," Poetry Foundation website, https://www.poetryfoundation.org/poems/58271/water-water-water-wind-water. Accessed 7 July 2022.

Inside/Out Prison Exchange Program website, https://www.insideoutcenter.org/. Accessed 7 July 2022.

Jackson, Spoon. "At Night I Fly." *Poetry* 217:5 (February 2021): 435–437.

Kios, Dan. "Was *Poetry* Magazine Really Wrong to Publish a Child Porn Convict in Its Prison Issue?" *Slate,* February 4, 2021. https://slate.com/culture/2021/02/poetry-magazine-prison-incarcerated-writers-kirk-nesset-child-pornography.html. Accessed 7 July 2022.

Knight, Etheridge, and Gwendolyn Brooks. *Poems from Prison*. Detroit, MI: Broadside Press, 1968.

Larson, Doran. "Toward a Prison Poetics." *College Literature* 37:3 (2010): 143–66. http://www.jstor.org/stable/20749607.

Lord [surname redacted], "Like Life Flowing." Cited and quoted with permission from the author.

Martise [surname redacted], "Life is Water." Cited and quoted with permission from the author.

Nadkarni, Nalini, Patricia H. Hasbach, Tierney Thys, Emily Gaines Crockett, and Lance Schnacker. "Impacts of Nature Imagery on People in Severely Nature-Deprived Environments." *Frontiers in Ecology and the Environment* 15:7 (2017): 395–403, doi:10.1002/fee.1518

Nesset, Kirk. "Once Place Is As Good As Another." *Poetry* 217:5 (February 2021): 458.

Nolan, Sarah. "Prison Ecopoetics: Concrete, Imagined, and Textual Spaces in American Inmate Poetry." *Green Letters* 18:3 (2014): 312–324.

Patterson, Orlando. *Slavery and Social Death.* Cambridge: Harvard University Press, 1982.

Perez, T.L. "Inmates Walk from Chow." *Poetry* 217:5 (February 2021): 428.

Pickett, David A. "Disaster Is in the Eye of the Beholder." *Poetry* 217:5 (February 2021): 432.

Price, Joshua M. "Spirit Murder: Reentry, Dispossession, and Enduring Stigma." In *Prison and Social Death*, 115–28. Rutgers University Press, 2015. http://www.jstor.org/stable/j.ctt15jjc08.11.

Prins, Seth J., and Brett Story. "Connecting the Dots Between Mass Incarceration, Health Inequity, and Climate Change." *American Journal of Public Health* 110:S1 (2020): S35–S36. doi:10.2105/AJPH.2019.305470

Solursh, Janine. "Forgotten Portraits." *Poetry* 217:5 (February 2021): 446.

12 Black Ecologies, the "Weather," and "Renegade" Poetic Sensorium[1]

Hanna Musiol

...the weather is the totality of our environments; the weather is the total climate; and that climate is antiblack.

—Christina Sharpe, *In the Wake: On Blackness and Being* (104)

...the earth is also skin.

—Katherine McKittrick (ix)

Excruciating reflections on the all-enveloping saturation of racism that cuts across bodies, systems, ecologies, and social welfare institutions prompt Christine Sharpe to recognize not simply that "the weather is the totality of our environments" (21) but that "the weather is the total climate; and that [the total] climate is antiblack" (21, 104). She argues, in other words, that "[a]ntiblackness" is literally, not simply metaphorically, the climate (Sharpe 21, 104). Such understanding of "racism as environmental" draws attention to how "sociopolitical forces generate landscapes that infiltrate human bodies," revealing its mutual, "trans-corporeal," body- and landscape-forming, flesh- and terraforming impacts (Alaimo 22). In her exploration of the "demonic grounds" of Black enspacement, Katherine McKittrick expands this line of inquiry and demonstrates how Black ecologies and their expressive arts, including poetry, reveal "an uncharted" and profoundly complex understanding of a "sense of place," of raced, gendered, and embodied geographies, of ecosocial political systems, and of temporalities we should reckon with (xxii). McKittrick lauds in particular how poetry, and other arts, can "unfix" (xxiii) supposedly stable paradigms of scientific knowing (xiii) and rework disciplinary thinking about seemingly "ungeographic bodies" and spaces (xi), without the established measurement protocols of "maps, charts, official records, figures" (xxii).

This chapter draws from these thinkers as it turns to such poetic knowing and the complex, biosocial understanding of space, climate, the environment, and the "fleshiness" of earth in Black *ecopoethics* and ecologies (McKittrick ix). Specifically, it focuses on how two acclaimed African American poets—Afaa Michael Weaver and Evie Shockley—engage with the "weather," space, and flesh in their "trans-corporeal" poetic meditations and landscapes, showing us how Black bodies are the geography and the "earth's skin" often missing in climate systems thinking (Sharpe 104; Alaimo 22; McKittrick ix). My approach is more narrative, retrospective in the case of Weaver's decades of poetic work—from *My Father's Geography* (1992) to *The City of Eternal Spring* (2014) and beyond—and more spatial, zoomed in on only two spatial poems by Shockley from her 2017's *semiautomatic* collection—":: in the california mountains, far from shelby county, alabama and even farther from the supreme court building, the black poet seeks

DOI: 10.4324/9781003399988-16

the low-down from a kindred entity ::." and ":: the way we live now ::." This is to account for the longevity of this "renegade" Black poetic ecothought practice and to attend to the specific affordances of spatial poetics more closely (Shockley, *Renegade*). I conclude with a short reflection on the pedagogies of such breathing, airy Black *ecopoethics*.

Black Ecopoetics as Embodied Systems Thinking

The place of literature in environmental humanities (EH), including climate studies, is now well established, as is the place of fiction and nonfiction in narrating, communicating, and teaching climate change (Heise et al.; Nixon; DeLoughrey and Handley; Iheka, *Teaching*). Poetry's very specific, spatio-textual, materially "condensed" (Dove 1), and embodied eco-thought—and especially the influence of Black, Indigenous, African, Asian, trans-American, queer, or diasporic ecopoetics on the EH and more mainstream understanding of "nature" or of climate, is still less acknowledged,[2] but not less vital. And yet if racism is "the total climate" (Sharpe 104), altering material spaces and "infiltrating human bodies" (Alaimo 32), and poetry is a spatial, bodily, "enfleshed," "animacious" medium (Sharpe 21; Chen, *Animacies*; McKittrick; Musiol, "Grieving"), it may be a particularly important, visceral "mode of [reflective] embodiment" or "embodied contemplation" (Chen, "Agitation" 551; Mauro Flude 219), not simply for theorising terraforming and transcorporeal ecologies but for "mattering" them in the poetic form and in the poet's and the readers' flesh (Alaimo 22; Chen, *Animacies,* 23; Musiol, "Grieving"). I want to explore the affordances of Black ecopoetry to speak, write, embody, and contain such sensorial climate systems thinking and "mattering," a decade after the publication of *Black Nature: Four Centuries of African American Nature Poetry* and at the time when artivists such as Mykki Blanco draw not simply links between "white supremacy" and "climate change" (July 12, 2022) but demand "decoloniz[ation of] the environmental movement" and development of "systems based on regeneration not extraction."[3] *Black Nature*, a long-overdue anthology of poetry engaging in a (un)*earthing* of Black environmental Anglophone poetics, was precisely an example of such effort. There are many others. Black and Indigenous spatio-environmental theorists—McKittrick, Sharpe, Robert Bullard, or Kyle Whyte, for example—also make this point explicit as they explore how racism and colonialism contribute to "the unequal distribution of environmental benefits and environmental harms" (Alaimo 22), how they literally "make landscapes" and "the weather" (McKittrick xiv; Sharpe 104; Bullard, *Dumping in Dixie, Unequal Protection*). They see the climate crisis as a crisis among many obscured systems of domination, exploitation, and extraction. Obscured, Jason Moore points out, "because we have been taught to speak in ways that avoid *naming the system*," especially when the system is gendered, racist, or "capitalogenic" (Moore n. pag.; emphasis mine).

Black ecopoets frequently foreground such de- or anticolonial systems thinking, engendering a decolonial reclamation of precarious bodies *and* their modalities of environmental knowing. This regenerative work often rests in bridging epistemic chasms via diasporic and fleshy *practices* of thought (Black and Indigenous; East Asian and African American; non-Christian and Indigenous, Daoist, Buddhist, and Muslim), which are not mediated or legitimized by intellectual traffic via European metropolises or by Western continental philosophies more broadly. Weaver stresses, for instance, that he "began to read and write poetry…the way [he] lived, from a black center outward" (in Burawa et al. 218). Importantly, poets Weaver and Shockley demonstrate how Black poetic ecologies transform, "undisciplined" environmental thinking, including climate work, by centering on Black "trans-corporeality" and "enspacement (McKittrick xxiii; Chen; Alaimo; Sharpe 13). As these poets activate what Shockley calls "renegade" poetic media, they attend to urban and sociopolitical environments and the vulnerable and defiant Black bodies as "trans-corporeal" biosensors at (or as) the edges, wastelands, landscapes, and epicenters of climate crises (Shockley, *Renegade*; Alaimo 18). In the process, they reframe and rescale the understanding of the "weather" or "climate" destabilization as always inevitably social, racial, classed, gendered, historical, colonial, and relational (Whyte). They also expose the way that Black bodies experience those climates and express them and write and breathe them into poetic landscapes that foreground ecological traumas as sociopolitical, biocultural, and epistemological crises (Alaimo; Armiero; Glissant; Sharpe 21, 104; Whyte). Ultimately they aim to take root and *placemake* to resist and alter the "weather." Later in this chapter, I reflect on how this might work for poets needing to reframe and reclaim their right to, and place within, the realm of "nature" first.

Black Poetry and the "discomfort with nature"

"For…nearly a century…African Americans have been collectively shelved under Uncomfortable in Nature," writes Shockley, and yet, the groundbreaking *Black Nature* "highlights" the importance of this "distinctive" Black biosocial ecopoetic "thread" (Shockley, "*Black Nature*" 763). This retrospective anthology of poetry pushes us, notes Shockley, to recognise that poems that treat "the natural world" in a less-than-celebratory manner are no less "nature poetry," and that, importantly, they anticipate "an increasingly complicated understanding" of the environment ("*Black Nature*" 763). Shockley also diagnoses a unique, triple marginalization of Black poetry, Black poetic aesthetic, and Black nature writing—within the American poetry, broader ecopoetic, and Black poetry traditions—yet to be fully redressed by this anthology or others. For Shockley, Black nature poetry's "disregard…within the…American literary nature poetry and ecopoetry canons" is "rooted in" Black poets' inability to participate "in the Romantic poets' reveries and ecstatic outbursts about Nature's mystery and majesty" ("*Black Nature*" 763). Black poets' unique "discomfort" with nature is one of the consequences of physical enslavement and a "dehumaniz[ation] through language," that is, a *narrative* dehumanization and animalization of nonwhite bodies (Weaver in Burawa et al. 229; Shockley, "*Black Nature*" 763). Moreover, the dominant "mononarrative of [what is poetic] innovation," restricting it "to the (white) avant-garde," further marginalizes the Black ecopoetic practice and thought (Ramazani xx, viii).[4] Yet this "disregard" has also something to do simply with the themes and environments on which African American poetry centers. In Shockley's view, the "association of black poetry with urban environments," which "helped African American poets break through exclusionary barriers and gain recognition within 'mainstream'…literary circles," is also partially to blame "for the…perception of African American poetry as being urban, and having nothing to do with Nature," making "the phrase 'black nature poetry'…an oxymoron" (Shockley, "*Black Nature*" 763).

Contemporary African American poets are viscerally aware of such literary exclusions, their lineages, colonial connotations, and violent, past and ongoing traumatic experiences, and in their works they, therefore, proceed with caution in embracing their "trans-corporeality" or animality in celebratory ways (Alaimo 22), "claiming and disclaiming nature" (Dunning 5). Yet urban or even working-class "industrial" poetry—that is, poetry that centers explicitly on the working-class racialized, gendered, embodied experience, on the ghostly urban (post)industrial landscapes—Black ecologists and ecopoets show us, is precisely the stigmata of the colonial and "capitalogenic" ecological devastation that undergirds the climate crisis but which many refuse to see (Moore n. pag.; Alaimo 22–37). Thus, this turning away from nonurban "nature," and the explicit urban thematic and aesthetics, has everything to do with climate. It is also what links

Black ecopoets' "undisciplining" and remapping of environmental and climate thinking with the work of other trans-corporeal ecologists who write on behalf of the poor or communities targeted for colonial extraction, or even of early 12th-century white working-class poet-critics of gendered industrial capitalism and exploitation[5] (Alaimo; Chen; Sharpe 13). In other words, the articulation of what Alaimo calls "sinister trans-corporeality" (30)—that is, the toxic "infiltration" of the body by colonialist, "capitalist…, Fordist [and post-Fordist], harvestable" regimes (Alaimo 30; Escobar 6–7)—is central to the understanding of climate change as systemic, spatial and planetary-scale, and intimately embodied. Extractive regimes, sensed, recorded, and expressed by precarious poetic author-bodies, are directly linked to the now widely recognized accelerations of contemporary climate change and extinction. Black nature and (or in) urban poetry often trace precisely how ruinous, violent, racialized, mega-scale socioeconomic systems work on the body, on the Black "biotariat," and larger nonhuman ecosystems (Moore n. pag.), without necessarily always engaging with climate change's usual list of large-scale ecological horrors. It is such embodied and systemic and decolonial engagements with climate that interest me in the poetic work of Weaver and Shockley.

Black "biotariat" and Embodied *Ecopoethics*

Afaa Weaver's long and rich archive of autobiographical narrative poetry—*Water Song* (1985); *My Father's Geography* (1992); *Stations in a Dream* (1993); *Talisman* (1998); *Timber and Prayer: The Indian Pond Poems* (1995); *Multitudes* (2000); *The Plum Flower Dance* (2007); *The Government of Nature* (2013); *City of Eternal Spring* (2014); and *Spirit Boxing* (2017), among others—is decades long and frequently referenced in the context of African American ecomaterialist and autobiographical poetry. This is despite Weaver not engaging instrumentally, or literally, with the mainstream understandings of climate or environment. In fact, Weaver would say himself that the aim of his poetics, especially after *Timber and Prayer*, was "the erudition of [his] interior [rather] than the exterior world" (in Burata et al. 221; Weaver, "The Eighth Man" 46). And yet Weaver can be considered an urban narrative and "enfleshed" climate poet of crucial significance in Christina Sharpe's understanding (21). Weaver insists that any practice of repair and reclamation must be deliberately epistemic, poetic, but also consciously carnal. It must disengage from the Eurocentric and Cartesian dichotomies, Western, white misogynist epistemic traditions, classed ecopoetics, and colonial regimes of extraction and dehumanization, but it must center on the body, too.

Weaver trusts poetry's capacity to be a vehicle for such embodied, *ecopoethical* knowledge-making and spatial work. He argues that "poetry holds the world to the imperatives of the deep compassion human beings can have for one another" but also that, in his own case, his "trauma has revealed itself in the exploration made possible by poetry" and that he thought of this exploratory work as "being driven by the *investigative light of the lyric*, as in mining" ("What Lies Inside of Us" 295; in Burata et al. 219 [emphasis mine]). He describes himself as a Black poet-"worker born to workers…who had emerged from the working class by birth and by occupation" and for whom poetry is an ethical *practice* of awareness, healing, and liberation ("The Eighth Man" 45).[6] Reading and writing poetry, he argues, helped him also recognize the spatial and systemic dimensions of his poetic work. As such, it also was a vehicle for environmental *systems thinking* including "a conscious awareness of cartography as [his poetic] modus operandi" ("The Eighth Man" 46), which enabled him to "see more clearly the complexities of [his] own experience," and it "unlocked the hidden *corridors* of [his] traumatic childhood, corridors that had held [him] hostage" ("The Eighth Man" 46; emphasis mine).

I am interested here precisely in what his Black spatial, autobiographical, and "trans-corporeal" poetic "I" and "we" teach us about architectures, cartographies, and networks of "environmental harm" *across* his diverse and occasionally bilingual English and Chinese poetic, philosophical, and translation projects (Alaimo 18, 22, 34). "Arts of living on a damaged planet" in an era of the Anthropocene, require, as Elaine Gain et al. note, that we recognize the "horror of our civilization—and yet refuse its inevitability" (in Tsing et al. G4). They urge us "to notice that the [Anthropocene's] "we" is not homogeneous" and that some of its humans are "considered more disposable than others" (in Tsing et al. G4). Resistance to the sociopolitical architecture of environmental harm in Weaver centers on the body for a reason, then; the "disposable" and "serviceable body" is central to the climate-devastation-causing capitalist regime (in Tsing et al. G4; Morrison 73). Yet, this Black body is often ignored as the locus of environmental knowing (Tsing et al. G4, Morrison 73). Like Shockley later on, Weaver places the reflecting and sensing Black (poetic) bodies and their subjectivities at the center of environmental corporeal worlds to heal and to meditate on large-scale ecologies and climate systems. This poetic task is not without challenges. Weaver states that while Walt "Whitman started out by celebrating his "self," Weaver "had to articulate [his] "self' [first] in the process of pursuing a poetic project" (in Burawa et al. 228). Yet he also searches for a new modality of being and of writing this self into nature bioculturally and on non-colonialist terms by engaging African American, Asian, and African embodied, decolonial, poetic, spiritual, and meditative philosophical practices of thought. In other words, for Weaver and other Black poets, such *ecopoethic* self-repair work foregrounds the Black body that knows, experiences, *and* withstands and resists the "total climate" of exploitation (Alaimo; Sharpe 104). Such *ecopoethic* work often demands reclaiming environmental thinking and the body from its racist and misogynist Eurocentric environmental, ecopoetic, and even posthumanist traditions (Blanco; Lynes 55; McKittrick).

For example, in *The Government of Nature,* the poet stages several failed epistemic encounters with the colonial actor, "a rogue disciple," "an apostate" ("The Ancestors Speak to the Cowboy," *TGoN* 20). The poem "Buddha Reveals the Apocalypse to the Cowboy" opens the volume, invoking the cowboy and his ancestors and descendants who "dreamed" "Americas highways," who "build [their] own ultimatums," but the poet is unable to comprehend "what drove [them] to speak holy names as convenience," ending with an admonishment to the cowboy "to exorcise this [violent and grandiose] thing in you" (*TGoN* 3). In "Ancestors Speak to the Cowboy," the ancestors themselves, Weaver writes, are at fault, as they "fell headfirst into some lust, a sadness,/misguided fingers turning to prophecies" (3) and gave the cowboy "a dream" that was "special," gave him "a map to outside worlds" (3); they failed to "teach" and to "guide" him. "Interpretation of Tongues," a later poem dedicated directly to the cowboy, is a litany of urgent questions, structured in disjoined couplets, pleading with god to "interpret the tongues," the "voices that speak" to the cowboy "from the dead wish of ambition." The poet cannot comprehend what made the settler "hear mayhem instead of magic" (*TGoT* 21). The poet pleads, therefore, for answers so that "we can chant the invocation" to avert further violence and "bind this Satan" (21). "Thought in reality spaces itself into the world," teaches poet-thinker Édouard Glissant (1), but in Weaver, the worldling power is not in the poetic chant. For Weaver to "decrescendo," "to mute," to resist "white noise," to engage with a different cosmology and political theory of self and the environment in poetry is a precondition for a poetic reclamation of the body and the world ("Flux," *City* 63).

If the climate crisis is a systems crisis, and the Black "biotariat"[7] is at the center of its mechanism, Weaver's poems honour the poetic, authorial, and trans-corporeal "I" as a biosocial agent who registers violent ecologies and networks and knows their infrastructures and cartographies. He does so by literally muting "the white noise" ("Flux," *City* 63) and publishing his work increasingly under several names, his American and his given and adopted Igbo name Afaa and Chinese name 蔚雅風,[8] and he frequently incorporates Chinese poetic and philosophical references in several volumes of poetry, *The Plum Flower Dance, The Government of Nature,* and *The City of Eternal Spring,* among them. At some point, he states, amusingly, that for him, it was "Chinese culture" that became his "starship[, his] Galactic Star Ship Plum Flower" (Akbar n. pag). In his poetic manifesto, biographical prose, and poetic pieces, Weaver writes explicitly about the way transnational epistemologies, spiritual practices, meditation, polylingualism, and translation can liberate the body and contribute to transnational epistemological pathways and to a transformative, humanist *ecopoethics* ("What Lies Inside of Us"; "The Eighth Man"; Burawa et al.). In particular, meditation, taiji, and Daoist practices became a vehicle for that but were also a lifeline, "help[ing him to] occupy the painfully complex and often contradictory spaces of race, gender, and class that would have otherwise torn [him] apart beyond any hope of healing" (in Burawa et al. 235). Most explicitly, in *The Plum Flower,* poems are divided into chapter-sections, "Gold," "Water," "Wood," "Fire," and "Earth," marked in two languages, following "five basic movements of qigong," mattering a planetary, bilingual, transnational geography into his texts (in Burawa et al. 235). But he also emphasizes that the body—the living, breathing, knowing Black male body of the poet—is also a miracle, "tender biopower" (Musiol and DeSoto, "Industry"), "a wish in disguise spun out from this celestial space to be poor/to be covered with black skin" ("Archaeology of Time: Waste," *City* 42). This eco-"poetics of...assembling" himself is a force to be reckoned with precisely because it pries the body from its instrumental, "biotariat" function (Akbar n. pag; Moore n. pag.).

Elsewhere, the poet meditates poignantly on tending to the weary body, "which knows its place within [an environmental, geopolitical, and] class system" and is able to speak it (Lewontin and Levin in Alaimo 22). In his 2013 epistolary poem "The Government of Nature," Weaver openly addresses his body tenderly as the "dear body of mine" (*Government of Nature* 26–27). The poem is not simply a tender letter to this body but also an account of the ways in which this body has been lettered, inscribed on, fragmented by childhood violence, "longing itself into being" and resisting violent ecologies (*Government of Nature* 26–27). In "Archaeology of Time: Convertibles," the poet finds solace in watching Asian "women selling/the whole cloth of the end of the world,/cloth we tear to shreds to weave again" (City 36). It is this "mesh of *black and yellow,*" this "pale slash Messiah flat fifths, fingers tapping/pulling our skin over oceans to save it," that also reconstitutes this body ([emphasis mine] *City* 36).

Ultimately, drawing on non-Western cosmologies, spiritual, and restorative meditative, movement, and breathing practices (such as taiji or qigong), Weaver engenders "the agencies" of the diasporic Black body. He finds, especially in his post-Taiwan and China travel poem series, that his engagement with non-Western thought offers a new way out of the Western human/nonhuman split and gives him meditative tools to reclaim the flesh, breath, and thought of the body outside the Western ways of imagining the planet and the Black body labouring within. This body, Weaver writes, can "raise from thought to be, being beyond thought/with energy as breath" in "City of Eternal Spring" (*City* 10). This body is also "a world with eyes opening inside light, inside knowing," he writes, "inside oneness" (*City* 10). He worlds this oneness in his poem, as he accounts for his post-traumatic healing, which "appears when the prison frees me to know I am not it and it is not me" ("City of Eternal Spring," *City* 10). In this poem, the Black flesh and its intimacies are not just dangerous vulnerabilities—though they are that, too, as the poem deals with surviving sexual trauma—the body is also the nexus for the embodied restorative meditative practice for political world-ecology, and a new embodied "poetics of [tender] relations" (Glissant). "Believing" in what the poet can "touch, see, feel, hear taste," Weaver implies, will "make a case for being alive" ("City of Eternal Spring," *City* 10).

In other words, to Weaver, the speaking, living, breathing, embodied, and weary "I" is cosmos but also an instrument of observation and repair. "I am a city of bones," he writes in "Flux," that can cherish its "trans-corporeal" (Alaimo) "enfleshment" (Sharpe 21), "deep inside my marrow," accessible only when "a song in electric chords decrescendo to mute, *rise/to white noise*" ("Flux," *City* 63; emphasis mine; Alaimo 31). In Weaver's work, the Black body is a target of sexual and racial violence, exhausting labour conditions under capitalism, and the toxicity of systemic environmental relations, but it is also a body that refuses to be "disposable" (Tsing et al. G4) and that *tends to itself* and learns how to emplace itself on this environmentally "damaged planet" and to heal it (Tsing et al.).

Apocalypses as Embodied Landscapes

"Every landscape is haunted by past ways of life," say Elain Gan et al. (in Tsing et al. G2), and every landscape bears traces of ruins and apocalypses. Like Weaver, Shockley draws attention to Black bodies who are "the whole world of difference" (Weaver, "Buying History of the Language," *The City* 19), and both live and, at various times are, apocalyptic landscapes. But she often experiments directly with the ecopoetic topography, worlding horrific and quotidian apocalyptic environments in her poetic landscapes in very deliberately spatial ways. Thus, my approach to Evie Shockley and her more recent work differs in focus and scale from my reflection on Weaver's work. I aim to zoom in on just two ecopoetic spatial experiments from her *semiautomatic*—":: the way we live now ::" (6) and ":: *in the california mountains, far from shelby county, alabama and even farther from the supreme court building, the black poet seeks the low-down from a kindred entity* ::" (52)[9]—in order to reflect how their transcultural ecothought is mattered by her "renegade" ecopoetics of space (Shockley, *Renegade*). Environmental violence and social injustice are spatial in Shockley; they are inseparable and co-constitutive in her work.

For example, ":: the way we live now ::" is one of Shockley's *semiautomatic*'s grimmer poems of ecological and racial devastation (6). "Black matters," argues Katherine McKittrick, "are spatial matters" (xii), and Shockley *matters* this point into and landscapes the racial-environmental apocalypses using poetical typographic tools as topographic tools: all lower-case letters, very deliberate lineation, and the title framed with and released by double colons [::]. Of interest is her particularly spatial uses of "::" to construct doorways, equivalencies, escape routes. In programming languages, :: has different functions—for instance to refine, rearticulate the main declaration in the C++ language—but most importantly, its use *builds* things; it is architecture. Similarly, in this poem, :: , which follows the title and precedes each attempt at the articulation of horrors in different stanzas, suggests a similar function. It enables syntactical analogies but also serves as a portal to, or a sequential doorway to another portal to another portal without a destination, a door leading to no place, and to no escape. In the two harshly enjambed stanzas, the poet shows that "the cultivators of corpses" who had done their historic violent deed to Black bodies are still at work, "busy seeding/plague across vast acres of the land" in the present time (6). They still make the current existence haunting, insufferable, exhausting, and also anticipatory (6). Like Sharpe, Shockley sees a horrific landscape as a "total climate" (Sharpe 104) or total landscape, a syntactical geography, in which colonial and contemporary regimes of biocultural and spatial violence collide and overlap, and where the past and present are impossible to tell apart.

As someone interested in the spatial affordances of the poem's form, Shockley literally builds this gruesome, confining landscape within two stanzas, double colons, repetitions, and four specific poetic lines in which the opening "when" operates as both an adverb, about the impossible temporal location, and a conjunction, linking impossible regimes of violence and devastation. She argues that when the navigational "there-/you-are" is simultaneously "where-you-were," the past and present environmental targeting and devastations collapse, and you end up facing "the sunset groans" and "the Atlantic" and "setting blue fire to dark white bones" (*semiautomatic* 6). If one of the crucial critiques of the universalising discourse of the Anthropocene is to abolish a uniformed human "we," responsible for climate devastation (Armiero; Moore; Tsing et al. G4), Shockley makes it clear that it is the "cultivators of corpses" who are "choking schools/and churches in the motley toxins of grief, breeding/virile shoots of violence so soon verdant even fools/fear to tread in their wake ::.," who are to blame (*semiautomatic* 6).

In this poem, the ecological doom appears to be "the condition of Black life"[10]—replaying in a traumatic loop, sonically, via repetitions, but also rigidly built in a poetic, syntactical line, spatially—and the poet notes that "all known tools of resistance [are] clutched in the hands of the vile" (*semiautomatic* 6). This seemingly "ungeographic" and trans-temporal poetic land-scape of violence, however, is an important corrective to linear Eurocentric and chronological narratives of the Anthropocene, whose devastation is to loom in the near future and affect a uniform "we" (McKittrick xiii, xix, xxi). In Shockley, there is no before and after the colonial devastation, nocommunal Anthropocenic "we," and the rhetorical question of "when" doubles up ambiguously as a declaration of inevitability. Her figurations point to the past inseparably linked to the present in an unending cycle of "breathing in the ashen traces/of dreams deferred" (*semiautomatic* 6). Shockley warns, however, that "the disempowered" are not so disempowered ('6). They may "slice smiles across their own faces," but they "hide the wet knives in writhing thickets of hair/for future use…," suggesting the simultaneous impossibility of telling the catastrophic environmental time with precision but also a possibility of violent insurrection (6).

In her poem titled ":: in the california mountains, far from shelby county, alabama and even farther from the supreme court building, the black poet seeks the low-down from a kindred entity ::," Shockley directly addresses the California drought and alludes to the legal attack on the Voting Rights Act in Alabama in June 2013 (*semiautomatic* 52). She uses similar punctuation devices, lower-case letters, although italicized, suggesting a nearly handwritten, urgent dispatch. In a sense, the environmental violence and desperate climate impacts are just as present and felt in this poem as they are in "in the way we are now ::" (6). And yet this poem worlds a new material realm of possibility via its experimental, airy poetic geography, and an open-breathing spatial structure of freer lineation and five quatrained stanzas, separated by generous line breaks. In this work, the lines interchangeably re-align, to the left, center, and more to the right, and its use of enjambment and punctuation is structured but liberating.[11] While in the previous two-stanza apocalyptic poem of consistent rhymes (ABABBCC), the symmetricality of the poetic stanza form, stanza structure, its rhythm, the tightness of lines, and its repeated syntactical form announced each time by the impending "when" of environmental doom supported a menacing sense of claustrophobic enclosure, here the poem structures "thought" to "spaces itself into the world," in airy, expansive, freeing ways within the poetic line, across different stanzas; making room, offering space to breathe, and reflect, between the lines, among the onslaught of political attacks on civil rights and the environment (Glissant 1).

The indictment of the culprits of the environmental devastation remains, and the poet warns that "whoever/says this weather's nobody's fault has/just bought a bridge they hope to resell" (*semiautomatic* 52). The poet, however, also moves beyond the colonial environmental rhetoric, metaphorically and spatially, and its apocalypses, and finds solace and inspiration in the comparison to incredibly resilient seep-spring monkey wildflowers, which know "how to get what [they] need…" to sustain themselves in and through crisis situations (52) and then return to bloom. Shockley acknowledges both the violent history of Euro-American environmental thinking and its extractivist and capitalogenic dualisms, partitions, and hierarchies (human/nonhuman, body/mind, whiteness/nonwhiteness) but also, like Weaver before, reclaims nonhuman nature as an ally, acknowledging that the seep-spring monkey flower looks like her and is her; it is a "kindred entity" that has answers and has shared an experience of animalising slurs and exclusions from the processes of political participation. It has "also been called *monkey*," she writes, "and didn't get to vote on that either" (52). In fact, the poem addresses the seep-spring monkey directly for survival tips, and this is not an accidental decision. The yellow seep-spring monkey flower is known to withstand poor soil and light conditions, equally, flooding and drought, and other severe weather, and, in Shockley's poem, is "growing/up from the scorched earth of last/year's planned burn," like a Black female poet (52). And, thus, Shockley acknowledges racist, "planned" colonialist practices and civilising discourses, which also dominate environmental work, and which dehumanize people of color, extract natural resources, and equate people of color with the realm of exploitable nature or animality to be dominated, trained, domesticated, civilized. Yet she also transcends it, drawing on a sense of "[B]lack abundance" (Laymon 66, 76) and transspecies solidarity that helps her return when "topsoil is ready for our comeback" (*semiautomatic* 52). The poem itself is one such comeback, offering new geographies of ecopoetic breathing space.

Poetic Climate Sensorium and Its Pedagogies

Ecopoetry certainly can and does narrate and *re-story* ecological crises (Tsing et al.), itself no small feat at a time when the climate crisis is recognized also as a narrative crisis (Tsing et al.; Nixon). Climate poetry, which is *recognized* as climate poetry, often deals thematically with particular understandings or symptoms of climate, and with specific bodies or stages of climate crisis (in)visibility: their extinctions, floods, biodiversity loss, heat waves, diseases, and so forth, especially as these crises begin to viscerally affect the Global North and its white residents in direct, palpable ways. Here, however, I have explored how Black poetic ecologies engage with climate in ways that are often not simply instrumental or thematic in a mainstream sense. I have also suggested, after Sharpe, McKittrick, Shockley, Alaimo, and Weaver, that we pay attention to the lyrical murmur, to the way that a poetics unearths and makes palpable the invisible, yet necrotic, ecosocial infrastructures and relations that destroy some human bodies, and not others; which terraform spectral climate landscapes and wastelands and scaffold ecological crises that eventually are felt elsewhere, belatedly, by white bodies, as "the brink of planetary inferno" (Moore n. pag.; Whyte). There is definitely no shortage of poems that directly and thematically narrate ocean acidification, species extinction, or extreme weather patterns.[12] Yet whether Weaver and Shockley explicitly or thematically address "climate change" in its mainstream, nonsocial, pre-UNSDGs' understanding, they both foreground environmental poetic knowing and sensorial systems thinking that emerge from the recovery of the conscious Black embodiment and from "Black geographies" (McKittrick), which are always at the core already "trans-corporeal" and human (Alaimo 31; UNSDGs). And if a racialized gendered body is an epistemic instrument, a social seismograph of ecosocial catastrophic climate-devastating systems, a Geiger counter made of flesh, of social toxicity, it knows well that "climate" is not just climate, or that "nature" is not just exterior to the human body. Uniquely socially emplaced, the body "registers" the cruel, insidiously exhaustive, "material agencies of place" (Alaimo 24). Ultimately, however, Weaver and Shockley explore not only the devastation that biosocial toxicity wrecks on different bodies and communities but how these bodies become aware of their emplacement within regimes of extraction and environmental social crises (Lewontin and Levins qtd. in Alaimo 22). Also, and perhaps more important, they focus on the ways that they endure, survive, adapt to, renege on, resits and "learn to live despite hatred," through socio-political violence and through climates of devastation (Weaver, "A Poem for Freddie Gray" 178).

Ultimately, another way in which Weaver's and Shockley's poetic sensorium performs climate work make space, extends to involve the reader. Since poetry is a spatio-somatic medium that acts on the human body, and it requires breath and space of the writer and reader, such embodied poetic breathing in and out, reading and listening to poems and bodies together, it enables is itself an environmental act of care and deep and focused attention (Musiol, "Grieving"). I such understood poetic climate work, we, readers, can experience the present-focused, fragile, grounding breathing spaces that are created when ecopoems are read aloud and recited collectively. This embodied readerly work is as important as the emphasis on the work of "transcorporeal" climate solidarity (Alaimo 30; Billington; Musiol, "Grieving"). If Black "renegade poetics" teaches us that climate is more than a networked system of scientific weather variables, and that the Black body registers and knows the infrastructure of extraction, these poets can and do engender reparative writing and reading experiences, and create a *climate* for breathing, for the "right to breath" (Allen et al., Musiol, "Grieving" 186), and for contemplative systems thinking. It may, therefore, be important for readers and learners to meditate on and activate the somatic and sustaining potential of poetry to act on the biosocial body, itself the target of environmental injustice that takes the breath away, to end delicately to our own and to others' breathing bodies (Alaimo; Musiol, "Grieving"). In our recent EH work, we did so together with students, scholars, and poets from many parts of the world.[13] Reading Shockley and other ecopoets of color chorally together, we practiced modes of socially and sensorially "reparative" reading (Sedgwick 6, 35). Tending delicately to our own and to others' breathing bodies, we extended their non-necrotic *ecopoethics* geographies, sensing and imagining other weathers, other climates.

Notes

1 Acknowledgements: This chapter owes its existence to polylingual poetic communities in Trondheim. I also thank Afaa Weaver, for sharing his poems at Simmons College—although it took me many years to comprehend the importance of his work, I am truly grateful for the encounter; Cajetan Iheka, for sharing the material from the Black ecologies seminar held at Yale on October 14 and 15, 2022; Shuhua Chen, for her translations; the editors and the anonymous reviewers, for their feedback on the earlier version of the draft; Tor Magnus Sjømæling, for his research assistance; and Kristen Ebert-Wagner, for her editorial help.

2 This is paradoxical too, since the impact of Indigenous or Black ecological thought—its understandings of space, environment, conservation, toxicity, the weather—in other media and fiction and nonfiction genres has been foundational to a rethinking of ecology, climate, and sustainability in EH (Whyte; Tsing et al.).

3 I thank Agata Kochaniewicz for sharing the 2022 recording of Blanco's performance in Malmö, Sweden.

4 Weaver speaks against this marginalisation in his poetry and interviews. As he says, he "could not accept the critical appraisal of black poetry as less than that of the white mainstream" (in Burawa et al. 218).

5 Stacey Alaimo writes incisively about earlier working-class women-poets—Meridel Le Sueur and Muriel Rukeyseyer, for instance—both "industrial," urban poets of the working class, hardly considered climate or "nature poets" and yet so crucial to the environmental and transcorporeal ecopoetics and to the understanding of "unequal redistribution of environmental harm" (22, 27–59).

6 Prior to his publishing and academic career, Weaver worked for Procter & Gamble and Bethlehem Steel, and he frequently writes and speaks about the impact of his working-class perspective on his poetry and worldview (Burawa et al. 223).

7 Jason Moore sees the climate crisis as one among many capitalogenic exacerbations. The system that produces it depends on and expresses itself, in his view, in "the paid and unpaid work performed by humans and the rest of nature"—which he calls "the proletariat, femitariat," and "biotariat"—"bound

together in the most *intimate* ways from the earliest strings of the capitalist world-ecology" (n. pag.; emphasis mine). While I don't share Moore's understanding of capitalism as the primary systems crisis, I find his work on capitalogenic violence illuminating.

8 After adding an Igbo Nigerian name, Afaa ("oracle"), given to him by playwright Tess Onwueme, to his American name, he added his Chinese name, given to him by the scholar Chinghsi Perng and modified by the poet Bei Ta (Akbar, n. pag). Weaver also credits his trips to Taiwan and China as revelatory, deepening his life-long engagement with a new language, epistemologies, poetic traditions, translation, and meditative practice, which in turn were all steppingstones to the development of his transnational *ecopoethic* ("The Eighth Man"; Akbar).

9 The volume was published in 2017, but both poems were completed in 2013 (Shockley, "::Account::" n. pag.).

10 I allude here to the poet Claudia Rankine's "The Condition of Black Life Is One of Mourning," *New York Times,* June 22, 2015, https://www.nytimes.com/2015/06/22/magazine/the-condition-of-black-life-is-one-of-mourning.html.

11 In her reflection on the writing process, Shockley talks about the impact of writing it during a poetic retreat in the Tahoe Basin of the Sierra Nevada. She notes that "[b]eing in that space—not only an amazing community, but a beautiful and . . . unfamiliar landscape—tends to bring out of me work that lies in the more metaphysical and attuned-to-'nature' zones of my poetic spectrum . . ." ("::Account::" n. pag.).

12 Margaret Ronda, who narrates environmental crises in traditional poetic genres of high and late capitalism, shows that poetic environmental discourse does not have to operate thematically or instrumentally, as does the "hortatory discourse of climate scientists and journalists" (Hunter 867), but rather as "enigmatic, refractory ecological imaginaries" (Ronda 5) or constructed poetic climate landscapes (Glissant; McKittrick).

13 These collective readings in postcolonial and transmodal storytelling took place during the Environmental Storytelling and Narrative NoRS-EH school at NTNU in Trondheim on June 4, 2021. For recordings or more information, contact the author.

Works Cited

Akbar, Kaveh. "'Can You See the Poetics of Me Assembling Myself?': AFAA MICHAEL WEAVER." *Divedapper*, 1 Sept. 2014.

Alaimo, Stacey. "Eros and X-Rays: Bodies, Class, and 'Environmental Justice.'" *Bodily Natures: Science, Environment, and the Material Self,* Indiana UP, 2010, pp. 22–37.

Allen, Tenille, Kellie Carter Jackson, Colin Dayan, et al. "I Can't Breathe." *Transition*, no. 117, 2015, pp. 1–15.

Bullard, Robert. *Dumping in Dixie: Race, Class and Environmental Quality.* Westview, 2000.

——. *Unequal Protection: Environmental Justice and Communities of Color*. Sierra Club Books, 1996.

Burawa, Christopher, Cynthia Hogue, and Stacey Waite. "An Interview with Afaa Michael Weaver." *Contemporary Literature*, vol. 52, no. 2, Summer 2011, pp. 212–235.

Chen, Mel. "Agitation." *South Atlantic Quarterly*, vol. 117, no. 3, July 2018, pp. 551–566.

——. *Animacies*. Duke UP, 2012.

DeLoughrey, Elizabeth, and George B. Handley, editors. *Postcolonial Ecologies: Literatures of the Environment*. Oxford UP, 2011.

Dove, Rita. *Playlist for the Apocalypse*. Norton, 2021.

Escobar, Arturo. "After Nature: Steps to an Antiessentialist Political Ecology." *Current Anthropology*, vol. 40, no. 1, 1999, pp. 1–30. https://doi.org/10.1086/515799.

Glissant, Édouard. *Poetics of Relation*. Translated by Betsy Wing. U of Michigan P, 1997.

Hunter, Walt. "Contemporary Poetry and Capitalism." *American Literary History*, vol. 31, no. 4, 2019, pp. 860–69, https://muse.jhu.edu/article/745446.

Iheka, Cajetan. *Teaching Postcolonial Environmental Literature and Media*. Modern Language Association, 2021.

Laymon, Kiese. *Heavy: An American Memoir.* Scribner, 2018.

Lewontin, Richard, and Richard Levins. *Biology under the Influence: Dialectical Essays on the Coevolution of Nature and Society*. New York UP, 2007.

Lynes, Katherine R. "'A Responsibility to Something Besides People': African American Reclamation Ecopoetics." *African American Review,* vol. 48, no. 1/2, 2015, pp. 49–66, 223.

Mauro-Flude, Nancy. "Performing the Internet: Post Internet Folklore." *Digital Humanities and Scholarly Research Trends in the Asia-Pacific,* edited by Shuh-han R. Wong, Haipeng Li, and Min Chou, IGI Global, Hershey, PA, 2019, pp. 200–227.

McKittrick, Katherine. *Demonic Grounds: Black Women and the Cartographies of Struggle.* U of Minnesota P, 2006.

Moore, Jason W. "Profits, Prometheanism & the Problem of Planetary Management." Anthropocene, Capitalocene & the Flight from World History, Part I, 24 May 2022, https://jasonwmoore.wordpress.com/2022/05/24/profits-prometheanism-the-problem-of-planetary-management/.

Morrison, Toni. *Playing in the Dark: Whiteness and the Literary Imagination.* Vintage, 1993.

Musiol, Hanna. "Grieving, Breathing, Keeping Time: Rights, Sequences, and Sonnetic 'Enfleshment.'" *Technologies of Human Rights Representation,* edited by James Dawes and Alexandra Schultheis Moore, SUNY P, 2022, pp. 183–204.

Musiol, Hanna, and Pablo DeSoto. "*Place by Co-Design*: Industry, Postcolony, and Disobedient Storytelling." *ASAP/J,* June 29, 2022.

Nixon, Rob. *Slow Violence and the Environmentalism of the Poor.* Harvard UP, 2011.

Ramazani, Jahan. "Poetry and Race: An Introduction." *New Literary History,* vol. 50, no. 4, 2019, pp. vii–xxxvii.

Ronda, Margaret. *Remainders: American Poetry at Nature's End.* Stanford UP, 2018.

Sedgwick, Eve Kosofsky. "Paranoid Reading and Reparative Reading; or, You're So Paranoid, You Probably Think This Introduction Is About You, Eve Kosofsky Sedgwick." *Novel Gazing: Queer Readings in Fiction,* Duke University Press, 1997, pp. 1–37.

Sharpe, Christina Elizabeth. *In the Wake: On Blackness and Being.* Duke UP, 2016.

Shockley, Evie. "::Account::." *The Account Magazine,* 2022, https://theaccountmagazine.com/article/two-poems/.

——. "*Black Nature*/Human Nature." *Callaloo,* vol. 34, no. 3, 2011, pp. 763–766.

——. *Renegade Poetics: Black Aesthetics and Formal Innovation in African American Poetry.* Iowa UP, 2011.

——. *semiautomatic,* Wesleyan UP, 2017.

Tsing, Anna, Heather Swanson, Elaine Gan, and Nils Bubandt, editors. *Arts of Living on a Damaged Planet: Ghosts and Monsters of the Anthropocene.* U of Minnesota P, 2017.

United Nations Sustainable Development Goals. https://sdgs.un.org/goals.

Weaver, Afaa Michael. *The City of Eternal Spring.* U of Pittsburgh Press, 2014.

——. "The Eighth Man: A Memoir Essay." *Obsidian,* vol. 7, no. 2, 2006, pp. 41–48.

——. *The Government of Nature.* U of Pittsburgh Press, 2013.

——. *Multitudes.* Sarabande Books, 2000.

——. *The Plum Flower Dance.* U of Pittsburgh Press, 2007.

——. "Poem for Freddie Gray, Baltimore." *Resisting Arrest,* edited by Tony Medina. Jacar Press, 2016, p. 178.

——. *Talisman.* Tia Chucha, 1998.

——. "What Lies Inside Us: Connectedness in Language and Being." *The Manifesto Project,* edited by Rebecca Hazelton and Alan Michael Parker, U of Akron P, 2017, pp. 294–297.

Weaver, Afaa Michael, et al. "Cave Canem: A Few Thoughts on African-American Poetic Form, an e-Mail Discussion." *Obsidian II,* vol. 13, no. 1/2, 1998, pp. 83–97. *JSTOR,* http://www.jstor.org/stable/44486364.

Whyte, Kyle Powys. "Our Ancestors' Dystopia Now: Indigenous Conservation and the Anthropocene." *The Routledge Companion to the Environmental Humanities,* edited by Ursula Heise et al., Routledge, 2017, pp. 206–215.

13 "Everything depends on us"

The Ecofeminist Vision in Naomi Shihab Nye's *Honeybee*

Sandra Lee Kleppe

All the worker bees are female,
why is that no surprise?
       —Naomi Shihab Nye

Introduction

The epigraph above is indicative of a contemporary poet's literary allusions questioning a preceding poet's ecocritical blind spots. The title poem of Naomi Shihab Nye's collection *Honeybee: Poems & Short Prose* (2008) is modeled on William Carlos Williams' poem number XXII (also called "The Red Wheelbarrow") in *Spring and All* (1923). The book, *Honeybee*, like *Spring and All*, consists of a mix of poetry and prose passages, and it can be seen as a 21st-century ecofeminist counterpoint to Williams' classic modernist volume. By employing "The Red Wheelbarrow" as a backdrop for her book, Nye makes a bold statement from the outset about what matters in poetry and life. In "Honeybee," Nye challenges Williams' authority by including the line, "You had no idea, did you?" followed by, "You kept talking about/ That wheelbarrow" (lines 7 and 9). The poem's placement makes it stand out even more as it precedes both the book's title page and table of contents. Nye's focus is on the "5 species of honeybee/ Among 20,000 different bee species" and her concluding lines are "everything depends/ On us" (lines 13–14 and 18–19). The pronoun "us" is deliberately polyvalent: in a very literal sense, if bees cease to pollinate plants, (human) life on the planet can be disrupted to the point of its extinction. Paired with the pronoun "you" that calls out Williams's blind spots in line 7, the "us" might also mean a (poetic) generation a century beyond the concerns of modernism—a generation that everything on the planet "depends/on" in real ways.

In *Honeybee: Poems & Short Prose*, a female poet of color questions an influential male Modernist, but her message about what matters—understanding, respecting, and connecting with the ecosystems of the planet—also develops Williams' depictions of nature as both stark and fragile in *Spring and All*. In Nye's volume, poetry is much more than aesthetically appealing. Her poems teach us about possible ways to approach the looming climate crises by promoting communication between the human and non-human worlds, by asking us to consider what matters, by criticizing systems of oppression and destruction such as patriarchy and industrial agriculture, and more. The book teaches us about the value of interdependence between men and women and between humans and the planet's ecosystems. Importantly, it inspires us to do something about the problems facing the planet. There is thus much to be learned from reading and teaching *Honeybee*; by following the speaker's journey across the volume, we can be sensitized not only to the plight of bees, but to the living conditions of a host of other species and how these interact with—and are interdependent on—humans of different genders and many

DOI: 10.4324/9781003399988-17

cultural backgrounds. Because of the strong strains of both ecological and feminist thinking in *Honeybee*, Section I of this chapter will employ a framework that draws on recent re-evaluations of ecofeminism, with an emphasis on the 2014 re-issue of the classic 1993 text *Ecofeminism* by Maria Mies and Vandana Shiva. Section II provides close readings of poems in light of this ecofeminist context and Section III sums up the ecofeminist vision of the book. The educational perspectives of poetry in general and Nye's poems in particular are reiterated in the Conclusion.

Ecofeminist Poetics for the 21st Century

Though there are many branches within ecofeminism, a central common tenet is that capitalist patriarchy is equally destructive to women and nature alike. In the foreword to the now-classic volume *Ecofeminism* by Mies and Shiva, Ariel Salleh points out that "women do 65 per cent of the world's work for 10 per cent of its wages" (xii). *Ecofeminism* explores how, in the global South, much of this work is women's subsistence farming to feed their families and communities. Women in such areas are particularly vulnerable to having their livelihoods and the ecosystems that sustain them exploited by extraction economies such as agricultural monocultures. As Shiva notes in the new Introduction to *Ecofeminism*, "Every crisis we mentioned is deeper; every expression of violence [against women and nature] more brutal" and "corporate globalization" is reducing "the world to monocultures controlled by global corporations" (xiii).

By employing honeybee colonies as the central metaphor of *Honeybee*, Nye points out this same type of double exploitation. In her poem "Girls, Girls," she brings up the fact that "all the worker bees are female" (male bees are expelled from the hive after mating) and in her Introduction to the volume she worries about the growing industry of migratory beekeeping for pollinating monocultures such as "the huge almond crop in California" (71; 1). Nye also cites bee colony collapse disorder (CCD) and chemical pollutants as a threat to honeybees and ecosystems alike. For example, she connects the decline of fireflies to this topic, "I had wondered about the loss of lightning bugs over the years [and] blamed their disappearance on pesticides" (7). Near the end of the book, she reiterates, "you have to look really hard for a firefly now" (157). Mies and Shiva also point out how toxic hazards go hand in hand with industrialized farming and that, "Patriarchal systems would like to maintain silence about these poisonous substances, but as mothers, women cannot ignore the threats posed to their children" because "the chemical pollution of the environment is ... clearly manifested in their ill-health" (82).

The modern environmental movement stems in large part from a seminal work on the devastating effects of chemical pollutants such as pesticides on ecosystems, Rachel Carson's *Silent Spring* (1962). Since then, both ecologists and feminists have embraced this work as a manifesto for change. One of the founders of deep ecology, Arne Næss, credits Carson for inspiring his work, and many of the concerns of deep ecology, such as the idea that all living beings have inherent value and that anthropocentricism has run its course, were particularly influential when ecofeminism arose in the 1970s.[1] From the 1980s onward, ecofeminist pioneers that built on Carson's work, such as Ynestra King ("What Is Ecofeminism" 1987), Val Plumwood (*Feminism and the Mastery of Nature* 1993), and Carolyn Merchant (*Radical Ecology* 1992) all combined the concerns of the environment with those of feminism. Though all of these philosophers are somewhat sensitive to the importance of intersectionality and the dangers of essentialism (conflating women with nature; more on this below), Mies and Shiva put the concerns of women in so-called developing countries and women of color at the forefront of their global analyses in *Ecofeminism*. Naomi Shihab Nye, a Palestinian-American, is also concerned with expressing the value of women of color in contributing to better social and ecological environments. This strain of *Honeybee* becomes more prominent in the final section of the book that concludes with a prose poem on a matriarchal figure, "An older woman in full traditional Palestinian embroidered dress, just like my grandma wore" (162).

Mies and Shiva's work contributed to rectifying the overrepresentation of the white, middle-class, Western focus of second-wave feminism, but ecofeminism, as Naomi Guttman and others have noted, has often been dismissed as essentialist because it is ostensibly "inherently problematic in reinforcing some of the stereotypes feminists have been fighting for the past 150 years, most particularly the idea that women are biologically and/or socially closer to nature than men" (44). However, Guttman and other scholars have begun to re-examine ecofeminism and its renewed relevance for the 21st century, disassociating it from simple essentialist assumptions.[2] Guttman's focus, as the title of her 2014 article indicates, is "Ecofeminism in Literary Studies," with a special emphasis on poetry. Reading several poems about the relationship between humans and agriculture, for example, she explores how the portrayal of such modern phenomena as monocultures and pesticides is rendered in complex, multivalent terms that go beyond binaries such as male/female or human/nature and concludes that ecofeminism is a "powerful force in artistic representation" (49).

In Emma Foster's recent essay, "Ecofeminism Revisited: Critical Insights on Contemporary Environmental Governance" from 2021, she notes that "affinity ecofeminists often use poetry and art to articulate their position…. This is one of the reasons they have been so easily dismissed" (2021, 195). Foster uses the term "affinity ecofeminism" to refute the "caricatured and simplistic critiques" that discredit ecofeminism on the grounds that it equates women with nature. She analyzes the many affinities women's experiences (rather than their biology) have in relation to environmental degradation and concludes that ecofeminism is a much-needed perspective to counter "the Anthropocene thinking that places its hope for environmental salvation in the market and technologies" (200). The prevalence of Mies and Shiva's groundbreaking study is clear in this section of Foster's review; *Ecofeminism* provides an in-depth analysis of how international corporations and new technologies destroy women's subsistence farming under the false flag of "development." In addition, Mies and Shiva point out that women's work and artistic work are often not considered productive in the economic sense of growth or profit, so such endeavors are therefore undervalued.

In this context, many ecofeminists promote art, literature, and poetry as particularly valuable expressions that counter the destructive forces of anthropocentric thinking, forces that include patriarchal capitalism. Mies and Shiva call their vision a "subsistence perspective" where value is measured by the mutual quality of earth's life and human life rather than exploitation of human and natural resources. As Mies sums up in the concluding chapter to *Ecofeminism,* "Subsistence work as life-producing and life-preserving work … is a necessary precondition for survival; and the bulk of this work is done by women" (297–298). The subsistence perspective of Mies and Shiva overlaps with the affinity perspective of Emma Foster—and other ecofeminists discussed in this section employ similar concepts to express the interdependence of humans and nature rather than binary relationships; keywords include integrative approach (Guttman 43), interconnectedness (Foster 202), continuum (Buckingham 152), and coexistence (Guttman 47). The ecofeminist poetics of *Honeybee: Poems & Short Prose* promotes precisely such a vision of interconnectedness of humans and non-humans, which is the topic of the next section.

The Ecopoetic System in *Honeybee*

Honeybee constructs a dynamic poetic system where bees play a starring role throughout the whole, supported by references to many animals and insects, including (but not limited to) bears, cats, chickens, crickets, fireflies, frogs, quails, a lion park, and a lone raccoon. The intertwining of animal and human communities throughout the book has affinities with an ecosystem in the ways all of the parts and whole function in symbiosis. The book creates an ecopoetic system not only through its references to the animal, plant, and mineral kingdoms, but also through a deliberate structure where the book's cover, graphics, punctuation, and section headings function as a scaffold for the content. In addition, there are several intertextual references to other poets and texts that bolster both the thematic and formal features of the volume.

One of the most prominent themes of the book is the value of communication. The language of bees is employed as a sustained metaphor of communication from start to finish, already apparent on the jacket of the book where the front cover showcases the drawing of a bee, surrounded by a variety of elements such as flowers and what appears to be a human village in the background.[3] On the back cover, the title poem "Honeybee" is reprinted, accompanied by more visual elements from the front. As mentioned earlier, this poem also precedes the title page, so its function as a framing device is abundantly clear. The table of contents follows; its sections are separated by small flower icons and a bee icon to introduce the middle section of the book, a sequence of ten bee poems (51–73). The small flower and bee icons are also repeated throughout the book to introduce sections and punctuate poems. These graphic elements support the theme of communication as interdependence between all the parts of the book, whether visual, linguistic, thematic, or intertextual. Immediately after the table of contents are two epigraphs with excerpts from bee poems by Carl Sandburg— "Let the bees go honey-hunting/…in the dome of my head"—and Antonio Machado—"Last night I dreamed.../that I had a beehive here/ in my heart." By intertwining the images of bee colonies and human organs, these poets underline the interrelations between different (bio) spheres such as insects and humans, art and fact, and illustrate how the boundaries are not binary but permeable.

The Introduction to *Honeybee* appears on the opposite page of these epigraphs. This is where Nye outlines some of the major concerns of the volume: "the language of animals"; bees as "fabulous communicators"; "bee problems" such as migratory beekeeping, CCD, and harmful pesticides; and "seeing things through a new filter, a changed light" (1–3). The language and behavior of bees, in particular, is what Nye will employ in the pages that follow to see things in a new light, to suggest models of how to improve communication, and to continue inviting other-than-humans into the human mind and heart, as the epigraphs so eloquently express. On page 4 of the Introduction, Nye picks up this thread again, paraphrasing Antonio Machado, who "dreamed a beehive in his heart could turn even flaws into something tasty" and refers to this creative process as "One thing becoming another, in the tradition of alchemy" (4). The poems after the Introduction explore such mysterious interrelations and transformations between many realms.

Such ecopoetic passages are strewn throughout all of the three parts of the book and there is a sustained metaphor of pollination that stretches across the volume as a whole. The first section contains 21 poems (a few in prose), the middle section is a sequence of ten bee poems (pp. 50–73), and this bee sequence is followed by 51 poems (some in prose). The book as a whole uses ecopoetic passages to embody and promote interconnections between humans and non-humans.

The second poem, "Someone You Will Not Meet," describes a woman who presents a handwritten booklet to her mother containing descriptions of "a few cats and plants" as well as "streams of bees swooping/ to the jasmine vine" (14, lines 25; 27–28). As these bees "dip into blossoms and fly away," she is surprised by a sense of jealously, but ultimately the scene conveys that even the smallest things are worthy: in the concluding lines she stares at "the sesame seeds" on a cookie, and "could almost give them names" (14, line 30; 15, lines 40–42).

Moving from the smallest to the largest entities in nature, the very next poem describes "A Stone So Big You Could Live in It." Here the speaker connects the stone of the title to the "blaze of bees" near the stone's "radiant moss" (16, lines 5–6), signaling in just a few lines interconnections between mineral (stone), insect (bees), and plant (moss) spheres. Just a few pages later, in "For My Desk," the speaker celebrates the bird kingdom, citing joyous "Sparrows," a "Gray dove" and a "purple martin mother/and purple martin father" who "solve it all" (23, lines 14; 15; 17–19). While the speaker leaves the solution a mystery, it is clear here and elsewhere that communication between birds, their singing "joyously" (line 14), can be a model for humans as well. Indeed, the poem that immediately follows "For My Desk" is titled "Communication Skills" and focuses on *mis*communication between human "[f]amilies, neighbors, best friends" (25, line 21).

Several poems throughout the volume describe various layers of a speaker's communication—and by extension interconnections—with non-humans. A few examples from the first section include the poem "Password" where the speaker "walked among train tracks/reading messages in the weeds" (31, lines 22–23); a sense of "pleasure" at hearing frogs "singing on six notes" in the poem "The Frogs Did Not Forget" (32, lines 9; 6), and an overwhelming feeling of belonging in the poem "The Crickets Welcome Me to Japan" (35). Near the end of the first section is a poem titled "Running Egret" in which the bird is personified as "nonpartisan" and the speaker claims that there "are days we wake and need an egret" (45, lines 5; 11). Personification is a type of affinity poetics that can project desired human traits onto birds, yet the sense of needing what nature has to offer counterbalances this anthropocentric effect, considering many facets of what nature can bestow on humans, be it mystery, pleasure, joy, consolation, or impartiality. To sum up this sub-section so far, the theme of communication in these poems offers multiple examples of how humans and non-humans might interact and thus teaches us possible ways of bridging perceived barriers in ecosystems.

The middle section of the book (pp. 51–73) is particularly important, as it is occupied by a sequence of ten bee poems. Each poem is punctuated by a bee icon, whereas in the other sections many of the poems end graphically with small flowers. As a whole, the sequence expounds on some of themes presented in the Introduction: we learn more about the threat to bees under the pressures of industrial agriculture and the consequences this might have for humans, bees as excellent communicators, and bee societies as a model for interdependence. In the opening poem "Pollen," a bee does a "waggle dance/in front of the hive" and the speaker feels soothed, even though she does not "know what that yellow machine/means exactly" (51, lines 5; 7–8). A few lines later she notes that "bees ventilate their homes/by hovering outside and fanning their wings," a fact that makes her hopeful in the closing line that humans will find their way back to nature, and "find the field again" (52, lines 15–16).

In "Pollen" and "Honeybees Drinking," nature offers parallels, comfort, and guidance to humans, though the latter poem introduces warning signals that our human activities are destroying bees, and by extension, ourselves as a species. The prose poem "Honeybees Drinking" opens by meditating on affinities between a child's early verbal discoveries and the language of bees; words are "nectar" on the tongue *"Like a swoon in a flower.... Words and voices, hovering, dipping down"* (53, author's italics). Yet as the poem progresses and the child grows up, the landscape suffers drought, forcing the bees to drink "water out of the cats' water bowls.... Sneaking in under the big tongues and teeth of the cats" (55). Here, we follow a degradation from the tongue and teeth being tools for communication in childhood to the same body parts becoming a threat bees must navigate in order to survive.

In the very next prose poem, "Weird Hurt," there is a long section on how the exploitation of bees in industrial agriculture forces them "to live and dive and drink in the same fields where poisons are spread," making a cat's water dish sound safe by comparison (57). The poem also suggests that the decline of bees is a mirror for "the disarray in the world of humans," intimating that there are more than just affinities between human and non-human activities (ibid.). Indeed, in another poem, "We Are the People," both frogs and bees are kinesthetically connected to humans. The frogs sing "so loudly you could feel a multi-layered frog chorus through your feet as well as your ears" (59), and when the bees are forcefully removed from their natural environment of "pastures and meadows" for managed agriculture the speaker muses, "in a world of disoriented honeybees, do you want to look locked out" of your own home (61)?

The next few poems employ metaphors, such as the "mind's hive" (63), clichés such as "busy bee" (65), and statistics such as "every four mouthfuls we eat or drink... benefit from pollinators" (66), to compare human and insect worlds—and their intersections. In "Bees Were Better," the speaker reflects on her time at college studying the language of bees, who "convey messages through dancing" and have "radar in their wings and brains/that humans could barely understand" (66). The volume as a whole is concerned precisely with understanding, with making connections to the bee world and other spheres in order to relate and function more symbiotically.

The final two poems in the bee poem sequence, "Girls, Girls" and "What Happened to the Air" sum up several of the themes discussed so far, and of the book as a whole. The ecopoetic system of "Girls, Girls" employs scenes from honeybee activities such as gathering pollen (70, line 6), "drinking from thousands of flowers" (line 23), and beating "wings fast to stay warm" (line 31) interspersed with metaphors humans borrow from the bee sphere.[4] In lines 14–15, the "cell phone in your pocket/*buzzes* against your leg," yet the speaker notes, it is "not a honeybee though" (line 16, italics added), drawing attention to how the language we normally take for granted points back to nature. The onomatopoeia "buzzes" is supplemented a few lines later with, "You're *stung* by messages from people far away" (71, line 1, italics added). The poem draws attention to the indefatigable work bees do "so you may have honey" (ibid. line 7) yet emphasizes human inconsideration for these efforts, "Maybe you don't want to think about it.... Pass the honey please" (ibid. lines 9; 11). The concern for the wellbeing of bees, however, turns nostalgic in the closing poem of this section, "What Happened to the Air," where the speaker used to feel the "buzzing" of the wind and now longs for a time "before the honeybees were in jeopardy" (72, lines 5; 21). This poem punctuates the bee sequence by foregrounding the theme of interdependence: we are "all so strangely connected/ and disconnected/ inside a vibrant web of signals" (73, lines 25–27). The poems discussed so far establish this web as a holistic tapestry of affinities between the linguistic and physical, communicative and symbiotic, as well as between animal (including human and insect), mineral, and plant spheres.

The final section of *Honeybee* is the longest, containing a mix of 51 poems and prose passages from pages 75–164. As with the first two sections, a wide variety of creatures that interact with humans appear here. In addition to some bee references, there are elements such as the wind, plants, and stones. There are poems with the titles "There Was No Wind," "This Is Not a Dog Urinal," "Bears," "Cat Plate," and "The White Cat." The sustained use of these motifs from different realms throughout the volume supports the structural metaphor of pollination—each poem brushes off on the next, accumulating significance and propagating yet more references. Although there are many motifs to choose from, one is of particular significance in this section of the book, the use of (clipped) wings and (dead) feathers to explore the themes of entrapment versus freedom, and human war versus nature's harmony.

Examples of this cross-pollination include a man at a Halloween party who "thought about coming as a honeybee but couldn't make the wings" (75) in the very first poem, followed by a description of a cockfight in the second, foregrounding wings that cannot fly. Indeed, the cocks are trapped by humans in a "bloody display" and the speaker vows to become "a friend of chickens" after viewing the fight (77–78). Several types of birds make appearances in this section, including "a crow with a post-it note" (97), underlining the theme of communication across spheres, a political critique of quail hunting that mourns each killed bird's "lungs/ and fancy feathers/ and elegant strong feet" (130), and "a lone ostrich" that stands by a fence with the words "INFO ON HUNTING" (133). The ostrich, like the cocks in the fight, cannot fly away, expressing how animals can become trapped in human structures. This theme comes to a climax in the poem "Ducks in Couples," where the serenity of the ducks is contrasted to human beings who "kill one another" because their imaginations are "broken sticks/ Without any feathers" (137), echoing the motif of entrapment as non-flight. Conversely, motifs pertaining to wings and flight, including airports as human hives, become sustained metaphors of freedom, harmony, and diverse communities across the volume, as opposed to the ostensibly patriarchal activities such as war and political dysfunction.[5] A complicating feature of this vision, however, is that airports are also hubs of pollution. In the context of *Honeybee* this might point to humans' complicity in CCD in hives or it might indicate possible solutions to the calamity, or both. When teaching and learning from poems, ambiguity and polysemy are important aspects of exploring meaning in a complex world, since they point to inclusiveness rather than dismissal.

The Ecofeminist Vision of Honeybee

The feminist and ethnic sensibilities in *Honeybee* are more subtle than the ecopoetic ones described so far, but they become intertwined as the volume progresses. This section will explore two poems that provide flippant commentary on patriarchy at the same time as they integrate motifs of wings and flight-as-freedom, and three poems set in multicultural airport hubs where the speaker is preparing for flight. Together, these poems present an ecofeminist vision of interdependence between humans and non-humans where the value of women's communities gradually gains more significance by the end of the book.

The first poem that mocks patriarchy is "Accuracy," which features a highly unconventional marriage where a 2.5-year-old child named Lyda Rose claims she has married a toy named "Sock Monkey": "I thought of him and/ married him in my mind," she exclaims (80, lines 1–2). The speaker of this narrative poem helps the girl hunt for her monkey husband in a pile of stuffed animals that includes a "snake," "yellow bunnies, battered bears, a small eagle ... a camel," and a bird "that makes a chickadee sound if you press its belly" (79, lines 9–12). When they find the spouse, the girl clutches him "tightly, singing the song of a chickadee trapped in/ a human body" (80, lines 4–5). A chickadee is a small bird, so morphing Lyda into the chickadee is an ecopoetic gesture that has affinities with other transformations in the book. The name "Lyda," according to several sources, means "small winged one," echoing both the chickadee, the wing/ feather imagery elsewhere in the volume, and signaling her agency as a free spirit.[6] The girl's very name references simultaneously the animal (Lyda) and plant (Rose) spheres. There is a turn of events at the end of poem: when the speaker says to Lyda Rose, "It's so nice that you love" Sock Monkey (80, line 9), the child responds, in the closing line, "I didn't say I love him! I said, *he is my husband!*" (80, line 11, author's italics). Thus, the meaning of the title "Accuracy" is revealed. Out of the mouth of this babe comes the understanding that the patriarchal institution of marriage is not necessarily based on love, and this girl will not have her wings clipped; her own agency demonstrates her freedom, and it also turns the concept of child marriage on its head. In addition, this girl transgresses norms by entering into an interspecies marriage. All of these factors contribute to a mix of feminism with ecopoetics. Lyda Rose is a strong, determined girl both in charge of her life and in communication with the non-human sphere.

Another biting commentary on patriarchy is presented in the opening and closing lines of "Girls, Girls," which juxtaposes the genders:

When the boys are alone,
They wash the dishes with facecloths.
          (70, lines 1–2)

....
All the worker bees are female.
Why is this no surprise?
          (71, lines 36–37)

The speaker's comment on boys suggests their awkwardness in the home, and the closing question highlights a parallel between honeybee colonies and human societies. In the hive, the function of the male drones is to breed with the queen; the female bees perform all of the work, including gathering pollen and nectar, feeding larvae, making wax, and keeping the hive clean. In the winter, the women workers "beat wings fast to stay warm (ibid., line 31), and in the summer they ventilate the hive "by hovering outside and fanning their wings" ("Pollen" 52, line 2). This emphasis on wings suggests, here as elsewhere, a strong agency on the part of the women workers. It also parallels the analyses of Mies and Shiva, who document how women, especially those in so-called developing countries, do most of the farming, housekeeping, and child-rearing; indeed, they write that "the everyday subsistence production of most of the world's women is the basis of our ecofeminist position" (*Ecofeminism* 19). The volume *Honeybee* as a whole also draws a parallel between the female workers in beehives who become disoriented and diseased due to industrial agriculture and women in third-world countries whose livelihoods are destroyed due to the "profit-oriented growth mania of the industrial system" (ibid. 15). Under the pressures of the same patriarchal capitalism, bees' and women's subsistence work become commodified in the market economy. Lines such as "All the worker bees are female" and they "beat their wings to stay warm" are not imaginative poetic gestures; they are based on factual information about bee societies. They can trigger a sense of curiosity and even awe in readers that can lead to the desire to learn more about the ecosystem of bees, in addition to sparking empathy for the hard work of bees themselves. Such poems can thus provide the first educational steps in caring and protecting the fragile balance between humans and the creatures we depend on for food and more.

Continuing with the motif of wings, Nye's three poems set in airports contribute to the subtle accumulation of an ecofeminist vision across the volume *Honeybee*. All human aircraft—planes, helicopters, drones, kites—are the result of biomimicry, where humans copy elements from birds and insects to create their flying machines. By choosing airport hubs and airplanes as scenes in several poems, Nye expands on the sustained ecometaphor of hives and flight as community and freedom (or lack thereof). In the first poem of the trio, "The United States Is Not the World," the speaker thanks the airport gate "D-4, Amsterdam to Delhi" for dissolving her "smug Americana" by placing her in a diverse crowd of "mamas in silk saris" (26, line 2), "Sikh boys with powder-puff topknots" (line 5), "braided girls" (line 6), and more. In keeping with the sensibility of 21st-century ecofeminism, the vision presented here and in the other airport poems emphasizes both gender *and* ethnicity.

A diverse community is a strong feature of the prose poem "Before I read *The Kite Runner*," which describes the boarding of an airplane to Cairo (142). The very title signals flight, ethnicity, and intertextuality as interconnectedness. While the speaker holds the book in her lap, several people on the plane connect with her: "Two men from Yemen" exclaim, "Good book!" and "Some women from Germany" pat the speaker's head while they pronounce, "We loved that book!" Even an American couple declare, "It opened our eyes!" The speaker feels befriended by everyone on the flight through the book in her lap, and she concludes the poem with, "Maybe we should just wander around other countries/carrying books" (142). The novel *The Kite Runner* by Khaled Hosseini is set in Kabul against the backdrop of the rise of the Taliban. The subtle suggestion here, and elsewhere in *Honeybee,* is that the values promoted by literature—empathy, imagination, interconnectedness—should replace war and political strife.

The prose poem that closes the volume, "Gate A-4," is a culmination of the theme of communication presented as an all-female society modeled on a beehive, where an Arabic matriarch acts as a metaphorical queen bee who strews sweet pollen on her community of women workers (162–164). When a flight is delayed, the speaker of the poem is asked to act as interpreter for "an older woman in full traditional Palestinian embroidered dress, just like my grandmother wore" (162). The Palestinian woman does not understand English well and is devastated because she believes her flight has been canceled. The speaker and the old woman chat in Arabic and form a friendship. The themes of feminism and ecopoetics merge when all of the women at the gate receive "*mamool* cookies—little powdered sugar crumbly mounds" from the elderly woman in a scene reminiscent of communion. This matriarch parallels the function of a queen bee, and soon all the women at the gate are metaphorically covered in pollen: "we were all covered with the same powdered sugar. And smiling" (163). There is also a metaphor for nectar; when the airline provides drinks, "two little girls from our flight ran around serving us all apple juice, and they were covered in powder, too" (164). Another striking ecopoetic element of this poem is when the speaker discovers that the Arabic woman "had a potted plant poking out of her bag," to which she comments, "Always carry a plant. Always stay rooted to somewhere" (164).

"Gate A-4"—the final poem of *Honeybee*—closes with the speaker proclaiming that the multilingual, communal bonding at the gate is "the world I want to live in .... This can still happen anywhere. Not everything is lost" (164). Although the volume ends with these lines about the strength of an all-female community, the ecofeminism in the poem—and in *Honeybee*—does not exclude any gender (or species). During the two-hour wait at the gate, the speaker and her new friend call a number of men so that the older woman can talk in Arabic: "we called her son.... She talked to him. Then we called her other sons.... Then we called my dad ... and found out of course they had ten shared friends" (163). Thus, the women in the poem retain agency by including men in their bonding, while still keeping them at some distance over the phone. In addition to all of these calls, the speaker thinks "why not call some Palestinian poets I know and let them chat with her?" (ibid.). By including poets in the conversation, the speaker draws attention to poetry as a communicative device for sharing experiences. It also points to the intertextual elements of the book that support inclusive ecofeminism.

As Mies and Shiva have noted, ecofeminism is an inclusive movement promoting "interconnectedness among women, among men and women, [and] among human beings and other life forms" (12). In *Honeybee,* Nye makes a point of contrasting men who are hunters, warmongers, and/or insensitive to the needs of nature, with male writers who embrace a holistic vision of interactions. In the title poem "Honeybee" (discussed above), there is a skepticism of the poet William Carlos Williams' version of what matters, at least in his famous wheelbarrow poem: "You had no idea, did you?/ You kept talking about/ That wheelbarrow" (lines 7–9), whereas the speaker is concerned with "5 species of honeybee" that are in danger (line 13). By contrast, the two epigraphs by male poets celebrate connections with nature; Sandburg portrays bees buzzing "in the dome" of his head, and Machado describes bees making combs in his heart. And of course Nye can simultaneously be offering homage to Williams: elsewhere in *Spring and All* he celebrates roots, branches, and healing. One sinister male figure in *Honeybee* is the speaker's president (Bush) who goes quail hunting in "My President Went" and is insensitive to the suffering of countries where he wages war in "Letters My Prez Is Not Sending" (130; 89). However, countering this, the speaker proclaims in another poem, "Ted Kooser Is My President," describing this poet as someone who is "not big on torture at all" and "could probably sneak into your country.... and say something really good about it" (36, lines 18–21). Preferring a poet as president is just one gesture that indicates how the intertextual elements of the book are intertwined with the ecopoetic and feminist ones. Other writers Nye pays homage to in *Honeybee* include the great nature poet Emily Dickinson, and Margaret Wise Brown, author of "Goodnight Moon"—a child's story about the loving affection between a bunny and the moon (161). Finally, as noted above, Khaled Hosseini's novel *The Kite Runner* provides a source of affection and connection between several strangers boarding an airplane. Here again the motif of flight, represented by the kite and the airplane, has affinities with all of the winged creatures presented in *Honeybee*, including bees, a chickadee, crickets, crows, ducks, fireflies, martins, quails, sparrows, and more.

Conclusion and Educational Takeaways

The volume *Honeybee* echoes the concerns of leading ecofeminists Maria Mies and Vandana Shiva, whose decades of environmental activism underline the connections between women workers, especially those of color, and the degradation of the planet through industrialized agriculture controlled by international for-profit corporations who destroy ecosystems through commodification of subsistence farming, a process that involves the massive use of pesticides, synthetic fertilizers, and monocultures. It is precisely such chemicals alongside monocultural beekeeping, as Nye points out in her Introduction and elsewhere, that have contributed to both bee colony disorder and the large-scale poisoning of our natural environment. Contemplating the fate of bees in *Honeybee* allows both poet and readers to see "things through a new filter" (Nye 3) and learn about new perspectives on the complex environmental problems facing humans and non-humans alike.

Communication is one the most central themes of *Honeybee*, and poetry, like the language of bees Nye describes in the book, is an undervalued form of transmission of knowledge, ideas, empathy, and inspiration that deserves a more prominent place in our toolbox of approaches to teaching about the environmental crises facing the planet. In a short article from 2021 titled "How Poetry Can Help Us Understand the Urgency of the Climate Crisis," Christina Thatcher points to some of the crucial functions poetry can have in the current discourse around climate: "poetry has the power to make abstract or diffuse issues, like climate change, more real to readers" (3rd paragraph). It can do so in several ways. For Thatcher, reading nature poems by women poets such as Ellen Bass and Gillian Clarke helped her feel "the full emotional impact of climate change" and triggered her to do something about it (by writing the article, for one).

For ecofeminists, this type of connection is often referred to as "embodiment."[7] This sense of embodiment appears throughout the volume *Honeybee*. Many such examples expand on the opening metaphors of the epigraphs—Carl Sandburg's bees "in the dome of my head" and Antonio Machado's "beehive/ here in my heart." In the Introduction to *Honeybee,* as noted above, Nye writes of poet Machado that he "dreamed a beehive in his heart could turn even flaws into something tasty" (49). Echoing Sandburg, in the prose poem "Help With Your Homework," the speaker writes that in "the mind's hive, chips and glimmers of language… sashayed gracefully" and in "Busy Bee Takes a Break," the speaker proclaims that "to stretch out on the bed with a single good book" is the "the honey of the mind time. Light shines through our little jars" (63; 65). Other lovely examples of ecopoetic embodiment in the book include frogs singing "so loudly you could feel a multi-layered frog chorus through your feet as well as your ears" (59), and the girl Lyda singing "the song of a chickadee trapped in/ a human body" (both discussed above, 59; 80).

Poetry is especially well positioned to teach humans how to connect, not just intellectually, but kinesthetically and emotionally with other humans and non-human others through sound, tone, imagery, simile, metaphor, rhyme, rhythm, and so on. Learning to connect bodily and effectively with the non-human is crucial if we are to have any chance at making a positive difference in the current climate crisis where species are disappearing at alarming rates. In the poem "Deputies Raid Bexar Cockfight," the speaker is forever changed after witnessing the bloody spectacle where humans force the animals to battle: "I pledged myself further to the strange life" as "a friend of chickens in general, friend of dust" (78, lines 2; 5). Such change starts with us, and so much depends upon us to avert the sixth extinction on the planet where not only bees and other creatures are threatened, but the human species as well. Humans all over the world are experiencing climate catastrophes from storms and floods to droughts and fires. In the poem "Click" Nye describes how on the same day as "One million acres of the Texas Panhandle" went up in flames and "ten thousand animals/ [were] scorched. Three people told me/ poetry saved their lives" (124, lines 8–11). If poetry only saves the life of one chicken or one bee or one human, we should welcome its potential in the challenging times facing all creatures on the planet.

Notes

1 "The international, long-range ecological movement began roughly with Rachel Carson's *Silent Spring.*" (Næss and Rothenberg 1989, 210).
2 See, for example, Seagar (2003), Buckingham (2004), and Guttman (2016).

3 Jacket art by Chris Raschka; Jacket design by Chris Raschka and Sylvie Le Floc'h.
4 The ecofeminist theme of "Girls, Girls" will be discussed in the section "The Ecofeminist Vision of *Honeybee*" below.
5 There is a strong anti-war theme in *Honeybee* in poems such as "Letters My Prez Is Not Sending" (89) and "Broken" (92). Though war is part of the military-industrial nexus of patriarchal capitalism that destroys both women's livelihoods and natural environments, the topic is beyond the scope of this chapter.
6 Lyda" can also be a version of "Leda" hence echoing the myth of Leda and the Swan but giving the girl real agency in this poem. On other meanings of the name see https://www.thebump.com/b/lyda-baby-name Accessed April 13, 2022. http://www.thinkbabynames.com/meaning/0/Lyda.
7 Sources on embodiment: https://www.europenowjournal.org/2020/03/09/ecofeminist-embodiment-in-the-anthropocene/ Accessed April 22, 2022.

Works Cited

Buckingham, Susan. "Ecofeminism in the Twenty-first Century." *The Geographical Journal* 170, no. 2 (2004): 146–154.

Foster, Emma. "Ecofeminism Revisited: Critical Insights on Contemporary Environmental Governance." *Feminist Theory* 22, no. 2 (2021): 190–205.

Guttman, Naomi. "Ecofeminism in Literary Studies" in *The Environmental Tradition in English Literature*, edited by John Parham, Abingdon, Oxon: Routledge, 2016, 37–50.

King, Ynestra. "What Is Ecofeminism?" *The Nation,* 12 December 1987.

Merchant, Carolyn. *Radical Ecology: The Search for a Livable World. Revolutionary Thought/Radical Movements*. New York: Routledge, 1992.

Merchant, Carolyn. Professor Carolyn Merchant Reflects on Legacy of Ecofeminism." Interview with Sydney Schoonover in *The Daily Californian*, April 22, 2018. Accessed February 7, 2022 at https://www.dailycal.org/2018/04/22/carolyn-merchant-uc-berkeley-ecofeminism/

Mies, Maria, and Shiva Vandana. *Ecofeminism*. Foreword by Ariel Salleh. London: Bloomsbury Academic & Professional, 2014. Originally published in 1993.

Næss, Arne, and David Rothenberg. *Ecology, Community and Lifestyle: Outline of an Ecosophy*. Cambridge: Cambridge University Press, 1989.

Nye, Naomi Shihab. *Honeybee: Poems & Short Prose*. New York: Greenwillow, 2008.

Plumwood, Val. *Feminism and the Mastery of Nature*. London: Routledge, 1993.

Seager, Joni. "Rachel Carson Died of Breast Cancer: The Coming of Age of Feminist Environmentalism." *Signs: Journal of Women in Culture and Society* 28, no. 3 (2003): 945–972.

Thatcher, Christina. "How Poetry Can Help Us Understand the Urgency of the Climate Crisis." *The Conversation*, November 5, 2021. Accessed February 4, 2022 at https://theconversation.com/how-poetry-can-help-us-understand-the-urgency-of-the-climate-crisis-170971

Williams, William Carlos, and C.D. Wright. *Spring and All*. New York: New Directions Publishing Corporation, 2011. Originally published in 1923 by Robert McAlmon's Contact Publishing Co.

Part IV
Global Juxtapositions

14 Mitigating Ecological Threats

Amplifying Environmental Activism in Gabeba Baderoon's Poetry

Niyi Akingbe[1]

Introduction

It may seem counterintuitive, but ecological threat as an unimaginable horror currently constitutes a much-debated global topic. Its continued attraction to different disciplines has often generated shifting, fragmentary, and contrary ideologies to complicate the world environmental disorder (Soper, 1995:2). Even though a crisis can illuminate how literature examines new challenges, the media visibility of these threats has ramifications for literary studies, accounting for the emergence of ecopoetry, ecodrama, and cli-fi (climate fiction) sub-genres. Living with the conviction that ecological disaster is a clutter of devastation and annihilation that require immediate representations, the cultural environment has moved through historical landmarks in the past decades to accommodate literary studies' intervention in shaping the templates of ecological mitigations (Wuthnow, 2010:2). What would it mean to seek justification for the literary representation of these threats, even at the expense of aesthetics?

Poets have interacted with nature over the centuries to account for the varied environmental changes on earth (Felstiner, 2009:xiii). If the environment has generated conflicting directions since the 1960s, individual nature scholars and writers of literary background have practically become eco-warriors in their participation in heated discourses of national and international environmental politics. (Carter, 2007:2). Often entangled and conflated by literature, ecology and poetry are co-mingled in the works of nature writers such as Henry David Thoreau and Rachel Carson and nature scholars such as Leo Marx and Raymond Williams who have successfully explored experimental engagements with nature (Lidstrom, 2015:2). Given his prodigious contributions to the right mix of empathy and sensitivity, Thoreau could be considered the father of the environmental movement in the contemporary world (Likar, 2011:77). Over the years, the climate change crisis has spurred critical interventions to elicit varied poetic voices of different racial and ideological backgrounds to unsettle Western Romantic orientations and to counterbalance the status quo of degradations. This chapter advances a new perspective on the South African poet Gabeba Baderoon, best known for her anti-apartheid work, as an artist and activist who is also focused on human interactions with the environment.

While the trajectory of ecocriticism is indebted to the exceptional intersection of literature and the environment as aptly illustrated in the American and English literary traditions, a broader approach would seek to probe the essence of ecology within the larger context of phases of the world literary history, to account for how interaction between poetry and nature has evolved from expressing individual passions to advancing ecological preservation campaigns. J. Scott Bryson has outlined that ecopoetry places a premium on the dialogue between humanity and nature (cited in Fisher-Wirth and Street, 2013:xxviii). Ultimately, fuelled by the understanding that global warming and climate change are the negative effects of a complex and complicated

DOI: 10.4324/9781003399988-19

aftermath of the disruption of the ecosystem, ecopoetry interrogates the relationship between human and other-than-human elements. The linking of this disruption to the much-publicised global environmental abuses has incontrovertibly invited ecopoetic interjections. Drawing on the evidence from the works of the romantic poets in their dependence on, and individual appeal to, nature through environmental appreciations, it becomes apparent how ecological consciousness is grounded in the seminal contributions of poets like William Blake, Taylor Coleridge, Percy Bysshe Shelley, John Keats, and William Wordsworth. By advancing a proto-environmentalism that allows for the criticism of eco-violations in their poetry, they have amplified the rhythms of nature while making activist stances more imaginable. In more contemporary times, the efforts of the romantic poets have been robustly complemented in the poetry of eco-poets like Seamus Heaney and Ted Hughes. However, the ecopoetic tradition would benefit greatly from more attention to living poets from beyond the British Isles. On the African continent, other concerns such as decoloniality and feminism once preoccupied many poets, but the environment has now become a more visible and urgent topic as well.

Arguments in this chapter coalesce around the significance of eco-activism in Baderoon's poetry to offer an eclectic reading that has not yet been advanced earlier, despite growing interest in climate change and emerging interest in environmental activism. The chapter explores Baderoon's commitment to nature's protection as it argues that Baderoon's eco-activism inaugurates a decisive engagement with ecocriticism, as the poet works to prevent climate change snowballing into climate chaos. Undoubtedly, quests for nature's preservation, campaigns against environmental degradation, and criticism of climate change tend to pervade Baderoon's poetry. Even though Baderoon's poetry continues to privilege a consummate discourse of the evils of apartheid as it affected the lives of Black majority and Indian minority during the era of Apartheid in South Africa, the impact of climate change on human existence is also given significant attention in all her poetry collections. Baderoon's environmental activism is temperate, consistently shunning radicalism and violence to engage with nature conservation, ecofeminism, environmental imagination, and ecological awareness. Invoking the environmental imagination, Baderoon's nature-oriented poetics blurs the complicated lines between nature and human interaction with it, to foreground factual detailing of environmental features in her four poetry collections. With ecocritical subtlety, these collections strive to identify, interrogate, and respond to the environmental complexities of both global and local concerns. It is in the spirit of concern for humanity, angry optimism, determined zeal, and unwavering commitment that Baderoon continues to advocate for environmental preservation in her poetry.

A Survey of Activism in South African Eco-Poetry

During the apartheid era, not much concerted efforts were made by South African writers to create awareness of ecological degradations in the country. Most literary works subordinated environmental concerns to political themes of racism complicated by the Apartheid system. Marginal environmental narratives are recorded in the works of early South African writers like Sol Plaatje, Dennis Brutus, Ezekiel Mphalele, Nadine Gordimer, Peter Abrahams, and Arthur Nortje. Beyond South Africa, save for limited representations of the environment in Ngugi wa Thiong'o's *Wizard of the Crow* (2006) and Sembene Ousmane's *God's Bits of Wood* (1970), the environment has also been under-represented – curiously – in the works of first-generation African writers like Chinua Achebe, Wole Soyinka, Athol Fugard, Nuruddin Farah, Ayi Kwei Armah, Bessie Head, or Nawal El Saadawi, amongst others. These writers did not privilege the environment as the major focus of their writings (Caminero-Santangelo and Myers, 2011:7). They were more focused on other political problems. As such, little or no attention was devoted to the contextualisation of the environment in their works. Universal environmental concerns, like global warming, desertification, drought, overfishing of oceans, and the disposal of toxic waste, affect a majority of African countries but are not addressed in the works of these writers. For foundational African writers, the tradition has been to privilege the human above the non-human and to discountenance the environmental problematic in African societies (Iheka, 2018:2).

At the level of policy, Ogaga Okuyade has contended that "the environmental crisis in Africa today spans beyond the moral depravity of government and the bureaucratic inefficiency with which the business of governance is run or conducted" (Okuyade, 2013:x). This implies that African governments have remained indifferent to the environmental challenges ravaging the continent. Due to uncontrolled population growth, non-availability of modernised agriculture, soil degradation, and pastoral economies, Africa's natural environment continues to suffer a decline and deterioration (Abbink, 2018:2). The imaginative and interpretative aspects of literature are what make it relevant for the construction of environmental discourses. In Africa, literature has often engaged with the environment primarily to expose the environmental disruption perpetrated by exploitative colonisers in the colonies. Most references to these exploitations refer to the theft of natural resources like land and other natural endowments embedded in the colonies. In the colonial history of Africa, land is all too often one of the concomitants of resource exploitation (De Loughrey and Handley, 2011:3). Revisiting debates on the colonial exploitation of the environment, De Loughrey and Handley have argued that literature testifies to the anxieties of land misappropriation by the empire and its attendant consequences on the African environment. Land and space are coterminous with African ancestral possessions, and their violation signifies environmental disruption.

James Ogude and Tafadzwa Mushonga have strenuously drawn attention to the interaction between literature and the environment when they acknowledged that "literature has consistently shown that the process of environmental globalisation is closely tied in with, if not altogether, overdetermined by a long and complex history of the empire" (Ogude and Mushonga, 2023:93). Ogude and Mushonga have incontrovertibly stressed that the literary imagination cannot be disentangled from its geographical location. Distinct from other genres, and due to its language reservoir, poetry has become prominent as a vehicle of African eco-poetics. With accompanying evocations of environmental degradations, exploitation, and resource theft grounded in the poetry of Niyi Osundare's *The Eye of the Earth* (1986) Tanure Ojaide's *Labyrinths of the Delta* (1986), Ibiwari Ikiriko's *Oily Tears of the Delta* (2000), and G'Ebinyo Ogbowei's *marsh boy & other poems* (2013), postcolonial African literature has begun to continually discuss the ecological concerns of the continent. In this context, Baderoon's oeuvre is worth exploring for its ecocritical dimensions.

With four collections to date, Baderoon has chosen to confront environmental hazards in her poetry without downplaying the other forces at work in South African politics and life. Through her environmental activism, Gabeba Baderoon has become one of the most visible eco-poetic voices in South African literature. Environmental activism – as well as advocacy for the preservation and restoration of the natural environment to search for the humane in the middle of ecological disaster – distinguishes Baderoon's poetry from other South African poets. While her peers such as Allison Claire Hoskins, Toni Stuart, Koleka Putuma, and Wilma Stockenstrom have contributed to the South Africa's ecopoetry largely within the narrow context of aqua-poetics, Baderoon stands out as she strives to engage with all areas of the South African environmental sensibility. Baderoon's overt depiction of environmental threats in her poetry marks a sustained adroitness and a radical departure and progression from the limited attention hitherto given to the environment in South African literary scholarship.

Even though not all the poems in Baderoon's collections deal with nature and environmental activism, a significant portion in each collection offers formidable inquiries into South African ecology. The poems in this chapter were chosen because they are informed by ecocritical and nature concerns. Baderoon's inclination to embrace environmental activism in her poetry stands out as exceptional; she is a South African poet who has continually sustained her interaction with nature while drawing the reader's attention to the larger frameworks in which environmental activism takes place.

Eco-Activism and Poetics of Environmentalism in the Poetry of Gabeba Baderoon

Who are environmentalists? Who are the eco-warriors? What qualifies a poet to be called an environmentalist? Few things are more daunting than having to chart the course of environmental transformation in a world populated by individuals who seem to be indifferent to environmental tensions (Hays, 2000:5). More immediately, agitations for environmental protection start with an undeniable notion that ecological apprehensions are obvious realities which constantly occur in different ways across social and geographical spaces. As narratives of environmental degradation spin wildly around the globe, people in specific ecosystems are stunned by the ferocity of climate change. Concerns about this phenomenon reflect ongoing, devastating upsets that can disrupt bioregions' populations and their ways of life. Environmental threats include the destruction of or loss of natural resources, as well as unsustainable practices that produce landslides, famine, and deforestation. Individuals, writers, and organisations who consider environmental degradation a threat are often referred to as green activists or eco-activists. Green activists are disquieted by the global ecological crisis whose precarity demands urgent action.

As an eco-poet, Baderoon is also an environmentalist who is intensely involved in nature's advocacy. But she is reluctant to describe herself as an eco-warrior, since she considers such an appellation negatively connected to martial metaphors. If such reluctance risks downplaying her fierce commitment to environmental activism, her passionate attachment to nature rooted in ecopoetics tends to offset this perception. Perhaps Baderoon resists warrior metaphor in part because she wants to highlight the task of nurturing nature, while resisting discourses that place this responsibility "exclusively on the bodies of women..." (Jacob, 2015:xvii). While radical and violent eco-environmentalism is characterised by eroticised or militarised representations of ecology, Baderoon's environmental advocacy is grounded in carefully measured poetic rhythms devoid of luridly melodramatic tendencies. Radical environmental literature can turn representation into pessimism when its fecund imagination is too crowded with violence that shapes the interplay between apocalyptic themes and military forms, depicting destructive acts, perpetrated by organisations or government, as irreversible or inevitable.

Elana Gomel has contended that radical narratives often "increasingly abandon the rhetoric of power, statehood, or global trends to focus on violence" (Gomel, 2003:xiii). Interestingly, radical environmental activists are often those who are contemptuous of the less-proactive policies of the government and organisations, even when said policies aim to ameliorate environmental degradation. Surprisingly, one immediately striking feature, marked by consistency in her poetry, is that Baderoon can be termed neither a radical ecofeminist nor a violent environmental activist, but a temperate eco-poet whose activism straddles humanism and the environment. Consequently, her moderate stand attempts to transform the earth while avoiding the insensitivity that can emerge with radical environmental rhetoric. Baderoon would rather embrace nature as a platform for disentangling ecology from its potential self-marginalisation by overly-strident voices. This perception is shared in "Two Autumns":

> I glance outside and expect
> a mountain to rise behind the house,
> sudden granite and trees
> in inlets carved by waterfalls,
> the air down the mountain slowing
> to honey above the sea.
>   (*The Museum of Ordinary Life*, 12)

For Baderoon, environmental restoration calls for nurturing, not constant battles. In this poem, a string of words is chosen to encourage greater empathy towards the environment with all its vulnerability and sweetness.

How does Baderoon enunciate eco-activism in her poetry? Green leitmotifs and water ecology are frequently present in Baderoon's poetry. Assuredly, eco-critical settings in Baderoon's poetry are shaped by the intertwining of eco-awareness and eco-activism. Notably, the principal means deployed to achieve this is through a degree of hedging that avoids aligning environmental concerns with global changes and events. Rather, Baderoon's eco-activism is situated in a rhetoric of personal motives as highlighted in "My Tongue Softens on the Other Name":

> In my mother's back yard washing snaps
> above chillies and wild rosemary.

The poet thus links plants with the emotional content of her home–both her mother's domestic work and the larger landscape of South Africa that produces certain flora:

> Kapokbos, cottonwool bush, my tongue softens
> on the rosemary's other name.
> Brinjal ...

Finally, she notices a wild plant, a witloof, that is thriving even though is affected by human incursions and technologies:

> At the edge
> of the grass by the bedrooms, a witolyf reaches
> ecstatically for the power lines.
>   (*The Dream in the Next Body*, 31)

Within a locale of environmental advocacy, the issue of ecological consciousness in the poem raises a few concerns, the most poignant being the compelling question of how humans must interact with the plants for their mutual sustainability. The connection between human and plant becomes increasingly apparent as witloof grows unhampered, earning the admiration of the poet as it sprouts besides the bedroom to clamber up the power lines. The interlacing of human and nature is broadened with the witloof's growth in a natural habitat which has also been appropriated for human use. Human and plant life are thus depicted as being complementary and beneficial.

The proximity of the witloof to the bedroom is best understood as a metaphor of vegetal growth that reflects the symbiosis between human and non-human agencies. Towards this goal, Baderoon leads her reader to believe that the world must come to terms with the understanding that the environment must be protected to encourage the interrelationship of human and non-human environments. Admittedly, the proximity establishes with certainty that the human interrelates closely with non-human agencies. The non-privileging of the human over the environment locks itself into a mutual partnership based on admiration and understanding between human and non-human entities in the poem. If we are to unhurriedly read Baderoon's commitment to the engagement with the environment in the poem, nature as an indispensable agent of sustainability is venerated and essentialised.

Exploring Ways in which Ecological Consciousness is Teased Out in Baderoon's Poetry

One way of measuring the degree to which environmental activism reverberates in Baderoon's poetry is to pay attention to details of how language is appropriated to illustrate, process, and analyse the lush greenery of the environment. She thus reveals the interconnectedness of two ecologically rich river basins of Antwerp and Thames in London in "The River Cities," while linking both to the (non-European) town of her childhood:

> Between the river cities, Antwerp and London,
> the train windows look out on green fields
> and a VW factory with its stalled cars
> waiting to leave, like the parking lots
> of Uitenhage, union town of my birth.
> (*The History of Intimacy*, 27)

Given its propensity to evaluate challenging environmental issues, Baderoon adopts an uncluttered ecological poetics to express her thoughts lucidly in the poem. When contextualised within an ecological framework, there is a need to acknowledge Baderoon's fixation with simple expressions, which are regularly used in her poetry to nudge the reader into understanding dangers posed by human activities to the environment. If language provides traditional bedrock values for literature, literature in turn makes a usage of multifunctional expressions embedded in language (Gersdorf and Mayer, 2006:132).

Given the global lacework of ecology formed by the confluence of environmental humanism in the poem, Baderoon's language is clear and engaging and does not intensify needless anxieties. Language has been effectively utilised in the poem to embody the intersection of the environment and human society. The poem thus illustrates how language seamlessly reflects an awareness of the personal impact of factories and globalisation on human societies. This represents a level of urgent and immediate concern that redefines 'ecological turn' in the humanities (Stibbe, 2015:7). Not only does she bring empathy, associated with ecofeminism, to bear on her poetry, Baderoon's eclectic literary background also facilitates her easy identification with multiple countryside landscapes. In this poem, nature triumphs over the obstructing Volkswagen factory ruining the rustic locale. Such a proclamation aligns with Ben Okri's underscoring of the importance of nature, when he quipped that "the poet turns the earth into mother, the sky becomes a shelter, the sun an inscrutable god…" (Okri, 1997:2). Recognisably, the simplicity of expression in the poem attests the task of (re)constructing a new wave of vocabulary for deciphering the intersection of nature and the environment in the poem.

Again, Baderoon would rather suggest a conservation blueprint for nature's reclamation than adopt the militancy of radical environmentalism that might send jitters through the very people who most need to receive her message. Violence in eco-narratives invites readers to misconstrue the intention of such writing and can snatch away the possibility of initiating a mutual dialogue between the writer and reader. If radical environmentalism galvanises unwarranted aggression, the rhetoric of conservation offers Baderoon a strategy to advance advocacy of the preservation of the environment across diverse cultures and bioregions. Baderoon's ecofeminist approach to environmental conservation is registered in "This is not my father's garden":

> The roses have given up,
> only one lingers at the edge of the path.
> The hibiscus is gone
> from the centre of the grass,
> now wild as veld.
>
> (*A Hundred Silences*, 46)

It can be seen from a concomitant depiction of the withering of the roses and hibiscus that Baderoon artfully teases out flagrant underminings of the environment. Her gripping path in the poem provides a refreshing counterpoint to radical environmentalism. Such subtle activism, as embedded in the poem, offers a distinctive and individualistic voice to the criticism of ecological disaster as a global concern which can cause mass hysteria and paralysis. Arguably, the merit of successful narratives of environmental destruction resides within less complicated codes of expression (Campos, 2019:ix). Therefore, by shunning melodramatic and sensational approaches in the poem, Baderoon stresses that humanity has a responsibility to protect the environment. Baderoon's rallying of readers to support environmental humanism is made more broadly appealing, even in national contexts where other political concerns absorb much of the focus. Ultimately, it can be argued that Baderoon is an important eco-poet, who has chosen poetry to connect with nature in ways that appeal to a range of readers across cultures. Using strategies of moderate language, Baderoon has positioned her poetry to be a voice for the environment.

Note

1 Excerpts from Gabeba Baderoon's *A Hundred Silences* (2005), *The Dream in the Next Body* (2005), *The Museum of Ordinary Life* (2005), and *The History of Intimacy* (2018) reprinted by permission of the author.

Works Cited

Abbink, John. 2018. "Introduction: Promise and Peril in Africa – Growth Narratives vs. Local Environmental Problems" in John Abbink (ed.) *The Environmental Crunch in Africa: Growth Narratives VS. Local Realities*, 1–28. Switzerland: Palgrave Macmillan.

Baderoon, Gabeba. 2005a. *The Dream in the Next Body*. Cape Town: Kwela Books

Baderoon, Gabeba. 2005b. *The Museum of Ordinary Life*. Cape Town: Kwela Books.

Baderoon, Gabeba. 2006. *A Hundred Silences*. Cape Town: Kwela Books.

Baderoon, Gabeba. 2018. *The History of Intimacy*. Cape Town: Kwela Books.

Caminero-Santangelo, Byron and Myers Gareth. 2011. *Environment at the Margins: Literary and Environmental Studies in Africa*. Athens: Ohio University Press.

Campos, Isabel Sobral. 2019. *Ecopoetics and the Global Landscape: Critical Essays*. New York and London: Lexington Books.

192   *Niyi Akingbe*

Carter, Neil. 2007. *The Politics of the Environment: Ideas, Activism, Policy*. Cambridge, New York, Melbourne: Cambridge University Press.

De Loughrey, Elizabeth and B. George Handley. 2011. *Postcolonial Ecologies: Literatures of the Environment*. New York: Oxford University Press.

Felstiner, John. 2009. *Can Poetry Save the Earth? A Field Guide to Nature Poems*. New Haven & London: Yale University Press.

Fisher-Wirth, Ann and Laura-Gray Street (eds.). 2013. *The Ecopoetry Anthology*. Texas: Trinity University Press.

Gersdorf, Catrin and Sylvia Mayer. 2006. *Nature in Literary and Cultural Studies: Transatlantic Conversations on Ecocriticism*. Amsterdam and New York: Rodopi.

Gomel, Elana. 2003. *Bloodscripts: Writing the Violent Subject*. Columbus: The Ohio State University Press.

Hays, Samuel P. 2000. *A History of Environmental Politics Since 1945*. Pittsburg, PA: University of Pittsburgh Press.

Iheka, Cajetan. 2018. *Naturalizing Africa: Ecological Violence, Agency, and Postcolonial Resistance in African Literature*. Cambridge: Cambridge University Press.

Ikiriko, Ibiwari. 2000. *Oily Tears of the Delta*. Ibadan: Kraft Books.

Jacob, Sharon. 2015. *Reading Mary Alongside Indian Surrogate Mothers: Violent Love, Oppressive Liberation, and Infancy Narratives*. New York: Palgrave Macmillan.

Lidstrom, Susanna. 2015. *Nature, Environment and Poetry: Ecocriticism and the Poetics of Seamus Heaney and Ted Hughes*. London and New York: Routledge; Taylor and Francis.

Ngugi wa Thiong'o. 2006. *Wizard of the Crow*. New York: Anchor Books.

Ogbowei, G'Ebinyo. 2013. *Marsh Boy & Other Poems*. Ibadan: Kraftgriots.

Ojaide, Tanure. 1986. *Labyrinths of the Delta*. New York: Greenfield Review Press.

Ogude, James and Tafadzwa Mushonga. 2023. *Environmental Humanities of Extraction in Africa: Poetics and Politics of Exploitation*. New York: Routledge.

Okri, Ben. 1997. *A Way of Being Free*. London: Head of Zeus Ltd.

Okuyade, Ogaga. 2013. "Introduction" in Ogaga Okuyade (ed.) *Eco-Critical Literature: Regreening African Landscape*, ix–xviii. New York, Lagos, London: African Heritage Press.

Ousmane, Sembene. 1970. *God's Bits of Wood*. New York: Doubleday Publishing Group.

Osundare, Niyi. 1986. *The Eye of the Earth*. Ibadan: Heinemann Publishers.

Soper, Kate. 1995. *What Is Nature? Culture, Politics, and the Non-Human*. Oxford and Columbia, SC: Wiley-Blackwell.

Stibbe, Arran. 2015. *Ecolinguistics: Language, Ecology and the Stories We Live By*. London and New York: Routledge; Taylor and Francis.

Wuthnow, Robert. 2010. *Be Very Afraid: The Cultural Response to Terror, Pandemics, Environmental Devastation, Nuclear Annihilation, and Other Threats*. Oxford and New York: Oxford University Press.

15 Capitalism and Environmental Activism in Selected Nigerian Poetry

Mariam Salaudeen and Rasaq Malik Gbolahan

...I sing of creeks with crushed dreams
I sing of ponds with decaying hope
I sing of rivers the cargo ships and supertankers sail on
(Marsh Boy and Other Poems, 2013)

Introduction

The poetry examined in this chapter moves beyond the attributes of aesthetics, or what is invariably regarded as "art for art's sake," opting instead to address the anathema of degrading atmosphere, climate and environment which affect the socio-cultural situations of humans. Hence, while affirming that poetry portrays a scene or recounts a tale in a lyrical arrangement of words, it should also be noted that poems are, more often than not, organized with rhythmic lines and meter to project the realities and complexities of human existence with more creative ingenuity than other genres. The foregoing excerpt from G'ebinyo Ogbowei's *Marsh Boy and Other Poems* (2013) underscores the horrendous situations in which human beings have found themselves, reflecting the uneasiness that comes with contemporary climate changes.

The above excerpt has explicitly foregrounded the environmental dislocations the Niger-Delta people of Nigeria experience, as captured by the poetry of Ogbowei. Although poetry uses meter, rhythm, and other literary devices to express literary aesthetics and thematic motifs, it is a potent mechanism through which poets amplify the realities of our existence – with regard to the socio-economic and cultural, and especially in terms of how the environment affects us as humans. The unceasing deterioration of the planet has been a topic of discussion in the field of literary studies for several years. Writers and critics alike in Nigeria have spent a significant amount of time and energy conducting in-depth analyses of the ecological destruction that plagues the planet and the people who live on it. Prominent writers like Niyi Osundare, Ogaga Ifowodo, Tanure Ojaide, Nnimo Bassey, and others have addressed in their creative oeuvres the haunting aftermaths of oil spillage and environmental pollution on the Nigerian ecology.

In the Nigerian experience, the first ecological riots broke out in the Niger Delta, this was especially the case after the widely condemned political execution of Ken Saro Wiwa, a Nigerian poet, journalist, and environmental activist, who was hanged alongside eight other Ogoni men (now referred to as the Ogoni 9) by the Abacha military regime in 1995, for fighting Shell's impunity. Like other eco-poets working assiduously to revolutionize through artistic and other means against the government's involvement in the destruction of the Niger Delta's ecosystem, Saro-Wiwa remains an unforgettable voice that stood unshaken despite the death threat and other injuries to his life and personality. Saro-Wiwa deployed the use of the Movement for the

DOI: 10.4324/9781003399988-20

Survival of the Ogoni People (MOSOP) to agitate fervently for the emancipation of his people from the dubious activities of Shell and the government.

Through MOSOP, the Ogoni people of the Central Niger Delta engaged the military dictatorship of Abacha and addressed environmental issues, particularly oil spillages and indiscriminate gas flaring, carried out by Shell. They also presented their plight to the Nigerian state through the drafting of the Ogoni Bill of Rights under the auspices of Ogoni Central Union in 1990 (Ojakorotu, 98). He and other leaders were however arrested and condemned to the guillotine in a dubious trial set up by the military regime of the time. This attracted wide international condemnation and Shell has always been implicated as conniving with Abacha's regime in an attempt to stifle the voices of Ogoni people against their economic impoverishment and worse still, ecocide of their land:

> The trial, which was conducted by a military appointed tribunal and included a serving military officer, was universally condemned as a sham (Birnbaum, 1995; ICJ, 1996)....
> Nevertheless, on 10 November 1995, Ken Saro-Wiwa and eight MOSOP leaders (now known as the Ogoni Nine) were hanged by the Nigerian authorities. After the executions there was worldwide condemnation of Shell (Wheeler, 1995; O'Sullivan, 1995; Hammer, 1996). Headlines appeared that painted Shell as callous and a supporter of dictators. In the months after the executions of the Ogoni Nine, Shell found its role in Nigeria the focus of much analysis in the media.
>
> (Boele et al., 81)

This singular occurrence has also been a veritable source of inspiration for both old and new generations of Nigerian writers. Amatoritsero Ede for instance poetically recalls how Shell and the Nigerian government were partners in orchestrating the death of Saro-Wiwa and his kinsmen in a bid to "shell-shock" the Niger Delta "into haunted silence," in section "v" and "w" of his *Teardrops on the Weser* (2021). Other civil society groups formed to counter the sinister activities of oil companies and the government on the land include Environmental Rights Action (ERA), the Ijaw Youth Council, Pan-Niger Delta Resistance Movement, the Movement for Reparation to Ogbia (MORETO) and the Movement for the Survival of the Ijo in the Niger Delta. After the execution of Ken Saro Wiwa, some of his writings (letters and poems) were discovered in which he addresses the continuous determination of the Ogoni people to fight the government and the murderous and oil-mongering Shell and Chevron. These realities emerging from the Ogoni people's fight against the government and oil ventures display humans' passion to protect the earth and in essence their own existence. This history forms the bedrock on which environmentalism in contemporary Nigerian literature emerged.

From its inception, Nigerian literature, particularly poetry, has been utilitarian. The critic, Ayinuola (35) meticulously captures how Nigerian poetry exhibits a direct relationship between literature and social institutions. He demonstrates that what is observed and experienced in the natural environment is translated into oral forms like praise poetry, songs, and chants, mostly to the accompaniment of musical instruments. It then becomes almost impossible to deny the instrumentalism of Nigerian poetry:

> Nigerian poets, across a span of some fifty to sixty years of the life of the nation, have served as recorders, censures of wrongdoings and advocates of change, especially in the appalling situations and circumstances the country has found itself.... The onus to call the leaders and the people to order has partly fallen on creative writers and the artists, especially the poets.
>
> (Solanke 60)

Nwagbara (17) also corroborates this when he notes that written poetry in Nigeria covers about six decades, from its birth, and has been a tool employed by poets to decry colonialism, cultural imperialism, socio-economic subjugation, and political brutality.

The emergence of environmentalism in Nigerian poetry further lends credence to the utilitarianism of Nigerian literature. Emulating the iconic ecological role played by Saro-Wiwa, numerous Nigerian poets have adopted environmentalism, promoting ecological awareness in an attempt to awaken Nigerians' obligations to their environment, and reassert the symbiotic link between man and his environment. Therefore, Sule Egya is right, when he states that:

> In the case of Saro-Wiwa, the notion of exemplariness stretches to the huge influence he turns out to be on Nigerian writers. Arguably, his execution in 1995 by the maximum ruler General Sani Abacha marked the inspirational impetus for the emergence of explicitly ecocritical writings in Nigeria. That is, the literature of the environmentalism of the poor took its life from the rage and angst that attended the widely condemned killing of Saro-Wiwa, who was not only an environmental activist but also a renowned personality within the community of writers in Nigeria.
>
> (121)

The rage against oil-extruding companies and the government remains a familiar trope in Niger Delta eco-poetry. Over the years, Niger Delta poets like Gabriel Okara, Ken Saro-Wiwa, Tanure Ojaide, Ogaga Ifowodo, Ebi Yeibo, G'ebinyo Ogbowei, Nnimmo Bassey, and others have critically revolted, through their poems, against the greediness and recklessness exhibited by oil companies (Shell and Chevron) and the Nigerian government concerning the damages perpetrated on the Niger Delta ecosystem. These poets document elegiac experiences and explore eco-themes that unravel the losses in their land. Through constant engagement of these heart-wrenching events, they serve as the voices of their people, narrators of their grievances and clarion advocates who admonish the government to address the ravaging effects of oil exploitation in the region.

Some of the literary investigations into the works of these poets have focused on the idea of ecological trauma and activism that has arisen as a direct response to humans' careless exploitation of the natural world. In modern contemporary poetry, however, neither the form of poetry nor its attitude to the violence inflicted in and on the earth has been subjected to an adequate amount of critical examination. The crux of this essay is, therefore, locked in the aftermaths of the capitalist acts that engulf the Nigerian environment with a specific focus on the Niger-Delta area of Nigeria. It considers how Nigerian poets like G'ebinyo Ogbowei and Magnus Abraham-Dukuma employ poetry to project and question the nauseating and unbearable experiences of the ordinary Nigerians who are invariably at the receiving end of the actions and inactions of ecological-cum-environmental foes. The *Marsh Boy and Other Poems* by Ogbowei (2013) and Abraham-Dukuma's *Dreams from the Creek* (2015) have been selected purposefully, as they unearth the complexities of environmental degradation and disillusionments that have reduced the Niger Delta, in Nigeria, to a region where oil-mongering multinational firms, with the support of the government, exploit resources to gain wealth for themselves.

Activism, Militancy, and Environmental Revolution in G'ebinyo Ogbowei's *Marsh Boy and Other Poems*

Niger Delta's decades of struggle and relentless agitation against ecological degradation started years ago. With the discovery of oil on the land, the government's source of income skyrocketed, as oil became a major resource of revenue. However, the government's failure to pay proper attention to the ecological decay occasioned by the constant exploitation of the land by its foreign partners signals the government's capitalist inclination, which serves as the genesis of many deaths, famine, despoliation, and other ill-health occurrences in Niger Delta. Accentuating the claim that the government has been using the discovery of oil to generate more revenues while eschewing the implementation of stringent environmental policies and installation of adequate infrastructures in oil-producing communities, Oyesola observes that:

> The Federal Government has been generating over 90% of its foreign exchange revenues from oil exploration, exploitation, and marketing by foreign oil companies. Yet, the contention has been that the government does not use a substantial part of the revenue so generated to provide the needed infrastructure in the oil-bearing communities.
>
> (62)

Here, the typical case is Niger Delta, where the inhabitants wallow in abject poverty, and their children wander the streets, looking famished and gaunt. The land, which according to Kadafa (19), is the largest wetland in Africa and among the ten most important wetland and marine ecosystems in the world, is now depleted owing to its gross plunderage through unsustainable exploitation of crude oil spillages and gas flaring carried out by multinational firms backed by the government.

In his paper titled Eco-Poetry and the Nigerian Poet: A Study of Some Selected Poems in Tanure Ojaide's *Delta Blues* And Christian Otobotekere's *Beyond Sound And Voice*, Jachukwuike (2021) traces the beginning of eco-decadency militating against the eco-dreams and the future of the Niger-Delta people to the discovery of oil in commercial quantity in Oloibiri now in Bayelsa State, on January 15, 1956, which placed the country among the rank of oil-producing nations from 1958. More importantly, critics like Cajetan Iheka have observed that oil exploration activities began to have impacts on the Niger-Delta vegetation as soon as Britain, through corporations like the Nigerian Bitumen Corporation (1908) and later Shell (1915) started prospecting for oil in the region relying on seismic surveys, long before 1956 when crude was finally discovered in commercial quantity (Iheka, 90). It may however be argued that the impacts of oil, during the periods of exploration, were not as evident as those following the years after full-blown international trading of crude started in the Niger Delta leading to countless spillages and gas flaring. It has been observed that in Ogoni land for instance, between 1976 and 1991, over two million barrels of oil polluted the land in 2,976 separate oil spills through Shell's operation (Friends of the Earth International, 2019). This gave additional impetus to the rise of Niger-Delta literature, which became dominated by inscriptions of exploitation, ecological problems, and corruption as induced by the activities of the multinationals and the exploitative trends of economic considerations which became a catalyst for the current crisis, tension, and varied responses from major stakeholders (Jachukwuike, 2021, 3).

These topical issues affecting both human and non-human populaces are prevalent in poetry emerging from the Niger Delta. Abba and Onyemachi lend credence to this when furthering their discourse on the literature of the region focusing on Tanure Ojaide's and Nnimmo Bassey's poetry collections which present the oil-rich region as "an endangered environment" that not only reflect the economic, social and political implications of eco-degradation, but also display eco-alienation, a term in use for describing the sense of severity between people and their natural environment (3). Tanure Ojaide and Nnimmo Bassey are two of the Niger Delta poets who fight defiantly against the injustice and maltreatment of the inhabitants of Niger Delta and their environment in their poetry. They address germane issues with poetic diction that embodies the despair of the people and engage how the once verdant and lush land became arid and grim with a view to effecting lasting solutions:

> Both Ojaide and Bassey are very prominent poets who have not only deployed their poetic weapons in the fight against environmental injustice in the Niger Delta region but have also inspired a good number of other poets. They seem to be aware that the struggle for the emancipation of the people of the area should not be left only in the hands of gun-toting militants working in the creeks. The intellectual angle of the war in a way was needed to complement the other forms of activism going on.
>
> (Abba and Onyemachi, 4)

Marsh Boy and Other Poems by Ogbowei follows on from the pioneering involvements of poets like Ken Saro-Wiwa, Tanure Ojaide, and Nnimo Bassey in actively exposing the ongoing ecocide of the Niger Delta while inciting a revolution against the government and its foreign oil producing companies. The collection begins with the title poem "Marsh Boy," which is made up of six incisive yet well-coordinated segments. The poem's opening section is an elegiac composition set against the backdrop of the Niger Delta's environmental and ecological catastrophe. The devastation of marine objects such as "creeks, ponds, rivers, and marshes" is personified to produce a vivid mental image of their desolation as a result of oil and gas activities in the area. The persona portrays himself as a crusader against all types of mistreatment directed toward his ill surroundings, as well as a voice for the mangled characters that suffer in silence. The persona laments from "the prison of poverty," a symbolic portrayal of the plundered Delta:

> i sing of rivers the cargo ships and supertankers sail on
> i sing of swamps sold to swindlers and rustlers
> i sing of swamps demanding dignity and opportunity
> (Marsh Boy, 21)

The persona assumes a melancholic tone in this section, describing the state of a fading world, complete with creeks of "crushed dreams" and ponds of "decaying hope." Humans have words like "dreams," "hope," "dignity," and "opportunity" in their vocabulary, but Ogbowei projects on the marine environment the traits of living entities capable of suffering afflictions and sorrows through his choice of words. On the other hand, Ogbowei's constant usage of lower case for the personal pronoun "I" might be seen as a dehumanization of the persona, which is typical of the people of his region.

In contrast to the first stanza of the poem, where we see a gloomy poet, the second stanza presents a character who has turned choleric and aggressive, as he declares himself a revolutionist entrusted with delivering justice to his tortured environment:

> i am the marsh boy
> quick and handy with a gun
> i am the marsh tiger
> (*Marsh Boy*, 21)

In portraying the marsh kid and his environmental justice-oriented efforts, the persona uses wildlife and metallic motifs such as "tiger," "dagger," "assegai," "gun," and "bomb." These images support the savagery of the "humble hungry hunter" who was originally described as such. In the face of injustice, he transforms into a gentle python who strikes with pinpoint accuracy. This section depicts the "marsh kid," the persona, as being on a quest to save his environment from the clutches of greedy businessmen, who are fittingly described as "beneficent tyrants" stalked by the marsh tiger,

> swept south by cruel storms
> to secure staked swamps
> (*Marsh Boy*, 21)

A closer examination of the text exposes the persona's reference to the exploitation associated with commercial endeavors. Petrol capitalists, according to the persona, are nothing more than "beneficent tyrants," whose initial outlook and demeanor suggest benevolence, but whose deeds are in reality tyrannical, concerned only about amassing fortune at any costs.

One of the prominent excuses of colonial domination was propagation of civilization in supposed savage communities; however, colonialism was only an excuse to advance the economic hegemony of colonial powers as evident in the Nigerian experience. It instated global capitalism and dichotomized the nations of the world into West/South, where the South has economically remained at the mercy of the West since the colonial era. In the Niger Delta for instance, economic contact with the outsiders started first with slave trade, later in palm oil for British industries and for lubricating railways, and then trade in crude oil after its discovery in marketable quantities. Iheka rightly notes that all these enterprises spearheaded by colonial Britain in the Niger Delta and much of Africa "demonstrated the economic inequality between Africa and the West in the insertion of the region into the global economic order" (90). It should be recalled that in 1938, prior to Nigeria's independence, the British Crown had given Shell D'Arcy (now Shell plc) the sole license to prospect for oil in the country, and when oil was finally discovered in commercial quantity, it was the first venture to begin exploitation and exportation of crude from Nigeria. Other oil-extruding companies from the West like Mobil and Chevron, quickly followed suit and still remain key exploiters of petroleum resources in Nigeria today. One would expect that the swift exploration and exploitation of "black gold" would bring development and stability to the host communities; however, the reverse seems to be the case as those communities have continued to languish in both human and environmental catastrophes of varying degrees, while the multinational corporations largely responsible seem to be oblivious of these consequences, as they favor accumulation of profits carted away to their mother lands, over the people's predicament.

The extract from "Marsh Boy" exposes that these imperial capitalists are "driven south" by "painful storms" – the need to advance the economic interests of their motherlands ("south" referring to the world's Third World nations). They then use the newly acquired fishing grounds, the Niger Delta in this case, to further their business interests amidst oil spillages and overall impoverishment of the people. Adam Vaughan seems to consent to this in a report where he states that:

> the rapidly expanding oil industry was dogged in controversy from early on, with criticism that its financial proceeds were being exported or lost in corruption rather than used to help the millions living on $1 a day in the Niger or reduce its impact on the local environment.

As a result, the marsh kid reiterates his resolve to blow apart the "quiet" of the "mugger," "stalker," and "pillager" in the last stanza of the second part.

The poem's third section is logically connected to the preceding segment. The persona's goal is to defeat the plunderers and replace them with the downtrodden. Capitalist exploiters are referred to as "bellicose bogs" and "cancer" that will be "carpet-bombed" and "cauterized clean." After evicting and defeating these plunderers, the locals, and revolutionaries, who are referred to as "mudbugs" and "mud hens" to describe their humble lifestyles and economic predicament, would be "honored," "held high," and "roost in palaces," where they truly belong.

In a similar vein, the persona goes further to emphasize the marsh boy's belligerency. His rage is fueled by the reality of his neighborhood, although it produces the resources on which his country is founded, it is economically marginalized and, worse, it is facing various levels of environmental degradation. In the words of Ogbowei (9), oil exploitation "fails to conform to internationally accepted standards," which aggravates the issue of pollution. The persona finds it creepy and ironic that people who should be adorned in "royal robes" are instead decked in "shrouds." The persona says that liberty and equality are what the people yearn for, but they only get to enjoy them in their deaths and graves:

> We desire liberty and equality, not bread
> But death a liberator
> The grave a leveller…
> *(Marsh Boy*, 22)

Drawing on the foregoing, it becomes apparent that the ironic scenario needs the quick involvement of the marsh boy, who represents a people who have taken control of their fates to transform their dire economic and environmental circumstances. The marshes, whose residents have grown "mutinous" and ready to ride on "violent waves" targeted at washing away all kinds of oppression, are introduced in the poem's fourth section:

> out of shadowy hills and baking sands
> vengeful cutlasses and foxy axes
> hack off the grabbing hands of a dying dominion
> *(Marsh Boy*, 23)

The territory is infested with furious rebels' intent on putting out the fires of exploitation that have engulfed their homeland. They are resolved to "hack off" the "grabbing hands" that continue to exploit without consideration, "a dying dominion"- a region which has almost become a wasteland, yet its plunderers are not willing to let it off. This section not only depicts a radicalized Delta fighting oppression but also criticizes the liberation struggle's saboteurs. They, too, would be washed away by the "angry waves" of real comrades. Similarly, the persona believes that these "quislings" are those who promote the success of the "cruel crowns," a metonymic image for the western countries particularly Britain, whose firms that are situated in the Delta have left the communities "outcasts on the fringes of society." According to the persona, "angry waves" will sweep away the covetous leaders of the battle who have abandoned their people by "clinging to privileges" that reject their "humanity":

> angry waves wash away turkey cocks
> commanders wrestling for control of oil
> clinging to privileges that deny our humanity
> *(Marsh Boy*, 23)

Having promised the exploiters and quislings a radical expulsion from the region, the persona once again praises himself at the beginning of the fifth part. He restates his commitment to the liberation of his land from all forces of oppression, by stalking

> stalking beneficent tyrants
> romanovs who see in our desolation their prosperity
> somozas who see in our destruction their security
> (*Marsh Boy*, 23)

The "romanovs" and "somozas" are historical allusions, referring to two influential political dynasties of the Romanov and Somoza families in Russia and Nicaragua, respectively. During their reign, the two families were prominent for their ruthlessness against opposition. Just like these dynasties see in the "desolation" and "destruction" of others, their "prosperity" and "security," so also do the exploiters of the Delta see wealth in the destruction of the people and their environment.

The last part of the poem makes a case for the revolution in the region. The persona emphasizes the fact that the peace of the region has been breached by its inconsiderate exploitation which engendered the current turmoil between "the avenging demons of destitution," the petrol capitalists and the Nigerian government. The persona further condemns the Nigerian system of government which permits the exploitation of some at the expense of others. To the persona, "Democracy" as it is being practiced in the country is a "gun-toting kleptocracy" which encourages the plunderage of national resources mainly by those in power. He further argues that "greed" has become a malleable tool in the hands of the leaders who wield it indiscriminately. As such, corruption within the political system, which is at the root of Delta's quandary, necessitates the reaction of the marsh boy and his fellow liberators who discover the "plasticity of greed,"

> seeing through the bizarre rituals of corruption
> we dynamite granite hearts
> that see us protesting only as brainless people do
> (*Marsh Boy*, 25)

The persona proclaims that the "battle" between the people and the oppressors is incited by the ill treatment of the former by the latter, in the last stanza of the poem. This proclamation foregrounds the marsh boy's resolution to continue all hostilities until his abode is treated fairly:

> hear the hyena howl
> the battle for land
> is the battle for life
> (*Marsh Boy*, 26)

To this "humble hungry hunter," the battle for "land" is the battle for "life." Apart from the physical despoliation of Delta through enormous oil spillages and gas flaring, which threatens the existence of all living organisms, the reverence of the people for their land is also underscored in this excerpt. As Iheka observes, the people till date still have a strong spiritual connection with the deities of their lands despite widespread practice of Christianity, brought with colonial incursion:

> One cannot discuss the spirituality of Delta communities without mentioning the significance of rivers. As Ken Saro-Wiwa explains, "To the Ogoni, rivers and streams do not

only provide water for life – for bathing, drinking, etc.; they do not only provide fish for food, they are also sacred and are bound up intricately with the life of the community, of the entire Ogoni nation." Saro-Wiwa gestures to the significance of the more-than-human world for these African communities. More pointedly, his astute observations suggest a relationship between the people and the rivers and streams that nourish them physically but also constitute a source of spiritual replenishment. In many Delta communities, people believe in the existence of water gods and goddesses that manage the affairs of humans

(89)

As such, the destruction of Delta is tantamount to the severance of the people from the gods of their lands which has undesirable consequences on their existence, and this contributes to their fight for emancipation. In addition, the suffering inflicted upon the people regardless of the richness of their land has made them learn to revolt against oppression. Thus "the place of suffering" has become "the place of learning" (*Marsh Boy*, 26). As the adage goes, since the hunter has learnt to shoot without missing, the bird has also learnt to fly without perching.

The persona predominantly employs sarcasm to convey the anger of his people against the despoliation of their environment, and their continuous exploitation by a few capitalists and their political cohorts in "Welcome to our Smouldering Swamps", another intriguing poem in Ogbowei's collection. In the first stanza of the poem, the persona welcomes all and sundry to a traumatized land. The anger of the people is contained in the description ascribed to the swamps of the region which have become "smouldering swamps", "swamps of death," and "boiling cauldron for loony leaders and dreamers".

It is instructive to note that in rendering this poem, the persona taps into the indigenous tradition of the Ijaw people of Delta. Ogbowei infuses the poem with a refrain directly adopted from an Ijaw battle cry: asawana/wana (an onomatopoeic expression conveying the ability of young Ijaw warriors to appear and disappear in a flash). The poem is a war song denouncing the ill treatment of the region and at the same time presenting the revolutionary activities of the people targeted at stimulating a positive change.

The exploiters are ushered into the region where they commit a lot of atrocities directly affecting the people and their environment. The persona depicts that the people are not only killed to attain oil wells and gas fields, but the environment is also "pounded" in the frantic search for wealth. These exploiters are dared to dance (waltz) with the revolutionists through the "starving swamps". To create a mental image of the region's lachrymal condition, the persona adopts historical allusions and compares it to "Choeung Ek" and "Tuol Sleng." Choeung Ek is popularly known as the "Killing Field of Cambodia" where the Khmer Rouge regime executed about 17,000 people between 1975 and 1979. Toul Sleng on the other hand was the notorious security prison where Khmer Rouge's prisoners were initially kept and tortured before execution. Toul Sleng is currently a genocide museum which chronicles the gory activities of the Khmer Rouge of Cambodia. The persona's comparison of the region's predicament to these Cambodian sites creates a pathetic picture of the torturous life in the Niger Delta.

To the persona, social amenities like schools, clinics, water pumps, and power mowers are of no use in a dying environment, as the consumers are already "vanishing":

> what are schools and clinics to the vanishing ones
> what are water pumps and power mowers
> what are cruisers and suvs to the swamp dweller
>
> (*Marsh Boy*, 28)

In this excerpt, the persona clamors for environmental conservation against amenities that are insignificant to an ailing environment. This fact is further foregrounded in the subsequent stanza, where the persona asks rhetorical questions like "what use is rembrandt to the blind" and "what use is tchaikovsky to the deaf." The fact that Rembrandt was an influential 17th-century Dutch artist, while Tchaikovsky was a celebrated 19th-century Russian composer emphasizes the uselessness of luxury to a dying wretch.

In subsequent stanzas, the persona recalls the Sabra and Shatila massacre of Lebanon in 1982, and the terrorist attacks on Khobar Towers in Saudi Arabia and the Twin Towers in the United States in 1996 and 2011, respectively. It can be deciphered from the composition that the persona views the two terrorist attacks as a revenge for the unjustified killings during the Sabra and Shatila massacre. Although the historical allusions in no way celebrate the gory events, it can however be deduced that Ogbowei employs them to showcase the possible aftermath of unequal relationship between the subjugated and the subjugators.

Having elucidated the plights of the swamp dwellers, which have made them become aggressive and their swamps become "smouldering" in the concluding part of the poem, the persona reiterates the revolutionists' resolve to turn the swamps of wealth into places of "death" for inconsiderate exploiters. The persona asserts that the plunderers might think they have the control of the region, but in reality, the people hold the key to their activities:

> You who think you hold the watches
> Discover now we've got the time
> Asawana
> wana
>   (*Marsh Boy*, 30)

"Welcome to our Smouldering Swamps" takes the reader on a tour through a despoiled region with a discontented populace. The violence depicted in the poem is a direct fallout of the ill treatment of the region by its exploiters in spite of the huge financial gains generated yearly. As such, it is not surprising that the creeks which have been pounded into "submission" have become vengeful and have turned to "sticky swamps" and "swamps of death" for the obnoxious debauchers.

In general, Ogbowei's poetry is dense with historical and political allusions, making it challenging to understand. Beyond that, the poet differentiates himself by criticizing both environmental and human exploitation while also encouraging radical revolution against the established order. Aside from allusions, the poet uses cohyponyms of fauna, mangrove habitats, and insects to crystallize pictures of the many settings depicted. Furthermore, Ogbowei's use of certain emotive terms highlights the irony and contradiction of Niger Delta's prosperity.

Capitalism, Activism, and Environmental Revolution in Magnus Abraham-Dukuma's *Dreams from the Creek*

Dreams from the Creek begins with "Invitation," a two-stanza poem. The poem invites everyone to come and witness the ecocide perpetrated by "gruesome guests" on the persona's "lands," as the title indicates. It also asks everyone who has been invited to judge "fairly and promptly":

> Come, see the lacerations on these paths,
> Peer through the membrane of these hearts,
> Days bleed on these paths
>   (*Dreams*, 13)

The persona arouses readers' emotions, causing them to empathize with the residents of the region, whose "gruesome invaders" have despoiled their grounds and driven them from their homes:

> Nature weeps for these lands,
> Smiling strands, suffering strands,
> Judge fairly and timely.
> (*Dreams*, 13)

"Invitation" emphasizes how capitalism disintegrates the persona's ancestral origins. The character alerts the readers to the region's distress and gently incites acts capable of improving its existing state by appealing to the guests to judge "just and promptly."

In addition, the poet persona in "Mining Fields" claims that the finding of "black gold" in the Niger Delta has elicited both "pain and joy" sentiments. The "black gold" made the area the center of attention, and "various feet" poured in to answer, "our black gold's call." While many people in the region where it was found have been in excruciating pain, the explorers and exploiters have continued to enjoy unrestricted pleasure. This is reflected in the poem's second and final stanzas where the persona expresses that in the mining field – "a field of pleasure and pain":

> Some are mining oil,
> Some have mined penury,
> Some have mined pains, …
> (*Dreams*, 17)

Based on the region's tragic experiences, it can be deduced that regular people are the ones who suffer the most in this situation.

Going forward, the poet alludes to Qatar, an oil-producing Arab nation where both the people and the environment benefit from oil and gas activity in "Native Qatar." The reference to this nation is intended to raise questions about why the Niger Delta's situation is so different. Even though the two areas have oil in common, Niger Delta is plagued by the "irony of Qatar."

The first five lines level an allegation at the leadership of the country, as Qatar is described as a nation "crafted" by the passion of its countrymen for indelible development. Today, Qatar "stands"/"weeping for this delta." The repetition of "here we are"/ "left with an irony of Qatar" reiterates Delta's impoverished state despite oil production. The region remains the exact opposite of Qatar although it also possesses all the qualities Qatar boasts of, including oil:

> She has men, we have men,
> She has marks of years,
> We have the marks of the years…
> (*Dreams*, 24)

The poet goes on to say that, unlike Qatar, Delta's oil has simply resulted in economic suffering and a weakened ecology, with little progress to show for these sacrifices:

> Our flora is gone,
> Our fauna is gone,
> No streets of gold to show
> (*Dreams*, 24)

The author ends the poem with a sardonic couplet, "No streets of gold to show,/ No victuals to throw," asserting that Delta is also Qatar; it's simply a different kind of Qatar known as "native Qatar." The poem is therefore, in a sense, geared toward engendering a lasting solution to the region's environmental challenges.

It becomes critical, therefore, to remember that the Niger Delta's economy was predominantly agrarian before the discovery of oil in the region. As a result, "Harvest Cry" is the lamentation of a Deltan farmer whose harvest was copious before oil exploration but has turned poor and meager in the face of oil activity. The poem depicts the region's environmental and ecological degradation, particularly as it pertains to farming. The farmer screams out, "What evil has been done to our lands?" Farmers do not appear to be reaping the benefits of their labor:

What evil has been done to our lands?
That now small are the works of our hands…
                    (*Dreams*, 25)

To the farmer, "nature's favor," the abundance of crude oil, has suddenly turned "evil" as a result of the region's exploiters' greed. Before this "evil," the character laments, the villagers had bumper harvest and "exchanged smiles with the sky." However, the situation has now flipped, with the inhabitants having little to harvest and now living in poverty. Every "spill" of this "gift" from nature is a threat to the region's natural environment:

Our gift now, by every spill, bids bye to its nurture,
And to our peril, men change its nature,
Who has done this!
                    (*Dreams*, 25)

The extract's last phrase, "Who has done this to my/ land," references the betrayal of the people by the oil merchants who promised that oil will bring prosperity but instead brought adversity upon the region.

The farmer stands his fading grounds, which were once fruitful but have now become wastelands:

My land is crying! Our harvests are poor,
My young ones are crowing! In their hearts is a sore,
See my harvest! Poor! Not enough! Poor yield!
                    (*Dreams*, 25)

It is noteworthy that the farmer is not blind to the perpetrators but rather urges them to accept responsibility for their acts and become more sensitive to the plight of the people.

Oloibiri, the first place where crude oil was found in Nigeria and commercially exploited by Royal Dutch Shell Oil Company is personified in the poem "Tears from Oloibiri." The poem depicts the community's intense sorrow even though it has for years provided prosperity for other geographical places. Oloibiri speaks out against its overwhelming plight in all of its forms; its resources have been plundered, and its environment has been polluted:

I am Oloibiri,
I have lost my essence;
I breathe a morbid hybrid air
                    (*Dreams*, 35)

It should be recalled that the initial oil well at Oloibiri has subsequently dried up after around 60 years of exploitation, and Shell has abandoned it in favor of other potential oil wells in the Niger-Delta area for similar endeavors. Samuel Oyadongha and Emem Idio's research about the developmental status of Oloibiri communities in 2016 reveal that:

> The discovery of black gold, instead of accelerating the growth of the host communities, has turned out to be a pain to the people as Oloibiri could best be described as an abandoned fishing port after the anglers had left with their catch. The communities, today, lack the basic necessities of life as the black gold, an exhaustible asset... has since dried up and Shell moved to another location regardless of the dislocation caused to the locals (2016).

Although "legions had thronged to drink my milk," Oloibiri complains that now that she is "ravished, forlorn, weak, and sick," none of them appear concerned. While Oloibiri languishes in filth, its resources are paradoxically put to good use in other places:

> ... The decay and putridity are mine,
> But some other places are fine,
> Gloss and magnificence are not mine
> 　　　　　(*Dreams*, 35)

With the use of horrible terms like "sores," "death," "squalor," "filth," "decay," and "putridity" Oloibiri becomes a vivid picture of the community's ugliness. Even though the earnings from the oil well have converted "other areas" into "beautiful places," Oloibiri lacks "gloss and splendor." Despite the fact that Oloibiri, who has lost her "essence, nature, and nurture," writhes in anguish, the repeating of "but some drink and dine" emphasizes the reality that the community's decline is to the exploiters' benefit:

> I have lost my nurture;
> Daily and yearly, I pine,
> But some wine and dine
> 　　　　　(*Dreams*, 35)

In general, the poem emphasizes the alienation associated with capitalist practices, regardless of whose ox is gored, individual satisfaction is prioritized over human and environmental welfare. The personification of Oloibiri is a technique adopted by Abraham-Dukuma to present the community's ordeal through the horse's mouth and restate the fact that the environment, even though non-human, also feels the pangs of exploitation.

In *Dreams from the Creeks*, Abraham-Dukuma employs relatively simple language, highly rhythmic rendition, repulsive images, and nostalgia to describe the destruction of Niger Delta and the resulting deprivation of the people. Similar to Ogbowei's *Marsh Boy and Other Poems*, Abraham-Dukuma implicates Nigerian authorities and capitalist corporations in this crime against people and the environment. He however urges, in contrast to Ogbowei, a stealthy revolt against these orchestrators.

Conclusion and Educational Perspectives

Environmental and ecological concerns continue to be a true wellspring of poetic inspiration for Nigerian poets. These theme structures in Nigerian poetry have been examined from a variety of perspectives, as evinced by the works evaluated in this investigation. Although academics such as Nwagbara (2013) and Aghoghovwia (2016) have highlighted the challenges of capitalism in Nigerian environmental poetry, this study investigates the interaction between capitalism and environmentalism in wholly separate collections of poetry. It is demonstrated that these collections by Ogbowei and Abraham-Dukuma not only document the ongoing ecocide of the Niger-Delta area but also deconstruct the capitalistic methods driving such despicable actions. Both collections adhere to the tradition of ecological Marxism, which projects that the tendencies of capitalism will damage nature as part of its process of expansion. Close examination reveals that the poetry collections depict environmental exploitation by capitalist corporations as a phenomenon that not only impacts the ecology, but also its inhabitants. Thus, the literary works strive to effect a positive change in both the environment and the suffering population.

As G'ebinyo Ogbowei noted in *Marsh Boy and Other Poems,* "the place of suffering/ is the place of learning." This chapter is useful in terms of teaching students how Nigerian poets like Gabriel Okara, Tanure Ojaide, Ebi Yeibo, G'Ebinyo, Ogaga Ifowodo, Magnus Abraham-Dukuma, and others play critical roles in shifting our gaze to the losses occasioned by ecological destruction in a place like Niger Delta in Nigeria and how this also bears a global burden in terms of how we think about land and the government's capitalist motif that affects it. Teaching this topic can also reflect how poetic intervention can be studied for the purpose of creating important conversations around the need to protect the land and animals, and also offering a space to think about how we can collectively work against ecological hazards.

Works Cited

Abba, A. A., and Onyemachi, N. D. 2020. Weeping in the Face of Fortune: Eco-Alienation in the Niger-Delta Ecopoetics. *Humanities* 9(54): 1–16. Retrieved from https://doi.org/10.3390/h9030054. Accessed 12th June, 2022.

Abraham-Dukuma, M. 2015. *Dreams from the Creeks*. Ibadan: Kraft Books Limited.

Aghoghovwia, P. 2016. Strategic Apocalypse and the Turn Towards 'Yasunization' in Nnimmo Bassey's Poetry. In Simon-Lopez, A., and Dunai, M. (Eds.), *Handmaiden of Death: Apocalypse and Revolution*. Brill, 85–95. Retrieved from https://doi.org/10.1163/9781848884137_009. Accessed 13th June, 2022.

Ayinuola, F. I. 2013. *The Natural Environment in the Selected Poems of John Keats and Niyi Osundare: An Eco-Critical Perspective*. PhD Thesis, Covenant University, Ota, Nigeria.

Boele, R. et al. 2001. Shell, Nigeria and the Ogoni. A Study in Unsustainable Development: I. The Story of Shell, Nigeria and the Ogoni People- Environment, Economy, Relationships: Conflict and Prospects for Resolution. *Sustainable Development* 9: 74–86.

Ede, A. 2021. *Teardrops on the Weser*. Winnipeg: Griots Lounge Publishing.

Egya, S. 2021. *Nature, Environment and Activism in Nigerian Literature*. New York: Routledge.

Friends of the Earth. 2019. *A Journey Through the Oil Spills of Ogoniland*. Retrieved from https://www.foei.org/a-journey-through-the-oil-spills-of-ogoniland/#:~:text=Over%20two%20decades%20after%20Shell,oil%20%E2%80%93%20that%20pervades%20the%20air. Accessed 14th October 2022.

Iheka, C. 2018. *Naturalising Africa: Ecological Violence, Agency and Postcolonial Resistance in African Literature*. New York: Cambridge University Press.

Kadafa, A. A. 2012. Environmental impacts of oil exploration and exploitation in the Niger Delta of Nigeria. *Global Journal of Science Frontier Research Environment and Earth Sciences* 12(2): 19–28.

Nwagbara, U. 2010. Poetics of Resistance: Ecocritical Reading of Ojaide's Delta Blues & Home Songs and Daydream of Ants and Other Poems. *African Study Monographs* 31(1): 17–30.

——. 2013. Nature in the Balance: The Commodification of the Environment in Niyi Osundare's *The Eye of the Earth*. *Nordic Journal of African Studies* 22(3): 196–212.

Ogbowei, G. 2013. *Marsh Boy and Other Poems*. Ibadan: Kraft Books Limited.

Ojakorotu, V. 2018. The Internationalization of Oil Violence in the Nigeria Delta of Nigeria. *Alternative Turkish Journal of International Relations* 7(1): 92–118

Oyadongha, S., and Idio, E. 2016. 60 Years after Nigeria's First Crude: Oloibiri Oil Dries Up Natives Wallow in Abject Poverty. *Vanguard News*. Retrieved from https://www.vanguardngr.com/2016/03/60-years-after-nigerias-first-crude-oloibiri-oil-dries-up-natives-wallow-in-abject-poverty/. Accessed 14th October 2022.

Oyesola, D. 1995. *Essentials of Environmental Crisis: The World and Nigeria in Perspective*. Ibadan: University of Ibadan Press. Print.

Solanke, S. O. 2013. Poetic Exploration and Sociological Changes in Nigeria: The 'handwriting on the wall' from Nigerian Poets. *The Journal of Pan African Studies* 5(10): 50–62.

Jachukwuike, U. B. 2021. Eco-Poetry and the Nigerian Poet: A Study of Some Selected Poems in Tanure Ojaide's *Delta Blues* and Christian Otobotekere's *Beyond Sound and Voice*. Retrieved from https://www.researchgate.net/publication/351873344_Eco-Poetry_and_the_Nigerian_Poet_A_Study_of_Some_Selected_Poems_in_Tanure_Ojaide's_Delta_Blues_And_Christian_Otobotekere's_Beyond_Sound_And_Voice4. Accessed 14th October 2022.

Vaughan, A. 2011. *Oil in Nigeria: A History of Spills, Fines and Fights for Rights*. Retrieved from https://www.theguardian.com/environment/2011/aug/04/oil-nigeria-spills-fines-fights#:~:text=A%20major%201970%20oil%20spill,spills%20between%201970%20and%202000. Accessed 14th October 2022.

16 Bugtong or the Philippine Riddle as an Ecopoem

Christian Jil Benitez

The Riddle of "ecopoetry" in the Philippine Tropics

Ecopoetry, as a particular subgenre, could be argued to have formally emerged in the Philippine literary landscape with the publication of *Sustaining the Archipelago: An Anthology of Philippine Ecopoetry* (2017), edited by Rina Garcia Chua. Although comparable literary anthologies commemorating and responding to particular contemporary disasters have been previously published (the most notable of which include *Agam: Filipino Narratives on Uncertainty and Climate Change*, commissioned and published by the Institute for Climate and Sustainable Cities (2014); *Verses Typhoon Yolanda: A Storm of Filipino Poets* (2014), edited by Eileen Tabios; and *Our Memory of Water: Words After Haiyan* (2016) edited by Merlie Alunan), it is Chua's anthology that first consciously consider the works it has gathered as indeed ecopoetry. In this sense, the anthology assertively extends the intersection between poetry and ecology beyond occasions of catastrophe, after which the poem is often taken merely as either an artful means to narrate the experience and insist upon the truth of the present climate emergency; or, at most practical, a material way to raise funds to provide aide for those who have been affected by such disasters.[1] And so, Chua's intervention effectually advances the ecopoem as a locus of more holistic shifts in perspective that maintain local connections while moving beyond the consideration of specific catastrophic events, and thus insisting that poetry circulates not just as a response to an event, but as a material with wider, and specifically ecological, historical, cultural, and pedagogical implications.

In her introduction to the anthology, Chua derives her definition of ccopoetry from what Anne Fisher-Wirth and Laura-Gray Street have already provided in their landmark *The Ecopoetry Anthology*, cited by Chua (2017) herself as "one of [her] models" for the project (xxxii). Differentiating ecopoetry then from the early manifestations of ecologically oriented poetry as described by Fisher-Wirth and Street (2013)—namely, nature poetry, which simply metaphorizes or personifies nature; environmental poetry, which overtly proclaims environmentalist positions; and ecological poetry, which attempts to embody ecology itself through the very form and language of the poem (xxviii–xxix)—Chua (2017) defines

> ecopoetry, as we know it now, [to be] not only hav[ing] form, meter, and/or content, but bring[ing] you [as well] *into* the environment and mak[ing] you, as a reader, more knowledgeable and intimate with the space recreated through the poet's words.[2]
>
> (xxxiii)

And for Chua, it is through such mediated engagement with the environment in "grassroots" instances of reading an ecopoem that it can ultimately render such text as a "concrete contributor

DOI: 10.4324/9781003399988-21

to the global environmental debate," and perhaps even a "part of the solutions (and not merely a response)" (xxxiv). This potency of the ecopoem, as a literary material that produces ecological knowledge crucial in activating hopes for sustainability, is what Chua terms "ecological literacy" (xxxiv; see also Chua 2014; Chua 2018).

As a foundational moment to the emergence of ecopoetics in the country, what bears emphasizing in Chua's efforts to outline a Philippine speciation of the ecopoem is the apparent derivation of her definitions from western paradigms rooted in linear literary history.[3] Granted that Fisher-Wirth and Street's anthology has been crucial in fortifying what ecopoetry might mean for the world, it does come from a particularly American history and sensibility. This accentuates its fundamental inadequacy for a context such as the Philippines, which is an archipelago in the tropics that has undergone, and is still contending with the lasting effects of, several colonizations, one of which is inflicted by the American empire itself. For instance, poems such as Jose Rizal's "A las flores de Heidelberg" ("To the Flowers of Heidelberg, 1866"), in Fisher-Wirth and Street's taxonomy, might simply be classified as a nature poem, given the harnessing of the persona to the flowers to express a human longing for the homeland. However, taking into consideration the Filipino folk intuitions on materials and the natural world—namely, that these matters are agents, too, in and of themselves, capable of causing things to happen, in their own manner (see Benitez 2022a)—"A las flores de Heidelberg" can be also appreciated as ecopoetic in a more contemporary sense, with its perceptible regard to the flower as a nonhuman botanical agent which facilitates the possibility of kinships spanning the globe.[4]

Thus, in the global project of thinking about ecopoetry, it is necessary that the Philippine tropics—similarly to other "postcolonial," "Third World," or "Global South" contexts—must be recognized not as a mere geographical location onto which predetermined notions of the ecopoetic are to be projected and deployed but rather as a critical sensibility from which ecopoetic concepts can be rearticulated. After all, such "decolonial critique is [also] precisely ecocritical" ("lubos na ekokritikal ang dekolonyal na kritika") (Benitez 2019a, 202), for history is as much a dimension of environment itself, especially in a milieu such as the Philippines, whose natural resources have been a primary object of interest to various colonizations (see, for instance, Bankoff 2013). And so, in the riddle that is "Philippine ecopoetry," it does not suffice to ask "What kind of 'body [of work]' does Filipino ecopoetry show to the world?" (Chua 2017, xxxiii); instead, it is imperative to dare examine the category of "ecopoetry" itself, and to ultimately redefine it somehow in terms more appropriate to Philippine sensibilities.[5] Doing so will ultimately allow a Philippine ecopoetry, whatever form it might take, to work in cultural and pedagogical contexts across the globe without losing its distinct rootedness.

To do so, it is instructive to consider what the queer Filipino writer John Iremil Teodoro (2012) says on ecocriticism as a theoretical paradigm: that in a way, it is both new and old in Philippine discourse, in the sense that despite its seemingly novel language, methods, and concerns, what it ultimately stands for is already most familiar to the Filipinos, given our inevitably intimate relation with the nonhuman world. In a similar manner, we can then wager that perhaps, Philippine ecopoetics is also embodied by texts that are "old," predating the term "ecopoetry" itself, despite their usual exclusion in the presently predominant ideations of ecopoetry such as that of Chua and of Fisher-Wirth and Street, in their historically-linear classification (if not simplification) of these older texts as merely "nature poems."[6] Such has been astutely demonstrated, for instance, by the critic Paz Verdades Santos (2011) in her reading of various Bikolnon rawitdawit or poems, ranging from folk verses such as the epic Ibalon and children's rhymes, to contemporary works written by poets such as Jaime Jesus Borlagdan (2009) and Kristian Cordero (2013). At the same time, as Santos's exegesis reaveals, although none of these texts have been previously identified as "ecopoetry," they nevertheless exhibit the characteristics of the subgenre.

As an attempt then toward syncopating the Philippine in a "Philippine ecopoetry," this essay turns to a species of Filipino folk poetry, namely the bugtong or riddle, and asserts its potency as a text that incites encounters with the environment. This is shown by shifting the primary focus of the bugtong from the instant of finally ascertaining its singular answer to the very process of thinking with the world. In this imaginative moment, the interaction with and reconsideration of things in the material world are recognized here to be acts of love, forms of erotic modus operandi, in the sense that these gestures allow these things to insist upon their own materiality and agency to the human riddler, and thus displacing the supposed anthropocentricism in the moment of reading. In other words, the bugtong is read here as an ecopoem that permits us to intuit the potency of the material world, as well as our most intimate and inevitable entanglement with it. In doing so, Philippine ecopoetry is ultimately salvaged from being merely another subgenre to be promoted as novelty within a western framework[7] and realized instead as a subgenre that can instruct how the world, especially the Philippine world, can be encountered anew.

Bugtong, or Philippine Ecopoetry in a Riddle

Historicization of Philippine literature, especially in the genre of poetry, often begins with the mention of the riddle (see, for instance, Cruz and Reyes 1984; Lumbera and Lumbera 1997; Tolentino 2007; Devilles 2017). This is largely due to its being a folk poetic form that is supposed to predate Spanish colonization and that has managed to subsist to the present times.[8] Crucial to its survival is its inclusion in a handful of colonial writings, most notable of which is Fray Juan de Noceda and Fray Pedro de Sanlucar's (1754) edition of the *Vocabulario de la lengua tagala*, a dictionary compiled for the purpose of teaching the Spanish friars designated to Tagalog provinces the vernacular, as part of the project of converting more natives to Catholicism. Considered "the most extensive collection of Tagalog poetry since printing was introduced in the Philippines in 1593" (Lumbera 1986, 1), this particular edition of the *Vocabulario* features in some of its entries' riddles, identified in their vernacular name "bugtong," as a means to define and exemplify the usage of the listed word.

For instance, in its entry for the word "bugtong" (spelled "bogtong" in old Tagalog), the *Vocabulario* offers the following riddles:

Naiysaysang anac,   (An only child,
Amat, Ina,y, ualan olat.   whose Father and Mother are countless.)[9]

Isang bogtong na bata,   (An only child,
di mabilang ang diua.   whose soul is countless.)[10]

(Noceda and Sanlucar 1754, 92)

The answer to these riddles is the bugtong itself, as a conundrum whose most singular ("naiysaysa," "isa") solution first appears multiple or even infinitely many ("ualan olat," "di mabilang"). As such, the second riddle is especially clever, as it already mentions its own answer in the first line ("isang *bogtong* na bata") and yet is able to hide it in plain sight, through rendering the word "bogtong" as a mere description—as in the adjective "bogto," meaning "to be severed like a rope" ("quebrarse como cordel") (Noceda and Sanlucar 1754, 92)—appended to another object, namely the child ("bata"). This recourse to the figure of the only child ("naiysangysang anac," "bogtong na bata") to represent the bugtong, however, is far from an arbitrary metaphorization in the riddles, for according to the *Vocabulario*, the word "bugtong" also refers to an "only-begotten son" ("hijo unigenito"), as in "ang bogtong na Anak nang Dios" ("el hijo unigenito de Dios," "the only son of God"). In other words, in these poems, the riddle and the figure of an only child are yoked through the homonym that is the word "bugtong" itself.

Even as these poems engage in ingenious play on the two senses of "bugtong," it is crucial to note how they also conform to the temperaments of Catholicism. Just as how, in Noceda and Sanlucar's *Vocabulario*, the definition of the word "bugtong" was seized as an opportunity to mention "el hijo unigenito de Dios" as a specific example—and perhaps, subtly, as the ideal, too—of an "hijo unigenito," the riddles can be also interpreted as hailing of key Catholic figures.[11] In the first riddle, for instance, the otherwise banal triad of a family is rendered as the Holy Family, through capitalizing the words "Ama" ('Father') and "Ina" ("Mother") in its second line. Meanwhile, in the second riddle, especially after reading the preceding riddle and the aforementioned definition of "bugtong" as "hijo unigenito," one is ultimately reminded of Christ, with his multiple essences ("di mabilang ang diua") that is being at one with the Holy Trinity, and by extension, the entirety of humankind, dogmatically believed to be fashioned after the likeness of the divine. And so, given the compatibility of the images in these riddles to the religious principles that the friars intend to preach to the natives, it becomes understandable why these poems were included in the *Vocabulario* and thus was deemed acceptable by the standards of the Catholic censorship.

The projection of Catholic sensibility onto these folk riddles is instructive toward recognizing that the bugtong, in how it has come to be predominantly appreciated in Philippine literary history, is analogous—if not causally related—to the ways that Christianity, entwined with colonialism, has executed its self-proclaimed divine imperative of suppressing pluralities of sexualities, races, knowledges, and even life forms in favor of its own worldview (Gaard 1997, 122). As a literary material, the bugtong has been primarily approached in terms of a single, predictable answer, so much so that riddles that are ambiguous enough as to yield more than one plausible answer are often ridiculed as "binayabas," which literally means boiled with guava leaves, and idiomatically pertains to the poem's being "not so well-crafted" ("hindi gaanong mahusay ang pagkakalikha") (Almario 2017, 275n11). The presumed unique answer of the bugtong is thus valued over the multivalent provocations it can offer. Such bias is demonstrated, for instance, by how in most studies and anthologies, the riddles have been arranged according to the alphabetical order or thematic cohesion of their solutions (see, for instance, Starr 1909; Manuel 1962; Hart 1964; Lua 1994; Eugenio 2005) instead of, say, the sources from which they were gathered (see, for instance, Vanoverbergh 1953). Moreover, in the case of "erotic" bugtong—that is, riddles that appear to have "innocent" and "naughty" answers (Hart 1964, 27)—if they are even included in such collections despite their so-called "coarseness" (138–139), they are mostly identified and classified in terms of their "innocent" solutions, with their sexual insinuations dismissed as mere "distractions" from the reputed "correct" answers.[12]

However, taking words as a "viable material premise" (Benitez 2022a, 3; see also Benitez 2019b, 459) to incite a contrapuntal, and perhaps revitalizing, understanding of things, a return to Noceda and Sanlucar's (1754) *Vocabulario* offers an alternative reading of the bugtong. For here, the butong is defined too as "adivinanza, ò cosi cosa" (92), where "adivinanza" can be construed as either signifying to the riddle or, more crucially, to the action itself of divining or guessing. This emphasis on the gesture of guessing can be further insisted through revisiting as well the earliest edition of the *Vocabulario*, compiled by Fray Pedro de San Buenaventura (1613), wherein "bogtong" is listed as an equivalent for the verbs "adivinar" (25), or the actio of divining; and "proponer" (499), or the action of proposing or suggesting. Furthermore, in the same edition of the *Vocabulario*, San Buenaventura also assigns as another equivalent for "adivinar" the word "turing" (25), which is curiously mentioned in Noceda and Sanlucar's (1754) entry on "bogtong" in relation to the one who has already figured out the riddle, as in "nacaturing" or "el que acerto" ("the one who ascertained") (92), instead of the one who still divines and proposes for a solution. And so, from these overlooked definitions of "bugtong," what now emerges is an intuition of it that syncopates not the commonly assumed unique correspondence between the riddle and its answer (and thus the certainty of the enigma's resolve) but the very gesture of working through the conundrum, the process grappling with it rather than the finality of deciphering it.

Such an affinity between the bugtong and the work of understanding itself is evinced as well by the other names of this folk poem in other Filipino languages. For instance, in Cebuano, the tigmo, as defined in Fray Mateo Sanchez's (1711) *Vocabulario de la lengua bisaya*, pertains not only to the "enigma" itself, but also to the action of "adivinar" (513). Similarly, the Hiligaynon paktakon is contemporarily defined as both the "riddle" or the "conundrum," and the acts of "solv[ing] riddles" as well as "giv[ing] each other riddles to solve" (Kaufmann 1989, 351). Meanwhile, according to the anthropologist E. Arsenio Manuel (1962), the Bagobo atukon derives itself from the verb "atuk," meaning "profetizar," or to divine or to guess (124); as such, the atukon can be likewise construed as ultimately founded, too, on the very work of figuring out the riddle. The same insight can be deduced to a number of other Philippine folk riddles, such as the Capiznon patugmahanon, the Waray patitgo-on, the Agutaynen pasigem-sigem, the Batak paigumun, and the Tausug tigum-tigum, with their respective roots tugma, titgo, sigem, igum, and tigum, which all comparably intimate an emphasis on the process of guesswork.[13]

Through this philological revaluation, the bugtong can thus be reconceptualized as a literary material that insists on the vitality of thinking—and more crucially, *re*thinking—precisely through looking at things in different manners. And, as further described in the following section, this act of thinking does not limit itself to an anthropologocentric rehearsal of mastery over nature but crucially necessitates instead forms of material encounter with our surroundings. In other words, the act of thinking that the bugtong activates is one that "subverts the dominant precedence attributed to the [human] head," as to perhaps "turn to the entirety of the body" (Benitez 2021, 69n16) that is not only our own, but instead enmeshed with others', the nonhuman matters included. It is in this sense that "thinking, most properly speaking, [becomes] love… the love for that which reaches experience… that gives itself to be welcomed" (Nancy 1991, 84), even and more so by nonhuman things with which we have always been inevitably entangled. It is in this way, too, that the workings of the bugtong as a Philippine ecopoem becomes most palpable: as an instance of coincidence for various material agencies, and thus, an ecology itself made manifest as a poem.

Bugtong, or Thinking with the World

Among the folk texts frequently invoked in narrating the earliest moments of Philippine literary history (see, for instance, Lumbera 1986, 3; Almario 2017, 181; Tolentino 2007, 31) is the following bugtong, which pertains to the banig:

Bongbong con liuanag   (Bamboo by daylight,
Cun gaby,e, ay dagat.   By nighttime, a sea.)
               (Noceda and Sanlucar 1754, 61)

Noceda and Sanlucar's *Vocabulario* defines the "banig" as "petate, ò estera" (61)—a "woven bedroll, or mat"—whose function in the daily life of the natives is concisely described in the above riddle: during the day, it is rolled like a tube of bamboo, kept or set aside, most likely standing upright; meanwhile, at night, it is expanded on the floor like the sea, laid out for sleeping. In her reading of the riddle, Jaya Jacobo (2011) notes that

> what is compelling here is not just the magical configuration of the object as it changes its material state from solid to liquid as the day progresses, but also the way in which the common object is made to showcase reduced and expanded spatialities with the passage of time
>
> (64–65)

In other words, the very materiality of the banig permits for an intuition of the fluxes of space-time itself. Similarly, for Rolando Tolentino (2007), the bugtong crucially intimates how in the "time of the natives" ("panahon ng katutubo"), one's dwelling—the locus where one imaginatively and habitually interacts with the banig—can be regarded as a "total space" ("total na espasyo"), where things, commonly differentiated as "natural" and "cultural," "primitive" and "domestic," are recognized to be entangled with each other (32–33).[14]

That such critical insights can be gathered from this bugtong, and by extension the species of bugtong in general, as somehow "elucidating of the worldview of its time" ("[nakapag]papal-iwanag… [sa] pananaw-mundo sa kapanahunan [nito]" (Tolentino 2007, 32), or at the very least, revealing of the "truth perceived or experienced [then] by humans within their surround-ings" ("katotothanang nadarama o dinaranas ng tao sa loob ng kaniyang kaligiran") (Almario 2006, 35). In this sense, the bugtong performs the foremost ecopoetic power of "bring[ing] [one] *into* the environment" (Chua 2017, xxxiii)—a traversal that happens in the bugtong not only in terms of space, but also time, given the specific historicity of the environment that the poem activates. In the case of the previous example, for instance, the riddle telegraphs a milieu in which human habitation is perceivably close to both bamboo groves and the sea, to the extent perhaps that these elements flux through and with the house itself, and thus evoking an "imagin[ation] [of] a space that enfolds the passage of time, of weather, through the rolling and the unrolling of the mat" (Jacobo 2011, 66). Although a dwelling like this still exists somewhere in the contemporary Philippines, what has changed in the present is the human attitude toward these elements: the entry of these "external" agents to the "interior" of the house is now typi-cally taken as an instance of disaster rather than, say, another passing instance in the tropics, if not an erotic encounter with the world.[15] In this regard, similar to how Chua (2015) understands contemporary Philippine ecopoetry, the bugtong acts as a "time capsule" (35), although one that is not confined to commemoration of immense tragedies, but instead expansive enough as to accommodate even the mundane everyday, such as the routinary transformation of the banig.

It is crucial to emphasize, however, that the other times and places—indeed, other environments—that the bugtong invokes are, at the same time, vital to the very process of fig-uring out the conundrum. In other words, these worlds are not mere passive atmospheres into which we are "brought" by the riddle, but instead material ecologies that we also need to interact with if we are to think about the bugtong at all. As Virgilio Almario (2017) writes, a "patient thinking" ("matiyagang pag-iisip") is necessary to solve the riddle—a gesture that involves not only literally "knowing how the bamboo and the sea look like" ("alam ang itsura ng bumbong at dagat"), for example, but also "exceptional[ly] discover[ing] the characteristics and connec-tions of these things" ("di-karaniwang pagtuklas sa katangian at kaugnayan ng bagay-bagay [na ito]") (181): the bamboo and the sea, daytime and nighttime, the banig itself, and ultimately the historical habitus of the natives, which all coincide in this riddle. In this sense, the bugtong as an ecopoem is not didactic, composed to simply "equip the individual for the perception of insights about the life around [them]" (Lumbera 1986, 4)[16]; instead, it critically compells us to meet these other lives, human and nonhuman alike, and somehow entangle with them, or at least recognize our being already enmeshed with them. It is only through such material encounter with the material world that we can commence thinking, guessing, and proposing about the bugtong—an erotic *modus operandi* of "plumb[ing] the [material] other's unsuspected enormity" (Mathews 2003, 19), that can lead us to a different manner of perceiving the world.

This practice of encounter that the bugtong incites and necessitates renders then the "active collaboration" (Lumbera 1986, 4) that is integral to such poetry to be inclusive even of non-anthropomorphic agents. Beyond the human interaction that a bugtong occasions (see Burns 1976), other forces in a given ecology are recognized to be partaking just as much in the construction of and thinking about the bugtong, considering that it is also their very materialities that permit these gestures to happen in the first place. Moreover, the instance of defamiliarization (Almario 2006, 36) typically associated with the bugtong is also displaced from its anthropomorphic role to "control... nature" (Lumbera 1986, 4) and be its "powerful lord" ("makapangyarihang panginoon") (Almario 2017, 182) and can be understood now instead as a phenomenon that emerges from complex and intimate engagements with the world.[17] In this sense, the authorless-ness of the bugtong can then be ascribed not only to its being a folk orature, but to its being a synergistic creation, too, between humans and the environment writ large. It is in this light, too, that the bugtong can be particularly regarded as a Philippine ecopoem: as a text that ultimately acknowledges and embodies the agency of the Philippine material world, making manifest how the nonhuman matter is inevitably entwined with the literariness itself of the poem.[18] In other words, it is a syncopation of poetry as indeed "more than mere words and imagery" (Chua 2017, xxxix),[19] considering its utmost material entanglement with things other than itself.

From these ideations of the bugtong as a species of Philippine ecopoetry, what ultimately becomes palpable is a certain love for the material world that is materialized in and through this poetic form—a love that is not merely anthropocentric or unfaltering in its environmentalist stakes, but more importantly, permitting us "to become shaken by doubt" (Butler 2002, 66), to be "interrupted by the indeterminable capacity of things" (Benitez 2021, 57), as to let emerge an alternative grasp of the world. Indeed, the butong embodies a kind of love that encourages us to encounter anew the things we commonly find in our surroundings, although not to simply "see each thing in a manner similar to other things also known" ("tingnan ang bawat bagay sa paraang katulad ng ibang bagay na alam din") (Almario 2006, 36). Rather than relying on easy analogies in terms of the physical attributes of these materials, the bugtong allows us instead to realize how materials are actually intimately entangled, and entangled with us humans, in many different ways amid the vast ecology of things.

Thus we can consider how the ecopoetic potency of the bugtong extends well beyond the particular moment of riddle contests, and with implications for how we read, teach, and learn. Perhaps the work of thinking about the bugtong, which involves a range of engagements with the world, does not necessarily end once the purported solution for the conundrum has been figured out. Instead, it can be imagined to continue as we, for instance, try to further plumb the riddle, asking what kind of environment it embodies and activates in us, and in turn, how this might move us beyond our often anthropocentric ways of perceiving things. And while it is never certain that we will acquire from our encounter with the bugtong a forthright environmentalist sentiment or a clear course of action with regard to the present environmental crises that the possibilities of what could come out of such poetic engagements are left to be guessed and proposed *is* the crucial point; it is the openness that, perhaps, also poses the riddle of the futurity of our world.[20] And after the Philippine bugtong, what becomes apparent now is that in classroom or in life, it is less so much about figuring out a single answer to the conundrum, than it is about being always in the process of thinking with the world.

Bugtong in the Contemporary Environment

This essay has attempted to expand the definition of Philippine ecopoetry through first problematizing its predominant definition in the current Philippine literary landscape, and then offering the bugtong as an instance of ecopoetry rooted in the vernacular. Through a brief philological reconsideration, the appreciation for the bugtong is moved away from the common impetus to find a single solution, as to stress instead the critical process of guessing and speculating. This process of interpretation is also intuited as a moving away from anthropologocentric readings, in its encompassing of a range of material engagements with the material world. In this sense, the bugtong becomes a materialization of love for things that displaces, or at least unsettles, our more anthropocentric assumptions, by asserting the agency of the nonhuman world as well as our inevitable and intimate interconnectedness with it. Thus, the bugtong, as a Philippine ecopoem, gifts us a new way to encounter the world, beyond the occasion of riddle contests.

It is then most unfortunate that in contemporary Philippine classrooms, the bugtong, along with other forms of folk poetry such as the salawikain (aphorism) and sawikain (idiom), are barely present in the K-12 curriculum that has been implemented in the country since 2012. Folk poems are mandated to be engaged here only four times in the course of 12 years: in Grades 1 to 3, wherein these poems are utilized as examples mainly for developing the student's communication skills (see DepEd 2016b); and in Grade 8, as texts that purportedly serve as "mirror[s] of yesterday" ("[mga] salamin ng kahapon") (DepEd 2016a, 153). And yet, even in this latter inclusion to the curriculum, the bugtong is hardly considered in relation to Philippine historical contexts, and much less so to the Philippine environment.[21] Such is the long-standing disvaluation that has been imposed on Filipino literature in general in the Philippine educational system, which can only be attributed to the incapacity of the institution to imagine how literature has been and will always be relevant for the nation—and any nation for that matter—especially in the midst of the present climate crises.

As a way to conclude, it is then worth turning to an example of how the bugtong can be also brought closer to more current experiences, especially for pedagogical purposes: in the form of what Tolentino (2007) proposes as a modern bugtong, which he considers as an "elaboration of the postcolonial condition" ("elaborasyon… ng postkolonyal na kondisyon") (34). While more commonly classified as a use-in-a-sentence joke—an arguably Philippine version of knock-knock jokes—Tolentino's treatment of the following text as a bugtong is noteworthy, as it effectively expands the form of the folk poem—for instance, allowing it do away with rhyme, meter, and recourse to figures of nature:

Use "vampira" ["vampire"] in a sentence.
Mayroon ka vampira?

(31)

The couplet in this bugtong operates as a call-and-response, with the first line giving the imperative to use the word "vampira" ("vampire"), and the second offering such a usage. The answer echoes the proper Filipino sentence "Mayroon ka *bang pera*?" which translates to English as "Do you have money?"—a double meaning that is only accessible to those who understand both languages. With this play on incongruent homophones, namely the Filipino "bang pera" and the English "vampira," what becomes apparent for Tolentino (2007) is how "the answer reveals the emergence of an unripe or 'quasi' postcolonial citizen, which more deeply symbolizes the bastardisation instead of regimentation of use of language and American colonialism" ("ang kasagutan ay nagsasaad ng pagsulpot ng hilaw o 'mala-malang' postkolonyal na mamamayan na mas malalim na sumisimbolo ng bastardasyon kaysa rehimentasyon sa gamit sa wika at sa kolonyalismong Amerikano") (34). In other words, through this pun, the bugtong embodies the contemporary postcolonial, if not *neo*colonial, condition of the Philippines, where both Filipino and English are most intimately entangled, rendering a hybridity of a language that is as much a material resistance to American imperialism as it is a lasting trace of it.

This recourse to the figure of the vampire as well as the usage of the word "vampira" in order to ask for money also suggests the Philippine social reality as a postcolony/neocolony, with its "liminality" (Lundberg and Geerlings 2017) that confounds the Filipino subject as much as it constitutes them. For Tolentino (2007), the vampire is a "curious figure, part primitivism in the age of cosmopolitanism that hints in turn on our being similar aberration figures of native and global habits" ("kakatwang figura, halong primitibismo sa edad ng kosmopolitanismo na siya namang nagpapahiwatig ng ating pagiging parehong mga aberasyong figura ng katutubo at global na gawi") (34). It is this vampiric abnormality of the postcolonial/neocolonial subject that is precisely embodied in the bugtong, particularly in the second line, as a sentence which responds to and frustrates the (American) English in the first line. In this way, the modern bugtong also tells something regarding the Filipino humor that subverts the empire, with its imperative that is turned here on its own head, becoming an occasion instead for a pun only intelligible to a Filipino.

That the layers of this modern bugtong are comprehensible only to those most entangled with the Philippine world makes it then as much of an ecopoetry as the previous examples from the "time of the natives." Extending the functions of older iterations, this bugtong activates an impetus toward encountering, too, the material world. In this case, however, the anthropocene—with its complications induced by imperialism, social inequalities, imperialist (particularly Catholic) schooling, and other sources of oppression—is foregrounded. And yet, as with the older bugtong, this new version presses us not to jump to a most singular solution, but to consider the practice of thinking with the world writ large—including nonhuman matters. After all, the riddles of violence and ecological devastation are not exclusively human problems with human solutions; they inevitably riddle, too, the nonhuman world.

Notes

1 All the literary anthologies mentioned thus far are somehow involved in raising funds for relief efforts and similar causes. Income generated from *Agam* and *Verses Typhoon Yolanda*, for instance, were donated to various nonprofit organizations (see Santa Ana 2018, 81n23; and Tabios 2017). Similarly, all the royalties earned from *Sustaining the Archipelago* were donated to the Philippine Animal Welfare Society (see Chua 2017, 262). Meanwhile, although *Our Memory of Water* does not have a similar disclosure as to where its proceeds would go during its launch on February 27, 2017, in Tacloban City, Philippines, the book was offered at a special discounted rate for those interested in partaking to its Adopt-A-School Program, wherein the second copy bought by a participant will be donated to the school of their own choosing. It bears underscoring, however, that all these anthologies cost no less than PhP 550.00 (~USD 11.00) each, with *Sustaining the Archipelago* as the least expensive.

2 Compare with Fisher-Wirth and Street's (2013) concise articulation of what ecopoetry might mean: "Ecopoetry enacts through language the manifold relationship between the human and the other-than-human world" (xxx)—a statement that can be read as their summation of Ed Roberson's (2009) wager on ecopoetry, as that which "occurs when an individual's sense of the larger Earth enters into the world of human knowledge. The main understanding that results from this encounter is the Ecopoetic: that the world's desires do not run the Earth, but the Earth does run the world" (5, quoted in Fisher-Wirth and Street 2013, xxx).

3 Emblematic to this derivation, perhaps, is how *Sustaining the Archipelago* opens with a short note from the Canadian Greg Garrard (2017), whose first words were, "I have never been to the Philippines," and then proceeds to briefly discuss W. H. Auden's "In Memory of W. B. Yeats" and Yeats himself, on a perceivable pretense of universalist stakes on environment and poetry (xxi). For a further reading of this foreword as symptomatic of dependence of the anthology to western paradigms, see Benitez (2019a).

4 A contemporary adaptation of such regard to the flower in Rizal's poem can be found in the punctuating sequence of the Filipino film *An Kubo sa Kawayanan* (*The Hut in the Bamboo Grove*) (2015) by Alvin Yapan. In the said scene, a zinnia floats down the Bicol River and heads toward the sea, as the protagonist—who resolves on staying in her deteriorating hut by the bamboo grove, despite the palpable pressure to migrate to the "modern" spaces of the metropolis and the Global North—reflects on the inevitable interconnectedness of all things (see Benitez 2021, 77n22).

5 Tangentially, it is also by the same rhetoric that a Philippine ecofeminism can be proposed, if not recovered: through looking at the "lines of Philippine critical thoughts that particularly attend to the mutual concerns of women and the environment, [albeit] these are often not explicitly labeled as 'ecofeminist,' but instead usually subsumed to other predominant critical nomenclatures such as the 'postcolonial'/'anticolonial'/'decolonial,' the 'feminist,' or even the 'Indigenous'" (Benitez 2022b, 37).

6 It is critical to note that Chua's *Sustaining the Archipelago* is composed purely of poems written by contemporary, living Filipino poets, unlike Fisher-Wirth and Street's *The Ecopoetry Anthology* which contains poems categorized into historical and contemporary sections, that is, before and after their assigned temporal marker that is the 1960s American environmental movement. In an interview with Kristine Ong Muslim (2016), Chua shares that what she originally envisioned was "a comprehensive anthology that would have indigenous, historical, and contemporary ecopoems that have been published or chanted in the Philippines," although this did not ultimately materialize due to the lack of "proper funding for the anthology." However, it bears underscoring that in Chua's (2017) introduction for the anthology, neither did these "indigenous" and "historical" poems were even mentioned to be a part of the Philippine ecopoetry being outlined. "Folk wisdom" was at least acknowledged to be something that is "beneficial to everyone" if explored (xxxvi), however always in the light of contemporary poetry.

7 In a podcast episode with the Forest Foundation Philippines (2021), Chua curiously cites *Agam* as "really the seminal eco-literary anthology in the Philippines": "Syempre, ang *promotion* natin is the first anthology of ecopoetry ang libro natin ['of course, our *promotion* is my book is the first anthology of ecopoetry'], [but] for me, *Agam* is occupying a space that is very special in eco-literature. It opened the doors for a project like mine to get attention and be able to reach your fingertips" (emphasis mine). Interestingly, if one looks up "Philippine ecopoetry" on the internet, it is Chua's anthology and critical works that firstly and predominantly appear.

8 While much of precolonial writings perished due to violent colonial purgings, Bienvenido Lumbera (1986) estimates that the folk poetry found in Noceda and Sanlucar's *Vocabulario* were, at least, "current during the latter part of the seventeenth and the first half of the eighteenth century"—a historical range that, considering the orality of these texts, can be pushed back to "a time early enough in the Spanish colonial period when folk poetry was basically what it was in 1570," and thus covering perhaps "the period of the first relations between the native and Spanish cultures" (2).

9 Compare with the Damiana Eugenio's (2005) prose translation: "He happened to be the only child, but his father and mother are not known" (1092). In the translation provided above, *ualan olat* is translated as "countless," after Noceda and Sanlucar's (1754) definition of *olat* as "Quenta. Pallilos, con que quentan" ("Count. Small sticks, with which they count") (361), and thus rendering the original phrase to be literally "no count." The crucial movement from the quantitative to the qualitative between the *Vocabulario* entry on *olat* and Eugenio's translation can perhaps be attributed to the definition of *ulat* in Pedro Serrano Laktaw's (1914) *Diccionario Tagálog-Hispano*, cited by Eugenio herself, in which the said word is defined as "cuenta; explicacion" ("account; explanation") (1344). In the present translation, however, the numerical definition of *olat* is preferred, given its resonance with the other riddle provided in the *Vocabulario* for the entry on *bogtong*.

10 Compare with Eugenio's (2005) prose translation: "Only one little riddle, but with innumerable meanings" (1092). In Eugenio's translation, it is crucial to note that the "bogtong na bata" has been ascertained as "one little riddle"—that is, the answer itself to this conundrum—instead of the literal meaning of the former as an only child. Furthermore, while Noceda and Sanlucar (1754) defines *diua* as "espiritu aliento" (188), that is, "spirit breath" (see also Serrano Laktaw 1914, 225), Eugenio translates the same word as "meaning," which makes more sense in relation to the answer of the said riddle, but ultimately diminishes its poetic ambiguity as, indeed, a conundrum.

11 That the *Vocabulario* particularly defines the *bugtong* as an only son also evinces the Catholic temperament that pervades the said dictionary, with its patriarchal prejudice projected onto an otherwise gender neutral word. Another instance of such masculinization would be on the androgynous diwata, which according to Rosario Cruz-Lucero (2007), "only… survived, because it transformed itself into a seductive nymph…. append[ing] 'Maria' into her place of origin… becom[ing] fairy godmother… That was perhaps the first sex change operation in the history of the Philippines" (18).

12 Archer Taylor (1951), for instance, describes the suggestiveness of riddles as simply "a trick characteristic… with the intent of confusing the hearer by an entirely innocent answer" (687). In her anthology of Philippine riddles, although Eugenio (2005) lists down exactly 39 riddles about the human genitalia—19 on the penis, and 20 on the vulva (xx)—the number is suspiciously small, considering the massiveness of the said volume, and thus intuitively pointing to the probability that a lot of other "erotic" bugtong were left out.

13 Other noteworthy examples are the Pangasinan pabitla, derived from the root "bitla," which pertains to the act of pronouncing or putting words in one's mouth. ("pronunciar ó echar la palabra de la boca") (Cosgaya 1865, 74); and the Bikolnon patototdon, from the root "totdo," pertaining to gesture of signing with one's finger ("señalar con el dedo") (Lisboa 1865, 408). From these examples, considered alongside the aforementioned ones, what can be crucially surmised—as to be demonstrated as well in the following parts of this essay—is that the work of figuring out riddles must also involve gestures beyond (anthropocentric) thinking.

14 Although for Tolentino (2007), this perceived entanglement of the "natural" and the "cultural" also presumes a linear progression from the former to the latter—that is, the often unexamined view of nature as necessarily "transformed by the humans to utilize for the development of their lives" ("natransforma… ng tao para magamit sa pagpapaunlad ng kanyang buhay") (32–33). In contrast, for Jacobo (2011), a sense of permeability between the two is at least intimated via the trope of the loob or inside (the "cultural," the "domestic") in relation to the outside (the "natural, the "primitive"): "in the riddle, the *loób* [inside] is not a permanent spatial structure or fragment. It is a quality, a virtue, a feature of spatiality… which ontologizes its moveable loci. Here the *loób* is less an effect of enclosures than a premise for openings. It is premised on possibility, not on limit" (65).

15 Consider, for instance, the following salawikain or proverbs which equates the entry of nature to one's abode as failure of human dominance that is domesticity:

Ang hindi tauhang bahay,	(The unmanned abode
Sinu-sino ay manunuluyan.	Will be dwelt in by anyone.)
Ang maruming bahay	(A dirty abode
Ay tirahan ng mga ahas.	Is home for snakes.)
	(Eugenio 2002, 281).

This resistance against encounter with nature—and the perception of such encounters as merely ravaging, instead of possibly ravishing, too, in some ways—can be further understood in relation to the historical transformations of the Philippine notion of sakuna, in its translation toward disaster—a crucial paradigmatic shift which, according to Alvin B. Yapan (2019), is mainly characterized by desacralization.

16 Similar to how the bugtong is commonly considered as didactic, Chua (2017) mentions among the "key parts" of ecological literacy of Philippine ecopoetry is its capacity for "educating the readers of the interrelationships [of things]" (xxxiv). However, what bears emphasizing in such moralistic regard of poetry is how notions of insight and education are not absolute: what one deems "insightful" or "educational"—or, conversely, "not insightful," "not educational"—might not be so for others, as in the case of "erotic" bugtong, whose "innocent" solutions are usually given precedence over the "naughty" ones. In the same manner, what counts as "pedagogical" in ecopoetry cannot be ascertained, thus rendering the attempt to define this poetic subgenre via such didactic quality to be ultimately unstable.

17 While the Russian formalist notion of defamiliarization that Almario (2006) evokes is mostly anthropocentric, in the way how the opportunity to reconsider things is mainly credited to the human capacity to harness art as technique (see Shklovsky 1965), a new materialist rendition of such defamiliarization can be intuited in the Filipino poetic proposition Bagay, whose "moment of creation is… instigated by an encounter with the things that surround us" (Benitez 2022a, 6).

18 The same can be said with Philippine vernaculars in general, with their onomatopoeic words that appear to be co-constituted by the nonhuman world (see Benitez, 2022c).

19 It must be noted, however, that Chua's (2017) articulation regarding the possible "transcendence" of poetry from itself regresses to a rather anthropocentric formalist universalism, albeit with an environmentalist stake: according to her, in such transcendence, "poetry becomes a universal language… that has the capacity to speak to individuals, one by one" (xxxix). What is crucially missed in such ideation is the opportunity to displace the obvious privileging of human agency; the potency of the poem as a material, for one, is simply reduced to being a vessel for delivering a "message… quickly, clearly, emotionally, and effectively" (xl).

20 Chua (2017), on the other hand, while similarly admitting of the limits of ecopoetry in inciting actions in relation to climate change, is more hopeful: "I know I cannot [save the world], but I want to try, because I know that someone who will read this anthology *may* and *will*. The ecopoems in this anthology will assure that anyone *can* save the world, if one is willing enough to stand tall despite the incoming tides" (xlviii). The cruelty in such optimism, however, lies in how much of contemporary Philippine ecopoetry, at least in terms defined by Chua, is mainly inaccessible to many Filipino readers; see, for instance, note 1 regarding the prices of few notable Philippine ecopoetry anthologies.

21 In the curriculum for Grade 8, the bugtong, salawikain, and sawikain are approached with the idea of them having singular meanings, and as such, only studied as to ultimately "guess the important ideas and answers" ("nahuhulaan ang mahahalagang kaisipan at sagot") that they contain, in order for students to deploy them eventually in other instances of communication (DepEd 2016a, 153). As such, the expected teaching of these folk poems in Grade 8 does not differ much from how it is expected to be taught in Grades 1 to 3.

Works Cited

Almario, Virgilio S. 2006. *Pag-unawa sa Ating Pagtula: Pagsusuri at Kasaysayan ng Panulaang Filipino.* Pasig City, Philippines: Anvil Publishing.

———. 2017. *Taludtod at Talinghaga: Mga Sangkap ng Katutubong Pagtula*, 2nd ed. Manila City, Philippines: Commission on Filipino Language.

Alunan, Merlie M., ed. 2016. *Our Memory of Water: Words After Haiyan.* Naga City, Philippines: Ateneo de Naga University Press.

Bankoff, Greg. 2013. "'Deep Forestry': Shapers of the Philippine Forests." *Environmental History* 18, no. 3: 523–556, doi:10.1093/envhis/emt037.

Benitez, Christian Jil R. 2019a. "Hinggil sa mga Salalayang Pamanahon: Isang Pagbasa sa *Sustaining the Archipelago.*" *Katipunan*, no. 4: 199–203, doi: 10.13185/KA2019.00412.

———. 2019b. "*Panahon* and *Bagay*: Metonymy and the Close Reading of Dictionaries to Understand Filipino Temporality." *Philippine Studies* 67, nos. 3–4: 457–488, doi: 10.1353/phs.2019.0023.

———. 2021. "Telepathic Visions: On Alvin Yapan's *An Kubo sa Kawayanan* (2015)." *Res Rhetorica* 8, no. 2: 55–81, doi:10.29107/rr2021.2.4.

———. 2022a. "*Bagay*: Articulating a New Materialism from the Philippine Tropics." *Rupkatha* 14, no. 1: 1–11, doi: 10.21659/rupkatha.v14n1.07.

———. 2022b. "Philippine Literature and Ecofeminism." In *The Routledge Handbook of Ecofeminism and Literature*, ed. Douglas A. Vakoch, 36–45. New York and London: Routledge.

———. 2022c. "Vernacular Virtual: Toward a Philippine New Materialist Poetics." *eTropic* 21, no. 2: 95–119, doi: 10.25120/etropic.21.2.2022.3903.

Borlagdan, Jaime Jesus. 2009. *Que Lugar Este Sa Sadiring Banwa: Rawitdawit.* Tabaco City, Philippines: Tabaco City Arts Council.

Burns, Thomas A. 1976. "Riddles: Occasion to Act." *Journal of American Folklore* 89, no. 35: 148–153.

Chua, Rina Garcia. 2014. "Speculating on the Ecological Literacy of Ecopoetry in a Third World Nation." Paper presented at the 6th Tamkang International Conference on Ecological Discourse, Tamkang University, Taiwan, December 19.

———. 2015. "Dismantling Disaster, Death, and Survival in Philippine Ecopoetry." *Kritika Kultura* no. 25: 26–45, doi: 10.13185/KK2015.02504.

———, ed. 2017. *Sustaining the Archipelago: An Anthology of Philippine Ecopoetry.* Manila, Philippines: University of Santo Tomas Publishing House.

——. 2018. "The Germination of Ecological Literacy in a Third World Nation." In *Environment and Pedagogy in Higher Education*, ed. Lucie Viakinnou-Brinson, 97–113. Lanham, Boulder, New York, and London: Lexington Books.

Cordero, Kristian Sendon. 2013. *Labi: Mga Tula*. Quezon City, Philippines: Ateneo de Manila University Press.

Cosgaya, Lorenzo Fernández. 1865. *Diccionario Pangasinan-Español*. Manila, Philippines: Colegio de Santo Tomas.

Cruz, Isagani R., and Soledad Reyes S., eds. 1984. *Ang Ating Panitikan*. Manila City, Philippines: Goodwill Trading.

Department of Education (DepEd), Republic of the Philippines. 2016a. "K to 12 gabay pangkurikulum: Filipino (Baitang 1–10)." *Department of Education, Republic of the Philippines*. http://www.deped.gov. ph/sites/default/files/page/2016/Filipino%20CG.pdf.

Department of Education (DepEd), Republic of the Philippines. 2016b. "K to 12 Curriculum Guide: Mother Tongue (Grade 1 to Grade 3)." *Department of Education, Republic of the Philippines*. https:// www.deped.gov.ph/wp-content/uploads/2019/01/Mother-Tongue-CG.pdf.

Devilles, Gary, ed. 2017. *Pasakalye: Isang Paglalayag sa Kasaysayan ng Panitikang Filipino*. 2nd ed. Quezon City, Philippines: BlueBooks.

Eugenio, Damiana L., ed. 2002. *The Proverbs*. Vol. 6 in *Philippine Folk Literature Series*. Quezon City: University of the Philippines Press.

——. 2005. *The Riddles*. Vol. 5 in *Philippine Folk Literature Series*. Quezon City, Philippines: University of the Philippines Press.

Fisher-Wirth, Anne, and Laura-Gray Street, eds. 2013. *The Ecopoetry Anthology*. San Antonio, TX: Trinity University Press.

Forest Foundation Philippines and Rina Garcia Chua. 2021. "Eco-literature in the Time of Crisis." Produced by Forest Foundation Philippines. February 26. Podcast, MP3 audio, 1:02:21. https://www. gubatbp.forestfoundation.ph/episode-2/.

Gaard, Greta. 1997. "Toward a Queer Ecofeminism." *Hypatia* 12, no. 1: 114–137, doi: 10.1111/j.1527-2001.1997.tb00174.x.

Garrard, Greg. 2017. Foreword to *Sustaining the Archipelago: An Anthology of Philippine Ecopoetry*, by Rina Garcia Chua. Manila, Philippines: University of Santo Tomas Publishing House.

Hart, Donn V. 1964. *Riddles in Filipino Folklore: An Anthropological Analysis*. New York: Syracuse University Press.

Institute for Climate and Sustainable Cities. 2014. *Agam: Filipino Narratives on Uncertainty and Climate Change*. Quezon City, Philippines: Institute for Climate and Sustainable Cities.

Jacobo, Jaya. 2011. "Mood of Metaphor: Tropicality and Time in the Philippine Poetic." Doctoral dissertation, State University of New York at Stony Brook.

Kaufmann, John. 1989. *Visayan-English Dictionary: Kapulúñgan Binisayá-Ininglís*. Iloilo, Philippines: La Editorial.

de Lisboa, Marcos. 1865. *Vocabulario de la lengua bicol*. Manila, Philippines: Colegio de Santo Tomas.

Lua, Norma N. 1994. "Butbut Riddles: Form and function." *Philippine Studies* 42, no. 2: 155–176.

Lucero, Rosario Cruz. 2007. *Ang Bayan sa Labas ng Maynila/The Nation Beyond Manila*. Quezon City, Philippines: Ateneo de Manila University Press.

Lumbera, Bienvenido L. 1986. *Tagalog Poetry 1570–1898: Tradition and Influences in Its Development*. Quezon City, Philippines: Ateneo de Manila University Press.

——, and Cynthia Nograles Lumbera, eds. 1997. *Philippine Literature: A History & Anthology*. Revised ed. Pasig City, Philippines: Anvil Publishing.

Lundberg, Anita, and Leenie Geerlings. 2017. "Tropical Liminal: Urban Vampires & Other Blood-Sucking Monstrosities." *eTropic* 16, no. 1: 1–4, doi: 10.25120/etropic.16.1.2017.3574.

Manuel, E. Arsenio. 1962. "Bagobo Riddles." *Folklore Studies* 21: 123–185.

Mathews, Freya. 2003. *For Love of Matter: A Contemporary Panpsychism*. New York: State University of New York Press.

Muslim, Kristine Ong. 2016. "Philippine Ecopoetry and Climate Change: Rina Garcia Chua on *Sustaining the Archipelago.*" *Chicago Review of Books*, March 28. https://chireviewofbooks.com/2016/03/28/rina-garcia-chua-sustaining-the-archipelago-interview/.

Nancy, Jean-Luc. 1991. *The Inoperative Community.* Minneapolis and Oxford: University of Minnesota Press.

de Noceda, Juan, and Pedro de Sanlucar. 1754. *Vocabulario de la lengua Tagala.* Manila, Philippines: Imprenta de la Compaña de Jesus.

Roberson, Ed. 2009. "We Must Be Careful." In *Black Nature: Four Centuries of African American Nature Poetry*, ed. Camille T. Dungy, 3–5. Athens and London: University of Georgia Press.

Sanchez, Mateo. 1711. *Vocabulario de la lengua bisaya.* Manila, Philippines: Colegio de la Sagrada Comp. de Jesus.

Santa Ana, Jeffrey. 2018. "Filipino Ecological Imagination: Typhoon Yolanda, Climate Change, and Imperialism in Philippine Poetry and Prose." In *Southeast Asian Ecocriticism: Theories, Practices, Prospects*, ed. John Charles Ryan, 61–86. Lanham, Boulder, New York, and London: Lexington Books.

Serrano Laktaw, Pedro. 1914. *Diccionario Tagálog-Hispano.* 2 vol. Manila City, Philippines: Lit. de Santos y Bernal.

Shklovsky, Viktor. 1965. "Art as Technique." In *Russian Formalist Criticism: Four Essays*, trans. and introduction by Lee T. Lemon and Marion J. Reis, 3–24. Lincoln: University of Nebraska.

Starr, Frederick, ed. 1909. *A Little Book of Filipino Riddles.* New York: World Book Co.

Tabios, Eileen, ed. 2014. *Verses Typhoon Yolanda: A Storm of Filipino Poets.* San Francisco, CA: Meritage Press.

———. 2017. "VERSES TYPHOON YOLANDA: A Storm of Filipino Poets." *VERSES TYPHOON YOLANDA*, July 9. http://versestyphoonyolanda.blogspot.com/2014/03/verses-typhoon-yolanda-storm-of.html.

Taylor, Archer. 1951. *English Riddles from Oral Tradition.* Berkeley and Los Angeles: University of California Press.

Teodoro, John Iremil. 2012. "Ekokritisismo: Bagong Luma." *John Iremil E. Teodoro*, July 27. http://jieteodoro.blogspot.com/2012/07/ekokritisismo-bagong-luma.html.

Tolentino, Rolando. 2007. *Sipat Kultura: Tungo sa Mapagpalayang Pagbabasa, Pag-aaral at Pagtuturo ng Panitikan.* Quezon City, Philippines: Ateneo de Manila University Press.

Vanoverbergh, Morice. 1953. "Isneg Riddles." *Folklore Studies* 12: 1–95.

Yapan, Alvin B. 2019. "Desakralisasyon ng 'Sakuna' Bilang Disaster sa Karanasang Filipino." *Katipunan* no. 4: 78–110, doi: 10.13185/KA2019.00406.

17 Poetry and Ecological Awareness

Inspiration from Pierluigi Cappello's Poetry

Marzia Varutti

Poetry and Ecology

In the poem 'Idillio', Pierluigi Cappello writes:

> A spiderweb, just after a thunderstorm,
> a clapping of light changing,
> unchanging, in the cool breeze [...][1]

The breeze, in turn, 'gives breath' to the leaves. In a few words, Capello's poem registers stillness in the changing light, crispness in the air and enlivening of the foliage; a few words make us 'feel' the past thunderstorm, partake in the essence of the moment. This is the power of poetry: words chosen with art can electrify our senses, ignite the imagination needed to envision and create a different world, and shake off some of the inertia of everyday living, which invites inattention and disconnection. All this has ecological relevance as these habitual human responses are a major obstacle to climate action.

The aim of this chapter is to show that poetry is uniquely positioned to pierce through inertia, apathy and denial. Poetry can enhance ecological awareness—that is, awareness of our deep entanglements with the planet—and in educational settings, it can lay the foundation for lifelong engagements. Ecological awareness is a necessary condition for ecological action (Chawla 2008; Angelovska et al. 2012). If ecology is essentially about inter-relatedness, about relationships between organisms and their environments, then poetry *is* ecology as it is intrinsically about relationships – with ourselves, fellow human beings, the planet; indeed poetry can be seen as the art and craft of putting those relationships into words. Given the inherently cross-disciplinary character of the argument, the chapter draws on debates on the concept of ecological awareness in the humanities (Morton, Ingold) and proposes a 'poetic affective methodology' based on full participation, attention and affective involvement of the writer with the poetic oeuvre.

I will draw on the works of Italian (Friulian) poet Pierluigi Cappello[2] to illustrate my arguments. A unique voice in contemporary Italian poetry, Cappello shows us how to practise attention to the world and how to tend to the human and other-than-human condition whilst acknowledging their deep entanglement. To my knowledge, Cappello has not explicitly positioned himself or his work as ecological or 'eco-poetic'[3]; I believe this does not detract from the pertinence of linking his poetry to ecological awareness, quite the contrary, it reinforces my argument that poetry – all poetry – is inherently ecological as it teaches us to notice, to pay attention and become aware of our connection to what surrounds us.

Poetry has shaken off (neo-)romantic bohemian stereotypes and is today perhaps more than ever popular. In January 2021, it was the moving performance of the young African-American

DOI: 10.4324/9781003399988-22

poet Amanda Gorman that caught global attention at the inauguration of the 46th President of the United States. Gorman's popularity comes in the wave of the Canadian Punjabi-Sikh poet Rupi Kaur, whose 2014 collection *Milk and Honey* sold millions copies. Kaur has become the emblem of a generation of 'Instapoets', young poets with a prominent media presence on platforms such as Twitter and Instagram, where they publish short, plain, confessional-style poems. Albeit raising concerns about the commodification of poetry (Miller 2019; Wilson 2017), the sudden and sensational popularity of 'Instapoetry' indicates that poetry – in new formats and through new channels – does have a readership, unprecedentedly large and young. Consistently, as Instapoetry flows from our screens, bookshops are replete (Ferguson 2019) with anthologies of poetry pharmacopoeia (e.g. Alma 2015; Sieghart 2017) offering to come to the rescue of our battered souls. It is not a coincidence if we turn to poetry in the hardest times, as poetry responds to a deep need to reconnect, to mend and heal broken relationships, including with the planet.

Poetry carries deep ecological relevance. Poetry matters to us as individuals, to our emotional and mental well-being, which directly affect our capacity to function and act in an ecologically responsible manner. Poetry matters to us as societies, and the relationship we entertain with each other, as the global scale of ecological degradation demands globally coordinated, concerted action. Poetry matters to us as a species, as it can indirectly inform our relationship with the planet we inhabit. And poetry matters also beyond us, beyond human presence, as it affects our capacity to imagine and shape the worlds we will leave behind as legacy.

A Poetic Affective Methodology

The affective turn in the humanities and social sciences (Clough and Halley 2007) has cast light on the pivotal importance of emotions in our lives. Whilst much research is exploring how affect and emotions as theoretical and analytical lenses change our epistemologies (e.g. Dukes et al. 2021), less attention has been paid to how the renewal of interest towards affect is transforming the way we do research: the way we observe, participate, reflect, interpret and write. To capture these dimensions, we need to turn the lenses of affect onto ourselves and our research endeavours. I experiment with this approach in this chapter.

My main argument – poetry fosters ecological awareness – informs the research methodology, whereby a poetic gaze permeates the way I read a poem and write about it, as I let the poem guide me into new forms of attention, of tending to the world and my deep enmeshment with it. I (the reader/academic writer) enter into an affective dialogue with the poet and the poem's subject matter in order to engender what anthropologist Tim Ingold (2021, xii) has called 'knowing from inside': "a method, that would join *with* the people and things with whom and which we share a world, allowing knowledge to grow from our correspondences with them". I am interested in exploring poetic ways of writing academically. I suggest that this is not so much a matter of writing style, as of positioning: I consciously wish to abandon the position of 'impartial' observer advocated by the scientific approach and intentionally put myself in the position of being a participant, 'being with', and therefore being affected (on affect as method see Varutti 2021). I share anthropologist Tim Ingold's (Spencer and Ingold 2020, 211) lament that in academic texts, words "have been sterilised, sanitised, cut off from the world whose praises they sing. We should not blame words for their academic incarceration". Rather, he continues "words, especially when they are written by hand, are feelingful, they well up from the body in manual gesture, and as every poet knows, they are laden with affective resonance." Writing academically about poetry should not preempt the possibility to write from a poetic standpoint, which I take to be a participant standpoint. In adopting this stance, I am inspired by a long tradition of academics writing poetically as affected participants, such as anthropologist Tim Ingold mentioned above (see for instance 2000, 2021), environmental biologist Robin Wall Kimmerer (e.g. 2020, 2021) and ecologist and philosopher David Abram (e.g. 1996, 2011) among many others. They all show that poetic academic writing is in itself a kind of *training* – both for authors and readers – in the skills of seeing, listening, noticing, paying attention, letting ourselves be affected and entering into dialogue with the surrounding animate world. These practices constitute the essence of what I call a 'poetic affective methodology'.

I suggest they carry ecological relevance. In a poem, metaphors and images are mobilised to convey a complex interplay of sensory, embodied, cognitive, affective and linguistic dimensions. Exposure to, and engagement with this composite grammar nurtures what Fritjof Capra (1995) has called 'ecological literacy' or ecoliteracy, that is "our ability to understand the basic principles of ecology and to live accordingly" (Capra 2007, 8), and more specifically 'sustainability literacy' "the skills, attitudes, competencies, dispositions and values that are necessary for surviving and thriving in the declining conditions of the world in ways which slow down that decline as far as possible" (Stibbe 2009, 11). Ecoliteracy is a crucial skill for young and future generations, and we should harness all resources available in order to instil it, especially in children, teenagers and young adults. Poetry is uniquely suited to the purpose. Whether we are teachers in public education institutions, pedagogues in informal educational frameworks, trainers in self-development courses or simply speakers in community events, poetry offers significant educational value and potential as the analysis of poetic texts can be used to educate to attention, to bring about and hone the skills of sensing and feeling, tending to, focusing on, tuning with and participating in. These are to a large extent innate skills and are most often intact and vibrant in children. It's therefore less a matter of teaching them to look and notice, as a matter of teaching them the *value* of looking and noticing, and teaching them the resilience it takes to keep up these skills, and the ethos that underpins them, in a society that tends to overlook them, or worse, devalues them. Teachers of all grades and kinds are called to play a critical ecological role; poetry can be another precious arrow in our quiver.

After a brief discussion of the concept of ecological awareness, I illustrate my propositions through the analysis of the poetry of Cappello, which I approach through the lenses of a poetic affective methodology.

Poetry and Ecological Awareness

Ecological awareness is awareness of what it means to exist – to live, think, act, feel, dream – in relation to, and together with other organisms and environments. It entails a (re-)awakening of the senses, alertness to sensory stimuli and a firm grounding in the present and in the soil right under our feet. Ecological awareness effectively counters inattention and indifference by developing more attentive ways of being in the world.

Poetry is advantageously positioned to foster ecological awareness. If we agree that poetry is a form of art, then we might subscribe to the argument of philosopher Tim Morton (2021) that art can ultimately awake us to the wonder and strangeness of the world. More to the point, the words of Tim Ingold offer a valuable perspective on the unique gifts of poetry to reawaken our senses:

Science does not teach us how to love the world. It is left to art to bring us to our senses, to show us how to open our hearts and minds to what surrounds us, rather than turning our backs on it in the name of objectivity. Art rekindles wonder and astonishment. (…) I do think that art can and should rekindle the senses, so that we can learn to attend directly, even lovingly, to the world around us, and to respond in kind—with precision, sensitivity and wisdom. That's what I mean by ecological awareness.

(Spencer and Ingold 2020, 214)

Following Ingold (2018, 225), writing and reading poetry become forms of inquiry in their own right, as each artwork/poem is an experimental form of 'ecological' investigation that "moves forward in real time along with the lives of those who are touched by it, and with the world to which both it and they belong" (2018, 218). Ingold's approach is based on what he calls (drawing on Miyazaki) 'the method of hope', that is, "the hope that by paying attention to the beings and things with which we deal, they, in turn, will attend to us, and respond to our overtures" (Ingold 2018, 218).

Ecological awareness is nested in the dialectics inherent in poetry: as we attune our senses and awareness in the act of writing and reading a poem, we also simultaneously engage with the world within and around us. The poet's attention is captured by an aspect of the world, the poem is written in response to that. When we read a poem, we are given the opportunity to live (again and again) the poet's response to a fleeting moment. Both writing and reading a poem then encapsulate the multiple acts of observing, paying attention to the world, marvelling at it and responding to it in words. The poem is a response in kind, as Ingold suggests, born out of precision, sensitivity and wisdom. As Aretoulakis (2014, 174 drawing on Bate) notes, "poetic discourse, almost by definition, constitutes an ecological language to the extent that it does not 'name things in order to make them available for use but rather in order to disclose their being in language'". In poetry, language becomes the vehicle for a specific ontology, a particular way of being in, and of this world, as the poem links author and reader in a journey from the illusion of being external, dispassionate observers, to acknowledging, even enacting, full entanglement and participation in the world. This 'enmeshed' ontology is condensed in the words of feminist and science theorist Karen Barad (2003, 829): "We do not obtain knowledge by standing outside of the world (...) we know because 'we' are of the world. We are part of the world in its differential becoming".

This stance entails a degree of humbleness. Humbleness is intrinsic to the poetic gaze, the poet will need to set aside their ego in order to observe in detail, listen deeply and transcend themselves in order to catch something that permeates the self and the stretches beyond. Crucially, humbleness is also inherent in ecological awareness, as this implies awareness of human limitations and of the place of human beings in the wider realm of life on this planet. As Tim Morton explains, ecological awareness "is awareness of unintended consequences" (2018, 11), that is, awareness that our human capacity of imagining and anticipating the consequences of our acts is limited when confronted with the scale of complexity of biological processes. In Morton's words, "ecological awareness is knowing that there are a bewildering variety of scales, temporal and spatial, and that the human ones are only a very narrow region of a much larger and necessarily inconsistent and varied scalar possibility space, and that the human scale is not the top one" (Morton 2017, 186). Writing and reading poems is then a training in paying attention, participating, being ecologically aware, and cultivating an attitude of humbleness. The crystalline poetry of Pierluigi Cappello offers an ideal illustration of these points.

A Journey Towards Ecological Awareness Through Pierluigi Cappello's Poetry

The poetry of Pierluigi Cappello reflects the depth of thought and intensity of feeling of a life claimed and savoured in spite of extraordinary difficulties: first, the childhood traumatic experience in 1976 of a disastrous earthquake that destroys Cappello's home and relocates the family to the small village of Chiusaforte, in the Friulian mountains, and then, when Cappello is only 16, a tragic motorcycle accident that condemns him to a wheelchair for life. Memory and sense of place are key perspectives in Cappello's poetry: appreciation for the local natural landscape, its colours and seasons, for the lifestyle and cultural identity of Friulian mountains, together with a tender nostalgia for childhood, permeate much of Cappello's work. Never self-victimising, Cappello continuously worked on his sensitivity and love of words, effectively turning his boundedness into a resonance box for insight, empathy and imagination.

Ecological sustainability demands an economy of means in the same way as poetry demands an economy of words. Both sustainability and poetry invite to shed the un-necessary, the super-fluous, in order to appreciate the simplicity of the essential. Cappello's poetry resonates strongly with this: simplicity is a stylistic signature of Cappello's poetry and in several instances, it becomes a theme of its own, as in the verse "the simplicity of the stone/ready to resolve itself into dust".[4] Simplicity is so central that to describe Cappello's work, the poet himself and liter-ary critics have used the expression 'bare words' (Linguaglossa, 2017).[5] Spirit of observation and sensitivity brought Cappello to perceive the extraordinary that lies just behind the veil of the ordinary; he never lost childhood's capacity to marvel at the most unremarkable details: the light on the garden's trees or a fly on his desk could become the protagonists of special moments, captured, frozen in time and then unfolded skilfully, carefully, laying down one by one – as Ingold put it, with precision, sensitivity and wisdom – the words that would bring his perceived and imagined universes to life, again and again, as we read his poetry.

It is possible to extrapolate from the literature in environmental studies and environmental philosophy a series of shifts and steps likely to lead to ecological awareness. Below I expand on some of these shifts and show, using examples from Cappello's work, how poetry can facilitate and promote these changes towards more ecologically aware individuals and societies.

Tuning with, Reawakening the Senses

One of the main tenets of ecological action is the need to reconnect with the natural environment through the activation of the senses. Awareness of the properties of the environments we live in begins with the rekindling of the senses, the very basis of ecological awareness. Art scholar Barry Bignell (2009, 193) explains this process as a "felt change of consciousness (…) it is about entering, in full consciousness, the experience of knowing and, in the experience, seeing the known and ourselves in a new light". To some extent, ecological awareness recalls children's innate capacity for wonder. As environmental scholar David Orr (2000, 19) observed

> Before their minds have been marinated in the culture of television, consumerism, shopping malls, computers, and freeways, children can find the magic in trees, water, animals, land-scapes, and their own places. Properly cultivated and validated by caring and knowledgeable adults, fascination with nature can mature into ecological literacy and eventually into more purposeful lives.

Wonder, fascination and the capacity to marvel at the world are not exclusive prerogatives of childhood, they are not lost opportunities, but skills one can nurture – also through poetry. In particular, poetry can teach us what poet Matthew Zapruder (2017) calls 'defamiliarisa-tion', the capacity to look at familiar, everyday objects and events through fresh eyes. Poetic compositions can achieve this through a range of tools, including metaphors and synesthetic constructions. Skilfully chosen, evocative metaphors are pivotal to attain a defamiliarisation effect as they make the reader both alert and a participant through acts of imagination. So for instance swift-moving nightingales in the sky become "a handful of gold pennies/thrown into the air who knows by whom".[6] Here Cappello layers the metaphor with a synesthetic dimension where the activation of one sense gives way to the automatic activation of another. In other words, synesthesia entails "a metaphorical process by which one sense modality is described or characterised in terms of another" (Poplavskyi et al. 2020, 303). In the poem cited, we come to 'see' in our mind's eye the nightingales flying in the sky, but we also come to 'hear' them, their crisp sound as gold bits that tickle our hearing.

Tuning Out, Decentring

Awakening the senses, tuning them to what surrounds us leads to locate the human within a broader network of relations where human and other-than-human coexist, and where not only does the human perceive but is also being perceived (Abram 1996). Developing ecological awareness implies acknowledging this interconnectedness and displacing the centrality of the human – a deep-rooted legacy dating back to Greek philosophy and reinstated in Renaissance Humanism. As social scientists Andrew Metcalfe and Anne Game (2014, 297) noted, "ecological awareness involves open response to a difference or otherness that is not locatable, that is inside-and-outside; ecological responsibility is this response. Our argument is that this responsiveness is not possible with a subject- and human-centred form of being".

The themes of participation, relatedness and embeddedness in the fabric of life emerge when poets inscribe themselves into the scene of the poem, as in this instance: "outside the sun/ blossomed on the tree branches, smiling/between me writing and the word nothing".[7] Here Cappello writes himself into the outdoor scene he is depicting, a sunny day in the outside garden. His participation appears to reach so deep that the sun rays permeate the poet's thinking and writing process, they inhabit the space between several thresholds: perceiving and thinking, the word written on the paper and the one not yet conceived, the humanity of the poet and the surrounding world. Another example of full, embodied enmeshment with life is the verse "and the February sky turns into breathing/inside and outside your lungs",[8] the body contours almost blur, merging with the outside air of February: that particular air of that particular day and season, is literally incorporated, it becomes part of us.

Appreciating interconnectedness does not mean reducing or negating the alterity of the Other. Quite the contrary, it means recognising alterity and encountering it on its own terrain and on its own terms; it means encountering what philosopher Tim Morton has called 'strange strangers' referring to entities that become increasingly unfamiliar as we get close to them. By offering opportunities for proximity with 'strange strangers', poetry can change the way we perceive and relate to the world. For instance, writing about a spider that made its cobweb in a corner of his studio, Cappello invites us to pay attention, to take in it's being different: "look at it closely/alien as a lunar module".[9] Through multiple little shocks of images and metaphors, poetry captures our attention and then sustains it by creating a space for personal, creative forms of intimacy with the other-than-human world.

Tuning in, Grounding, Slowing Down, Belonging

Poetry teaches us to tune in with our feelings, to feel that we belong in our body and our world. Philosopher Tim Morton proposes that we develop an awareness of ourselves and/in the world around us that "is still and moving at the same time, a ground state of feeling or doing or mentating or being embodied. Awareness rocks" (2017, 188). The type of awareness Morton refers to is of very special quality: it is an elastic, flexible, fine-grained, penetrating attention; it defies the superficial, short-lived glances fuelled by the mediaspheres (Citton 2014).

Tools for nourishing the special kind of attention Morton is proposing can be found in Cappello's poetry. Cappello was acutely and patiently attentive to the material world and to his thinking and feeling body – he, who could feel his body less than others, yet could feel more than many. In the poem 'Poiein', Cappello writes about being grounded in his body and being in the present. The opening words firmly set the poet in his reality: "you are from here, from this world" and almost as evidence of this, he observes the shadow his own fingers cast on the writing paper. But his being grounded goes *through* and beyond the material world, as he lives 'within the words', in the shape of things when they catch his attention, his awareness imma- nent and evenly distributed between his material and immaterial being and the world around him – an awareness still and moving, as Morton noted. From this expanded, diffused awareness he/we can attempt to grasp the present (almost stolen to the wind, he writes) by refocusing on the materiality of the body, and it is from this bodily materiality that we can look beyond and imagine eternity: "the present of these hands/as if it were eternal".[10]

Poetry nurtures a kind of attention that can only emerge when we change pace and slow down. As Cappello put it, "time is a host in a hurry".[11] It is not surprising then that Cappello's poetry brings us to decrease our speed and impatience, and coaxes our awareness to hang at the threshold of the instant, as in these lines: "between the last word said/and the first new one to be said/that is where we live".[12] Cappello brings us with him at the edge of the present, right at the point when the moment that is present is about to drop into future. This bears witness to Cappello's skill, and lesson, to take notice of, and even try to dwell in that interstitial and ephemeral space that we call present. This meditative, contemplative slowing down is at the essence of poetry, as much as it is at the essence of ecological awareness.

Taking Responsibility

Engaging in sustainable action and cultivating ecological awareness involve claiming rights and facing obligations: the right to a home, the continuation of life in and around us, a future; as we do so, we are faced with the responsibility of taking care of this home, the present life and its future.

In his self-description as a human being in whom "a God precipitated the whole Earth/the Earth wholly distanced that God"[13] Cappello conceives of the human being as a condensation of the whole Earth but also acknowledges humanity's distancing itself from a deep sense of the sacred. Yet, it is of no use to succumb to 'anthropic guilt' (Smyth 2022), far more construc- tive is to think of responsibility as the response, the consequence of becoming ecologically aware (Metcalfe and Game 2014). Barnett (2018, 992) noted that taking responsibility for eco- logical degradation is to 'realise we are the culprits of a crime we have been investigating'. Whilst this realisation is crucial, the investigation must continue, and it must involve our own selves. This is precisely the unique gift of poetry: its ability to hold up a mirror to ourselves and give us a tool to ponder our depths, however intimidating or uncomfortable that might be. Poetry is the vessel for us to become, as Cappello put it, 'archeonauts' of ourselves (Cappello 2018, 117), it encourages us to take full responsibility for the consequences of our decisions, even when, as Morton warned, we cannot foresee all the consequences because the scale of complexity is unimaginable.

Healing

Ecological awareness does not come to an end with taking responsibility for our decisions, we need to move further towards healing in order to find motivation for ecologically responsible action and problem-solving. We can find in poetry venues and instruments to shift from despair to hope, such as opportunities for venting our rage, sharing our grief, shedding the non-essential and finding a mental space and inspiration to nurture a re-enchantment for the world. Writing and reading poetry provide stimuli and frameworks for these healing processes.

On the one hand, we can imagine that the writer will find some kind of relief in giving names, verbs and images to knotted feelings; for instance, Cappello translates a feeling of anxious wait through the desperate bouts and flights of a hornet in an enclosed space, 'a dollop of rage' drawing 'spikes of air'.[14] On the other, the reader might find solace in reading of a familiar pain, or perhaps surprise at finding a secretly held grief magistrally explained there, black on white on the page. Feelings that we believed were ours only turn out to be a shared experience; from this, emerges a sense of understanding towards others, as well as a feeling of being understood. The poem creates a dialogue between writer and reader, and imagined communities of shared feelings among readers.

One of the strengths of poetry that make it ecologically relevant is that it can bring about healing through connection with the other-than-human by fostering a sense of participation in a composite world – a broader community. It can help us perceive the life that is breathed into the cosmos, as in Cappello's poem 'The Starry Sky' where the stars turn into infinite fragments of ourselves and "a still breath of shadows, light/contours the dim embryo of the moon".[15] We find ourselves scattered in the universe, contained and dispersed into infinite distant, celestial bodies. It might be a terrifying image but Cappello infuses it with the warm glow of life, as the cosmic breath brings the moon alive, even, it turns it into the very emblem of life, the embryo, perpetuating the everlasting promise of life. Even in his acknowledgement of human limitations and fears in front of the unknown, Cappello never leaves the reader in despair. The force and artistry of the poet is in finding the silver lining, the leverage point that upturns the mood and tips it towards opportunity and hope. In one of his last prose compositions, Cappello reflects on the future of humanity offering us a shining image of hope: "Tiny, just a seed facing the unknown, the human being is nothing but a cub, whose eagerness to know has been bearing fruit for millennia. And so, the pensive nakedness of a child from the back, faceless and therefore with all possible faces, we might as well call it future".[16]

Conclusion: The Ecological Relevance of Poetry

Ecological sustainability will remain an unrealistic goal unless the current levels of ecological awareness and engagement are swiftly and significantly heightened. A paradigm shift in current epistemologies, axiologies and actions is urgent and imperative if we are to avert an ecological collapse. What is needed is an epistemology that is no longer human-centred and no longer driven by growth but by a more respectful relationship with the other-than-human. I hope to have shown in this chapter that poetry is deeply nested within this thinking (and feeling) and therefore uniquely positioned to make a substantial contribution to this task of paradigm shift. Notably, poetry contributes to forging an alternative to the current epistemology paradigm, an alternative where ecological awareness lies at the core of more organic and more sustainable approaches to the very notion of humanity, now re-envisioned through its deep interrelatedness with the other-than-human.

The ecological awareness engendered by poetry has a unique power as it is based on a re-awakening of the senses, a decentring of the human that enables more equal relationships with the other-than-human, slowing down in order to notice and ground in the present, taking responsibility for our (in)actions and, finally, finding solace and healing in sharing the journey. The ecological awareness fostered by poetry nurtures a vision geared towards action and wild imagination steeped in hope, as the ultimate form of resistance. In our damaged world, ecological awareness is a civic duty and a social responsibility; poetry a vessel to that.

In times of ecological degradation, the poet takes up a demiurgic role: poetry is a tool for envisioning and re-worlding, for making the world anew as a form of resistance and militance. In a prescient statement, science-fiction writer and poet Ursula Le Guin (2019, 113) cautioned "Hard times are coming, when we'll be wanting the voices of writers who can see alternatives to how we live now, can see through our fear-stricken society and its obsessive technologies to other ways of being, and even imagine real ground for hope. We'll need writers who can remember freedom – poets, visionaries – realists of a larger reality". Pierluigi Cappello was 'a realist of a larger reality', an artist who could see alternatives to how we live now and suggest new ways of living our humanity, and of relating to the other-than-human – a poet demiurge. That we can read his poems and find generous clues on how to be better, or just more, human beings and give ourselves a chance to survive as a species, bears witness to the extraordinary gift that Cappello left us: words that travel across boundaries – geographic, disciplinary, cultural and temporal, generational – and reach to the heart of the human condition and its prospective future.

We can open a poem and find inspiration and guidance to become more ecologically aware and sustainable inhabitants of this planet; this bears witness to the power of poetry in all its multiple voices and formats. This is the power to talk to and from the core of our humanity, the power to re-inject our senses with wonder and emotion. Without these, ecology is just scientific data with little or no traction on our hearts – the current ecological situation, more than half a century after scientific data provided us with evidence of the imminent collapse, is a sad illustration of this. Poetic thinking should have a prominent place in ecological education, as poetry opens to understandings of the world and our place in it that are not cognitive but emotional. Ecological awareness is then felt, embodied and appropriated, it becomes a personal experience, a skill, an ontology and a part of who we are as we recreate ourselves as ecological beings.

Acknowledgements

This work was supported by a EU-Marie Skłodowska-Curie funding grant no. 101022941.

Notes

1 From the poem 'Idillio' by Pierluigi Cappello. Original text in Italian: 'un battimani di luce che varia, non varia, al fresco di brezza che ha messo respiri alle foglie' (Cappello 2018, 116).
   All translations of Cappello's poems by the author, unless otherwise stated.
2 All Cappello's poems have been gathered in the posthumous anthology *Un Prato in Pendio* (*A Meadow on a Slope*, Cappello 2018, in Italian). The volume *Go Tell It to the Emperor: The Selected Poems of Pierluigi Cappello* translated by Todd Portnowitz (2019) includes a significant selection of Cappello's poems in English. Several English translations of poems also feature in De Thomasis et al. 2017, and in journals such as *Poetry, Asymptote,* and *Narrative Magazine*.
3 I refer to ecopoetry here following Samantha Walton's definition: "Ecopoetry can be defined as poetry that addresses, or can be read in ways that address, the current conditions of our environmental crisis" (Walton 2018, 1).
4 Untitled poem. Original Italian: 'la semplicitá del sasso/pronta a risolversi in polvere' (Cappello 2018, 132).
5 The expression 'bare words' ('parole povere') featuring in the title of one of his most well-known poems has been appropriated by critics to refer to the key characteristic of Cappello's production: the neat, plain, essential writing, deprived of verbosity. *Parole Povere* is also the title of a video documentary devoted to Cappello, directed by Italian director Francesca Archibugi in 2013 (52 minutes, Italian with English subtitles).

6   Untitled. Original Italian: 'una manciata di spiccioli d'oro/gettata nell'aria chissà da chi' (Cappello 2018, 128).

7   From the poem 'Il Calabrone' ('The Hornet'). Original Italian: 'Fuori il sole/è fiorito sui rami, sorridente/fra me che scrivo e la parola niente' (Cappello 2018, 120).

8   From the poem 'Febbraio' ('February'). Original Italian: 'e fa del cielo di febbraio un respirare/dentro e fuori i tuoi polmoni' (Cappello 2018, 385).

9   From the poem 'Un Ragno e Altre Cose' ('the Spider and Other Things'). Original Italian: 'vedilo da vicino/alieno come un modulo lunare' (Cappello 2018, 192).

10 From the poem 'Poiein'. Original Italian: 'Tu sei di qui, di questo mondo', 'stai dentro le parole', 'e il presente di queste mani/come se fosse eterno' (Cappello 2018, 283).

11 From the poem 'Febbraio' ('February'). Original Italian: 'il tempo è un ospite che ha fretta' (Cappello 2018, 385).

12 Untitled poem. Original Italian: 'fra l'ultima parola detta/e la prima nuova da dire/è lì che abitiamo' (Cappello 2018, 134).

13 From the poem 'Al Sole' ('In the Sun'). Original Italian 'un organismo dove/un dio precipitò tutta la terra/la terra allontanò tutto quel dio' (Cappello 2018, 121).

14 From the poem 'Il Calabrone' ('The Hornet'). Original Italian: 'il calabrone è un acino di rabbia./Ha descritto da parete a parete/spigoli d'aria' (Cappello 2018, 120).

15 From 'Il Cielo Stellato' ('The Starry Sky'). Original Italian: 'un respiro immobile di ombre, luce/ contorna il fioco embrione della luna' (Cappello 2018, 111).

16 From the prose 'Oceano Indiano'. Original Italian: 'Minuscolo, appena un seme davanti all'ignoto, l'uomo non è che un cucciolo, la cui ansia di conoscere fruttifica da millenni. Allora la nudità pensosa di un bambino di spalle senza volto, quindi con tutti i volti possibili, chiamiamola pure futuro' (Cappello 2018, 409).

Works Cited

Abram, David. 1996. *The Spell of the Sensuous: Perception and Language in a More-Than-Human World.* New York: Vintage.

Abram, David. 2011. *Becoming Animal: An Earthly Cosmology.* New York: Vintage.

Alma, Deborah 2015. *The Emergency Poet: An Anti-Stress Poetry Anthology.* London: Michael O'Mara.

Angelovska, Julijana, Snezana Bilic Sotiroska, and Nina Angelovska. 2012. "The Impact of Environmental Concern and Awareness on Consumer Behaviour". *Journal of International Environmental Application and Science* 7 (2): 406–416.

Aretoulakis, Emmanouil. 2014. "Towards a PostHumanist Ecology". *European Journal of English Studies* 18 (2): 172–190.

Barad, Karen. 2003. "Posthumanist Performativity: Toward an Understanding of How Matter Comes to Matter". *Signs: Journal of Women in Culture and Society* 28: 801–831.

Barnett, Joshua Trey. 2018. "The Ecological Awareness of an Anthropocene Philosopher". *Environmental Communication* 12 (7): 989–993.

Bignell, Barry. 2009. "Beauty As a Way of Knowing", in Stibbe, A. (ed.) *The Handbook of Sustainability Literacy: Skills for a Changing World.* Totnes: Green Books, pp. 191–195.

Cappello, Pierluigi. 2018. *Un Prato in Pendio. Tutte Le Poesie, 1992–2017.* Milano: Rizzoli.

Cappello, Pierluigi [translated by Todd Portnowitz] 2019. *Go Tell It to the Emperor: The Selected Poems of Pierluigi Cappello.* Brooklyn, NY: Spuyten Duyvil Publishing.

Capra, Fritjof. 1995. *The Web of Life.* New York: Anchor Books.

Capra, Fritjof. 2007. "Sustainable Living, Ecological Literacy, and the Breath of Life". *Canadian Journal of Environmental Education* 12 (1): 9–18.Chawla, Louise. 2008. "Participation and the Ecology of Environmental Awareness and Action", in Reid, A., Jensen, B. B., Nikel, J., and Simovska, V. (eds.) *Participation and Learning: Perspectives on Education and the Environment, Health and Sustainability.* Dordrecht: Springer Netherlands, pp. 98–110.

Citton, Yves. 2014. *Pour une écologie de l'attention.* Paris: Le Seuil.

Clough, Patricia Ticineto, and Jean Halley, eds. 2007. *The Affective Turn: Theorizing the Social.* Durham: Duke University Press Books.

Dukes, Daniel et al. 2021. "The Rise of Affectivism". *Nature Human Behaviour* 5 (7): 1–5.

De Thomasis, Sandro-Angelo, Gurisatti, Damiano, and Giovanni Miglianti. 2017. "Friulian Poems by Pierluigi Cappello". *Journal of Italian Translation* 12 (2): 174–197.

Ferguson, Donna. 2019. "Poetry Sales Soar as Political Millennials Search for Clarity". *The Guardian*, 21 January 2019. https://www.theguardian.com/books/2019/jan/21/poetry-sales-soar-as-political-millennials-search-for-clarity.

Ingold, Tim. 2000. *The Perception of the Environment*. London: Routledge.

Ingold, Tim. 2018. "From Science to Art and Back Again: The Pendulum of an Anthropologist". *Interdisciplinary Science Reviews* 43 (3–4): 213–227.

Ingold, Tim. 2021. *Imagining for Real*. London: Routledge.

Kimmerer, Robin Wall. 2020. *Braiding Sweetgrass: Indigenous Wisdom, Scientific Knowledge and the Teachings of Plants*. London: Penguin.

Kimmerer, Robin Wall. 2021. *Gathering Moss: A Natural and Cultural History of Mosses*. London: Penguin.

Le Guin, Ursula, 2019. *Words Are My Matter*. Boston: Mariner Books.

Linguaglossa Giorgio, 2017. "Pierluigi Cappello (1967–2017) Poesie scelte". *L'Ombra delle Parole Rivista Letteraria Internazionale.* https://lombradelleparole.wordpress.com/2017/10/02/pierluigi-cappello-1967-2017-poesie-scelte-con-un-commento-impolitico-di-giorgio-linguaglossa/.

Metcalfe, Andrew, and Ann Game. 2014. "Ecological Being". *Space and Culture* 17 (3): 297–307.

Miller, Alyson. 2019. "'Poetry's Beyoncé': On Rupi Kaur and the Commodifying Effects of Instapoetics". *Axon: Creative Explorations* 9 (1). https://dro.deakin.edu.au/view/DU:30122389.

Morton, Timothy. 2017. *Humankind: Solidarity with Nonhuman People*. London: Verso.

Morton, Timothy. 2018. *Being Ecological*. Cambridge, MA: MIT Press.

Morton, Timothy. 2021. *All Art Is Ecological.* Penguin Random House.

Orr, David. 2000. "A Sense of Wonder", in Barlow, Z. and Crabtree, M. (eds.) *Ecoliteracy: Mapping the Terrain*. Berkeley: Living in the Real World, p. 19.

Poplavskyi, Mykhailo, Yulia Rybinska, and Taisia Ponochovna-Rysak. 2020. "The Specific of Synesthesia in Contemporary American and English Poetry and Its Impact on the Reader". *Cogito* (12) 3: 297–315.

Sieghart, William. 2017. *The Poetry Pharmacy: Tried-and-True Prescriptions for the Heart, Mind and Soul*. London: Particular Books.

Smyth, Richard. 2022. "Nature Writing Should Strive for Clarity Not Sentimentality", *Aeon.* https://aeon.co/essays/nature-writing-should-strive-for-clarity-not-sentimentality.

Spencer, Antonia and Tim Ingold. 2020. "Ecocriticism and 'Thinking with Writing': An Interview with Tim Ingold". *Ecozon@: European Journal of Literature, Culture and Environment* 11 (2): 208–215. https://ecozona.eu/article/view/3666.

Stibbe, Arran (ed.) 2009. *The Handbook of Sustainability Literacy: Skills for a Changing World*. Totnes: Green Books.

Varutti, Marzia. 2021. "Affective Encounters in Museums", in Pétursdottir P. and Bangstad T. R. (eds.) *Heritage Ecologies*, London: Routledge, pp. 129–144.

Walton, Samatha. 2018. "Ecopoetry", in Castree, N., Hulme, M. and Proctor, J.D. (eds.) *Companion to Environmental Studies*. Abingdon: Routledge, pp. 393–398.

Wilson, Carl. 2017. "Why Rupi Kaur and Her Peers Are the Most Popular Poets in the World". *The New York Times*, 15 December 2017. https://www.nytimes.com/2017/12/15/books/review/rupi-kaur-instapoets.html.

Zapruder, Matthew. 2017. *Why Poetry*. New York: Ecco/HarperCollins.

Conclusion

From Poetry to the World

We cannot fail to learn the lessons of climate change; indeed, the climate itself is teaching us. Formal education often takes place "inside" classrooms, but no classroom is truly cut off from our shared global environment. Schools are demolished by floods and hurricanes; paper comes from downed forests; and—even in remote parts of the world—every student's body is full of toxins and microplastics. Educational practices are often (and rightly) hyper-local, but in the context of climate change, teaching also has a global dimension. The climate crisis transcends every border, no matter how vigilantly policed it may be. In this volume, then, we have avoided reifying borders and binaries such as North/South, East/West, settler/native, or art/STEM, instead opting for a both/and approach that honors multiple perspectives. From these perspectives, however, a common goal has emerged: every essay in this collection aims to expand the range of contemporary poets, poems, and ecocritical approaches available to eco-conscious educators.

In the opening chapter, Janet Newman frames poetry as a cross-cultural educational opportunity, rooting her analysis in Aotearoa/New Zealand. Newman shows how settler (Pākehā) and indigenous (Māori) poetries speak to each other and about/with nature, finding common ground without denying the violent legacies of colonialism. Newman includes a glossary of over 40 Māori words, many of them describing nature, fish, and animals from the region. Newman suggests that students everywhere can learn (without appropriating) to read differently—more ecologically—as Māori words reframe the natural world. Indeed, perspectives from Oceania span this volume: Chapters 2 (Høvik), 4 (Coleman), and 10 (Stuart) treat various aspects of Australian poetry, from indigenous collaborations (Chapter 2) to migratory birds (Chapter 4) to vegetation in Australian ecopoetry (Chapter 10). Such essays serve educators by implicitly challenging them to explore—and to teach—through the cultural lenses of many traditions and knowledge bases.

Just North of Oceania, in Southeast Asia, Chapters 5 (Brink) and 16 (Benitez) present short poetic forms—the haiku and the bugtong, respectively—as genres with generative pedagogical potential. Brink moves between readerly and writerly subject-positions, modeling for students the ways that haiku forms can stage eco-aware "conversations," across cultures and ages. Benitez's discussion of the *bugtong* invites teachers and students from other culture areas to understand the "agency of the Philippine natural world," while learning to ask questions about their own local ecosystems. Both Brink and Benitez showcase poetry that engages with climate issues using irony, subtle humor, and indirection. This makes their work especially useful to instructors who wish to move students beyond reductive or didactic reading practices.

Views from Europe can be found in Chapters 4 and 17, where Scottish migratory bird poetry (Duckworth) and Italian verse (Varutti) promote an awareness of environmental issues that

DOI: 10.4324/9781003399988-23

transcend national or nationalist mindsets. Like the migratory birds that cannot be contained by national boundaries in Chapter 4, many of the poets discussed in this volume define themselves through multiple identities. For example, Naomi Shihab Nye writes from a Palestinian-Swiss-German-American background (Chapter 13, Kleppe), while poet-artist Shaun Tan was born in Australia and is of Malaysian-Chinese and Anglo-Irish background (Chapter 11, Moen). Tan's diverse origins are likely an important influence on his visual-verbal works that seem concerned with a type of universal human who also relates to, and empathizes with, more-than-human life forms. As students struggle to locate themselves as readers, poetry can help them explore the politics of their individual (national, ethnic, and racial) identities while also understanding the ways that—perhaps especially in the era of climate change—identities can be mutable and contingent.

Poetries of Africa and the African diaspora are another key feature of the book. Chapter 12 pursues ecopoetic readings of select African-American poets, positing the "total climate" as infused with anti-Blackness while imagining the Black body as a locus of climate resistance and transformation. From a vantage point in sub-Saharan Africa, Chapter 14 (Akingbe) explores the South African poet, Gabeba Baderoon, framing her as an eco-activist who embraces rhetorical moderation as a way to promote pragmatic and inclusive environmental change. Also situated in Africa, Chapter 15 (Salaudeen and Gbolahan) considers how Nigerian poets like Gabriel Okara, Tanure Ojaide, Ebi Yeibo, G'Ebinyo, Ogaga Ifowodo, Magnus Abraham-Dukuma, and Amatoritsero Ede depict and protest the losses occasioned by ecological destruction in places like the Niger-Delta. They link these losses to global capitalism. Teachers and students unfamiliar with contemporary African poetic traditions will find ample materials to learn more, as well as to consider how all of the continents represented in this book (even Antarctica!) are inspiring poets to write about local environmental issues that also resonate globally.

Not all borders are national. The lines between "human" and "more-than-human" are also shifting as species disappear, and several chapters in this volume tackle the issue of anthropomorphism. Poets from many global traditions have long ascribed so-called "human" characteristics to animals and plants, while scientists have (until recently, at least) rejected anthropomorphic perspectives as non-empirical. Several chapters of this book address the way poetry can frame human/animal encounters, going beyond the merely romantic; these include Chapters 6 (Thatcher), 8 (Scarano), 9 (Moen), and 10 (Stuart). Animals are a popular topic for discussion in classrooms at all levels, including among adult learners, but these essays ask students to go deeper, using poems to think harder about how we "see" animals, what we owe them, and what they can teach us.

The educational potential of eco-aware creative writing is another thread running through this volume. Chapters 5 (Brink), 6 (Thatcher), 7 (Kalinowski and Van der Voet), 8 (Scarano), and 11 (Sorby) are all written by practicing poets who teach. These essays illustrate how writing poetry about/within specific ecosystems can give students access to agency and hope. In some national educational systems—particularly at the college level—creative writing is not taught at all, or is confined to specialized courses. In the spirit of blurring boundaries, these essays by poets implicitly invite teachers in all kinds of classrooms (not just "creative writing" classes) to assign poetry writing. When students are asked to write poetry, they get a chance to actively practice against-the-grain thinking, to engage in close observation, and to articulate emotional attachments beyond the self—all "habits of mind" that can support climate awareness and ecological problem-solving.

As a whole, the essays in this volume offer not a fixed educational program or curriculum but a broad invitation to teach the poetry of planetary climate change. The range of contemporary eco-poems available in English (or English translation) is dazzling, and poetry as a genre models inventive ways to challenge ingrained assumptions about progress, about "nature," about ourselves. *Poetry and the Global Climate Crisis* offers educators, students, and general readers multiple ways to engage with poetry eco-critically. This is work worth doing because poems can help all of us move past paralyzing binaries and boundaries into a world of kinship, agency, and action.

Index

Note: Page numbers followed by "n" denote endnotes.

Printed in the United States
by Baker & Taylor Publisher Services